SPIRITUAL EXPERIENCES

Emanuel Swedenborg's Diary,
recounting

SPIRITUAL EXPERIENCES

during the years 1745 to 1765

FIRST VOLUME
including indented paragraphs from
The Word Explained, and numbered paragraphs
from *The Bible Index*

General Church of the New Jerusalem
Bryn Athyn, Pennsylvania
1998

Copyright ©1998 by The General Church of the New Jerusalem.

Library of Congress Cataloging-in-Publication Data

Swedenborg, Emanuel, 1688-1772.
  [Diarium spirituale. English]
  Emanuel Swedenborg's diary, recounting Spiritual experiences during the years 1745-1765.
      p.   cm.
  Includes bibliographical references and index.
  ISBN 0-945003-17-x (set). -- ISBN 0-945003-11-0 (v. 1 : alk. paper)
  1. Swedenborg, Emanuel, 1688-1772--Diaries. 2. Swedenborgians--Sweden--Diaries. 3. Spiritual life. I. Title.
BX8712.S71998
289'.4'092--dc21   98-46231
[B]   CIP
First Edition 1000 copies

Some of the Scripture quotations in this translation are from *The New King James Version*, ©1979, 1980, 1982, Thomas Nelson, Inc.

TRANSLATOR'S PREFACE

In recent years a compelling demand has arisen world-wide for a modern and at the same time reliable translation of Swedenborg's work properly called *Spiritual Experiences*, formerly known as *Spiritual Diary*. This translation has been undertaken in response to that need.

Swedenborg's Claim

The reason for this demand is undoubtedly to be found in the abundance of detailed description in Swedenborg's accounts of spiritual and heavenly life. While intrinsically indescribable and ineffable (2 Cor. 12:4), that life nevertheless reached his consciousness, and empowered his pen, with a clarity sufficient to transmit a salutary message to any receptive human mind.

In the hope for such a reception, Swedenborg wrote paragraph 2894 of this work:

> In general it must be maintained that all things I have written in this book[1] have not been written in any other way than from actual experience, from conversation with spirits and angels, from thought communicated as tacit speech; then when I was writing, from things imparted by those who for the most part were together at the time while they were being experienced, and from their guidance of my thoughts, the things written, my hand. So everything written in these three books and elsewhere, though here and there disconnected, are nevertheless experiences, and everything in its own way from spirits, or angels—this likewise having been guided by spirits next to my head. For I have in every case perceived their presence. 1748, 23 Aug.

Much of Swedenborg's detail is enigmatic, such as the locations assigned to angels and spirits of various character in the Great Human Structure of God's Kingdom. Much is frightening, when we see the inevitable consequences on the plane of spiritual life of man's corrupt, self-centered, greedy, carnal, violent qualities of life.

---

[1] See the preface to *Experientiae Spirituales*, pages viii and ix.

TRANSLATOR'S PREFACE

Even if salvable, people entering the other life will have to pay for their every iniquity! Spiritual law is as constant as the law of gravity, and the wages of sin as certain as the speed of light. But the qualities of love to God and belief in Him as the only Source of life, and of love and mercy toward the neighbor, draw all souls who are striving for them upwards to a place in God's eternal Kingdom.

The spiritual experiences Swedenborg recorded in this large work are his own documented testimony, from day to day and year to year, and the intimate account of his introduction into the higher life, spanning twenty of the twenty-seven years following his call in 1745 to serve as the human instrument of new Divine revelation to mankind. In response to that call, Swedenborg undertook a detailed indexing and study of the Divine Word culminating in the writing of an explanation of the Old Testament, known as *The Word of the Old Testament Explained* (hereafter referred to as *The Word Explained* and abbreviated as *WE*. The Latin will be referred to as *Explicatio*).

The Title[1]

The first occurrence of this title is found in an annotation in the margin of his Schmidius Bible (in the upper left corner of page 62, above Genesis 49–50):

De *Gade* et *Aschere*, vide Experient: Tom: III: ad finem.

The English translation of this is:

About Gad and Asher, see Experiences Tome III at the end.

The Rev. A.W. Acton interpreted this—I believe *wrongly*—to mean: ". . . see the experience in Tome III [of *The Word Explained* (Codex 61)] at the end." For "Experient:," being capitalized, is not referring to one single experience, but to an entire work Swedenborg is here calling "Experiences" ("Upplevelser").

---

[1] This article is excerpted from the translator's preface to *Experientiae Spirituales*, pp. iv to ix.

TRANSLATOR'S PREFACE

That Swedenborg did conceive of a distinct work that would include all the experiences recorded in the indented paragraphs and on the end pages of the *Explicatio* volumes, is confirmed in the first place by the fact that the index of the "Diary" refers back to these paragraphs, as in the examples that follow:

Notice tome number followed by paragraph number and in the case of Tome IV, which was not numbered, the page number. Notice also references to the "missing numbers" starting with nos. 15, 16.

For what other reason would Swedenborg have included all these in the index than because he viewed them as an integral part of that work?

iii

TRANSLATOR'S PREFACE

In the second place, as regards the title, there is a statement found in Codex 6 (*Bible Index of Isaiah and Jeremiah*, the author's page A1), which, when rightly interpreted, shows not only that Swedenborg intended to gather the experiential material from *Explicatio* together into one work, but *also that he had a name for it.* It is a crossed-off item of an agenda in Swedish prepared for his departure for London about November 1748:

Taga ut exp. sp. och sen legg dem ehop.

Faulty interpretation of this note has helped to obscure the true composition and title of the work that has traditionally been known as "Spiritual Diary."

Dr. R.L. Tafel interpreted it to mean: "To take the Ex[positionem] Sp[iritualem] (the Spiritual Explanation), and lay it on top." By "Spiritual Explanation" he understood the manuscripts of the *Arcana Coelestia*. Dr. Acton, realizing that this could not be referring to the *Arcana*, interpreted it to mean: "To take out [the volumes of] the Spiritual Exposition and then lay them together." By "Spiritual Exposition," Dr. Acton understood the work *Explicatio*; and by "lay them together" he understood: "put them in order."

Our interpretation of "exp: sp." is "experientias spirituales." (This reading was also suggested in a letter written by Curator Lennart O. Alfelt to the Rev. Donald L. Rose on Sept. 16, 1964, and supported by Dr. Hugo Lj. Odhner—my father.)

The most reasonable conclusion is that this directive concerned the composition, and indicates the name, of the manuscripts containing Swedenborg's spiritual experiences in their totality. For the directive was followed up: the first $148^{1}/_{3}$ numbers of the "Diary," subsequently lost, were indeed "taken out." These pages were "legd ehop" with the end pages of the *Bible Index of Isaiah and Jeremiah* containing those paragraphs we know as 149 to 205. Swedenborg then continued the numbering from 206 to 972, in the paragraphs written in reverse order at the back of his *Index to the Prophetical Books*. Then all these paragraphs from 1 to 972 were duly indexed.

TRANSLATOR'S PREFACE

Of course, the indented paragraphs in *Explicatio* could not be "taken out and combined" like the final pages, without having to be rewritten and renumbered. Perhaps there was not time for this in view of the imminent commencement of the *Arcana Coelestia*; but they, too, were indexed in the only way possible: by tome number and paragraph number, or by page number, as they stood, interwoven within the text of *Explicatio*.

The Word Explained

It was during the writing of this work that Swedenborg's spiritual vision was opened into the spirit world. These visions were so strikingly distinct from his laborious explanations of the Biblical texts, that he began using generous indentation to set them off. (An example of "indented paragraphs" in the work *The Word Explained* is inserted on the next page.)

Because these indented paragraphs form an integral part of *Spiritual Experiences*, I have excerpted them and include them at the commencement of the present edition. There are other paragraphs that were not indented in *The Word Explained*, but are identified as belonging to *Spiritual Experiences* by their inclusion in the index Swedenborg composed of this work. To each of these paragraphs he assigned a number, but because the numbering is not sequential, I have assigned them the *SE* numbers [1a] through [403a]. The brackets indicate these as my numbers, not Swedenborg's. The numbers that A. Acton assigned these paragraphs in *The Word Explained* are also indicated for the reader's reference.

Although these indented passages are numbered paragraphs of *The Word Explained*, they were later referred to in the indexes of *Spiritual Experiences*, a clear sign that the author assigned them to that work. And in fact further experiences were jotted down at the end of the four tomes of *The Word Explained*, as well as parts of his *Bible Index* tomes. These, numbered from 1 to 148$^1/_3$ were subsequently taken out, and lost. They were reconstructed from the index by the previous translators, Bush/Smithson and A.W. Acton, and in this edition I have similarly reconstructed the lost passages.

The subsequent growth of the record of Swedenborg's spiritual experiences followed a complex manuscript trail. After he ran out of paper in that tome, he wrote further spiritual experiences at the front ([148$^1/_4$] to 148$^1/_6$]) and back (149 to 205) of the voluminous *Bible Index* he was assembling. Soon out of space again he took

TRANSLATOR'S PREFACE

Example of indented paragraphs: *Explicatio* III 3771-72

TRANSLATOR'S PREFACE

another, largely empty, volume of his *Bible Index* and began writing spiritual experiences from the back of the tome toward the middle, eventually filling half of the book in reverse order (206 to 972½).

Perhaps realizing by then that experiences yet to be extracted from the *WE* might fill at least half a tome, he took a fresh tome of blank pages, wrote until he came to the end (973 to 1789). Having left the first half blank, he then started at its beginning and continued writing until it was full (1790 to 3427).

Beginning with paragraph 3428 Swedenborg devoted a whole fresh tome to his experiences, filling it for the first time from cover to cover. For a period after he had written paragraph 4544, however, the manuscript was not available to him, and he therefore started afresh with paragraph 4545 in a new, smaller (octavo) blank volume. Its paragraphs he numbered up to 4715, leaving some at the end unnumbered. I refer to this text, formerly called the "Minor Diary" as the "Interim Diary," differentiating it from the main text by adding an **a** to its numbers. When Swedenborg again had access to the main tome, he continued documenting his experiences in it, resuming with the number 4545 and continuing to number 6096, along with 15 unnumbered paragraphs and a notation in Swedish.

The Index

To unify this large and varied body of text, the author now and then paused to create an index. He first laid out blanks for each letter of the alphabet, larger or smaller depending on its projected frequency of occurrence. He soon filled these areas with entries, and continued on subsequent numbered pages, entry by entry—no longer in alphabetical order, but keyed by the original alphabetized section. This first index, titled Index I in the Second Latin Edition, covered paragraphs [1a] to [403a] and 1 to 4644a. A second index, titled Index II and covering paragraphs 3428 to 6110½, had an alphabetized key at the end. These indexes fill two volumes, i.e., V and VI, of the Second Latin Edition, but simplification of the large amount of repetition may enable the translator to reduce these to one volume, allowing the sixth volume to accommodate the A. Acton Numerical Index (Bryn Athyn: 1954) to be discussed later.

The New English Translation

The new translation is based on the Second Latin Edition prepared by the present translator and published by the Academy of the New Church in the years 1983 to 1997. Only one complete

TRANSLATOR'S PREFACE

English version preceded this one, namely *The Spiritual Diary of Emanuel Swedenborg, Being the Record during twenty Years of his supernatural Experience*, published by James Speirs, 36 Bloomsbury Street, London, in five volumes (Volume I, numbers 1 to 1538, Volume II, numbers 1539 to 3240, and Volume III, numbers 3241 to 4544, in the year 1883, translated by Professor George Bush, M.A. and the Rev. John H. Smithson; Volume IV, numbers 4545 to 5659, in the year 1889, translated by Professor George Bush, M.A. and the Rev. James F. Buss; and Volume V, numbers 5660 to the end and index, translated by the Rev. James F. Buss, in the year 1902.)

A second English version of paragraphs 1 to 1538 was translated by A.W. Acton and published by the Swedenborg Society, London in 1962 under the title *The Spiritual Diary, Records and Notes made by Emanuel Swedenborg between 1746 and 1765 from his experiences in the spiritual world.*

The portions of *The Word Explained* extracted and translated here as integral parts of *Spiritual Experiences* were translated previously by Alfred Acton, M.A., D.Th. and published by the Academy of the New Church, Bryn Athyn, Pa. (1928–48) in eight volumes plus index under the title *The Word of the Old Testament Explained, a Posthumous Work by Emanuel Swedenborg.*

Scored out Passages

Many passages of this work were crossed out by the author with transverse lines, not intended as deletions, but in most cases as an indication of transfer to another work (see the preface to the Latin text of this work, *Experientiae Spirituales*, pp. xxii and xxxix). A reproduction of this type of lines is inserted below, p. x. These portions are indicated in the Second Latin Edition by a marginal vertical line, and in the First English Edition by parentheses scattered throughout the text. They are not indicated in the present English translation, since this information can be obtained by researchers from the Latin edition.

Symbols used in this Translation

Marginal notations in this edition are indicated by a superscript ^{m} at the beginning and a superscript ^{n} at the end. In the original manuscript, the place of insertion of marginal notes is usually clearly indicated. When not clearly indicated, I have inserted them where they seem to belong.

TRANSLATOR'S PREFACE

Ellipses with four dots indicate the omission of a segment ending with a full stop, and if occurring as a separate line, the omission of a paragraph.

A right-hand square bracket] at the left margin indicates a sub-section designated by John Faulkner Potts in *The Swedenborg Concordance* (Swedenborg Society, London: 1890).

I often need to refer to the A. Acton translation of *The Word Explained*, in which he renumbered Tomes II, III and IV, not adhering to Swedenborg's paragraph arrangement. The asterisks * starting at [39a] indicate paragraphs bearing a number in the original manuscript of *WE* but not assigned a separate number by A. Acton.

Editorial Practices

A general principle observed in this edition is fidelity to the author's style where practicable. Capitalization, for example, is for the most part carried over to the English.

Type Conventions employed in Text Extracted from *The Word Explained*

Volume I of this work, which consists of extracted material originally written in other works, presented certain problems of layout. The indexed paragraphs from *The Word Explained* that were indented, I have accordingly indented. Nonindented paragraphs that were nevertheless indexed, I have left unindented. Both of these types of paragraphs, as well as the third type—indented paragraphs that were not indexed—are printed in roman. These constitute the text of *Spiritual Experiences*, further identified by the bracketed numbers in bold type above-mentioned, [1a] to [403a], and, if indexed, by the bracketed index words under them, whether or not they are indented.

Nonindented paragraphs in italics are from *The Word Explained*, included to give the context needed to understand the indexed passages in roman. In cases where Swedenborg underlined passages, if they are biblical quotations, the underlining has been indicated by quotation marks, and if they are simply used for emphasis, they are printed in **bold** throughout this part of Volume I.

Bracketed index words are translations of Latin words having a variety of English equivalents, and we insert the meaning offered by context, e.g., if the reference were to *Vox* (voice, word, expression) and the context asked for "voice," this meaning is inserted. The original Latin is to be found in the Latin edition.

TRANSLATOR'S PREFACE

Acknowledgments

In closing I would like to acknowledge a debt of gratitude to my consultants for Volume 1, the Rev. Dr. Jonathan Rose (Latin); the Rev. Kurt Nemitz (Latin); Carroll Odhner, Director, Swedenborg Library (English); and Dr. Stuart Shotwell (Preface), for their many valuable suggestions; also to Rachel Longstaff for a fine job of layout, proofing and preparation of the final copy.

J. Durban Odhner

Scored out passages: *Experientiae Spirituales* **3745 ff.**

SPIRITUAL EXPERIENCES

[This is the first section of threshold materials clearly belonging to *Spiritual Experiences*, extracted from *The Word of the Old Testament Explained*][1]

[Paragraphs from *The Word of the Old Testament Explained*, Tome I (Genesis 1 to 35), numbered by the author from 1 to 1713.]

[See what precedes, especially WE 315 to 317 up to this point, explaining Genesis 24:48–52.]

317. ....

[1a.] (These things were written in the presence of saints who were confessing their iniquity. I was told at the time that they were so completely in the heavens that they were in God's Kingdom, praising Jehovah God together.) Whether these words should be inserted will be seen later.

[See also WE 448–58, explaining Gen. 27:41 to 28:9.]

[2a.] 459. These words [Gen. 24:2–9] make it quite clear now that this precept was such a very strict legal and religious obligation that if their descendants should fail to observe it, they would entirely nullify every promise and blessing given to Abraham and Isaac. Certainly, they would not possess the land of Canaan, much less have the Messiah born from their lineage; consequently they would be outside the Kingdom of God.

Since the hope and the actual attainment of that promise and blessing depended on their keeping this precept most sacred thereafter, it is no wonder that everyone was commanded to enter into marriages within their

    1. own families or stock. But how the Jews later observed it will appear from their history.

---

[1] See also the Preface to *Experientiae Spirituales* under the heading "Additional 'Diary' Materials," as well as the Preface to VOLUME I of the same under the heading "The indented paragraphs in Codices 59–62."

That this precept was a matter of the strictest law was, as said, solely on account of the Messiah. He was the seed in which Abraham and Isaac and Jacob, and all their descendants, as well as all the nations of the whole world, would be blessed [Gen. 18:18, 22:18], as so very often said above.

Now this stem, from which the Messiah was to come, was later called the stem of David. And being a root and stem, it was likened to a tree into which the descendants of Abraham and Isaac would be ingrafted as branches. So there would surely come forth a tree like the one which had been in the midst of the Paradise at the first creation, called the tree of life.

Now to insure that those branches, and thus the whole tree, would not be spurious, but legitimate, like the one in the Paradise of old from which Adam was cast out lest he touch it [Gen.] 3:22, they had to observe most strictly the law limiting marriages only to the closest relatives. This was the reason why the Jewish and Israelitish people were so severely forbidden to marry Canaanites and strangers. For in that people the Messiah willed to bring back, and thus to create anew, not only the Tree of life, but also the whole Paradise. The tribes of Israel would be like the trees of that Paradise, but the tribe of Judah, the Tree of Life Itself in their midst. This could never have been accomplished without marriages from closest relatives.

2. (These words, together with those above starting with verse 41, were said to me verbally, and practically announced, and in fact by little children who were with me at the time and even spoke through my mouth, and also guided my very hand.)

[Marriage; Little child (Infant); Hand]

[See WE 472–74, where the explanation of Gen. 28:10–22 begins and the Kingdom of God in general is discussed.]

[3a.] 475. But what the Kingdom of God will be like is evident from the writings of the Divine Word. Its deepest level of meaning contains nothing else but what regards the Kingdom of the Messiah. Here I will only mention that when the higher path is opened up in anyone's mind, the Kingdom of God comes to view, and one sees what it is like. For there are in everyone two passages leading to the understanding part of the mind. One is from the world through the outer senses; the other is directly from Heaven, through the highest mind specifically termed the Soul. The latter is to be called the higher or inward way, but the other the lower or outward way.

The higher path, through the soul, is quite unknown to the human race; for ever since Adam himself after his fall, it has been closed in all who have not been admitted into the Kingdom of God itself while living on earth. It has lain open only to those who have been introduced, as many were

in the earliest times who spoke with the Messiah Himself—such as Abraham, Isaac, and others told of here and there in the Divine Word itself.

If, therefore, it should be described at this day what the Kingdom of God is like, it would transcend all human belief, especially for those who acknowledge nothing but the kingdom of the world, that is, the world. Those blinded by the love for it and for themselves, acquire wisdom by the outer senses alone. At merely hearing that there is in man a way opening to heaven other than the way through their senses, which are called external, they would reject this as fable.

3. For this reason, in such people the higher way directly into heaven cannot be opened until those loves, for the world and for self, have been dispelled, and only the love of the Messiah, and of His Kingdom, takes their place. Nor can this path ever be opened by anyone who is in the Heavens except the Messiah Alone, to one whom He sees fit to admit to Himself, or into His Kingdom. Then for the first time they can behold what His Kingdom is like.

To tell it in a few words, it means that one is allowed to hear and to speak with those who are in Heaven, in fact, with heavenly spirits, with saints who died long ago, even with Abraham himself, Isaac, and Jacob, and through them, indirectly, as well as even directly if such boundless grace be granted, with the Messiah Himself—indeed, even to see Him. The speech itself is entirely like speech with companions on earth, but coming down so clear from Heaven, from above, from every direction, far and near, as well as from within, that it is heard in the same way as speech of the mouth, but so that none of the bystanders hears or perceives any of it. This is the case even in an actual group, whether consisting of many persons or few. And every such individual hears it in their own native language.

The eyesight also is like ordinary sight, but unless one is admitted into the [very] inward heaven, one sees only symbolic displays, especially when the eyes are closed, and above all in a state midway between waking and sleeping. One sees them as clearly as we see with our eyes at midday. This happens as often as the Messiah sees fit to grant anyone to behold it.

As well as by hearing, sight and speech, their presence is made known—not vaguely, but clearly—by touch. What the Kingdom of God is like, therefore, is plainly discerned at such a time by the senses just mentioned, to a degree that no one could believe such immense happiness could ever exist.

But lest these accounts be rejected as fables, I can testify sacredly that the Messiah Himself, Savior of the World, Jesus the Nazarene, has introduced me into that Kingdom, and I have spoken there with heavenly guardian angels, spirits, dead people who have risen again, even with those who called themselves Abraham, Isaac, Jacob, Esau, Rebekah, Moses, Aaron, and the Apostles, especially Paul and James. This has gone on now over a period of eight months almost uninterruptedly [see 8a below], except on my journey from London to Sweden, and continued while I have been writing these things which now come out in public. In fact, they themselves, or else their angels and others, brought in the very words from closest by.

Hence you may now realize that there is a Kingdom of God, and, from what is to be said later here and there, what it is like. This only I am prompted to add, that somehow I have been introduced into Heaven itself, not only with my mind, but almost my whole body, that is, my bodily sensation, and this when I was completely awake. This might strike everyone as so strange that they cannot help calling it into question. But because I have seen, heard, and experienced it with the very senses of my body, I cannot help affirming it now, upon Divine consent, and testify to it.

(Those words written about me, I cannot yet affirm so strongly as to be able to swear to them by God; for I cannot be sure whether every single word of the description is right and accurate enough to entirely agree with the facts. Therefore, they must be amended at some other time, if God sees fit, so that I am really satisfied that the words I am speaking are entirely true.)

[Speak, Speech; See, Vision]
[See also WE 476–540, continuing to discuss Gen. 28:10–22, and the Kingdom of God in general.]

[4a.] *Experience*

541.   Now as for the Kingdom of God described here and above from the Divine Word, and to be further described below, let me say the following.

In order that everyone may believe that it will be such as described, I would like to make it known to them that it has been shown me several times. This first happened during a quiet sleep, but later in broad daylight when I was awake and able to discern it most clearly with my very senses. I actually saw how Angels, from Jehovah, the Only-begotten Son of God, descended and ascended as if by a ladder, conveying their own voice from on high through ever repeating voices, right to my ear.

Then also I could see how countless heavenly Spirits together, among them also saints who had died, were associated together so as to form one body, as if they were one person, and how they streamed in so harmoniously that not even the least discord could be felt. And this reached my very senses as clearly as objects normally reach the external senses, together with a clear voice and announcement, as if by one person, saying that this was an effigy of the Kingdom of God itself.

The sweet pleasantness and deep happiness I felt resulting from this was so great that I cannot express it in words. In a manner indescribable, it deeply penetrated my tissues and innermost marrows, and stirred them.

Because the Messiah in His infinite mercy and grace has granted me, His most unworthy servant of all, plainly to see this

effigy on several occasions—but so often to experience those feelings of sweet happiness during the past two years that I will refrain from numbering the times—therefore I cannot keep from testifying to this.
[*Angel; Heaven; Happiness; Harmony; Inflow; Kingdom; Ladder; One (Union)*]

[*See what precedes from WE 913 on, where the explanation of Gen. 30:39 begins, but here especially 933–42.*]

[5a.] 943. Yet who will believe it that human minds, and thus people in the whole world, are controlled entirely at the Messiah's will, by means of spirits; and that human minds, consequently the human beings themselves, are mere instruments?

But to the end that everyone may believe this, I can earnestly declare by God that I have experienced it so clearly that I am sure there could not be a clearer sensation in these matters. This has lasted now for a period of almost eight months [*see* 8a *below*]. During this time, by the Divine Grace of the Messiah, my mind has been governed by spirits of His heaven, with whom I have spoken throughout that entire period by day, almost without interruption.

At such times, these spirits streamed into my mind, bringing spiritual light together with the mental images themselves and the least points of thought, and even the actual words themselves, which no bystander was able to hear. Their inflow was so plain that I knew I was not thinking anything at all, not the least thing, that was not thus consciously streaming in. I could not produce even one idea by my own effort, even though I was conceded the appearance that I could. Yet all the while, during a period of five months, I was going around as before with friends in my country and with others socially, and no one noticed that such a heavenly association existed.

Just as they did into my intellect, spirits also streamed into my will and into my very actions. I was led wherever they pleased—through roads and streets, to an inn, and all around—to the point that I was just like a mere passive instrument. So perceptibly did they control the very movements of my feet, arms, head, eyes, and bodily joints, during conversations, according to the pleasure of the Messiah Himself, that the Spirits of His Heaven, who likewise by their own confession were controlled as passive instruments by the Messiah, were amazed themselves that I scarcely strayed by a footstep. This happened in the same way as when one is driven along by a plainly felt power.

Through all this, by the Divine grace of the Messiah, I have learned most clearly that all human thought, will and action is guided by the Messiah Alone, according to His will. Some of His Servants, from pure mercy and grace, He leads by means of His heavenly Spirits; and some He leads by permission, through other spirits who are not heavenly, all depending on each person's life.

(See whether it will be allowed to insert the above when the time comes for printing.)

[Action; Angel; Think; Go around (Associate); Body; Step; Spirit; Will]

[See WE 944–66, where the explanation of Gen. 30:39 in general continues, but here especially 958–66.]

[**6a.**] 967. Uninterrupted and constant are the feelings that govern our mind devoted to understanding, and, in fact, all its thoughts and mental images, right down to the least details in the mental images. And so constant are the changes of the feelings, that they perform unceasing spiralling movements having now a wider, now a narrower range, going to almost opposite extremes, or from falsities to truths themselves. The wider the range is, the more perfect and thus the happier is the state when one is governed by the Messiah. And this all happens in such an amazing way that it is most difficult to describe even in general terms.

I have experienced this, by the Divine mercy and grace of the Messiah, so strongly that I can declare and testify from actual, most lucid experience, that it is nothing else but feelings that govern all thoughts, and that without them, there is no life of the understanding, and consequently no understanding.

If I were to tell everything that I have been allowed by the Divine mercy and grace of the Messiah to learn from actual experience, as well as from regular conversations with heavenly beings and thus from living proof during a period of several months, about feelings of every kind (both those that govern our mind devoted to understanding and its will, and those that govern our moods and even our body) if I were to tell but a few proofs of actual experience from among these instances, people should be amply convinced that nothing else but feelings or loves govern the whole mind and all its ideas, thoughts, efforts and actions, the least as well as the greatest.

[Feeling (Affection); Love; Range (Field); Falsity; Opposite; Truth]
[See WE 968–85, which continues the general treatment of Gen. 30:39, here especially 973–85.]

[7a.]   986.   There cannot be more than one love, thus more than one life, and this comes from the Messiah Alone. The life that appears in human minds since the fall is a nature-based life. It is like the life of demons who are let into Heaven[1] in order to sustain and arouse life in those human minds concordant with the state of each person's life. These demon spirits, regarded in themselves, are earthly, being inwardly angels of shade, but outwardly appearing as angels of light; so they live an entirely upside down life.

These words were said to me by those who are in the Heaven of the Messiah Himself.

[Love; Demon; Person (Man); World; Spirit; Life]
[In WE 987–1002, see the continued explanation of Gen. 30:39 in general; see 1002 especially.]

[8a.]   1003.   There are a great many people who say to themselves that they could not believe such claims unless they themselves were allowed to enter Heaven, and then see the things that exist there, or speak with the dead who have risen again. Well, I am able to testify that for a period of eight months now, by the pure mercy and grace of the Messiah, I have been associating with those who are in heaven just as I do with acquaintances here on earth. This has gone on almost uninterruptedly, to the point not only of experiencing this, but also of being

---

[1] In all the index references to this passage, the term *world of spirits* is substituted for *Heaven*.

instructed by them by actual proofs and accompanying discussions, so that it has been absolutely corroborated to me.

For this reason, I wish to share these seemingly so miraculous experiences, so as to strengthen belief in regard to me—one who has been in heaven for so long, while at the same time on earth among friends. Specifically, this lasted from April, 1745, to the 29th of January, i.e. the 9th of February, 1746 new calendar, except for the one month that elapsed when I was on the journey to Sweden, arriving on the 19th of August, old calendar.

[Die, Dead]

[See in WE 1004–30 the rest of the explanation of Gen. 30:39.]

1144.[1]   *"And the angel of God said to me in the dream, Jacob, and I said, Behold me!" [Gen. 31:] verse 11. It is apparent that these things had indeed been seen in a dream, but that it was not a true dream such as occurs in sleep, is clear from what he says above, that at the time when the flocks were conceiving, he raised his eyes, and saw in a dream. So he first raised his eyes, then he saw in a dream. True*[2] *dreams are described in a different way.*

Here, a dream means the kind of visions that take place at a time of wakefulness, when the mind is withdrawn from outer sensations and passion. At such a time, the mind, left alone to itself, sees everything displayed to it as if before the eyes. Such dreams as these are elsewhere called visions, and they occur in full daytime, when a person is wide awake. One really sees mentally the symbolic displays themselves, not as thought sees, but as external sight does, outside of itself.

It is clear that such visions existed in the earliest Church, especially with these patriarchs, and indeed, in full wakefulness. They are portrayals of the Messiah Himself and the things that must come to pass. I can affirm that such displays do occur, even in the daytime, and in fact, so vividly that one may see the spirits themselves and many things that take place in heaven. This has often happened to me, and at the same time, angels spoke

---

[1] Paragraph 1144 is included here because it is mentioned in [9a] and [10a].
[2] The original has *visa*, where *vera* seems to have been intended.

[9a.] SPIRITUAL EXPERIENCES

with me. This was also the case in the earliest Church among the patriarchs. Heaven and earth were joined together so closely that those who were in the heavens spoke with those on earth, and the reverse, and thus portrayed symbolically those things which would come to pass. This is how revelations took place at that time.[1]
[See WE 1145–46, where the explanation of Gen. 31:11 continues.]

[9a.] 1147. Angels are simply instrumental means, and God Alone lives in them, but good and truly heavenly angels, who live the true order, draw their life from the Messiah Alone. I have had this made plain to me and even proven in various ways so often while in their company, that not one of them would call it into doubt. But evil angels deny it, and are even almost ignorant of it, for they wish to be governed by themselves and so think of themselves as the masters. This is how good and evil angels and spirits, as well as people on earth, are recognized; there are general distinguishing characteristics. For the children of the Messiah do not want to govern themselves, as do other spirits in various ways depending on the character of the spirits.[2]

Over a period of eight months, not the least particle of thought, feeling, conviction, came to me, as I was able to feel very clearly—not even the least bit—that did not originate from an outside source. Yet in the company of people on earth, I was like anyone else. I was so sensitive to this inflow that I was aware of the smallest details through my own senses.

ᵐThe Messiah guides people on earth directly, as well as indirectly by means of heavenly spirits. This is plain from the human soul itself, which is guided by the Messiah alone, for no one is given the power to guide the human soul itself but the Messiah alone. And because the soul is the all in everything of its body, therefore He guides the whole person also indirectly by means of spirits, in accordance with His Will. But there is this difference, that in His own children He is the life of love

---

[1] In the original this paragraph was emphasized by the word *Obs.* written twice in the margin.
[2] In the original, there is a marginal notation beside this paragraph that reads, "See above on this page, where it is marked *obs. obs.*" [WE 1144, see footnote].

flowing in through the soul; in all others is His higher than heavenly Divine Light without love, as very often said above [*WE* 851, 941].

The reason why angels stream in is because of their energy, which makes them active forces. Such also will those on earth become, after death; but while they live in the body, their powers are bound up by tissues and vessels, which is not the case in spirits.[n]

[Feeling (Affection); Angel; Think, Thought; Inflow; Spirit]

[**10a.**] 1148. The Messiah works directly into the human soul —this is an unchanging truth. For the soul is the soil into which Divine light streams. Relative to the soul, this is higher than heavenly light. But into their minds, He works indirectly through spirits.

In the children of His Church, however, such as Abraham, He works through love, which likewise streams in through the soul; but in others He works only through higher than heavenly light, enabling the mind to be spiritual and to contemplate heaven, and to lift itself up toward heaven. So the Messiah guides the rest of his children by means of light alone. What the difference is may be seen from the corresponding effects of light and of heat in the world.

But the reason why angels and spirits are instruments, and therefore mediating forces, is that the powers in them are not bound up by blood vessels and their ramifications as they are in people on earth. In man, the vessels themselves pass from the innermost to the outermost parts, and from the outermost to the innermost, and bind together all things, even to the very least. This is not the case in spirits, who do not consist of flesh and bones, that is, of blood vessels, muscles and similar hard substances.[1]

Such also will humans on earth be after their passing, when that bond with flesh and bone, or with blood vessels, withdraws from their inward powers and

---

[1] In the original, there is a marginal notation beside this paragraph that reads, "See above, *Obs. Obs.*" [*WE* 1144].

abilities. They, too, will become forces like spirits are, but more perfect, because in them the sequence from the innermost elements to the outermost, or from the higher than heavenly to the earthly, has been established, and so, their mind is developed by the interactions between them.

ᵐHeavenly spirits are minds, whose own body-like structures interact with our earthly minds whenever they enjoy the use of those body-like structures, as we are calling them. So after the life of the body, they resemble people on earth. In another respect they are minds that govern human minds indirectly, and so, through the person's will, govern his or her actions. In this respect they are mediating forces, and then do not have use of a body-like structure, which is a substance midway between a spiritual and an earthly one.ⁿ

ᵐThe speaking of spirits among themselves is really quite like the activity of the higher human mind devoted to understanding; but when human minds are not kept aloof from the earthly mind, the person does not hear that speech, for it contains innumerably more [elements] than can be expressed by words. So, in fact, does human thought, but because this is not separated from the earthly mind, the person does not grasp the true nature of that speech. For this reason, when Spirits spoke among themselves, I clearly noticed, but did not grasp the countless thoughts they uttered within a few moments. However, when the Messiah sees fit, it is understood by a different method.ⁿ

[11a.] 1149. The things I am telling are amazing, yet I have experienced them so often that I have stopped numbering the instances when heavenly spirits have so controlled the actions of my whole body, that I have gone wherever they wished, so responsively that I went without resistance and not against my will. They directed my footsteps, every one, and my gait and other movements of my body, of my hands, fingers, arms, eyes, head, completely at their pleasure, as if they themselves were moving my body. I did retain the ability to resist, and to turn from their leading to a different one, but this was because power was given to me by the Messiah.

Moreover, they even informed me how they were able to do this, namely by simply willing it for themselves, as if it were their will. This communicates completely with our mental faculty, causing us to think that something is our own, when yet it is the spirits'— and not even theirs, because they are only instrumental means, while it is the Messiah Himself through spirits Who controls and tempers all things down to the very least. So spirits suppose it to be their own will; in fact, evil spirits themselves think the very body they are controlling is their own, and do not know differently. This is how they rule the will of a person who has yielded to their passions.

Whatever freedom people then have consists in being able to resist; but this the Messiah gives them. If they do resist, then indeed there arises a combat and [the spirits] withdraw, but they come back, and so they continue life in those who are bound to them through passions. Such is the human state, and I cannot help being amazed that it is unknown, when yet it is so clearly declared in the Divine Word that no one ought to have any doubt. But they interpret it differently because they are unaware of this state of mankind, and are afraid to hear that they are led in this way by the devil and his demons.

The experience is so clear that there is nothing I can affirm with greater certainty than that I have undergone this so often and so consciously. Sometimes it lasted for a whole day, together with conversations on this very subject, and about the effort and the resistance, and the fact that I then got away, and many more details I pass over on account of their number.
[Step; Mankind (Man); Foot; Spirit]

[**12a.**] 1150. In fact, I have even written whole pages, and the spirits themselves were not just dictating the words, but were entirely guiding my hand, and thus writing. As an experiment, they even wrote words that I myself had not

[13a.] SPIRITUAL EXPERIENCES

thought of, but only their meanings. Besides this, they also dictated words.

^{m}It would be too much to tell how thoughts stream in before they are spoken, instantaneously, and how at times one is unaware what is to be thought, but it follows from its own context, and is then understood from what follows. So also it is too much to tell how all those deeds are summoned up that correspond [to their thoughts], as, for example, from the people while talking together, when their very least evil and good acts, from childhood on, are brought to light. Every single deed appears down to the least details that were thought to be forgotten, and this in a long sequence, so that I almost wanted to withdraw myself from their company. But it was in vain—for I could not restrain myself from appearing as if in judgment before them. To recount all this would be a large undertaking.^{n}

^{m}There is nothing that is not driven by actual energies, even when it comes to the smallest things. Thoughts are nothing but energies. These become visible when the door is opened into heaven, as has clearly shown itself to be the case with me.^{n}
[Hand; Write]

[See also WE 1203–13, explaining Gen. 31:19.]

1214. **In the deepest sense**, *this means the whole world since the beginning of days. Those yet to live, therefore, and those who have died, as well as all those who have clung to this idolatrous worship, are to be judged, and that worship abolished, which flourishes and persists in heaven as on earth.*

[13a.] 1215. But that Peter their God [was cast] from heaven (whether he is to be restored, I do not yet know), this I do know for certain. And that he was deprived of his key, that is, his privilege, and now walks about like a poor spirit, this I can assure you with certainty. For he has very often asked me to pour out prayers for him before Jesus Christ, but this I was not allowed to do. I could tell much more about this if this were the place for it; but at some other point, if God the Christ sees fit, more will come.
[Peter]

[See also WE 1216, which concludes the explanation of Gen. 31:19.]

FROM *WE* TOME I [15a.]

[See WE 1266–67, explaining Gen. 31:28.]

1268.   After *[Laban] had poured out these deceptions, he then said, "Surely you have done foolishly in so doing," that is, in doing this thing secretly, as he had tried to persuade Jacob. But Jacob had an entirely different feeling, as appears from what follows. This is usually the case among those who easily understand the deceptions of another, especially when they let themselves be led by the Messiah. Then nothing can be said that is so cunning as to go unnoticed. For the attitude and mind of the deceiver slips into the least words, and is then secretly exposed.*

   This is a gift of the Messiah Alone, so that His very inward and innermost Church can never be deceived by the evil. The evil themselves do not know this, for they are so blinded as to think that they have deluded the good, as if they were little children and innocents, but just the opposite is the case. It is the evil themselves who are deluded in spite of all their cunning, which they call good judgment; for their deceit is very apparent behind their flatteries. It is different in the case of evil people among themselves.

[14a.]   1269.   From the pure mercy of the Messiah, I have very often experienced what a providence there is in these cases, seeing to it that the innermost qualities of demons become transparent, and then show themselves even through pretended truths and goodness, so that their real character is exposed in everything. For they were allowed to pour out their tricks in a most subtle manner, but they were nevertheless clearly exposed, as if betrayed by their very words—when yet it was by means of their innermost thoughts that their intent was noticed in a remarkable way, instantaneously, after certain occurrences, and finally for certain.
[Trick (Deceit)]

[See WE 1346–50, explaining Gen. 32:1–2.]

[15a.]   1351.   How these things appeared to Jacob, and perhaps no one else but Jacob, is clear from many particulars.

   1) Jacob saw the angels with open eyes, which occurs with those who are of the very inward Church. These see them almost as they see people on earth, as did many we read about in the Divine Word.

15

2) They appear also in another way, when one is in a wakeful state and the inner senses are more or less removed from the external senses. Then symbolic displays are also visible, but not as they were to Jacob and Abraham and others.

3) It is different, however, in the state nearest to wakefulness, when one believes one is awake, yet it is not true wakefulness. In this state, angels appear as clearly as if in the daytime, unless they are symbolic portrayals of matters brought to view instead, like what was frequently seen by the prophets, like Ezekiel, etc.

4) Fourth are visions when the eyes are closed in a wakeful state, which are as clear as in broad daylight.

5) Lastly, there are dreams.

[See, Vision]

1352. *But visions and the like having the purpose of portraying Heavenly angels and things in heaven, will be discussed elsewhere, as God the Messiah sees fit, for they occur everywhere [in the Word].*

[16a.] 1353. Visions of the second, third, fourth and fifth types have happened with me, and, in fact, those of the second type often, those of the third also several times, those of the fourth most often and as vividly as in daytime, and those of the fifth over a period of several years. To this I can solemnly swear. By this means I have, by pure mercy of the Messiah, been given a definite knowledge of visions and thus of inspiration through the Messiah's angels—and I pass by the rest, only mentioning visions [of the first type,] before the sight.

[See, Vision]

[See also WE 1354–65, where, prior to the explanation of Gen. 32:3 ff., the gentiles are discussed in general.]

1366. The reason why there are as many nations as there are in the entire globe, having so many forms of Divine worship, and why the Church of Christ is gathered from the whole world, is clearly this, that in that Greatest Society which will constitute the Kingdom of the Messiah, there must exist a perpetual and inexpressible variety. From this variety, brought together into a most perfect form, results the true perfection of that whole Society, which, by the Divine Providence of the Messiah, is being chosen from the entire globe, from Noah's time even to the end of days. Providence itself is especially concentrated upon this, for it is looking to the final goal in just as many means as there have been and are people on earth, spirits and angels.

[**17a.**] In order that all of mankind may be arranged in this way, so great a range of spirits and guardian angels is provided that from Love alone, that is, the Messiah, every variety, and thus Divine harmony, is obtained.

[See WE 1393–94, explaining Gen. 32:9.]
1395. The descendants of Jacob likewise turned away from the Messiah, and while acknowledging out of fright the God who did miracles, they still bowed down to many other Gods. And they were brought back to the recognition and worship of the Messiah, Who is God Himself, Who created both heaven and Earth, Who is the new creator of Heaven and Earth, without Whom there could no longer be a Heaven and Earth, nor a human race other than a bestial one, worse than any wild animal, that would be entirely torn to pieces by wild animals. These facts are so clear that they can never come into doubt.

[**18a.**] 1396. Without the Messiah, the human race would no longer be a human race, but bestial and viler than the wild animal; and, having been dismembered by the Devil Himself, would have been tossed to the wild animals of this earth. They would have been torn to pieces, and there would never again appear anything human. This is a truth so obvious that it should never be called into doubt.

From my point of view, having had so many visions and having examined the nature of so many evil spirits that have encompassed me time after time, I am obliged to conclude for certain that if the Messiah should relax His control the least bit, mankind would immediately be cast headlong to its destruction, etc. It could never again be human. See the accounts given below[1]. If I were to recount all those particulars, it would fill many pages, even sheets[2]; and indeed, they would be nothing but pure experiences, not just theories.
[Lord; Mankind (Man); Universe]

---

[1] The reference here is probably to *SE* 27; see the heading entitled "The 'missing numbers'" in the Preface to the Second Latin Edition.
[2] A sheet or *membrana* = 4 folio pages.

[19a.] SPIRITUAL EXPERIENCES

[See also WE 1397–99, concluding the explanation of Gen. 32:9.]

[See WE 1408, explaining Gen. 32:12.]

[19a.] 1409. Hence it is now said, "Doing well, I will do well with you," where it does not read "to you" as applying to Jacob alone; for by him now, his family is also meant, since he was now a husband, implying also wives and children. Earlier, Chapter 28:14, Jacob did not have wives who had to be taken into account; but here where it says "I will do well with you," is meant to those who are with him, so that these words can be applied to those meant in the very inward and innermost sense by Rachel and the children. Thus the very words are inspired by the Messiah, so that the persons are forced to say what they should, and not whatever they want.

This has happened to me also several times, by the Divine mercy of the Messiah, that is, that I had to say words containing truths which were afterwards explained, and then understood. Thus truths are pronounced by the mouth of man that altogether symbolize the things which God the Messiah wills to have, so that they may symbolize what is true.

[Ignorance; Inspiration; Truth]
[See also WE 1410, which concludes the explanation of Gen. 32:12.]

[See WE 1452–60, especially 1455 on, explaining Gen. 32:24.]

[20a.] 1461. This is the real explanation of the wrestling of the Messiah's angel, that is, of the Messiah Himself by means of an angel with Jacob as Jacob, then with his descendants, with whom He likewise wrestled even until by wrestling not anything more could be achieved. For they abandoned the Messiah and worshipped other gods, and thus their own loves, and consequently they were abandoned.

For this reason, they await no other Messiah than one who will favor those loves, and will hand over to them world dominion and the world's riches. As for heaven and the heavenly kingdom, they do not care to hope for this from him, their king.

[Jacob; Wrestle; Temptation]
[See also, for the connection, WE 1462–68, explaining Gen. 32:25–26.]

1469. But Jacob was well aware that it was the angel of the Messiah who was wrestling with him (although we do not read whether he understood that this wrestling symbolized temptation). And he said, "I will not let you go, unless you bless me," realizing in that anxious state in which he still was, that an angel had been sent down from heaven, from whom he was urging a blessing. For such a realization dawns quite clearly in the human mind, when the Messiah finds it fitting, and, in fact, so clearly that one feels it in oneself to be the Messiah's will. This can be known to one who

[21a.] 1470. has experienced it several times, especially in that state in which, by the mercy of the Messiah, I have been for so long. I have also had to undergo spiritual temptation for many weeks, which are to be told about elsewhere if the Messiah sees fit.

[Jacob; Wrestle; Temptation][1]

[See also WE 1471–72, which conclude the explanation of Gen. 32:26.]

[See also WE 1507–10, explaining Gen. 33:8.] [2]

[22a.] 1511. This was written by my hand, only acting as an instrument. Spirits who were like Jacob were present, and I do not doubt that Jacob himself also hears these words, whose face I saw portrayed to me, not in a dream, but in wakefulness, and entirely real, but while my eyes were closed.

For at that time, these spirits were portrayed to me entirely as if in clear daylight, and it was said aloud that Jacob was like this. Therefore I was able to describe him. He had a handsome face, was then young, tall in stature and clothed in neat but rustic garments. Nor was there any such [deceit] apparent from his face, as I am also obliged to admit in order to defend him against myself, who am able to judge only from the face about those things that I could not help bringing forward against him [*WE* 1510], because they entirely agree with the Word of the Messiah. (As to whether these words are

---

[1] These also clearly refer to *WE* 1469.
[2] This portion is referred to in the index under *Jacob*, where it is said: "Jacob was seen, and is described; he wrote by my hand about the Lord. I Vol. 1511, *and what immediately precedes it.*"

[23a.] SPIRITUAL EXPERIENCES

to be inserted, see when the time for printing arrives whether it is permitted).
[Jacob; Hand; Write]

[For the sake of context, see also WE 1512–25, explaining Gen. 33:9–12.]

[23a.] 1526. Further regarding Jacob, who dissembled and did not yet show a right face towards the Messiah his benefactor, it had indeed been foreseen that this quality would be in his descendants. Whether it was in him when he had grown older, will appear in what follows, for this is known to the Messiah Alone, Who knows the deepest things. (Whether it was from ignorance of the Messiah, or some other reason, cannot be known.

This was written by my hand as an instrument. It was said, in fact, to have been written by Jacob himself, who was somewhat indignant that I was writing such things about him. He did admit that he had not known the Messiah was his God, but that he had later found out. Whether this is true, I myself cannot confirm, but I am writing these words as if they were from him because he, or someone in his place, has been permitted to insert them.)[1]

[m]They should by no means be inserted. Whether it is permitted to insert them below in this book, and from it in the material to be printed, is not as yet clear to me, who am only a tool, just as Jacob himself. If they do come from him such as he has been described, then anyone can decide how much faith is to be put in them.[n]

1526[a]. Jacob now admits, and regrets, that he had been of that character, but still says and insists that he had repented before his death. This no one but the Messiah Alone knows. These are the words spoken by Jacob himself, as I am now being told.

[Jacob]

[24a.] 1527. Now Abraham himself is speaking through an angel to the Jews who are meant by Jacob, saying they should repent, and not be such as they had been and continue to be, for the Judgment of God the Messiah is approaching.

This they may know from the things that have now been written, for He is the Father of all believers, not only

---

[1] The portion in parentheses is deleted in the original.

among the descendants of Jacob, but also among the nations of the entire world, from the time of the flood even to the end of days. He is therefore urging them each and every one, to repent. These words were written by my hand as an instrument, but are the decrees of the Messiah Himself, through Abraham, His Father as to the human nature.
[Abraham; Hand; Write]

[25a.] 1528. If they are not willing, he gives them notice of a harsh judgment, even though he himself continually pleads with the Messiah on their behalf. These words were written by my hand and dictated by Isaac, Father of the Jews and of all the faithful in the Church of the Messiah. The words said by Jacob [1526] can be inserted if he wishes together with those written alongside [see 1526a].
[Abraham; Hand; Write]

[26a.] 1529. That not even the slightest word of those just above is my own, I can solemnly swear by Jehovah God.
[Abraham; Hand; Write]

[27a.] 1530. The rest of the words written by me are such that I cannot yet say for sure that they are from God the Messiah through Abraham or Isaac, but are the kind of things still in need of correction, for reasons to be spoken of elsewhere, if God the Messiah sees fit.
[Abraham; Hand; Write]

[See WE 1637–43, explaining Gen. 34:17–18.]
[28a.] 1644. How great a man Melchizedek, King of Salem—who yet was uncircumcised—was in the eyes of Abraham, is so evident that there is no need to corroborate it except from the story itself, Chapter 14, verses 18, 19, 20. Not only did Abraham hold him in higher veneration than himself, but in him adored God the Messiah, giving him tithes, verse 20. And Melchizedek blessed him, as we read in verses 18, 19, 20, being called "a priest to God most high," verse 18, so that he was then above Abram.

Melchizedek, however, was still uncircumcised, for circumcision was instituted later, as appears from the Word itself of God the Messiah; for it is read about after the many acts of Abram recounted in Chapters 15 and 16. After this he begat Ishmael, and

[29a.] when circumcision was given to him as a sign of the covenant, we read that he was a son of ninety and nine years, Chapter 17, verse 1.

Besides Melchizedek, just mentioned, Abram's Father Terah was also uncircumcised, and his Brother Nahor, from whom [his descendants] took their wives, so they had children from the uncircumcised. Why, if circumcision had been so necessary—unless this was the case only for the Jacobean people and those who were admitted into their house—would Abram himself have to do with the daughter of an uncircumcised man, as did Isaac also? not to mention many other cases, such as all those from Noah even to Eber, and from him even to Abram, who were all uncircumcised. And yet it was from these that [the Jacobeans] descended. Who would have been left, since one conceived and born of an uncircumcised person is thus condemned? So the matter stands, and

[Abraham; Circumcision]

[**29a.**]   1645.   these things can never be more evident to any person than to one who, by the infinite mercy of the Messiah Himself, the God of Abraham, is His servant in the lowest place, whom He has allowed to write these things in the presence of Abraham himself, His parent as to the flesh, who sees this very document, who is now speaking with me, and wishing it to be witnessed to as though he himself had written it.

[Abraham; Circumcision]

[**30a.**]   1646.   From the above it now clearly follows that circumcision was not a matter of necessity, except for the Jewish and Israelitish people, that is, the posterity of Abraham through Jacob. There are numerous other reasons for this, which cannot yet be brought to light here, and have not yet been told to me, but have been revealed to Abraham himself, the Parent of God the Messiah as to the flesh, as Abraham himself, through an angel, now tells me, thus bearing witness that the things are true that have been told above.

These words are to be considered like those indented, as they say, on this page, above [29a].

[m]Abraham is speaking of the matters contained in the paragraph just above, namely, 1644 [28a].[n]

[Abraham; Circumcision]

1649. ....

"Hamor came, and Shechem his son, to the gate of their city, and spoke to the men of their city" [Gen 34:20], ff. These things are so wicked that for now, they are passed by, and perhaps even until the time for printing, if that seems good. They cannot yet be inserted here,
[**31a.**] for numerous reasons, which must be kept silent.

It must be observed, however, that the sons of Jacob brought their wives from there, so that they might be saved.
[See WE 1650–55, explaining Gen. 35:1, especially 1651.]

[**32a.**] 1656.[1] There is an incalculably great number of those who call themselves gods, and who want to be worshipped as gods, and, in fact, all of them being really of the character to love themselves and the things of this world. I have been witness to the truth of this, and have learned by actual experience that there are a great many spirits roving around who, wherever they come across people of like character, attach themselves to them and then lead them as if they were those people themselves. This has, of course, been told before [11a], but I wish to affirm it once more.
[Gods; Spirit]

1694. "And God appeared to Jacob again, after he came out of Paddan-aram," [Gen. 35:] verse 9. It is quite clear from the first verse of this chapter that God did speak with Jacob, but it is not said that he appeared to him. Therefore, in that same verse 1 of this chapter, a distinction is made between His having spoken with Jacob and His having appeared; for speaking is a different thing than appearing. God the Messiah speaks with a person in various ways, namely, in sleep, in wakefulness, and speaks as clearly as one person with another, and for a long time, as said above [15a], but without any vision.

Thus it may be learned how familiar this phenomenon could have been at that time, when sincerity and simplicity reigned as it did in the earliest Church—familiar to many people who lived at that time, and are spoken of in the Divine Word, and to very many others of whom no mention is made.

So it was to Adam himself, and to Noah while he was building himself the ark, etc., so that nothing could have been more

---

[1] A. Acton numbered this paragraph 1655. See his footnote 4.

[33a.] SPIRITUAL EXPERIENCES

familiar among those whom God the Messiah saw fit to speak to through angels.
[**33a.**] 1695. About that speaking with man, occurring over such a great period of time, much has been written above, and then testified to; see above [3a–6a, 8a, 9a].
[See WE 1696–1700, concluding the explanation of Gen. 35:9.]

1711. "Jacob set up a pillar in the place where God had spoken with him, a pillar of stone; and he poured a libation upon it, and he poured oil upon it," [Gen. 35:] verse 14. Now
[**34a.**] 1712. if these words are to be taken in such an unfavorable sense as that set forth above [*see WE 1679–82 and* 1710], I cannot answer for these statements, for so the words were inspired into me, that is, that Jacob himself was the very one who had to be cast down from heaven [13a, 67a], consequently was the serpent himself who would bruise the heel of God the Messiah.

If this is so, then all the preceding, from verses 11 and 12 on, must be expressed in that unfavorable sense, so as to apply to the descendants of Jacob as the serpent himself. But I myself shudder at saying or writing these things. Therefore they must be the sayings of those [spirits] who were permitted to bring them in.

If they are to be taken in this sense, then it is obvious for whom Jacob set up this pillar, and many other objects, as idol worshippers do, imitative of those that have been placed in the very Church of God the Messiah. Let us now pass on to the words that follow.
[Heel; Jacob; Serpent]
[See WE 1713, which concludes the explanation of Gen. 35:14–15.]

[Paragraphs from *The Word of the Old Testament Explained*, Tome II (Genesis 35:16 to Exodus 14:28), numbered by the author from 1 to 2476, by A. Acton from 1714 to 4001.]

[See WE 1762–64, explaining Gen. 36:2–3.]

1765.   So now it is clear that Esau had three wives, and in fact, one from Abraham's nearest kin, namely, a daughter of Ishmael. The other two were from families that were related, especially spiritually, that is, through faith, and indeed, to the same extent as the different levels in the Church are related, and thus in the Kingdom of God the Messiah. The innermost level is meant by the "daughter of Ishmael"—for by daughters Churches are symbolized—the next level by the "daughter of the Hivites," among whom Hamor and Shechem had been; and the outermost level by the "daughter of the Hittites." So there are three classes that are thus symbolized by those daughters, or steps of the Church from the last to the innermost, where Esau is, together with Ishmael.

[**35a.**] 1766.   If it is allowed to say more about Esau and Ishmael, [namely,] that one is seated at the right hand and the other at the left of God the Messiah, this may be determined when the time comes for printing.
[Right hand; Esau; Ishmael; Left hand]

[**36a.**] 1767. ^{m}Those who sit at the right hand of God the Messiah are also meant by Ishmael, and those who sit at His left are also meant by Esau; for "to sit at the right" is to be the closest to God the Messiah.^{n}
[Right hand; Esau; Ishmael; Left hand]

1771.   "After this Esau took his wives, and his daughters, and all the souls of his house, and his cattle, and his every beast, and all his possession which he had acquired in the land of Canaan," [Gen. 36:] verse 6. Here everything that belonged to Esau is put into six classes, headed by Esau himself. For now the Messiah Himself is portrayed by Esau, who had been ruddy and hairy from his very birth, thus unsightly like a beast, as is quite evident from his description in Chapter 25, verse 25, as well as in Chapter 27, where Jacob was like a kid goat when he was clothed with its skins. Then also Ishmael was a wild man, like a beast, from his very birth, as is evident from the mouth of God the Messiah, Chapter 16, verse 12. But by

25

order of succession, they became the first; while Jacob, on the contrary, was a perfect man, dwelling in tents, Chapter 25, verse 27, but by an upside down order, became the last. This is what is meant by those words of God the Messiah, that the last shall be the first, and the first shall be the last; see the passage in the Gospel [Matt. 19:30, 20:16, Mark 10:31, Luke 13:30].

[**37a.**] 1772. But regarding the fact that sons of such opposite character are born of one parent, consult the things that were written and dictated at the end of this volume about the procreation of character (which may be inserted here, if it is later permitted)[1].

The same thing is confirmed in the case of the sons of Adam, who were Cain and Abel, and also Seth, as well as the sons of Noah—Ham, Japheth and Shem[2], who were of opposing character, though from one parent.

But that the twins Esau and Jacob possessed such [a difference of character] was of the providence of God the Messiah, which at that time transferred iniquity to Esau, and integrity to Jacob. But at a later period of their lives, this was changed in accordance with the character of each, received from the Father and the mother, just as that character was at birth, as said in that passage [83]. For the character of the father comes later, developing in the course of time, while that of the mother comes more quickly, and at first conception, thus in the unborn and the baby.

[Hereditary, Heredity; Character; Mother; Father]
[See also WE 1773–74, continuing the explanation of Gen. 36:6.]

[See WE 1799, explaining Gen. 36:19.]

1800. *It is said once more, "The same is Edom," that it may be known in the strictest sense that the Edomites arise from this source, and in a broader sense, that Esau is the father of the Edomites. In the very inward sense, it is said for the sake of the true Church of God the Messiah in all those generations and thus nations; in the innermost sense, for the sake of the true Church of God the Messiah in the entire globe, going back to Esau as parent. In the highest sense, however, it is*

---

[1] The reference here is to paragraph 83 of the missing portion. See the Preface to *Experientiae Spirituales*, Volume I, pp. xxx-xxxii.
[2] The original has *Seth*.

said for the sake of the Messiah Himself, Who found it fitting to be called "Edom."

The reason why He did find it suitable to be called "Edom," as shown above in paragraphs 1760 and 1780, is that spoken of above at Chapter 25, verse 30, [WE 356,] where it is obvious that Jacob had imposed this name upon Esau because Esau was partaking of the red stew when he sold his birthright. But it is quite apparent that God the Messiah turned this very thing that Jacob had done in mockery, into good.[1]

So it is always: when an evil person intends evil, God the Messiah Himself turns it to good, and this is the rule in all and the least cases, namely, that whatever evil is intended by demons is turned to good by God the Messiah.[2]

[38a.]   1801. Not any evil whatsoever has yet been injected by demons that was not turned by God the Messiah to good. This is clear from so many proofs that there could never be any doubt about it. For it has always happened with me, and so often that I cannot number the occasions, that whatever evil was injected by them was turned to good, and whatever falsity, to truth; likewise whatever sadness, into cheer.[3]

From this, one may easily enough deduce that with the corrupt, both spirits and men, as regards their state after death, the opposite occurs—as with individuals, so with a community, therefore with the greatest community.[4]

[m]This is said from experience of many months, now nine, and day by day, so often that I am unable to number the instances. It occurred so frequently and in such a remarkable way that they have never yet, not even once, been able to succeed in their attempts.[n]

[Good; Evil]

[See what precedes from WE 1835, treating in general of Gen. 37:1–11, but especially 1845–46, treating of Gen. 3:15.]

---

[1] In the original this paragraph was emphasized by the symbol ND. written twice in the margin.
[2] In the original this paragraph is emphasized by the symbol NB. written twice in the margin.
[3] In the original, this paragraph is emphasized by the marginal notation, "These words must be well noted."
[4] In the original, this paragraph is emphasized by the marginal notation, "These words must be properly noted."

[39a.]

1847. *But as to how the devil can "bruise the heel" of the Messiah, this happens only through human beings, and was actually done through the sons of Jacob at the city of Shechem, as well as when they sold Joseph [Gen. 27:12–28], and their own descendants did it likewise. For the devil and his gang lead human beings in the same way as they lead themselves, and they do not know that they are not those people, just as all spirits who are attached to people, even upright spirits and those of the Messiah Himself. They also, at such times, when guiding a spiritual person, are scarcely aware that they themselves are not people on earth. This is known to me from actual experience; for the spirits themselves,*

[**39a.**]   *[1]   as I have also noticed, admitted that they do not realize that they are not the person, though it was different in my own case. I was able to reply to them, and they to learn in this way that they were not earthly humans.

I have been surrounded, by turns, by a multitude of many kinds and species of spirits, and even by some who had died many centuries ago, so that I might learn, by the Divine mercy of God the Messiah, what the spirits are like, and how they operate, and that God the Messiah arranges and controls them all entirely at His will. This experience of so many months' duration, could not but make these matters known to me, as well as the fact that certain spirits see the least details of thoughts and immediately inspire feelings and convictions concordant with their own character, doing so in such remarkable ways that it cannot at all be described.

I have also and especially learned that no evil was ever injected by them, or any falsity, that was not wonderfully turned to good and truth, which both surprised those spirits and made them indignant, even angry. But the experiential evidence is more abundant than anyone could ever be brought to believe; for it has been continuous over such a long period of time, now nine or ten months.

As far as people after death are concerned, however, this is a different matter. They are not then instruments of spirits as they are while living in the body, for a

---

[1] See the explanation of the asterisk in the Preface.

reason to be discussed elsewhere, for then they are spirits themselves, and indeed, more perfect. But that perfection will be spoken of elsewhere, by the Divine mercy of God the Messiah. For this matter is in itself so subtle that it cannot be explained in a few words. Indeed the spirits themselves do not want to acknowledge it. Therefore the matter will be discussed else-where, if God the Messiah sees fit.
[Feeling (Affection); Good; Person on earth, Earthly human (Man); Evil; Earthly (Natural); Conviction (Persuasion); Spirit]
[See also WE 1848–54, treating of the rule of the devil.]

1855.	Now it has already been told above how spirits operate into people *[cf. 5a, 10a–11a, 39a]*, namely, by their actual presence, as well as by the presence of light itself and of brightness. That is called light which flows into the part of the mind dealing with understanding; and brightness, which flows into the earthly mind.

This latter kind is a mixture of solar and spiritual brightness, and by its means spirits operate at a distance, so that even if they are away from that mind, they are nevertheless able to operate into its faculties as if they were present, though not as effectively. They are like shining bodies, so to speak, because they are laden with energy, and so they spread light and brightness toward that mind.

How this can occur is also evident from experience in nature in respect to sub-heavenly forces. If applied to heavenly and above-heavenly ones, it clearly illustrates what the influence of spirits on every faculty of a person on earth is like. Moreover, they are there in such abundance that they fill up the whole region around this world; but they are arranged entirely at the will of God the Messiah Himself, in accordance with every use and every purpose He has in view.

[40a.]	1856. That there were thousands around me, was obvious from many circumstances, especially from their influence, which, by the infinite mercy of God the Messiah, was actually shown to me. And I was shown how the variety of spirits produces every kind of effect in the reasoning mind, and in its will. But to speak here about the experience itself would be too much.
[Influence (Inflow); Multitude]

[**41a.**] 1857. When the prince of the world together with his angels fell away, and from being an angel of light became an angel of shadows [Is. 14:12], then he wanted to be worshipped as god, and deeply within him clung the desire to be like God the Messiah Himself. Thus whenever he was granted the freedom (which was done for numerous reasons spoken of here and there in our text), he wanted to establish his kingdom, exactly like the Kingdom of God the Messiah. That desire clung to him most deeply.

For the Kingdom of God the Messiah is inscribed on human minds—and there is nothing in the created universe which does not concern the Kingdom of God the Messiah. It is especially inscribed on angels of light, whose every act is an image of that Kingdom of God the Messiah, or a portrayal of it—

this also I have been taught by much experience.
[Kingdom; Portrayal (Representation)]
[See also WE 1858–66, concluding the explanation of Gen. 37:1–11 in general.]

[See WE 1890–91, explaining Gen. 37:5 in particular.]
1892.   As for the dreams themselves, here by "dreams" in a more inward sense are meant all revelations given before the Word of God the Messiah was made known to the people. For later it is said, namely in verse 8, "Therefore they hated him yet more because of his dreams, and because of his words." Thus these are two distinct matters, that they hated him because of his dreams, and because of his words.

Therefore "dreams" here stand for all those things that had been revealed since the earliest time from which it could be inferred that God the Messiah Himself was worshipped, such as from the time of Adam himself, after the serpent had deceived him. At that time it was realized immediately what was involved in Abel's sacrifices, and later in those of many others—after the flood, in those of Noah, then of Abraham, etc.

That these matters were revealed to them, both in dreams and by spoken words, and also through revelations of angels themselves, is clear. For it is fairly obvious that angels of God the Messiah spoke at that time with people who were of His Church, who were then of a simpler nature and let themselves be guided by truths. It was different in their posterity, when wickedness increased, and evils were added to evils, which then gained strength and became hereditary. Then in place of truths, falsities and lies succeeded, and obviously, this type of revelations as well as conversations of people on earth with the angels of God the Messiah ceased. This I can even less call into question,

[**42a.**] * since such actual conversations have been carried on with me over such a long period of time, and in fact continuously, by various methods, just like one earthly human speaking with another. Consequently, the conversations of Jehovah through angels with Adam, Abel, Noah before and after the flood, with Abraham, Isaac and Jacob, with Moses, and later with those spoken of in the Word of God the Messiah, are so undoubtedly factual, that no one should ever call them into question—nor the fact that there are many methods of revelation, spoken of elsewhere [3a, *WE* 1144, 15a–16a].

As a matter of fact, all that has been written up to this point, was written in consultation with many who died of old, with many spirits and angels of God the Messiah, even to the extent that they spoke with me about these matters beforehand and afterwards.

However, I am allowed to add here that I have not been permitted to say anything here that was dictated orally to me by any of them (when this did take place, as it sometimes did, it had to be erased), but only the things that streamed in from God the Messiah Alone, indirectly through them, and directly. This was very plain to me (but this will be spoken of elsewhere, if God the Messiah finds it fitting).

[Close; Heaven; Earthly human (Man); Speak, Speech; Revelation]

[**43a.**] 1893. As for dreams in particular, I would like to say this, that they are brought upon a person by spirits. Dreams by which future events, as well as truths, are revealed, are brought on by spirits of God the Messiah, but the rest by spirits who are not of God the Messiah. But dreams by which people are deceived are caused by evil spirits, thus by the devil's gang.

Furthermore, dreams are brought on either by means of actual voices, or for the most part by displays in their countless forms. One who is not acquainted with these can never learn the meaning of symbolic dreams. For the portrayals of realities in heaven are effected by means of the same sort of things as there are on earth, especially those which are gazed upon, thus objects of nature. Sometimes they are composed in such a way that they can hardly be unraveled unless one is acquainted with the individual types of displays.

That dreams are of this nature appears very clearly from the dreams of Joseph, as well as of the Pharaoh, and notably those in the books of the prophets, where much is read about dreams. This is not to mention actual visions when people are awake. These visions are also altogether like dreams, being the same kind of displays, just like real life, as if in clear daylight, also at times of wakefulness before and after sleep, as well as other times [*see* 15a]. There are likewise actual portrayals, when the spirits are presented in person just as one person would be to another on earth; but this happened to me when I was in a different state.

^m^With some, the dreams brought on by spirits are only illusions amounting to almost nothing but games. They seize upon whatever is brought to mind by the blood and by thoughts that have slipped by.^n^

[Dream, Sleep]

[44a.] 1894. That the above matters are as stated, I can swear so that they may be doubted that much less. For they have happened with me, by the Divine mercy of God the Messiah, so frequently that they have become entirely familiar to me. It took place both by means of dreams—this came first for a period of many years, during which I learned their actual meanings to some extent—and then the other revelations mentioned, and more besides, such as the very letters being written before my eyes and read by me, etc. etc. But I am not yet permitted to say more about this.

[Dream, Sleep]

[45a.] 1895. As for dreams specifically, they are brought on, as said before [43a], by spirits themselves, and this was made so plain to me that

I came to know it for certain. I even got to speak quite often with the very spirits who had been present and had introduced the dreams, being fully informed in this way that they originate from no other source. But they are of a twofold, in fact, a threefold kind, as has been said [43a], just like the spirits themselves who are permitted to bring them on—which is in the hands of God the Messiah Alone.

[Dream, Sleep]

[See WE 1926–27, explaining Gen. 37:13.]

1928. One who is acquainted with heavenly portrayals, knows of the instantaneous substitution of one person for another, and even of a good spirit in place of an evil one, and so on. He will not be surprised that the same phenomenon occurs in the Word of God the Messiah, namely, that now Jacob is named, now Israel, thus in place of an evil spirit, a good one.

This was such a frequent occurrence with me, in the beginning, that I was absolutely unable to tell whether a spirit was evil, or good, except from

[**46a.**] the drift of his utterances, and thus not until he had been examined. Since this phenomenon is unknown, it cannot easily be explained to the understanding. The same is now *being done in regard to Jacob, in that he is now called Jacob, now Israel. When called Israel, there is a substitution of this kind, that is, of a good angel in place of an evil one. So it was Israel who sent Joseph, for Jacob could not have said these words, as is likewise evident from what follows, namely, that he inquired concerning peace, and did not know whether Joseph had been killed. Yet Israel as Jacob also sent Joseph, but then in a different sense—for he had been sent on account of Jacob, who was thus the cause of his being sent. For this reason both aspects are meant here.*

[**47a.**] 2067. "And Judah acknowledged them and said, She is more righteous than I, because I did not give her Shelah, my son. And he never knew her again," [Gen. 38:] verse 26. Judah was moved to having to say these words by God the Messiah Himself so that Tamar would be freed. All hearts whatsoever are moved at the will of God the Messiah, for God the Messiah governs the thoughts of all, and moves them to whatever feelings He pleases, just as it is said that He commands the water [Luke 8:25]. So now He also moves the heart even of Judah to utter the words, "She is more righteous than I, because I did not give her Shelah, my son."

This is so much the case, that not even the least thought, or even the least beginning of a tiny feeling, flows into the mind of anyone, except from God the Messiah Alone—something
[Think, Thought]

[**48a.**] * I have experienced over so long a period of time, almost continually, that [I have learned things] amazing beyond anyone's ability to think of and express

[48a.]

in words—about changes of feelings, about their spiralling motions, their harmonies, their falling away from opposite feelings, and matters of this kind.

They are ineffable, and if I brought them out, it would fill up entire volumes. Therefore, I am able to speak from actual experience.
[Think, Thought]

[See also WE 2068–70, concluding the explanation of the above verse.]

2119.[1]   "*And when his Master saw that Jehovah was with him, and Jehovah made all he did to prosper by his hand,*" *[Gen. 39:]* verse 3, "*Joseph found grace in his sight, and served him; indeed he put him over his house, and all that he had, he put into his hand,*" verse 4. Here again, the Egyptian, that is, the earthly person, is called Joseph's Master; here, as before, we read only "the Egyptian," and Potiphar is not mentioned by name, so that here is meant only the earthly part of Joseph.

What this is in a person being reformed can be well understood from what was said above *[WE 2100, 2108, 2117]*, namely, that the outward elements in a person, or earthly elements, are those which constitute the very kingdom of the devil. For the lower mind, together with its passions, thus the body itself, is the house of the devil. That lower mind, therefore, was formed altogether in the image of his kingdom prior to the devil's fall, so that he might direct that part of the human being—but under the auspices of God the Messiah through the guidance of heavenly spirits and angels.

After the fall, however, an entirely different state existed within mankind, which was turned upside down, as was order itself. The lower or earthly mind, together with the body, had become the kingdom of the devil, who invaded heaven itself in mankind, that is, the mind devoted to understanding, and thus mixed up the higher things in us with the lower.

Now so that we would not be without any life, and also could be reformed, it was granted to the devil and his gang to appear outwardly like angels of light. Then he was able to rule the human mind also, just as he does the lower mind, and inject his life into them.

---

[1] Along the margin of the upper half of the paragraph, the author wrote: "See paragraph 2147, as to whether what is there said should be appended here, or below; also 2146."

But in order that ==mankind may be reformed, it is neces-== *sary that the* ==devil first be cast out of our heaven, that is, out of our== ==reasoning mind.== *When he has been cast out of this, an entirely different state ensues, in which at first the earthly or lower mind seemingly becomes the master, for the order has to be completely turned about, and before it has been turned about, it cannot be otherwise but that the earthly part holds dominion for a time. But this takes place in such a way that different angels and spirits succeed the former, as arranged at the will of God the Messiah, and that finally the very spirits and angels of God the Messiah are put in charge.*

[49a.] 2120. As for the remaining words, they are certainly clear in themselves, but there remain some obscurities. Therefore, if God the Messiah finds it fitting, let them be left for another time. And if it is permitted at that time, let those matters be reported in the sequence which, by the Divine mercy of God the Messiah, took place from the first time to the last, if so permitted—and this in a form pleasing to God the Messiah when the time comes. I refer to the temptations, and the things that follow later one after another, but in a general way, if that is His pleasure. Then those points can be extracted, concerning these words and those that follow, that are able to be explained with greater clarity.

[See also WE 2121–26, concluding the explanation of Gen. 39:3–4.]

[See WE 2207–10, explaining Gen. 40:14.]

[50a.] 2211. Strange things occur in heaven when speech is addressed to man, and likewise through man, for one person comes and speaks, replacing another, so suddenly that it happens in an instant. Sometimes this is clearly noticed, sometimes only by the direction of the discourse. In fact, one spirit may sometimes present himself as another, and counterfeit the other so skillfully that one cannot tell the difference except by searching into the matter.

Sometimes many speak at the same time, thus forming a compound person. And they speak in various other ways impossible to recount here specifically, that are so strange that if told about in detail, scarcely anyone

[51a.] SPIRITUAL EXPERIENCES

would lend them credence. But these ways depend entirely on what matters are to be revealed.

These are the switches and like phenomena that occur in the Word of God the Messiah. How those interchanges take place cannot at all be explained to anyone unless he is acquainted with them, and cannot but seem strange to one who does not know about them. That it is so, however, it has fallen to my lot to learn, by the Divine mercy of God the Messiah, from long experience, without which interchanges of this kind, and many other things, could never have been understandable to me.

[Speak, Speech]

[See WE 2212–25, treating in general of Gen. 41:1–49.]

2226. Now consider those who hold that the works of the law are their Divine worship, believing they are made righteous by works of the law alone, and believing they are worshipping Jehovah, the Creator of Heaven and Earth, and consequently, as they say, the God of Abraham, Isaac and Jacob. As for these, it is obvious from what has been said, that they cannot possibly in this way come near to Jehovah, the Creator of Heaven and Earth, the God of Abraham, but that they are professing Jehovah [only] with the mouth.

Furthermore, there is no approach to Jehovah except through the One Only Son. Tell how what is impure can approach to what is holy, how can a human so profane approach to Jehovah Himself, except through a mediator who has taken upon Himself the impurities and sins of men, and thus became Righteousness! This is quite impossible. That profane human is as far from Jehovah as Heaven from the earth, as they say, or as the infinite from the finite, between which there is no ratio, as they say. There is no conjunction except by means of the Son, Who is God, and became human for the sake of mediation, so that mankind could thus be led to Jehovah, (but let me set forth these things in a better way, for here they are confused, being disturbed by impure spirits—I surmise, by Jews).

[51a.] 2227. Here should be inserted, if it pleases God the Messiah, the conversation held with Jews, with whom I spoke yesterday [*see* 147], and stands written down on a separate sheet.

[See also in WE 2228 the conclusion of the above.]

[See WE 2256, explaining Gen. 41:12 in particular.]

2257. *God the Messiah interpreted the dreams and the revelations in His Word, as everyone knows. This He did in the Temple itself, and then later before his disciples [cf. Luke 9:47, 20:1, 21:37, 24:27].*

[**52a.**] So also at this day, for I have not the least thing from myself.

2258. *And indeed, "to everyone according to his dream," that is, according to the prophecies; for Moses and the prophets treat of nothing but Him. About the interpretation itself, we have spoken above [WE 2197 ff.].*

[See WE 2376–80, explaining Gen. 41:47 in particular.]

2381. *It can be inferred from this that similar bunches exist in the Church of God the Messiah, and that its people are divided up into bundles according to spiritual knowledge, so that the good are mixed in with the evil and they are gathered into one, but with a definite government, on earth and in heaven.*

[**53a.**] 2382. For there are evil spirits now in heaven, let in for reasons spoken of above [7a, *WE* 1852, 2119], among whom good spirits and angels are indeed mixed in. But their arrangement by God the Messiah is such that they are nevertheless separate from each other, and the evil ones are not allowed to know there are good [among them] or to do them the least harm.

This is all very familiar to me, who by the Divine mercy of God the Messiah, even though densely surrounded by them for a length of time, have nevertheless been so protected that they were not able to bring the least evil upon me, although they were constantly attempting to. For if even the least leeway were given them, they would tear a person entirely apart in a few short moments. They breathe nothing but our destruction, unless we completely lowers ourselves to take their side so that they may imagine they are earthly humans. Yet toward each other they are most hostile.

From this source comes the inner hatred people bear against their own companions in society if they do not strive for the same goals and serve them as instruments for their passions by indulging and favoring them.
[Passion (Desire); Kill; Spirit]

[See WE 2527–30, explaining Gen. 42:27–28.]

[54a.] SPIRITUAL EXPERIENCES

2531. That the character itself may be called a memory [WE 2528], is evident from many considerations, for thoughts originate from feeling and take on the shape of the character, and then proceed into words that express whatever that character has prompted. The words themselves follow spontaneously, and are stored up in the memory. How these matters stand, or how the words themselves

[54a.] * are aroused when the feelings are aroused, may be seen in the material—which may be transferred to here, if it so please God the Messiah—which I learned from spirits. See at the end of this volume, at the sign ⊖⊖ [see SE 85].

2532. But whether such a conversation had passed among them is indeed another matter; for what is portrayed spiritually by the events of life does not come to their knowledge unless it so please God the Messiah. Sometimes this takes place a long time afterwards, as happened in my case, by the Divine

[55a.] * mercy of God the Messiah. I did not realize at the time what the events of my life involved, but afterwards I was taught about some of them, indeed, many of them. The result was, that I could at last plainly see that the firm hand of the Divine Providence from my very childhood had directed the events of my life. It had so governed them that I would finally arrive at this goal of being able, through a deeper knowledge of things of nature, to understand—and then by the Divine mercy of God the Messiah, to serve as an instrument to reveal—those things which lie concealed more deeply in the Word of God the Messiah.

So now things are coming to light which until now had not been disclosed.
[Goal (End); Providence]

[See WE 2617–18, explaining Gen. 43:15.]

2619. This is the innermost meaning of the words, though they may appear differently to human eyes at this day, which look only at the very outsides, judging a person by his clothing, not looking at his inward qualities. But I can assure you that when these words appearing in their literal meaning are read before those in heaven, who are truly spiritual and able to understand earthly things spiritually, they do not grasp it

[56a.] * in any other than its spiritual meaning. This is so much the case, that they do not see and are unaware of the literal sense, just like those who judge a person not from the face and outer adornment, but from his inner qualities. For them, therefore, it is as if there were no literal meaning, and they grasp only those things which lie very inwardly, and inmostly, concealed. On this matter I could also bring forth testimony, but because it would, perhaps, go beyond the belief of most, I think it best to pass it by for now.
[Letter; Word]

[See WE 2620, concluding the explanation of this verse.]

[See WE 2759-66, treating in general about Jacob and his sons, after the explanation of Gen. 47:13-26.]

2767. *From the very [nature of] the human being one learns what this generation was like. Without a deeper knowledge of humans in general, in regard to their faculties in their proper order, these matters cannot at all be grasped. For this reason, it is saddening, and heavenly spirits are also very sur-*

[57a.] * prised, that mortals live in such great blindness, and this just because of their philosophy and learning, as they call it, which lead them into dense ignorance. For they are unaware that there are four human faculties, and do not know how to distinguish the human soul from their reasoning mind, and not even from the soul of brute animals. They even might, just because of the philosophy of their minds, come into such blindness that they would hardly know how to distinguish the human soul from the soul of the lowliest insects, or even, finally, from the soul of inanimate objects, and of plant life, seeing similar reproductive processes there.

So it is saddening that at this day, they imagine they are living in such great light in matters of understanding, when yet it is a darkness so thick that none could be thicker. As a result, as soon as they consult any philosophy, they fall into the worship of nature and are turned backward, and the proper order becomes so distorted that belief becomes null, thus almost irreparable, unless all their philosophy is first shaken from their minds.

So there must be a belief opposite to their own state of mind—which is not the case, for a spiritual knowledge must come first. One must know what is to be believed, and that something is there that can be believed. For belief is not possible without knowledge of these matters. That would be a believing without the understanding and reason, which is not human.

[Soul; Wild animal (Beast); Blind; Ignorance; Philosophy]

2768. *Without a knowledge of those human faculties, there is no knowledge of what takes place in every society, smaller and larger, in the entire globe, in the Church of God the Messiah, in the Kingdom Itself of God the Messiah. For the Kingdom of God the Messiah will be just like a human being in most perfect order, from the innermost to the outermost parts, having all the human faculties.*

The state of this Kingdom of God the Messiah, thus the state of Heaven, is absolutely not known, not in the least respect, without spiritual knowledge of what the human being is like per se, and what when reformed. Without it, therefore, one cannot grasp, and thus cannot believe, anything at all about how we are reformed, that is, regenerated, created anew, made righteous, and so brought back into perfect order for our level, from the distorted order in which and into which we are born.

[See WE 2780–81, explaining Gen. 47:31.]

[58a.] 2782. But that *these words* are so difficult to understand makes me sad at the changes of the times. At that time, when Abraham, Isaac and Jacob lived, they were so easy that everyone understood. Therefore such an utterance by them was ceremonious—by them, that is, who were led by God the Messiah and spoke as His mouth.

[See WE 2798–2805, explaining Gen. 48:8–10.]

2806. *Here, because God the Messiah had spoken through the mouth of Jacob, who was therefore called "Israel," he could not help but love them and bear witness to his love by kisses and embraces, which are the effects of love in a human being. For when God the Messiah speaks through anyone, and sees those whom He loves, then that very person himself displays this by kissing and embracing*

them, these being the bodily effects that necessarily follow the feeling of love. I can certainly affirm that this is true,
[**59a.**] that is, that certain bodily gestures follow of their own accord from feelings, responding in a remarkable way.
ᵐSee whether these words are to be inserted, or not.ⁿ

2823. *[Gen. 48:] verse 16. Angel properly means "One sent by Jehovah," thus one who represents Jehovah Himself, so God the Messiah in this sense is called "an Angel," and also for the reason that He speaks through Angels, as in Chapter 31, verses 11 to 13, above. For truly heavenly Angels are only instrumental means through whom God the Messiah speaks as if it were He Himself. In fact, they*

[**60a.**] * are to such a degree merely instrumental means, that they themselves do not know what they are about to say until they are speaking or have spoken. They only understand the things after they have been uttered, and it appears to them at that very moment that they themselves are speaking. Such is the state of spirits properly so called. But there exist different grades of spirits, which here it is not the place to discuss.
[Understand; Speak; Prophet]

[See WE 2824–32, concluding the explanation of Gen.48:16, especially 2824–25.]

[See WE 2962–70, explaining Gen 49:17–18.]

2971. *Since, therefore, this is so dangerous, namely, by means of natural sciences to search out and investigate spiritual and heavenly matters, it has been granted me, by the mercy of God the Messiah, to venture to do this, not from*

[**61a.**] * my own daring, but from the inspiration of God the Messiah, as you may see above [4a, 29a, 42a, 52a]. Nevertheless, I must confess that every time I wished to involve my understanding in matters that are heavenly, I seemed to fall backwards, so plainly, and on so many occasions, that had I not, by the Divine mercy of God the Messiah, been brought back on the path at once, I would have quickly fallen backwards. So I have an actual and

[62a.] SPIRITUAL EXPERIENCES

very clear experience to keep in sight. Therefore, human philosophy can never enter into the spiritual and heavenly regions, but spiritual and heavenly things themselves must bring in earthly ones.

[Blind; Ignorance; Philosophy; Spiritual things]

[For the sake of context, see also WE 2972, continuing the explanation of Gen. 49:17–18.]

2973. Those are called "Dans" who are like "serpents in the way and asps on the path" [Gen. 49:17], that is, who want to comprehend everything by reasoning and science, and to place faith in nothing but that which they grasp with the understanding. But those matters which are above the understanding, or which are only to be derived by intellectual processes through sublime comparison—those they reject; for they "bite the horse's heels," and thus "fall backwards from the horse." Indeed, they fall into that nature-bound state, into idol worship, and so into the loves of self and of the world, thus into all errors, so that they are worse, and more uneducated, than the brute animals themselves—which, on the contrary, live aright and quite in accordance with nature, from their own character.

Now because this is the cause of all errors, as well as the corrupted state of human minds and the loss of belief in God the Messiah Himself, therefore, lest

[62a.]   *   mortals err and continue to fall backwards, thus from life into death, by the Divine mercy of God the Messiah, heaven has opened up to such a degree that it has been granted me now almost for a whole year to carry on conversations with the heaven-dwellers, and thereby to derive experience in spiritual matters, as well as higher knowledge. This was done so that my earthly knowledge could be joined to spiritual realities.

But I must confess the fact that whenever I was permitted to involve my understanding, I would have fallen face downward had I not, on every such occasion, been lifted up by God the Messiah, only by His mercy, and thus been kept on the path.

[Blind; Ignorance; Philosophy; Spiritual things]

[See also WE 2974–78, concluding the explanation of Gen. 49:17–18.]

[See WE 3021–31, explaining Gen. 49:25.]

3032. *However, intermediate blessings*[1] *are those that concern society, for in order that there might be happiness and prosperity, which are meant by "a blessing," it must absolutely exist with a plurality, who together must bring about that happiness and transfer it to each other by a wonderful communication arising from the harmony of many. What the resulting happiness is like,*

[**63a.**]   *   and what heavenly happiness is like, may be seen described below [*SE* 86], which passage may be transferred to this place if it is permitted; namely at the sign ⊙.

[See also WE 3033–36, concluding the explanation of Gen. 49:25.]

[See WE 3037–39, explaining Gen 49:26.]

3040. *Likewise all spirits and angels in heaven; for all their speech, which is produced by means of symbolic portrayals, regards only the Kingdom of God the Messiah, presenting a kind of image of it, so that there is nothing in them which does not long for these "hills," or these highest points, and summits.*

[**64a.**]   *   How heavenly angels and spirits bring to view in everything that which regards the kingdom of God the Messiah, would take too long to tell.

[See also WE 3041–48, concluding the explanation of Gen. 49:26.]

[See WE 3099–3109, explaining Gen. 50:4.]

[**65a.**]   3110.   When the Messiah is understood by "Joseph" in this passage, then He Who constantly prays and intercedes for the Church, and for the coming of His Kingdom, arises as the supereminent meaning. Then by "the house of Pharaoh," the very house of God the Messiah is understood, which must constantly pray to God the Messiah Himself that His Kingdom may come, and indeed, using the Prayer of God the Messiah Himself, in which nothing at all is contained that does not concern this Kingdom.

That prayer you may, by the mercy of God the Messiah, find explained elsewhere [*WE* 826]. For whoever prays to the Father in the name of God the Messiah, shall receive [John 15:16, 16:23], that is, whoever prays through God the Messiah Himself, directing the prayer to Him, but not to Jehovah His Father—for no one no one can approach Jehovah the Father except through the Son [John

---

[1] That is, "the blessings of the breast and of the womb" (verse 25).

[66a.]

14:6]—he shall receive. This is to pray in the name of This is to pray in the name of God the Messiah.[1]

The human race, and those who have died, both the saints and others, as well as spirits and angels, can never approach Jehovah the Father except through the one only Son—this is clear from what has gone before. For without the Son, the world is entirely cut off, and would perish in an instant. To do so would be like trying by some higher faith or sight to see into a bottomless pit where nothing is encountered but the thickest darkness; or like trying to approach Him by outward obedience, that is, by the works of the law, while inwardly being like a most filthy vessel, and like dung. By such obedience some do try to approach Jehovah the Parent. How absurd this is, I have just now discussed
[Lord; Jews; Mediation]

[66a.] * with those who are likenesses of the Jews, and were still persisting, like the Jews on our earth, in trying to approach Jehovah the Parent apart from God the Son; and they became silent.
[Lord; Jews; Mediation]

[See WE 3113–15, explaining Gen. 50:7.]

3116. By the "Pharaoh" here, all are understood who make themselves God, who want to be worshipped as a god, but they are the gods of Babel, etc. For they regard themselves as all-powerful over Heaven and Earth, looking only to worldly and earthly possessions and how to obtain them, just like the devil himself, who does likewise. It is the same in the case of those who make themselves out to be God the Messiah and want to be worshipped as Him—they are likewise gods of Babel, and devils.[2] So also are those who put their faith in saints, as they call them, and so, corrupt the faith, diverting faith in God the Messiah to those who were but human beings, and among them, impure ones whom they had wished to declare pure by their own willful authority. But to what extent they are, on this account, put up with in Heaven, may be evident

[67a.] * from Peter himself, who for this very reason was cast out of the company of the other apostles. I

---

[1] In the original, this and the next paragraph were emphasized by the symbol *NB*. written twice in the margin.
[2] In the original, the first portion of this paragraph was emphasized by the symbol *NB*. written twice in the margin.

spoke with them for quite a long time during the past month, when Peter was deprived of all his crowd—and it was also shown what he had been like—and so is wandering about miserably, as said above [13a].

[**68a.**] 3117. With Solomon also I have been allowed to speak several times, who has retained his style of speaking as in proverbs; but still he had been admitted into Heaven, and continuing in his ancient dominion was therefore arrogant. But his wisdom was now poor, and such as could be compared to a shadow of intelligence. For in the middle of a saying, he left off, so that one might guess the rest of it, when yet he himself could guess nothing when I spoke in the same manner. But I was told that those who are presently being let in are still not those who are to be admitted into the Kingdom of God the Messiah,

[**69a.**] * for they have as yet no joy. It is different in the case of those who are worshippers of God the Messiah: they get a picture or glimpse of the joy to come, whenever this is pleasing to God the Messiah. They therefore live with a perpetual longing for the Kingdom of God the Messiah.

[See WE 3139–41, explaining Gen. 50:15.]

3142. *They are here called "the brothers of Joseph" for the reason spoken of above [WE 1925, 2466, 2898], which is that from the posterity of Jacob and in the tribe of Judah the Messiah was born. All in the whole world will also speak in this way, both he who is called Jacob and he who is called Israel, for everyone will acknowledge, because in his own conscience he knows, that he has held God the Messiah in hatred; because man is evil from infancy, and loves nothing but the world, and thus rejects love toward God the Messiah.*

Then those who are called Israel will likewise say, "Perhaps Joseph will hold us in hatred, and repaying will repay us for all the evil that we did to him." For they do not know their own judgment before it has been pronounced, and everyone is called to account for the crimes he has committed and then thrust down, so to speak, into damnation. From this damnation, however, those are snatched away by God the Messiah who, through belief in Him, are children of

[70a.] SPIRITUAL EXPERIENCES

Israel. This is confirmed in the Word of God the Messiah, as I was also allowed to observe

[70a.]   *   from events in Heaven, where portents of the last judgment are constantly appearing, so that the greatest part do not know what judgment they will bear. From their present life in Heaven, it cannot be deduced that they will be among those who will enter the Kingdom of God the Messiah, except for some, such as Abraham, and Isaac, and certain others. For they who are evil still believe they will be lords over all of heaven, and want to be hailed as lords, just as the Jews living today do in their hearts. Even the devil and his gang are left in this opinion, for many reasons to be discussed elsewhere.

[See WE 3156-58 to this point, explaining Gen. 50:20.]
3158.[1]   ....To this it should be added that while, indeed, some are reformed more quickly, and even at the moment of death, yet these are such persons as have been prepared earlier in an unusual way, of which they themselves are unaware. It is another matter if it happens by way of the sheer mercy of God the Messiah, in which case they must undergo hellish torments, as I was told regarding Judas the betrayer,

[71a.]   for whom there is nonetheless said to be hope, because he was among the chosen, who were given by Jehovah the Father to God the Messiah, as God the Messiah Himself says [John 17: 6].
            [Judas]

[See also WE 3159–60, continuing the explanation of Gen. 50:20.]
3161.   This, too, is so common in human life that nothing could be more so, and it holds good in every particular case as it does in general, namely, that like the devil, mankind also thinks [evil] upon God the Messiah, but God has thought it into good. For the devil is permitted to intend evil, even to bring it forth, in a person, but for the purpose mentioned above [WE 3160], that this evil may be bent and thus turned into good. It sometimes happened to me that within several hours,

[72a.]   *   his attempts at evil, and his falsehoods also, were turned, by a different way, into good, and into

---

[1] In the original, paragraphs II 1477-85 (Acton 3156-63) are emphasized by the symbol *NB.* written 32 times in the margin.

truth. So I am permitted to speak from actual, indisputable experience.
[Good; Falsity; Evil; Truth]

3162. *The Word of God the Messiah abounds in cases of this kind, of which the Messiah Himself was the example and the effigy. He allowed the devil to carry Him away even unto death on the cross, and yet this evil inflicted on Him by the Jews and, at the same time, by the devil, was turned into Good itself, for it resulted in the salvation of the human race.*

3163. *For this reason it is now added here, "That He might do as at this day, to make a great people alive." By "a great people" is meant Israel, which is thus made alive. No other people can be meant here, and certainly not the descendants of Jacob as long as they remain outside of the faith and thus outside the gates of the Kingdom of God the Messiah. These words were very distinctly brought in from heaven, though*

[73a.] not dictated, as I could clearly perceive.
[See WE 3164, concluding the explanation of Gen. 50:20.]

3229. *[Exod. 1:] 20. Now that care and providence which God the Messiah observes in regard to His Church is described, that is, by His blessing the midwives and, in spite of the fact that they had made use of cunning, as well as cruelty and even death, setting them free. Such care and providence has God the Messiah toward His Church, that he protects her in the midst of dangers, for He is aware of all the tricks, and He has pity on them.*

[74a.] 3230. At times, spirits of evil character have been permitted to give vent to their anger and revenge upon me, and to rush upon me violently, and sometimes even to make cunning attacks. But I remained in their midst, protected by God the Messiah, and they were not able to carry out anything at all beyond the attempt. So they withdrew, astounded and spouting abuses, but admitting that their cunning, violence and fury were of no avail.
[Trick (Cunning, Deceit); Anger]

[See also WE 3231, concluding the explanation of verse 20.]

[See WE 3271-73, explaining Exod. 2:6.]

3274. *The daughter of the Pharaoh is said to have had compassion on the child, saying that this was one of the children of the*

[75a.] SPIRITUAL EXPERIENCES

Hebrews, because the "daughter of the Pharaoh" means the Church of the gentiles, which is loved by God the Messiah. Therefore, as she was acting in the same manner as God the Messiah Himself, from love and mercy, because such a feeling was inspired into her, she is said to have "had compassion," and this because the child had been exposed to death and placed at the river's bank.

For the Church of the gentiles loves the Jewish Church, because from it they derived their knowledge of God the Messiah Himself. The gentiles are moved by love toward the Jews, but the Jews, on the other hand, are moved by hatred toward those they call gentiles, meaning Christians.

How that Church declared its love toward the Jews is expressed by her words, "this is one of the children of the Hebrews," which she said despite the fact that the Hebrews were an abomination to the Egyptians, as we read above [Gen. 43:32]. She also bore witness to it by acts of love, in that she gave him to a nurse to be suckled [Exod. 2:7], and adopted him as her own son [verse 10].

They who are led by God the Messiah are like this, but just the opposite are those who are led by the devil. They have compassion for no one, and least of all for Christians, whom, if they had the power, they would condemn to death as they did Christ Himself, and would close the sepulcher with a great stone, meaning that they would cast them into the place symbolized by a sepulcher, and would stop up the sepulcher itself, rolling a great stone up to it [Matt. 27:66]. Such are the Jews, and such they have been since ancient times,

[75a.] * as was symbolically portrayed to me just now, while I was writing these words, by dreadful rebellious disturbances on the part of those who had been Jews.

But these things are so horrible that I would prefer to cast them utterly and forever out of my memory. From this experience, by the Divine mercy of God the Messiah, I was given to learn what their disposition had been, and is. I could then see clearly what the Heavenly Kingdom would be like if they had Moses as their leader, whom they wanted to raise up above God the Messiah Himself, and so gain control of Heaven. That is how wicked it was. ⊙
[Jews]

[76a.] 3275. Since, therefore, by the "daughter of the Pharaoh" here, the Church of the gentiles is portrayed, and by the "child of the Hebrews," the Messiah Himself, it is clear whom she understood to be in this box, namely, in the more inward and innermost sense, the Messiah Himself, Who was born of that Hebrew stock. On account of her acknowledgment of Him in this ark, she says, "This is one of the children of the Hebrews."

⊙ With those spirits [75a] I also carried on conversations for a long time, and I heard and saw the wickedness of their heart, for they were speaking in character, and cunningly. But these matters would fill up many pages.

[*Jews*]

[**77a.**] 3276. Obs.: I also had a conversation with those who were in charge of them about the descendants of Abraham, Isaac and Jacob, and, in fact, about those of Abraham not only from Isaac, but also from Ishmael, as well as from his six sons by Kethura; also about his other children who were sent to the east [Gen. 25:6]. It further concerned the descendants of Isaac from Esau, as well as the descendants of Jacob himself from his ten sons, who were afterwards called Israelites, that is, the ten tribes that were scattered over the whole world, first over the northern quarters of Europe, and from there into the whole of Europe and its islands, and some into Asia besides.

Thus the whole world, except for the peoples of Africa and the Indies, must be of Abraham's seed as to the flesh, which has therefore multiplied as the sand of the seashore and the stars of heaven [Gen. 22:17]. There is only one Tribe (together with Benjamin) living separated from them, which is a mere current in so great an Ocean, yet which stirs up so many disturbances, as if they alone were the sons of Abraham! Indeed, it was this current that aroused that great disturbance spoken of above [75a], and would constantly arouse one, if they were in heaven, against the children of Israel, that is, against their ten brothers and their generations descended from Jacob, against those of their uncle, Esau, and all his posterity, from whom also arose so many princes of the gentiles—eleven, to be exact [Gen. 36:40–43]—

against Abraham's own seed through Ishmael, from whom likewise princes arose twelve in number [Gen. 25:13–16], and also against the other children of Abraham by his lawful wife, Kethura, as well as those from Abraham's other children.

Thus that one Tribe, together with Benjamin, who are so few, would arouse a disturbance against the whole world, like a current against the Ocean; yet that current is so malignant that if its water were mixed into the Ocean, it would infect its waters like a ferment.

As for the rest of the peoples, such as those of Africa and the Indies, who, like the descendants of Ham, were exiled, their condition on the day of judgment will be better, because they live in continual darkness, and are not in any light. For this reason, there cannot be in them such a mixture of light and darkness and the consequent corruption of the spiritual state itself, and therefore, no crucifixion of the Messiah, as there is with those who live in broad daylight, and turn it into black darkness.
[Abraham; Jews]

[See WE 3322, explaining Exod. 3:4.]
3323.   By "Moses" here, all those are meant through whom God the Messiah will speak, and whom He will address, as He now addresses Moses from the bush.

[78a.]   *   Regarding voices: they are heard so clearly, from any location whatever, from afar, or wherever it pleases God the Messiah, and just as clearly as if they came from actual people on earth. And answers are given likewise. This phenomenon has been discussed very often above [see 3a:3, 4a], and testified to. Therefore, anyone who wishes to raise doubt about it, let him raise it, in regard to almost continuous experience of a year's duration!

But it is God the Messiah Alone Who speaks through spirits and angels, for no one lives but He, and all beings, whether angels, or spirits, or even people living on earth are only instrumental means. This I have experienced for the period of a year, so that not anything could possibly be said more truthfully.

But how it is that evil spirits are permitted to speak evilly, in fact, even to utter blasphemy against God the Messiah, shall be told later, for everyone is allowed to speak in accordance with his own nature and character for countless reasons which it would fill up many pages to present. So not a word that I bring forward and write is mine, and to this I can solemnly testify. Therefore, if anyone should ascribe to me even one jot of these writings, which are Truths, whether that person be on earth or in heaven, he or she commits such an offence against God the Messiah as to be unpardonable except by God the Messiah Himself.

^{m}But see how these matters might be put in a different way; for we are all so utterly weak as to ascribe things to ourselves, or to the human being. So as not to burden peoples' conscience, therefore, see when the time comes in what way it may be allowed, by God's Divine Mercy, to express them, and to change the wording.^{n}

[Good; Speak, Speech; Evil; Character (Nature); Instruments (Organs); Substance]

[See also WE 3324–26, explaining Exod. 3:5.]

[**79a.**] 3327. Whether I may be allowed later to say something about the washing of feet, and the things I was commanded to do, may be seen when the time comes [*see* 165a].

[See WE 3339, explaining Exod. 3:11.]

3340. *It certainly seems that Moses was permitted to speak in this way so that he would receive the signs and then persuade the people, who were without belief. But the same signs could have been given to him, and the same words spoken, without Moses replying, who, if he had been possessed of faith, would have kept silent and would have obeyed, as is well known from the case of Abraham and others.*

[**80a.**] * Moses himself is now present with me, and admits that he had not believed at that time, saying he did not want these words to be written—not for his own sake, he declares, but for the sake of that unbelieving people whom he later led.

[81a.] SPIRITUAL EXPERIENCES

What further passed between us, I do not wish to mention here. It can be gathered somewhat from the things heard and seen by me recorded above, paragraphs 75a ff.
[Moses]

[See WE 3341–44, continuing with the explanation of Exod. 3:11–12.]

3345. The very sign itself that someone has been sent is that God the Messiah Alone is preached and worshipped. So this will also serve as a sign for those who will be sent at the end of days, and this is a sign for me, that I have been sent. About this

[81a.] mission, if it be pleasing to God the Messiah, something will be told elsewhere—also about how far the mission is to go.

3346. Here God the Messiah tells Moses, as He earlier told Jacob [Gen. 46:4], "I will be with you," that is, that Moses himself would not lead the people out of Egypt, but God the Messiah, Who is all in all things. Moses was not capable of leading that people, as is obvious from all the subsequent events. For he could do nothing at all on his own, but was like a bare instrument or tool that can do nothing of itself, not even speak, as he confessed further on, Chapter 4, verse 10. This is why Jehovah gave the reply we read in verse 11. Neither could Moses do anything at all in the way of a miracle, but it was God the Messiah Alone Who performed all and the least of them. This is clear from the very words I said this day, in the presence of Moses,

[82a.] * speaking with those spirits who were around me: that they are not, and we are not, anything at all but instruments or tools—a fact which we were able to put to a test and find out so clearly that nothing is clearer.
[Good; Evil; Nature; Tools (Organs); Substance]

3347. How must they feel, now, about Moses, who is to lead them out of captivity into the land of Canaan, seeing his condition, that he cannot bring forth even the smallest word on his own, or utter any other word than that which God the Messiah allows him to say?

I confess the same thing of myself—something which I could not help testing and acknowledging in view of an experience of such long duration, now about a year. Even if I am in the company of other people, I speak exactly as anyone else, so that no one yet has been able

[**83a.**]   *   to tell any difference in me from my old self, or from another person. Even if I was in the midst of company, I have sometimes spoken with spirits, and with those who were around me, who perhaps were able to get something out of it. But I do not know whether they have noticed anything, for at these times the inner senses are sometimes withdrawn from the outer ones—yet not so much that anyone could draw conclusions. They could only have been able to tell that I was lost in thought. The speaking itself is heard by no one but myself and by those present in the heavens who are permitted by God the Messiah to hear. But sometimes it is as clear and distinct as the voice issuing from the lips of a person on earth (although not as highly pitched and rough-sounding), so that the spirits themselves, etc., were sometimes afraid they might be heard by those who were present in the world.
[Speak, Speech]
[See also WE 3348, concluding the explanation of these verses.]

[See WE 3388, explaining Exod. 4:11–12.]
3389.   *From hearing and sight is born all human understanding, so we take the will itself here in place of hearing, and understanding in place of sight. So in the innermost meaning, these verses concern will and understanding in the human mind. From will, by means of the organs, proceed all actions, consequently also the act of speaking. In these actions, as in the will, understanding is present.*[1]

This is expressed here by the words, "Who has given a mouth to the human being, Who has made the dumb, or the deaf one?"—thus coupling speaking with hearing. Understanding is expressed by the words, "Who has made the seeing, or the blind one?"—by which is meant that no life belongs to the human being, but that Jehovah God Alone lives, for which reason it is also added, "Have not I, Jehovah?" that is, He Who Is, as said in verse 14, Chapter 3.

[**84a.**]   3390.   That human beings do not think and understand, nor will and then do, anything whatever from themselves, has been so clearly witnessed, [see] above [5a,

---

[1] In the original, this paragraph is emphasized by the symbol *NB.* written three times in the margin.

[85a.] SPIRITUAL EXPERIENCES

9a, 47a–48a], that nothing could be truer. On the other hand, everyone thinks, and then acts, from the feelings that agree with their character acquired by training and then made their own, which is likewise as true as anything can be. One can of course also be forced to speak in a manner at variance with one's own character, but since this is false and put on, no one is permitted to do this before God the Messiah, when He is present in this way.

3391. To "be with the mouth" of someone, and to "teach him what he shall say" [verse 12], involves that He would not only cause him to speak without impediment, but also impart to him a living understanding, so that he could see and perceive what was true. For

[85a.] * when it pleases God the Messiah, such a light is imparted to the mind devoted to understanding that it is indescribable. Likewise, when it is permitted, such a darkness is brought on, but in this case by demons, that a person cannot see any meaning in the words—in fact, that one even views the subject matter as if from a different point of view, indeed a divergent one—even a contrary one. That is a very strange thing, which has become familiar to me by much experience, over a long period of time.[1]

This, therefore, is to "make someone seeing, or blind," etc. [verse 11].
[Ignorance; Understanding, Understand; Light]

[86a.] 3407. As for the statements made thus far concerning Moses, he himself, and many others—in great number, as I learned from the murmur—admitted without exception that they are true. They had been unable to seize on anything in what has been written that was not in entire agreement with the truth.
[Moses]

[See WE 3413–16 up to this point, treating of Exod. 4:22–23.]
3416.   ....

---

[1] In the original this paragraph was emphasized by the word *Obs.* written twice in the margin.

54

[**87a.**] Obs. Obs. (The meaning of the words in these verses from 22 to 26 inclusive may be seen in paragraphs 3439 to 3448 under the sign ⧘⧘ ⧘⧘. When writing the above, I was in obscurity.)
[See also WE 3417–19, continuing the explanation of Exod. 4:23.]

3420. *In the same way also later on, when God the Messiah wished to pass over from the Jewish people to the Gentiles, Moses, by his supplications, held God the Messiah so bound that Balaam, who was a prophet of God the Messiah, was unable to curse the Jewish people itself. About this matter, see Numbers, Chapters 22–24, and elsewhere [see Deut. 23:4-5, Josh. 24:9–10]. But how Moses interceded on that occasion on behalf of the Jewish people may be seen in that place [Num. 14:13–19].*

There was also Abraham, who was then permitted to intercede on behalf of the people of Jacob; for no one can intercede for anyone except it be by permission. This, however, is happening in remembrance of his belief, when he was alive. For Abraham hears no person in the world, nor is he able to hear anyone except one such as myself, in whom heaven has been opened—but even then, with the
[**88a.**] permission of God the Messiah.[1]
[See also WE 3421–28, concluding the explanation of Exod. 4:23.]

⧘⧘ ⧘⧘

3439.[2] *But the things said in [Exod. 4] verses 22 to 26 are in themselves obscure, unless, by the Divine mercy of God the Messiah, they are revealed. For they are secrets which can absolutely not be laid open except by God the Messiah Alone. For this reason, let the same words be taken up again.*
[See also WE 3440–44, again explaining Exod. 4:22–24.]

3445. *Here the subject is now the son of Moses, whom [Jehovah] could not slay because of blood, exactly as we read about the descendants of Jacob, namely, that the destroyer or smiter could not slay the children of Jacob upon seeing the blood [Exod. 12:13,23]; therefore those descendants were saved by it on that occasion. What the universal meanings are when the subject is the son of Moses, who was to be slain, cannot be told at this time by reason of the fact that*

---

[1] This short line appears in the original indented, below a full line which left little space, and therefore may not constitute an "indented paragraph." We include it as one, because its subject has the nature of an experience.

[2] This paragraph is inserted because it is referred to in paragraph 87a.

[89a.] * I am still in obscurity about the words here—also permitted, but for what reason, I do not yet know.
[See also WE 3446–48, again explaining Exod. 4:25–26.]

[See WE 3473–78, treating in general of Exod. 5:20 to 6:9.]
3479. *However, certain seemingly opposite passages occur as well, indicating that Moses had still been subject to many weaknesses, and had given in to them. For example, he had not holily given honor to Jehovah at the rock (see the passages, and quote the words [Num. 20:2–13]). And in anger, he had broken the tables of the law, which had been written by the hand of Jehovah (see the passage, and quote the words [Exod. 32:19]). Because of his earlier actions, he was not admitted into the land of Canaan, but died with the others (see the passage, and quote the words [Num. 27:12–14], and then, if it is permitted, tell what they symbolize), still less was he carried up into heaven like Enoch and Elias.*

From these passages, then, it can be inferred what Moses was like in real life, that is, what he was like in the beginning, when he was called and chosen to lead the people out of Egypt, what he became later on, and finally what he was like at the finish—for every life is judged by its end—and consequently what it means that he was allowed to see the land of Canaan, but not to enter it, Num. 20: verses 11 and 12, Num. 27: verses 12, 13, 14, Deut. Chap. 1, verses 37, 38, 39, Deut. Chap. 31: verses 2 and 3, Deut. Chap. 34: verses 1 to 6, Deut. Chap. 3: verses 23 to 29[1]*. In these passages we read, **first**[2]*, *that Jehovah became angry against Moses on account of the people, though also (as is stated elsewhere) on account of Moses himself, because he did not give honor to Jehovah, either. Many matters are left unmentioned, those only being told that happened at the waters of contention*[3]*, namely, that they did not believe, and Moses did not believe. Thus it was exactly*

[90a.] * as I heard it, by the Divine mercy of God the Messiah, to wit, that He became angry against Moses on account of the people, and on account of Moses himself, for the reasons spoken of above [WE 3479].
[For the sake of context, see 3480–82, treating further of Exod. 5:20 to 6:9.]

---

[1] The original has "13–29."
[2] The *second* and *third* points are discussed in *WE 3480 ff.*
[3] *I.e.* of Meribah (Exod. 17:1–7).

FROM *WE* TOME II [92a.]

[**91a.**] 3483. Just now I heard Moses lamenting, when he saw what was just written [*WE* 3481–82], and saying something which it is not permitted to bring in here.

Meanwhile, after his lamentation, and after an entreaty to God the Messiah, I noticed that he had been snatched away from those in whose company he was at that time. This was, as he also said, in order that the words we read in Deut. Chap. 34 might be fulfilled—but in their deepest meaning—that "Jehovah buried him," that is, hid him away, as well as those words which follow in the same verse, 6—but, as I said, in their deepest meaning—that he was removed from the company of those who wickedly wished to set him up as their Messiah. This is what is said also in the same Chapter verse 5, namely, that "he died according to the mouth of Jehovah."

He says he does not remember having been present with the Messiah together with Elias on the mountain, about which event the Evangelists speak [Matt. 17:3, Mark 9:4, Luke 9:30], because no one can ever recall anything of the past to remembrance, unless this is granted, and the memory imparted, by God the Messiah.
[Moses]

[See also WE 3484, concluding the explanation of Exod. 5:20 to 6:9 in general.]

3499. The accounts commencing with [Exod.] Chap. 6 verse 10 to the end of the Chapter, then commencing with Chap. 7, verses 1 to 7, are nothing but a summary of events up to this point. In a way, they also include things yet to take place, for starting with verse 8, the signs themselves begin. Here there is only description, such as a summing up of what Jehovah had spoken and had commanded Moses and Aaron to do, as well as of what Moses and Aaron had replied. Further, there is a description of the progeny of Reuben, Simeon and Levi down to Moses, who is described last.

[**92a.**] 3500. Here it should be observed that much speaking had intervened (as is usual when God the Messiah is speaking with anyone, although this speech takes place through angels, as it does with me), and so, perhaps, lasted over a period of many days. This is also evident from verse 13 of Chap. 6, as well as from the subsequent passages, in that the events are briefly reviewed here that had previously been told in detail.

But how long a time had elapsed from the first revelation on the Mount of God, Horeb, up until they performed the signs, is not apparent from the Word Itself. In verse 7, Chap. 7, we read that "Moses was then a son of eighty years."
[See also WE 3501–03, concluding the explanation of these verses.]

[See WE 3546–56, explaining Exod. 8:1–15.]
3557.   And so these frogs are what went forth from the river spoken of above [Exod. 7:15–25], and were gathered together into the river that is damned, in the region of the Egyptians [cf. WE 3539], that is, Armageddon [Rev. 16:16]. Thus the subject here is unclean spirits of the lowest sort, that is, the kind who control the lowest or outermost parts of the human being, and who arouse those passions pertaining to the body and blood that are called pleasures of the senses and merely bodily enjoyments—*strictly, the various bodily luxuries due to taste.* It is these unclean spirits that control the outermost or merely bodily regions of the human being, and are therefore called "frogs," which are larger insects of diverse shapes and sizes. They likewise

[93a.]   *   appeared once to me, when they were going out [of me], really clearly, so that I saw them creeping before my eyes, and presently gathered together into one mass. Then they were like fire, and exploded with a noise that came to my ears like a bang, as they broke to pieces. That spot was later cleansed. And this took place in London in the month of April, 1745. Bursting through my pores, they appeared like smoke, but on the floor, like so many crawling worms, in great abundance. [See 397.]
[Appetite; Eat; Fire; Worm]

3571.   [Exod. 8:] verse 11[1]. These words are also understood as [explained] above [WE 3560–61, 3569]. However, that frogs would be

---

[1] In the *Schmidius Bible*, this is verse 7.

left in the river means that they who have been rejected [WE 3557, [93a], WE 3570] live in their own swamps; for in swamps
[94a.] * *are their homes, thus also in rivers that stink like swamps, because of the dead.*
3574. *[Exod. 8:] verse 14*[1]. *Here it came about that the Egyptians "gathered the frogs into heaps," and that "the land stank from them." But these words were written down because they also involve other things, that is, that those gatherings, symbolized here by "frogs," are not only unclean spirits, but especially whatever is aroused by them, namely, bodily enjoyments. When these grow stale, then the whole body stinks from them. For although they are deprived of power, and dead, they still remain, so that the Egyptian, that is, earthly person,*
* *can breathe. A stench to the nostrils corresponds to their unclean nature, as has also*
[95a.] * *been made evident to me; for things in nature, even a stench such as comes from unclean things in nature, interact with such spirits.*

[See WE 3589–91, treating in general of Exod. 8:20–32.]
3592. *But these harmful flies, or fantasies, can only come up in earthly people, meant by the Egyptians, not in spiritual people, or children of Israel. For the latter are not weakened by such pangs of conscience [WE 3591], but rather strengthened. Such pangs are beneficial in causing one to know oneself and to admit one's faults, which God the Messiah then heals from most deeply within, like wounds that have first been opened up.*

This is the reason why it is first said here that this swarm of harmful flies would not appear in Goshen, where the children of Israel were, but only in Egypt, verse 22[2], *and this for the plain reason that God the Messiah shall bring them help and heal them. This is meant in verse 23*[3], *where we read, "For I will set a redemption between My people, and your people." What is redemption without a redeemer? Man is redeemed by God the Messiah Alone. Thus no power to hurt them is granted, according to what was written below, at the end [of this tome] at the sign* ה ה, *where*

---

[1] In the *Schmidius Bible* this is verse 10.
[2] In the *Schmidius Bible* this is verse 18.
[3] In the *Schmidius Bible* this is verse 19.

[**96a.**] * the cunning of many spirits is discussed.[1]

3594. *[Exod. 8:] verse 21*[2]. *To* "*send on Pharaoh, on his servants, on his people, and into his houses,*" *means the same as what was said above about the frogs, which you may see [at WE 3560-61]. For it is evil spirits that arouse those fantasies, and they desire nothing more than to tear a person apart miserably, by operating through dreadful fantasies,*
[**97a.**] * and like practices. For what this gang is like when, by permission, it is led by such a leader as is spoken of in the paragraphs marked ℞ ℞, no one can believe except from actual experience. For they aim at nothing else but to corrupt everything of one's mental landscape and thinking. When the person is absorbed in fantasy, then they really awaken, as if they begin to realize that they themselves are not those people [they are with]. Hence their brutality.

3641. *[Exod. 9:] verse 24. By* "*fire*" *here is described anger being enkindled, namely, how it mixed itself in with profanities, for we read,* "*and fire mixing itself in the midst of hail.*" "*Hail*" *is blasphemous words, but* "*fire*" *is that burning feeling which is said to reside* "*in the midst,*" *that is, within the words. That it does reside within them is noticeable in the speech of an angry person.*

The process of growing angry, when the angry person is one whose feelings and words spirits see, as they do mine, appears before them no different than
[**98a.**] * *as sparks going out in the form of a heavy, flaming rain. But this depends on the nature of the anger, which sometimes exists for a just reason, as was once the case with me—at which they were greatly astonished.*
[Fire; Anger]

---

[1] This refers to the "missing numbers," 1 to 148⅓, which were originally written at the end of the tomes of the *Word of the Old Testament Explained*. According to the index, paragraph 77 treats of the malice of evil spirits, paragraphs 143–44 of many spirits together and how they are kept in a bond. A. Acton refers to paragraph 77. However, the words "evil spirits" are an erroneous reading for "many spirits" (the Latin being *multorum*, not *malorum*). That the reference is more likely 143–44, is seen in [97a], which mentions a "leader."

[2] In the *Schmidius Bible* this is verse 17.

[**99a.**][1]   [....] He called them the children of Israel so that in them He might remember the gentiles [*cf. WE 3337–38, 4070*].

How the life of all who live on earth, as well as the life of the human body itself, is guided by God the Messiah Alone, is evident not only from what has been said above [*cf. WE 644–50*]. It was told how the human Soul lives, and therefore is ruled, by God the Messiah Alone, and the life of the subsequent faculties by spirits in a proper arrangement, who are only instruments of life, but not lives in themselves. But it can also be seen clearly, by comparison, from man-made instruments in which there is only one single acting force, as in pendulums, and in other mechanisms that are set in motion by the single force of a wheel, a spring, etc. Other powers that follow one upon the other, in whatever order they succeed and are consequently increased, are still activated by that single force. But this is only by way of comparison, to aid the understanding.

This also shows that in the last power, all the prior powers and forces reside, dependent and focussed upon the one force, and are thus together. The same applies in every action, to all the lives of a person, from his very first—for there are as many distinct lives as there are faculties. But when these are in a corrupted order, they are not guided in the same way as when they are in a reformed order. When in corrupted order, they are guided, upon permission, by evil spirits, who nevertheless have no power in them, but power is given to them as instruments, for various reasons that have been spoken of here and there [*5a, 7a, 10a–11a, 39a, 53a, WE 1852, 1855, 2119*]; namely, depending upon the state of the person on earth, both present and foreseen. Evil spirits, like men, think they are under their own control, but how miserably mistaken they are, I have very often observed, and it has been

[**100a.**] granted to me by God the Messiah to prove it to them vocally, as well as by various experiences, even to their extreme indignation.

But we read about this experience so often in the Word of God the Messiah—how He cast them out, and at His will sent them into the swine [*Matt. 8:30–32, Mark 5:11–13, Luke 8:32–33*], etc., as well as how they were cast out by His disciples—that there is no need to bring in other proofs, of which there are very many.

---

[1] The portion [99a–100a] is the content of a fragment of manuscript glued to the inside back cover of *Explicationes in Verbum Veteris Testamenti*, Tome II. See A. Acton, *The Word Explained*, Vol. III, p. 341, footnote 6, and Vol. IV, p. 320, footnote 1.

[100a.] SPIRITUAL EXPERIENCES

> *How the soul gives the will permission to go off into an act, should be considered; for nothing can pass into the will without the soul permitting it, but it is the soul alone that gives the power to act, whether it agrees or does not agree.*[1]

---

[1] In the original this paragraph is emphasized by the symbol *NB.* written once in the margin.

FROM *WE* TOME III [100a.]

[Paragraphs from *The Word of the Old Testament Explained*, Tome III (Exod. 14:29 to Deut. 34:5 as well as the Biblical books from Lev. to II Chron.), numbered by the author from 1 to 7762, by A. Acton from 4003 to 7566]

Why the Jewish people were so often tempted in the wilderness

4005.[1]   The people of Jacob, or of Moses, were tempted so often, and as often yielded in temptations—not ten times, as we read [Num. 14:22], but obviously many more. Therefore, one asks, why were they led so many times into temptations, when yet it was foreseen that they would succumb? Would it not have been better for them if they had not undergone temptations?

But the answer was given that while in Egypt, they were not only idol worshippers, like the Egyptians, but also, as one can see from Moses' prayer [Exod. 32:11–13], of a haughty spirit, looking upon the whole world as nothing, and condemning it, just because they themselves were of the seed of Abraham, Isaac and Jacob, and therefore the only ones who would be in charge, not only on earth but also in the heavens. For Moses prayed for himself and the people, that they might be greater than all peoples on the face of the earth, and that the soil might be their inheritance—and this at the very same time when they were worshipping the calf and carrying it in their hearts, having drunk its dust.

Therefore, since they ambitioned so much, and indeed to be the only ones, it is a necessary consequence that they should undergo temptations, and through temptations be corrected, for without temptation, no one can ever become better, so that they would not only see what they were like, but realize that they were not the chosen ones. For to let idol worshippers into the kingdom of God, is this not the same as letting in the devil, whose kingdom they harbor within them? Therefore, since this was their nature, they were subjected to temptations, and, in fact, of the lightest kind, as, for instance, when they were lacking water [17:1 ff.] and yet had seen so many miracles, and were seeing them every day; and as when Moses tarried for forty days, and yet they had seen the glory of God on the mountain [24:15–18], and so on.

---

[1] This paragraph is unnumbered in the original. See *The Word Explained* 4002, footnote 2.

[101a.] SPIRITUAL EXPERIENCES

[101a.] * This is the reply to the things said to me by those who are standing with them; for a multitude of them crowded around me for a long time, whose wicked deeds I do not dare to disclose.

[See WE 4020–22, explaining Exod. 15:2.]
4023. *As for Jah, however, this is an abbreviation for Jehovah, occurring in songs. About Jah, see elsewhere, in the Psalms of David. Here something should be pointed out which perhaps few know, if anyone. The speech of Spirits*
[102a.] * is one which falls mainly into a one-syllable ending; thus it is a kind of singing, though not having those rhythms that are very displeasing. Nevertheless, it is a kind of singing—not a song, but its endings are similar to those usually found in the Psalms, but of one syllable. ᵐThey are monosyllabic, even if the word is rather long, but [their speech] does not have the endings of hexameter verse[1].ⁿ And they do this with such great skill! For entire days they spoke with me in no other way, and afterwards, I spoke in the same way with them, for later this cadence came spontaneously. From this, inferences can be drawn regarding the Psalms of David, etc. etc.

But all the conversation of this kind between us flowed of its own accord, making me realize that I was speaking nothing whatsoever from myself, just as I was likewise not thinking anything from myself. Thus the thought went forth into such speech. But the speaking was not always like this.

They said, moreover, that the ending should be in a single syllable for the sake of unity.[2] From this also one may infer that the word "Jah" is a word of singing, and means Jehovah, because He Alone is to be sung, that is, worshipped.
[Speak, Speech; Rhythm; One (Union)]

[See WE 4037, explaining Exod. 15:9.]
[103a.] 4038. These next words [verse 9] apply to an enemy, that is, one who is constantly pursuing, with the result that there is combat, and who constantly thinks he is overtaking. With such peo-

---
[1] That is, with long or stressed syllables.
[2] See *TCR* 8.

ple it is always the case that they believe they have convinced others. For upon obtaining a forced agreement, they immediately boast that they have "overtaken," as I have learned by many experiences. It appears as if there is agreement
[Agreement; Persuasion; Spirit]

[**104a.**] * when spirits are permitted to pour in convictions, together with feelings, and at the same time to snatch away anything that refutes them. But they do not realize that in spite of this, they still have not overtaken the person, for that evil is turned by God the Messiah into good, so that they are compelled to admit afterwards they had not overtaken him at all.
[Agreement; Persuasion; Spirit]

[See also WE 4039–42, concluding the explanation of this verse.]

[See WE 4069, explaining Exod. 15:22–27 in general.]

4070. *Now although the [sons of Jacob] were of this character, still God the Messiah did not wish to abandon them, both because of the promise [made to Abraham] and, especially, because of the portrayal in them of the sons of Israel [see 46a, 99a, WE 2806, 3142, 3337–38, 3392]. For when God the Messiah saw their external rites and the statutes He had commanded them, He did not see them with human eyes, but with Divine ones, that is, He saw the Heavenly things they portrayed, thus calling to remembrance the Church of the Gentiles, both the earliest one and the one to come, that is, the sons of Israel; and so he did not wish to forsake them.*

Outer things entirely interact with inner ones—but [only] with Him Who is in the innermost regions and in the highest. For there is such an interaction that whatever exists on the earthly plane and is named, is understood entirely spiritually by those who are spiritual—as I once found out when I was telling in a series

[**105a.**] * a number of things that had a connection, but they were natural data; and yet, by those who were hearing them, I saw that they had been understood entirely spiritually. Their causes also come to view, for the causes of all natural phenomena lie in spiritual ones, and the beginnings of those causes in heavenly ones.
[Interaction (Correspondence); Speak, Speech; Earthly (Natural); Spiritual things]

[See also WE 4071, concluding the explanation of these verses.]

[106a.] SPIRITUAL EXPERIENCES

4106.   ....
[106a.] NB.*   ***Now begin the things which took place in the garden*** on May 2, 1746 [*cf.* WE 2072–74].[1]
[*See 4103–07, explaining Exod. 16:1–3.*]

[107a.]   4108.   That these things are so, I happen to know, by the mercy of God the Messiah. For I was sent into the wilderness, in that I was writing devoid of feeling, so that I was even compelled to grumble against those who were snatching feelings away from me—may God the Messiah forgive them. But many things took place at this point that cannot be told in regard to how these matters stood, because they involve secrets. There was grumbling for several days.

[*See WE 4109, concluding the explanation of verses 1–3.*]
[*See WE 4110, explaining Exod. 16:4.*]

4111.   That this bread was to be gathered "every day," that is, every morning, involves many things, namely, that they should have no care but for each day, for God the Messiah wills to provide for His own day by day, and to take care of them in this life, as in the other.

In the other life, as they are unaware of things future, as also of things past, no one thinks about what is to come, except they whom God the Messiah allows to remember past events, or to view those to come. This is the condition of the angels of heaven and of the happy in the other life.

[108a.]   *   Therefore no grief touches them as it does here in the world, where the grief comes only from the memory of things past, and from so-called human "providing" for future ones. He wills, therefore, that by their "gathering each morning"—as He also says in His own Prayer, "give us this day our daily bread" [Matt. 6:11, Luke 11:3]—that condition of the heavenly beings may exist on this earth, and thus, that heaven may be with those living here.

But what worries they can have, and over what kind of things, because remembrance is granted to them, will be told elsewhere. For these words involve more things than anyone could possibly bring to mind without their being revealed.

[*Happiness; Future; Memory; Past; Providence*]

---

[1] See *WE* 4106, footnote to these words.

[See WE 4112–15, concluding the explanation of Exod. 16:4.]

4129. *[Exod. 16:] verse 10. What is meant here is that no one knows when the bridegroom will come, in glory, with the angels. That this glory would appear in a cloud, is also foretold by God the Messiah [Matt. 24:30, Mark 13: 26]. "In a cloud" means Heaven itself, thus in Heaven. Whether He will come into individual human minds, in a miraculous manner, with a sound, and such things, we must wait and see. It was foretold [Rev. 1:7] that also the sons of Jacob will see His glory, thus even unbelievers, for which reason it is said here to both— that is, to the sons of Israel and the sons of Judah[1], "Behold, the glory of Jehovah appeared in the cloud."*

The "cloud" here is man's heaven, that is, the human mind, which is like a cloud, but in different ways. It is like a bright cloud to the sons of Israel, but like a dark and black cloud to unbelievers. For a human mind, one in which there are truths, is comparable to a cloud, and appears like a cloud, but for the sons of Israel, it will shine like dawn in the morning. That truths are portrayed
[109a.]   *   *by a bright cloud is abundantly evident.*
[See also WE 4130–31, concluding the explanation of Exod. 16:10.]

4160. *[Exod. 16:] verse 27. This passage confirms that in the other life, people will not find anything but what they had collected the preceding day [see WE 4156]; for as one's character then is, so it remains. This also has become clear to me in many ways while I was in company*
[110a.]   *   with spirits and those who lived after death. These had not been able to change their mind about things they had accepted in their bodily life. No matter how strongly I was permitted, so to speak, to suggest to them that they be of another mind, and thereby become happy, it was quite useless. They still remained the same as they were before, even if they acknowledged that the things said were true; in fact, there was seemingly a kind of will to live in a different mind, but as far as I could find out, by then it was in vain, for their own mind soon returned.
[Good; Character (Nature); Truth]

---

[1] Probably meaning Jacob; see *WE* 4097–4101, 4107–09.

[111a.] 4207. [Exod. 17:] verse 12. "When his hands were heavy," in the deepest sense, means that he had no more strength, that is, that in regard to belief he began to waver. Then the hands become heavy of themselves. When they are light, and are raised up by themselves, then there is belief. For it is human nature that the outward gestures become spontaneous and effortless when we are being our deepest self, for then we are sustained, because strength is proportionate to love. I have also quite often experienced, in various ways, how
[Love; Gesture]

[**112a.**] * outer strength, that is, power of mind and body, have followed with unrestrained ease when I was being my deeper self. It was evident in many ways. Furthermore, everyone experiences this same thing just from Love: when there is a love for something, nothing is heavy. The reverse is true when a person is struggling.
[Love; Gesture]

[See also WE 4208–10, concluding the explanation of Exod. 17:12]

4251. [Exod. 18:] verse 26. Likewise [it is confirmed that the words in verse 22 must be true]. Thus all the "weighty matters" would be referred to Moses—they must consult God the Messiah Himself and must receive answers. This has also happened many times,

[**113a.**] * in an image of that procedure, namely, that they went off to someone who held the position of a prince, and consulted, and they also brought back answers, which they told to me. This took place very frequently, in the image of the Kingdom of God the Messiah, so that the words that I wrote I am allowed to swear to.

It also happens the other way around, that they convey things I have said. They even consult among themselves, for instance, about the words I was writing, supposing as people on earth normally do that the consultation came of their own initiative. Then they were also allowed to bring their consultations into my mind—this I clearly observed.

However, these did not start from them, as I was also able to see plainly. Not the slightest thing that I saw coming from them, were they allowed to bring in;

indeed, their very thoughts were also corrected. So they did not realize that all counsels come from God the Messiah, though adapted to each individual's character and understanding. I have not been permitted, however, to insert anything whatever dictated aloud by them.

The reason they are unaware of these facts is so that they may suppose that they themselves live, for without this notion they would believe they had no life.

This also showed to some extent of what belief and character they were who were consulting and were allowed to bring in the consultations.
[Lord; Answer]

[See WE 4260, explaining Exod. 19:3.]
4260. When Moses went up to God, it is said that "Jehovah called to him"; elsewhere [verses 9, 10, 21, 24] it is said that "He said to him." A call is a louder voice, so that he would hear, and indeed, "from the Mountain," that is, in the deepest sense, from heaven. "A mountain" is heaven, because of the height, for it is in the highest places, God the Messiah being Heaven Itself. One can hear which place voices come from, such as

[114a.] * even several times from on high, through mediating voices of angels, as well as other voices also, at different heights, as I was allowed to observe. A voice was heard amid a moderate murmur, and indeed, from the height of the temple, etc. [cf. 4a].
[Speak, Speech; Ladder; Spirit]

* A mountain is also a temple, whence Heaven is called a Mountain; and in the highest sense, God the Messiah is the Mountain.
[See WE 4261, concluding the explanation of this verse.]

[See WE 4352–54, explaining Exod. 20:13.]
4355. This commandment applies likewise to all those who see and look on when any kill, torment, torture, revile, innocent people, and, although they are able to give help, do not give it—such as their leaders, who look on with composure, and do not in any way come to their aid. It is these, then, who kill, torment, for they consent to it, though not daring to do it themselves. There are many things that hold them back, but these are loves opposite to true love. They put

[115a.] SPIRITUAL EXPERIENCES

first what is their own or self-love. About this matter I also conversed with those who spoke
[**115a.**]   *   with me, one of whom, I take it, had looked calmly upon very wicked doings and had nevertheless made no move to render help, when yet he could have done so, for he possessed very much authority (if it was he). Thus (it seems to follow), by consent if not favor he would have condoned war, at least, and thus victory, with no regret at heart.
         [Abraham; Agreement (Consent); Jews]

[**116a.**]   * ^{m}See whether these words are to be inserted, that is, whether they are of any use in the elucidation of this commandment. If not, this must be blotted out.^{n}
[See also WE 4356–57, concluding the explanation of Exod. 20:13.]

[See WE 4384–86, explaining Exod. 20:17.]
[**117a.**]   4387.   [These words were said] because self-love and love of the world clung to the seed of these descendants, from Jacob. For from that time, it had been the nature of that people to despise all in comparison with themselves, to want themselves alone to be the chosen, and everyone in the world, even heaven, to perish, just so that they would be lords of it all; and would hardly let in the rest, even as the vilest servants. I am in a position to know this so very well, from so much
[Jews]
[**118a.**]   *   association and conversation with them after death, that I am convinced of it. Nevertheless, there must be nothing less likely, since they hold God the Messiah in hatred; in fact, they would tear each other apart like wolves and tigers, for this is what they regard each other to be, etc. etc.
[See WE 4388–93, concluding the explanation of verse 17.]
[See WE 4394–99, explaining Exod. 20:18.]

4400.   When God the Messiah speaks, He is acting from the very essence of things, because from what is higher and prior, as it is called. His words themselves then follow from the very essence of things. From that comes the understanding of the words; for it is the understanding that is then aroused, and the words that give expression. So the mind is kept in a state of understanding, not by the words that follow, but by the things which the words express. It is different when a human being speaks; then it goes the other way around, and the meaning, or thing, must be gathered from the words. That this

[119a.] * is the case, could be illustrated by so many examples and actual proofs, that if the abundance of proof within myself would accomplish anything, no one would be able to raise a doubt about this matter. For heavenly minds are in the very essence of things, whence they bring forth meanings into words, the words following from the things. Angels, when speaking, do not even know what words follow, or to which language the words belong. Yet they know very well everything that lies within each word, as I have very often observed, and on which subject I have spoken with them on several occasions. Even when I was speaking other languages I had learned, they did not know which language it was, unless I took thought that it was this particular language; besides other examples showing that understanding flows in, sometimes more abundant, sometimes more limited, entirely according to the will of God the Messiah, Who disposes the state of minds, imparting to them whatever will serve a use, etc. etc.

From this it may be evident that it was an understanding of things at that time that caused the people to tremble, to stand afar off, terrified; and thus that by "voices" are meant the words of God the Messiah, understood, etc. etc.

[Essence; Inflow; Inward; Speak, Speech; Things; Voice (Words)]

[120a.] 4401. Nor could it have been otherwise, when the Law was being decreed by God the Messiah Himself, than that voices and words spoken to the more inward parts, adapted to the understanding of each mind, should be heard. It therefore follows that the Law was not decreed at that time on the outside, but on the inside; for, as said above [*WE* 4395], there is no Law separate from the inner parts. Nor should anyone imagine that that voice, or those sounds, came through the air, and then through the ear or hearing, into the minds; for they came through a higher and prior way into the minds, because from an actual understanding of things. But that voice is exactly like a voice that flows in through the ear, so that the hearer, that is, the seer, could not possibly think of it as coming in any other way than through the ear. For it is just as clear and, in fact, just as

[121a.] SPIRITUAL EXPERIENCES

loud—although no bystander hears it—as speaking by the mouth of man when it passes by way of the ear. About this matter, I have gained such an intimate knowledge
[Speak, Speech]

[121a.] * that I can testify to it before everyone; on which subject you may read more above [78a, 83a].
[Speak, Speech]

[122a.] 4402. Moreover, how an understanding of things flows into the vocal expressions when some prayer, such as the Lord's prayer, is recited from memory, can also be told in a few words. It comes from above, and is poured in, sometimes more abundantly, sometimes in a more limited measure, depending upon the state of the human mind. This I clearly saw and could feel when I said that Prayer—to this I can solemnly swear—like today, the 16th day of May, 1746; and one who was speaking with me was both amazed and gladdened by it.
[Essence; Inflow; Inward; Speak, Speech; Prayer; Thing; Expressions (Words)]

[See also WE 4403–06, concluding the explanation of verse 18.]

[See WE 4412–14, explaining Exod. 20:20.]

[123a.] 4415. What this fear [*WE* 4414] is like, and in what way it is coupled with that other fear [*id.* 4413], and in what way separate from it, is difficult to describe. The sight of God the Messiah is, indeed, also feared, not because one is frightened by it, but because one fears for one's own impurity, and for one's own powerlessness to do and carry out those things which are ordered by the now present God the Messiah, the Very Holy One Himself. For the person sees that he should now cast away everything profane that is in him, and all that resists, and that is not holy; and seeing in himself the powerlessness, or the apparent inability, to put these things away from him, in thought, will and act, therefore he fears the sight, that is, the presence, of God the Messiah, or that God the Messiah should speak with him. Therefore, this speaking takes place through others, all depending upon the character and capacity of the person in question. I describe this fear from my own experience; whether it would also be like this
[Fear]

[124a.] * in others, if they had been in the same state, speaking with the Spirits of God the Messiah, and with so many other Spirits, I do not yet know.
[Fear]
[See also WE 4416–18, concluding the explanation of this verse.]

[See WE 4428–31, explaining Exod. 20:2;5.]
* Also, it is clear that everything which goes forth from the human being, as if the human being were its origin, is evil, because from an evil root; and therefore that we must not evoke such things, as if they were from ourselves.
* This is the reason why we do not obtain anything we ask for from ourselves, as is
[125a.] * evident from many cases, in which, as I was given to realize, I would not obtain anything that I wished. Of this matter, if God the Messiah sees fit, more will be told.
[Wish (Will)]
[See also WE 4432, concluding the explanation of verse 25.]

[See WE 4455, explaining Exod. 21:8.]
* This commandment also concerns the Church of God, specifically, that it must not be handed over to a strange Church, this being for reasons I am as yet not able to set forth due to the obscurity of my understanding. For it has been so greatly confined
[126a.] * that I am unable to expand my thought, because, as it seems to me, I was being delivered into the bondage of those who wish to dominate, who are not good.

[See WE 4460, explaining Exod 21:11.]
4461. Other matters which these words have to do with, I dare not tell in so many words—namely, those to do with the Jewish Church, which had indeed been put away, but still not sent away; for He will provide her with food, a roof, and the rest. But as for being sent away, if they wish, they may go away "for nothing, without paying any money," and choose themselves a different leader.
[127a.] * But Abraham, with a voice that I heard, altogether refused this; presumably Jacob likewise, who had

[128a.] held onto the heel of Esau–which subject you may see discussed earlier [*WE* 351].

[See WE 4476–77, explaining Exod. 21:5-6.]

*   A state of bondage is also seeing and recognizing the best goal, yet not being moved by it, but wishing to be moved by it, and not being able. This state of bondage existed with myself, when these things

[**128a.**]   *   were written; for I could in no way be freed as yet from spirits who wished to force me into writing them. Therefore, they brought on darkness when I was trying to grasp them in thought, and thus arouse love for the goal, that of serving the public and having regard for uses. I felt this state come upon me, as I could write nothing else with clarity but those words which were quietly dictated to me, so to speak, and yet I did not know with any conviction whether it was true and good, or not true and good—not with any conviction, still less feeling. I found out that truths had been mixed with non-truths. This was the reason for the prayer indicated below by the sign ⊖⊖ [*see SE* 81].

[Good; Ignorance; Use; Truth]

^mThe words here said about "a servant" also regard what is within a person, that is, the earthly or servile part, and the spiritual or free part, whence also the origin of these laws could be learned, as is evident from verses 20 and 21.ⁿ

[For the sake of context, see also WE 4478, concluding the explanation of Exod. 21:5–6.]

4479.   As for the punishment now spoken of, that is, for preferring anything above that freedom—that is, if one loves anything above God the Messiah, Who is Freedom Itself, as was said above [*WE* 4442]—one is punished by becoming a servant forever, but not in the service of God the Messiah Himself, which is called servitude, but is Freedom, for to serve God the Messiah Alone is to be most free; for then one is moved by what is best, and so is led by feeling, as if on one's own or as a free agent. That this is

[**129a.**]   *   freedom and, in fact, no bondage at all, so does not derive in the least from bondage, could be corroborated by many points; but they must be passed by, etc. etc.

[See also the last paragraph of WE 4479, concluding the explanation of these verses.]

[See WE 4573, explaining Exod. 23:8.]

4574. Hence "the seeing are blinded, and even the just are corrupted," for they cannot know the mind of the deceiver who is speaking and acting; nor does the deceiver himself know his own character and mind, which he sees even less than someone else—especially that dissembler, the serpent, who does this as if from his nature, on its slightest approving nod. Thus the deceit flows as if spontaneously,[1]

[**130a.**]   4575.   at which I have at times been amazed in spirits, who do not deliberate on the deceptions they are weaving together, but seize on them at the slightest nod, and then, as if unaware, spin together poisonous deceptions. So it is their nature, like that of serpents, that is acting. It had appeared to me that they were acting deliberately, but later I realized that it was from a nature that wholly dominates, and then draws every least thing into the whole, and thus corrupts it. For where a general purpose is regnant, all the least things are looked upon and seized upon as being for that purpose, which the spirits constantly harbor in themselves, and thus look to. This seemed to me to be the cause of their extreme shrewdness, which I have noticed at times.

[See WE 4576–77, concluding the explanation of Exod. 23:8.]

[See WE 4584–85, explaining Exod. 23:13.]

4586.   Thus one must extremely "beware" of thinking those things which are profane and damned, for then they infest the mind's thought, such as those which I have very often experienced,

[**131a.**]   *   when the bare mention of swearing and profanity so harmed my mind that I did not know which way to turn, so as to get rid of them. For when they who are spiritual, and must therefore return all and the least things to God the Messiah, hear such wickedness, it upsets their minds as much as if someone should beat their body with whips and clubs. I can solemnly testify that this has been happening to me for a period of a year, so that I could hardly be in company where things were

---

[1] In the original this paragraph is emphasized by the symbol *NB*. written in the margin.

[132a.]   SPIRITUAL EXPERIENCES

repeated that are so dreadful, and cause such very grave pains, etc. etc.
[Swearing; Profanity]

4605.   [Exod. 23:] verse 22. *"Hearing to hear" is to obey, as before [WE 4603], which is also explained here when it says, "if you do all that He speaks."*
*   *For when God the Messiah speaks, all in the least and greatest things must be carried out. Therefore, lest He be provoked, He speaks in various ways through angels.*
[132a.]   *   These matters can be set forth in many words, by the Divine mercy of God the Messiah, but whether this is the place, I do not yet know.
[See also the rest of WE 4605, concluding the explanation of verse 22.]

4620.   [Exod. 23:] verses 29 and 30. *These words in the more inward meaning signify secrets, namely, as to how a person is reformed. For evil is not driven out all at once, but little by little; and the evil that is clinging to one and has become fixed through acts, is gradually rooted out, and then an opposite, or better, character is put on. Meanwhile, evil is also turned to good, and in the place of evil feelings come good ones, and so it goes in all and the least remaining qualities, for a person's state changes through successive stages, but how it does, and what state is put on, is known to the Messiah Alone, because it is the work of God the Messiah Alone. How evil is turned into good, and*
[133a.]   *   how opposites are raised up to serve for a person's betterment, and many more particulars relating to reformation—something of which I was permitted to recall earlier [103a–04a]) may be seen discussed in an account about temptation [*see SE* 66], if God the Messiah sees fit to allow me to set it forth.

4621.   From this it may be evident how *"the earth would become desolate,"* if evil were driven out all at once; and how *"the beast of the field would multiply,"* that is, natural vices, that have become natural through acts; consequently, how it is driven out little by little. For when
[134a.]   *   evil is being driven out, it is called back several times, even until it is blotted out, and gives way to good.

This is a secret, and I do not know whether anyone knows it; etc., etc.
[Evil; Regeneration]
[For the sake of context, see also WE 4622, concluding the explanation of these verses.]
[See WE 4623-24 up to this point, explaining Exod. 23:31.]

* .... *"They will be driven out from their faces" means that they afterwards do not appear, while still contributing to a comparison, and thus to a sense of goodness, and to a recognition of truth. For without evil, there is no feeling of goodness, and without falsity, there is no recognition of truth. Hence, the words which were now* [**135a.**] * *said have to do with these matters, namely, why evil must be driven out so slowly, and "not in one year,"* etc. etc. ^mThis can be illustrated to some extent by fruit, which being at first unripe and tasting badly, later ripens, fills out, becomes sweet; thus [there must be] temptations, etc. etc.[n1]

[Evil; Regeneration]
[See also the rest of WE 4624, concluding the explanation of verse 31.]

4625.   *[Exod. 23:] verse 32. Evils must never be united to goodness, that is, "you shall make no covenant"; for if they are united, the person can never become spiritual. It must be as if he did not know evil, although it is present in some form, so secretly that it contributes, as has been said [above], to the feeling of goodness and to the recognition of it, and of truth.*

[**136a.**] * These points can be illustrated by some examples, if God the Messiah finds it fitting—some, perhaps, by what I have been allowed, by the mercy of God the Messiah, to learn through experience.

4626.   *[Exod. 23:] verse 33. "They shall not dwell in the land," that is, in the mind, for unless the form of the mind is brought back entirely into a spiritual form, in accordance with [WE] paragraph 4622, they do in some way live in the land.* More

[**137a.**]   *   can be said on this matter from the same principles, if it is permitted.

[See the rest of WE 4626-27, concluding the explanation of verse 33.]
[See WE 4628-29, explaining Exod. 24:1-2.]

---

[1] In the original, this marginal notation is emphasized by the symbol *NB*. written to its left.

[138a.] SPIRITUAL EXPERIENCES

4630.   As to whether the "seventy elders," who were to go up at the same time, portray the lower mind, this appears to be the case, for it is from that mind that a person is lifted up to God the Messiah. This may be better evident from what

[**138a.**]   *   I previously learned from experience, by the Divine mercy of God the Messiah [*see* 10a]. For the order is that the things in that mind must be lifted up into the mind devoted to understanding, so that from it must be brought forth what is to be of service to that mind. As for the feelings, whether and how they are to go up is still a mystery to me. It does seem to me now that the feelings of the lower mind are joined on like a body to the feelings of the heavenly mind.
[Feeling (Affection); Body]

[See also WE 4631–32, concluding the explanation of verses 1 and 2.]

[See WE 4633–34, explaining Exod. 24:3.]

4635.   However, [take note] that it is said—for it seems to be interjected by spirits,

[**139a.**]*   who now as before, are being answered, as has usually been the case—

*   that the people do not say, "all the words which Moses has spoken," but "which Jehovah has spoken." In everything which Jehovah speaks, there is order, from the very innermost elements toward the outward ones, so that one element cannot exist without the other.

As to how the people understood the words, see above [WE 4399–4400, 119a–20a], where the Law is discussed; for the people heard and saw when the Law was being decreed—which cannot take place without an understanding of inward matters, as you may see confirmed in the passages just referred to.[1]

[See also the rest of WE 4635, concluding the explanation of verse 3.]

[See WE 4646, explaining Exod. 24:11.]

*   From this it can be learned that they indeed "saw" the God of Israel with their eyes, but with eyes that had been opened, that is, opened from most deeply within, so that they could see when others could not, just as takes place when the eyes are opened, mean-

---

[1] In the original, this paragraph is emphasized by the symbol *NB*. written twice in the margin.

ing when all the sight comes from most deeply within. Then to the eyes it is dark in respect to worldly objects, and the person sees only things which are more inward. This may be clear from many

[140a.] *   of the particulars that are told elsewhere about the inner sight, if God the Messiah finds it fitting [see 3a, WE 1144, 15a–16a].*

[See the rest of WE 4646–47, concluding the explanation of verse 11.]

[See WE 4648, explaining Exod. 24:12.]

4649.   The "tables" are spoken of in what follows [Exod. 32:15–19, 34:1–4, 29]. Of these there were two, symbolizing the old and the new covenant.

[141a.] *   As to what the tables are, consult, if it is allowed at that time, what is hidden away, and not yet permitted for me to draw on [SE 39, 40, WE 5384].*

[See WE 4650–53, concluding the explanation of verse 12.]

[See WE 4657, explaining Exod. 24:16.]

4658.   Here again that is called "a cloud" out of which Moses was called to; thus [it is clear] what "on the seventh day" means, namely, that when the glory of Jehovah had appeared for six days, on the seventh Moses was called to "out of the midst of a cloud." But these matters are still too deep. If it is allowed to make public the

[142a.] *   things that appeared, and to draw conclusions from them, there are some matters that concern Moses, and that people—but perhaps this is not yet allowed—to the effect that they are still profaning (but I do not know whether Moses is among them).*

[143a.] [m]*4659.   On the 8th day of June, 1746, profane things were said to me, toward evening; also in the night in sleep, likewise wicked things were said, to which I would like to pay no attention.*[n]

[See WE 4662, on the general subject of Exod. 25:1–22.]

4663.   God the Messiah is everywhere, but in holy things He is more present than elsewhere, and with a different power, namely, with truth and love. Therefore it is said that He can dwell with someone, or, as later, that He can "not go with them" to the land of Canaan [Exod. 33:3], when yet He is everywhere present. Therefore also, in the prayer of benediction [Num. 6:24–26], He is implored to look upon them, when yet He is seeing them always, as well as the

[144a.] SPIRITUAL EXPERIENCES

tiniest things in the universe. But when they are sinners, He is said to "turn His face away," because there is not this kind of presence, namely, together with light and flame, that is, together with truth and love—which presence, by the Divine

[**144a.**]   *   mercy of God the Messiah, I have been allowed to experience, such as in London, on the street, at home, in a temple at Stockholm, and which presence I am thereby able to recognize, and thus to describe. It is a very deep feeling, which can never be described, and if it were described in many words, still nothing of it would be expressed.
[Lord]

[**145a.**]   *   Moreover, there are other presences, which manifest themselves by peace, by happiness, by a more inward sensation which I have experienced quite often over a period of two years; nor can these presences be described, for there is a clear sensation of happiness, which will be spoken of in a description, if it please [God the Messiah].
[Lord]

[See also the rest of WE 4663, concluding this general commentary.]

[See WE 4670, explaining Exod. 25:4.]

[**146a.**]   4670. "Hyacinth" is a cerulean color, also called sky-blue, or like the sky when it is clear, in which bright clouds appear. So it portrays clarity of the mind devoted to understanding, in which truths are shining. For this reason, that hyacinthine color, cerulean sky-blue, is greatly loved by the heavenly, as I have also experienced
[Color]

[**147a.**]   *   on many occasions, and I know that they value that color very highly, and not so much the color green, except insofar as it partakes of sky-blue.
[Color]

[See the rest of WE 4670, concluding the explanation of this verse.]

[See WE 4702–07, explaining Exod. 25:28–29.]

4708.   Whether these descendants of Jacob could have been saved by a mere observance of the Law in externals—as to this, doubt is now indeed being raised; but the answer is given that

[**148a.**] * external observances are nothing, unless they originate from inner qualities. Externals can certainly lead a person to inner things, but only when God the Messiah is leading the person, and moving him away from the loves of the world and of self; and then the person does not place righteousness in outer acts. But this only in passing.[1]

[See WE 4709–11, concluding the explanation of these verses.]

[See WE 4776–78, explaining Exod. 28:1–14 in general.]

4779. There are heavenly displays that appear to a person admitted into heaven, and

[**149a.**] * indeed, a diversity of them, when heavenly matters concerned with the Kingdom of God the Messiah are depicted as if before the eyes, in a long series, by various figures which, when brought down to something actual, would denote the exact same things as do the garments of Aaron here, with the mitre, the cloak, etc. But because these are still secrets, they are not to be made known as yet in particular—only this, that nothing whatsoever of this kind is depicted that does not involve something mysterious, and does not in the highest sense denote the Kingdom of God the Messiah. They are presented by means of the same things as appear before the sight, such as pyramids of various forms, most beautifully decorated, crowned, etc. etc.

[Earthly (Natural); Pyramid; Kingdom; Display (Representation)]

[For the sake of context, see WE 4780–81, continuing the explanation of these verses.]

4782. But how such portrayals *[as the garments of Aaron, and the ark]*, when looked upon by human eyes,

[**150a.**] * appear in an entirely different form in the presence of God the Messiah, namely, in a form truly Spiritual and Heavenly—thus being as though withdrawn from the things placed before the sight, and converted into forms truly spiritual—I could likewise speak of from experience. For example, when I have thought earthly facts in a long series, they were understood spiri-

---

[1] In the original, this indented paragraph and paragraph 4708 are each emphasized by the symbol *NB.* written in the margin.

[151a.] SPIRITUAL EXPERIENCES

tually; so, likewise, particulars in the Word of God the Messiah which are not at all understood according to the letter in the Word of God the Messiah in the Old Testament, but are understood according to the innermost meaning of the letter, wherein is the life of the Word of God the Messiah.

[Earthly (Natural); Kingdom; Portrayal (Representation); Spiritual things]

[See WE 4783, concluding the general explanation of verses 1–14.]

[See WE 4789–92, explaining Exod. 28:2 in particular.]

4793.   In that heaven, namely, in the third, where such speech exists, is the human soul; but because the door has been closed, like the door to paradise, it cannot be grasped by our mind's understanding.

[151a.]   *   About this speech, I can also testify that I have heard it in an almost waking sleep, and in fact, at the time, I seemed to understand its meaning; yet upon thinking back on it, it was inexpressible.

But these matters cannot be told about in a way that the understanding may grasp them, for they are above its realm, and what is above this is not understood. Who, for example, can believe that the soul, which is properly human, simultaneously and as though instantaneously, holds all and the least elements in order in the greatest and in the smallest parts [of man], where so many, such a countless number of different elements exist?

[Angel; Speak, Speech]

[See WE 4794–96, concluding the explanation of verse 2.]

[See WE 4910–11, explaining Exod. 28:8.]

4812.   As to what "bands" symbolize in general, many things could be said, but it is not yet clear

[152a.]   *   whether it is allowed to divulge them. Thus they stand for protection, when a person is girded with a band, etc. etc.

[See the rest of WE 4812, concluding the explanation of this verse.]

[See WE 4838 up to this point, explaining Exod. 28:15.]

*   Thus in this case, [colors] involve the righteousness of God the Messiah, which is accounted to man through saving belief.

[**153a.**] 4839. As regards colors in general, during spiritual temptation I have seen much; for example, what color portrayed universal grace, namely, a yellow golden color verging toward purple; further, which color portrayed mercy, love, etc., namely, purple and blood red; what a bright white portrayed, namely, integrity, truth, etc. Besides these, colors have been shown to me very often with a great deal of variety, and have also been the subject of conversation—and this has happened so frequently that the occasions could hardly be enumerated. They were shown with such beautiful variety that anyone would have to be amazed at it. Sky-blue is especially lovely, being heavenly, but this color also is distinguished according to its brightness, the whiter variety pertaining to truth, and the less white, verging toward purple, to love; etc. etc.
[Color]
[See also WE 4840–42, concluding the explanation of verse 15.]

[See WE 4864, explaining Exod. 28:30.]
4865. What "Light and integrity" are, in the deepest meanings and in the highest one, may be evident by an **unwrapping of the spiritual elements from earthly ones**. "Light," in the nearest meaning, is earthly sight like that of the eye. In a deeper meaning, it is spiritual light together with earthly, which so much resembles the light of nature, when a person is sleeping, dreaming,
[**154a.**] * that it appeared to me countless times, when my eyes were closed, exactly like the light of day, together with various objects, as if in broad daylight.
[For the context, see the rest of WE 4865–67, continuing the explanation of verse 30.]
4868. Thus "Aaron carried the judgment of the children of Israel before Jehovah," which words can now be understood from what has been said [WE 4864–67], after this has been put into order. Here they are sparsely touched upon, for several
[**155a.**] * reasons, for [it must be explained] what the "Urim and the Thummim" are, etc. etc.
[See WE 4869, concluding the explanation of verse 30.]

[See WE 4907 up to this point, beginning a general explanation of Exod. 29.]
* ....What I am being allowed to set forth here are secrets of heaven. It was told above [64a, 149a–50a], that angelic choirs of

[156a.] SPIRITUAL EXPERIENCES

God the Messiah, by various kinds of displays, portray to each other the Kingdom of God the Messiah, and in fact, such amazing ones, that I am unable to describe them, for they are very numerous, and continue in a long series, sometimes one continuous

[156a.] * display lasting for an hour, two hours, as I know well enough from experience. For it was granted me to follow those displays quite clearly by a like mental display, and sometimes for so long a time that it completely wearied my mind before it came to an end.
[Kingdom; Display (Representation)]

[See WE 4908-16, continuing on the subject of displays in general.]

[157a.] 4917. But what these displays are like, and what they look like, cannot be described so as to be clearly understood, for this requires experience. They are of such a nature that the person sees the things very inwardly, as if there were a sight rising above everything, and when they appear, they do not come in together with thoughts, but are entirely seen, deeply within; so that I was able to follow them with a kind of sight, which I cannot at all describe, and this in a long series from beginning to end, for even an hour, or two hours, until everything had finished.

So that if it were allowed to make known just one of them, namely, about the pyramid so marvellously constructed and decorated [149a], if this should be described, it would fill up very many pages; and its formation does not take place all at once, but successively.
[Kingdom; Display (Representation)]

[158a.] 4918. As for the very deepest sight, however, while it is not so familiar to me, nevertheless it has also been granted me once or twice to have the use of that sight, although very faintly; etc. etc. But then those who were in any of the lower classes could not take notice of that portrayal, etc. etc. These same things are what God the Messiah says, that if they did not understand earthly things, how would they understand if He should tell them heavenly things [John 3:12]? If, indeed, people do not perceive the inward portrayals that are presented to a person, with his eyes closed, as if in broad daylight, how would they perceive more inward ones? and if not these, then how the innermost ones? and if not these latter, which have incalculably many things within them, how, then, would they perceive the providence and omniscience etc. etc. in Jehovah God, in Whom are infinitely many things?

[Outer (External); Inward]

[159a.] * And still, people do not wish to believe anything that they do not perceive with their senses, and thus with their reason.

4919. Hence the order now followed, of explaining the words of the holy text first in the nearest meaning, then in the inward meaning, in the more inward, then in the innermost, and then how they regard God the Messiah in the very highest meaning.[1]

[160a.] 4920. The flow is from the innermost class into the more inward, as it is called, and from this into the inward class. One who is not in order never perceives innermost elements, that is, as He says, ...Divine ones[2].

But one who is held in order, perceives the very least agreements and disagreements between the true feelings and the feigned ones, no matter what shape they are given by evil angels, or by those who harbor evil in themselves; thus there is a certain discord most deeply within, although the appearance is persuasive.

This has happened to me so often that I cannot count the times. Thereby, the inflow of heavenly beings could be identified—but on these matters, it is not allowed, because of the length of the subject, to say much more—as it was today, when I was being thus enticed by the persuasions of one of them regarding a certain matter, into believing it to be so, but I still sensed deeply within, so to speak, that it was a trick, and turned away from him; the 23rd day of June, 1746, old calendar (it concerned a man-servant).

[Outer (External); Inward; Order]

[161a.] [m]4921. The power of symbolic displays raised up from a person by God the Messiah is most amazing, when a heaven is thus arranged round about him. Otherwise, they effect nothing. And the way in which the angels are arranged providentially guards against any [merely]

---

[1] In the original this paragraph was emphasized by the word *Obs.* written in the margin.
[2] The reference here, indicated by dots in the original, is probably to John 3:12, alluded to in [158a].

[162a.]   SPIRITUAL EXPERIENCES

visual pictures having some effect, or some power. This is the same thing as the **cherub**, or the **cherubs**, who guard the way to the tree of life [Gen. 3:24]. But while much more could be said about these matters, it is enough to tell of them in a general way.[n]
[Angel; Order; Spirit]

[See WE 4922–25, explaining Exod. 29:1 in particular.]

4926.   As for a "young bull," its nature is servile, because it is later put under the yoke, thus standing for servitude in general, and here, for the third class, to whom exclusively this sacrifice—and more to be spoken of later—was strictly adapted. It must, indeed, serve the middle class, just as this must serve the first or innermost class, and this last, God the Messiah directly; exactly as in man, the earthly mind must be of service to the mind devoted to understanding, and this to the soul, for the sake of which both these minds exist. So it is in heaven, which constitutes the greatest, heavenly human being.

[**162a.**]   *   Nevertheless, each class supposes that it serves God the Messiah directly. They are kept in this ignorance for several reasons, namely, so that they may believe they also are in the deepest region, and so may feel delights, at their own level, without any cause for envy—which could arise if they pictured to themselves the high estate of others, etc. etc.

[See also WE 4927–29, concluding the explanation of verse 1.]

[See WE 4930–33, explaining Exod. 29:2.]

4934.   About the fact that childlike people such as these [WE 4933] are instructed later in heaven, when they are among those who are truly Christian,

[**163a.**]   *   I could mention something here, for there have very often been little children who were being instructed, to whom that instruction was most pleasing; but it is an entirely different matter with those who have lived in the light of spiritual knowledge, and who had not been child-like people and innocents, ...(but see that nothing is brought in that might upset the minds of some people on account of the common church code that without spiritual knowledge and faith no one can ever be saved).[1]

[Little child (Infant), Innocence]

[For the sake of context, see WE 4935–36, continuing the explanation of verse 2.]

4937. "Unleavened bread" is the kind commonly prepared with water, and so we learn that this bread stands for the nourishment of the third class. This class is nourished in its own way by Heavenly bread flowing in at the different levels, when it is unleavened, that is, when the loves of self and of the world, which produce a boiling up of bloods or the human vital forces, are removed. These having been removed, which is the doing of God the Messiah Alone, then at the various levels, and thus adapted to the capacity of the subjects of this class, the heavenly bread flows in, that is, a teaching of belief in God the Messiah, Whom they must necessarily acknowledge as the Savior of the World, to be able to enter the Heavenly Kingdom. Those who, from an ignorance they cannot help,

* as it is called, do not know this during their bodily life—such as little children and other childlike and innocent people, thus myriads, who were not born in Christendom and cannot possibly be condemned for it—are instructed in the other life, and, because of their nature, imbibe the teachings easily, and with joy, and are educated. I could bring in many particulars about how little children were taught, as well as others also who, by the mercy of God the Messiah, had lived an unleavened life.

But it is another matter entirely when it comes to those who had been born in the midst of the teachings of [Christian] belief, and had been informed here in the world; their minds are entirely different. For they do not eagerly receive the teachings of the faith, because their attitude of mind had long been averse to them, and therefore leavened, etc. etc. So it was among the Jews of old in the symbolic Church, who did not know God the Messiah's merit and righteousness, that were figuratively portrayed.

It is different with those who certainly know about it, yet who entirely spurn it, and continually cru-

---

[1] In the original a notation appears in the margin of the upper part of this paragraph, "See whether it is permitted to tell something about little children."

[165a.] SPIRITUAL EXPERIENCES

cify the Messiah in their heart. In this life, these latter can change their minds, and those from among them can again be delivered who, living in blind ignorance—being made blind by their leaders—nonetheless, sighing, surrender themselves to the One God, Jehovah the Father, acknowledge His goodness in spiritual matters and place their trust in Him, without hatred toward God the Messiah, the Savior of the World.

[See the rest of WE 4937–42, concluding the explanation of verse 2.]

[See WE 4945–48, explaining Exod 29:4.]

4949. Above all, washing of the feet was also introduced by God the Messiah, and I am amazed that it is not in use among Christians, in remembrance of the washing away of sins and the cleansing by the suffering of the Messiah, which it just preceded.

[165a.]   *   I could say very much, in general terms, concerning the washing of feet, which it was also commanded me to observe, when I was in that state. But perhaps they will not understand the mysteries, like Peter when he refused to be washed, to whom God the Messiah replied that they did not understand the secrets of heaven, nor could they enter into the Kingdom of God unless they were washed [John 13:5–10]. But I am not speaking of an absolute necessity for those among whom this has been abolished, although they might be urged to carry out and to believe all that was instituted by God the Messiah, even if they do not understand the secrets of heaven, or how they are thereby portrayed as clean before the angels, who raise these symbolic acts to what is deeper, etc. etc.

If by the mercy of God the Messiah it is allowed at its own time, these matters are to be better examined, as to whether this act is a necessity, and whether it has been commanded, like the holy supper, and thus whether it has a use; because it was not explained what would thereby be called to mind. [*See* 79a].

[Wash; Foot]

[See also WE 4950, concluding the explanation of verse 4.]

[See WE 4960–63, explaining Exod. 29:8.]

4964. *For everyone in heaven serves One, that is, God the Messiah, and really does not know that it is done indirectly. Thus not a single one is the servant of any other than God the Messiah Alone, Who is the Lord of all. The*
[**166a.**] * fact that they are unaware of intermediaries, and thus any who are higher, except the One God the Messiah, I have also discussed with them, etc.
[See also WE 4965, concluding the explanation of verse 8.]

[See WE 4981–82, explaining Exod. 29:13.]
4983. *As for the "kidneys," they, too, are purifiers of the blood, for they carry away what is filthy, and this in a different way. Here those points may be brought in that were written by me about the kidneys, and a comparison be made.*[1]
* *Then it can also be told why the kidneys*[2] *are said to be "searched" [Ps. 7:9, 26:2; Jer. 11:20, 17:10, 20:12; Rev. 2:23], and how they symbolize these things in their different levels of meaning, etc. etc.; for everything falls together.*
* *Let there be also some description here of these [meanings] in a series.*
* *Then also let there be a description of how regeneration is recognized in things of nature, if it is allowed here. If it is allowed, I would then also tell what happened when I was thus*
[**167a.**] * *setting forth, by thought and visualization, the complete chain of regeneration in the liver, namely that all and the least particulars were taken up, and were understood, in the inmost heaven; I, of course, did not perceive them, except for what was pointed out to me in a miraculous manner, etc. etc.*
[Nature, Natural; Spiritual things]
[See also WE 4984, concluding the explanation of verse 13.]
[See WE 4985–86 up to this point, explaining Exod. 29:14.]
* .... *"Dung" here means what is even more [to be cast off]; thus the text is proceeding in order toward the most unclean things. Therefore the abode of the devil in man is depicted by the back parts, where the drain is, or where the filth is cast out. Such*

---

[1] See *Animate Kingdom* 284 *ff.*, especially 288, 294.
[2] *KJV* has "reins," archaic for "kidneys," and *NKJ* has "minds."

[168a.] SPIRITUAL EXPERIENCES

[**168a.**] *   portrayals are familiar to evils spirits themselves, when they are being cast out, when they are being arrogant, etc. etc.
[See also WE 4987, concluding the explanation of verse 14.]

[See WE 5002–03, explaining Exod. 29:19–20.][1]
5004.   But as to what the *"tip of the ear,"* the *"thumb of the hand,"* and the *"big toe of the right foot"* symbolize in this passage, I learned the following from certain things that had happened to me, which were, at that time,
[**169a.**] *   amazing displays that I would never dare, nor am I able, to recount. I learned this, that the right side of man is considered holier than the left, and, in fact, so much so, that the right side may never be touched except by those who are holy, while the left may be by others. If I should bring in my experience in these matters, besides being abundant, it would also be unbelievable.
[See also the rest of WE 5004–06 up to this point, continuing the explanation of these verses.]

*   But the *"big toe of the right foot,"* like the foot itself, stands for humiliation. This also could be testified to by much
[**170a.**] *   experience, but here there is no need for it as yet.
[See also WE 5007, continuing the explanation of verses 19–20.]
5008.   Since these are the kind of subjects recounted in God the Messiah's Word, and there is not even a jot that does not involve an infinitude within it, and since none can unravel it without revelation, who, then, in order to acquire belief, would wish to resort to intelligence, which certainly cannot comprehend these matters, even though they have been revealed to me through much experience? And even though I affirm them here positively,

---

[1] There is some doubt as to whether the last words of WE 5000 consititute an "indented paragraph":
[See WE 4998–5000, explaining Exod. 29:18.]
*   For the more knowledge and intelligence there is, the more difficult is the approach to what is holy, just as the more riches there are, the more difficult it is to enter heaven. For human intelligence closes the gates to heaven, and fastens the doors, which it is very difficult to break through, except for those who are not intelligent; but about this, if God the Messiah finds it fitting, we will speak elsewhere, as well as
[**168½a.**] *   about what intelligence ought to be.
[See also WE 5001, concluding the explanation of verse 18.]

[171a.] * yet who will have faith in them? Will they not still doubt about their meaning because they do not grasp it with understanding? Heavenly things are such that if they were revealed, anyone who puts his trust in understanding would never believe.
[See also WE 5009–10, concluding the explanation of verses 10–20.]

[See WE 5012, explaining Exod. 29:22.]
[172a.] * That a "shoulder" stands for what is most excellent in spiritual things joined to heavenly ones, was revealed to me (in sleep, when I was allowed to enter the very inward Church, as a result of supplication).
[Shoulder]
[See also WE 5013–16, concluding the explanation of verse 22.]

[See WE 5024–26, explaining Exod. 29:26.]
5027. *Further regarding the life symbolized by "waving," I can bear wit*ness that
[173a.] * a similar waving of spirits also reached my senses on several occasions; thus a waving of this kind is common among spirits. But this waving felt by me was undulatory, and it was also given me to consider what it involves, namely, that it is a common life, or a life of many, so harmonizing and conspiring toward a single thought, etc. etc., that it came more gently to the higher classes, and the mysteries within these symbolic acts were more fully extracted, and they grasped what the "odor of rest" [verse 25] is more fully, etc. etc.[1]
[Waving; Breathing]
[See the rest of WE 5027, concluding the explanation of this verse.]
[See WE 5028–29, explaining Exod. 29:27.]
5030. *Further in regard to the "waving," which I said was felt as a quite pleasant undulation in the Brain [173a], I could clearly,*
[174a.] * and as a witness, describe it in a most general way as consisting of various degrees; for the undulation was felt variously. One was in the brain itself, about which I spoke with spirits, saying that it was like the

---

[1] In the original this paragraph was emphasized by the word *Obs.* written three times in the margin.

wave-like creeping of cortical substances in the brain, in respect to which amazing things occurred, namely, that myriads of spirits together composed it, but there was [an undulation] in my brain corresponding to their waving. Then again [it was felt] in another way, with a great deal of delight; then differently again.

Therefore, it is the pleasantness of the undulation, which must be unutterable, and thus effigies the common life of spirits harmonizing together, or a general harmonious form, that is meant by "an odor of rest" after the offering had been set on fire [Exod. 29:25], etc. etc. For there is a general waving, symbolizing the particular waving of each spirit, and then the most individual waving in each—thus a harmony commencing from the very least things.[1]

[Waving; Brain; Inflow; Creeping; Breathing]
[See WE 5031–34, explaining Exod. 29:28.]
5034. ....

[175a.]   *   See what follows concerning the Theruma.

What follows must be taken note of, because memorable things happened at this point.
[See WE 5035–43, further explaining Exod. 29:28.]

[176a.]   5044.   **These words must be taken note of, because memorable things happened to me in connection with them. So that I might realize that the subject is privilege in the Kingdom of God the Messiah, namely the relative privilege of the old and the new Churches,** gifts were sent to me, such as a bundle of letters, a basket with apples and citrus fruit, which basket was not admitted: [signifying] delights. 1746, the 28th day of June (old calendar).
[See, Vision]

[See WE 5062–66, explaining Exod. 29:33.]

---

[1] In the original this paragraph is emphasized by the word *Obs.* written three times in the margin.

5067.   That an "unclean person"[1], if he should eat of it, would be cut off from his people [Lev. 7:20], figuratively portrays the same thing, namely, that whoever does not eat and drink [the elements of the Eucharist] in a right way, eats and drinks for himself death, and not life. For heavenly and worldly things may by no means be mixed

[177a.]   *   together, but must be kept separate, what is worldly submitting like household servants to what is heavenly. If they are mixed together, there is death. In man they follow one after the other and are not mixed together, for which reason it is providentially guarded against lest they should be mixed. About these secrets, if God the Messiah finds it fitting, [more will be said] elsewhere.

[See also WE 5068, concluding the explanation of verse 33.]

5075.   [Exod. 29:] verse 35. Not even the least detail was Moses allowed to change from what had been commanded, for there was not the least thing in the ritual of sacrifices, in the garments, in the tent, etc., that did not portray something distinct and thus refer to something in the teachings of the faith, that is, in the teachings on the acquisition of righteousness through belief.

*   For every single part of this ritual has an infinite content, just as does every single mental image, as

[178a.]   *   I can affirm from much experience.

[For the sake of context, see also the rest of WE 5075–81 up to this point, continuing the explanation of verse 35.]

*   ....Guardian spirits after life in the world believe they are equipped with a body, and are more convinced of nothing, and even that they are equipped with bodily parts, when yet such parts, which they are convinced that they have, like all parts of the human body, are of no use to them [there]. But in what form they are, they do not know at all; it depends

[179a.]   *   on how they are portrayed, so that they seem to take on whatever form is induced upon them by portrayal.[2]

[See also WE 5082, continuing the explanation of verse 35.]

---

[1] *KJV* has "stranger."
[2] In the original, this and the preceding paragraph were stressed by the notation *Obs. obs.* written three times in the margin.

[180a.] SPIRITUAL EXPERIENCES

5083. The portrayals of such secret matters, discussed earlier [149a–50a, 156a–58a], come forth continually among heavenly spirits and angels, in a continuing series and with unlimited variety: and nevertheless they do not at all understand what they mean (except for those who are in the innermost regions, to whom this is revealed by God the Messiah and Holy Spirit). Such were the displays that were mentioned [there], which
[**180a.**] * were seen by me in many series and over quite a long period of time,

5084. and still, those angels or spirits who portray these in a person do not at all know what they mean, but they are driven to depict them as if it were their own essential nature to do so, just as birds, if it is allowed to make a comparison, which are driven by instinct, portray the secrets of marriage by what they do, namely, building nests, laying eggs, hatching them, feeding their chicks, all in a most marvellous way; yet they are driven by nature to do these things. So, on a higher level, they who enjoy spiritual life, as do spirits and angels, portray such secrets with unlimited variety. That displays of this kind had existed in the earliest times in the first people, there can be no doubt; for speech cannot be cultivated, and cannot be devised, except from objects. Thus He spoke by means of such portrayals. That they can also
[**181a.**] * speak by means of portrayals has also become known to me; for it was allowed me also to speak through certain portrayals, of which few, except those who are innermost, knew the meaning. One display can[1] involve an infinitude, such being the speech of those who are in the innermost regions, for they see more at one look than can ever be expressed on paper. In fact, a person's whole life, with its every variation, feeling, together with the words and the very least contents in each word, can be thus presented by a single display, so that nothing at all is missing that has been written down.

[Display (Representation)]

5085.[2] The whole first creation is but a symbolic depiction of Jehovah God, this by means of God the Messiah and Holy Spirit. Hence all things of creation down to the very least regard the Kingdom of God

---

[1] At the top of a new page, the indentation of this passage was overlooked.
[2] In the original, the unindented portion of this paragraph is emphasized by the words *Obs. obs.* written three times in the margin.

the Messiah. *Those depictions cannot but come forth as the effect, because they come from Him Who Is, and Who Alone lives, and from Whom and in Whom all things are. From this, then, is the first*
[**182a.**]   creation, which involves the second creation, and so the new heaven and new Earth.
As for what eating and drinking with Abraham, Isaac and Jacob means, see what follows *at the sign (☉) [WE 5088].*

[See WE 5088, explaining Exod. 29:36–37; specifically, what eating with Abraham, Isaac and Jacob means.]

5089.   This spiritual eating is what is called eating and drinking with Abraham, Isaac and Jacob in the Kingdom of the Heavens [Matt. 8:11]. For as Abraham represents the first, Isaac the second, and Jacob the third class of the blessed in the Kingdom of the Heavens, it is understood what eating with Abraham, Isaac and Jacob symbolizes:

5090.   namely, that this spiritual eating may ascend step by step. For they who are in the innermost regions love all in the whole world on account of their belief in God the Messiah, being moved by His love, so that they do not regard, with feeling, the love of themselves, or of their own families, except as a love below them, which they therefore put aside: these are called the children of Abraham.

One who does not feel this in himself, but is touched by the love of those who are his own, which arises from the love of oneself, such a one is not in the innermost regions. About this matter it was granted me to speak with those who
[**183a.**]   *   were in the innermost regions, or who supposed they were in them, so that they might see whether they were in the innermosts, as they believed. But from the above-mentioned characteristic, they would know whether they are there. For all do not know differently, before being instructed, than that they are most deeply [there], in which matter they are of course mistaken, but are still kept in this opinion. For they cannot penetrate into what is unknown to them, just as is the case with people on earth.
[Inward]

[See also WE 5091–93, continuing the subject of eating with Abraham, Isaac and Jacob.]

[184a.]

[184a.] 5094. Today also it was granted to speak with those in heaven around me about the character of those who are there, that is, that they do not derive their character from any other source than their life in the body wherein it is developed; for they then continue to desire in the same way, that is, to have the same feelings. This being the case, they are worse than animals, which form a society and behave according to inscribed laws, such as bees, etc.; whereas if people should act from the nature so acquired, not any society could ever be formed, in heaven, for the society would go to ruin, each one would trouble, even drive the other out.

Therefore as a result of this and many other considerations, it was confirmed that if God the Messiah, Who is Love, were not controlling everyone by supreme and absolute power, then heaven would go to ruin, consequently human societies also, which are governed by God the Messiah through angels and spirits; so also would each person individually. They could not help affirming this conclusion, because it was granted them to see the truth.
[Lord; Nature]

[185a.] *   ᵐ**[Tell] how the more perfect ones are on a higher level, and know where a feeling with those at a lower level comes from, which they therefore control; for a heavenly society is governed as one person, by higher powers**, etc. etc.[1]

Therefore, one who cannot control a feeling of his own that is lower within him, cannot control the feeling of another who might be beneath him. For in heaven, it is the character that is ruled, and character arises from feeling; and from feeling arises understanding. But how it is in this life in those being regenerated, I do not yet know.ⁿ

[See WE 5137–39, explaining Exod. 29:42.]

---

[1] In the original this paragraph is emphasized by the word *Obs.* written three times in the margin.

5140. *Therefore it is here said, "at the door of the tent," as well as "throughout your generations," for they still wish to remain in the same Church, in the same shadow, in their sleep.*

[**186a.**]   5141. Something amazing happened to me today, in order to prove this to those who were around me from among the Jews who died of old; for they are the same after life as during life in the world, when left to themselves. I dreamt, and indeed, in a way that it appeared as if in wakefulness, as usual, and they were then so convinced that I was awake that they answered me as if I were awake.

Then, suddenly awakening, I realized I had been dreaming, and that they had spoken with me while I was asleep, and, in fact, believing me to be awake, which then embarrassed them exceedingly. One became indignant, another astonished, a third one loved it, because I then said that it shows from this how they live in a sleep, and their life was a sleep, and they believe that they see, hear, even live, when yet they are deceiving themselves, as they do not live from themselves, and yet likewise believe they do.

Then I wrote down the words in this verse [Exod. 29:42], and was thus allowed to demonstrate to them that they were still living their life in sleep; so they were able to say nothing. However, sometimes it happened that they knew a person was asleep, but in this case it was to prove to them in a different way in what shadow, and in what an illusion they are living—both those from among the Jews [of old], and those who are still living. See the continuation below at ⇉.

[Jews; Dream, Sleep]

[See also WE 5142–43, concluding the explanation of verse 42.]

5150.   ⇉ *It is amazing that man considers his life to consist in outer sensations and bodily*
[**187a.**]   *   pleasures, whereas the life of outer sensations, thus that of the body, is mere shadow, and consequently a sleep, compared to the life of inner sensation, that is, of the earthly mind, where fantasy and mental imagery as well as passions reside. Then again, some consider

life to consist solely in passions, whereas this is but a sleep compared to the life of a more inward faculty, which must be properly human—and yet which is nothing but a kind of sleep in us relative to our innermost life, or that of our soul. But this in turn is nothing but a sleep relative to Very Life itself, which is of God the Messiah, Who is Life.

So all things down to the very least in us are nothing but shadow and sleep. It is known that human life is sleep. Thus there are levels of sleep, just as there are levels of angels and spirits in heaven; but it is a wonder that people consider the densest sleep to be life, where there is mere darkness, as in the sensations and pleasures of the body. Therefore they do not know that the life which is thought to be life arises from a succession of more inward lives, and that into the innermost life, and then from this into all a person's faculties, comes life solely from God the Messiah.

5151. That the life of one faculty flows in succession into that of a second, and therefore, the life of the soul into that of the mind devoted to understanding, anyone may see quite plainly if he only attends to the innumerable elements in that mind, namely, those by virtue of which people are able to think, to judge, to conclude, to choose, and this analytically, in accordance with so many very deep and, in fact, unsearchable laws—this even in earliest childhood. Of these laws, some have been investigated, and are set forth in physiological hypotheses, but very few, and only the most general ones, which were able to be arrived at only by attentive contemplation of one's own mind.

These things could never exist unless they flowed in from a higher ability, that is, from the properly human soul, which is so much above the ideas of the mind devoted to understanding, that it composes those mental images and analytically arranges them in sequence, and thus composes the thoughts of the mind and their intelligible shapes. The same takes place in regard to feelings, which govern the will.

FROM *WE* TOME III [192a.]

[See WE 5167–72, explaining Exod. 30:3.]
[189a.]   *   About those auras [*WE* 5169 *ff.*], I once had a conversation with certain of the spirits.
[See also the rest of WE 5172–74, concluding the explanation of Exod. 30:3.]
[See WE 5175–78, explaining Exod. 30:4.]
5179. Order itself in general is portrayed by a "ring," but in that case order is viewed as arising from the innermost and descending to the last, then ascending from the last; thus as a descent and ascent through a circle. But here this is not the case.
[190a.]   5180. The angels do not reach through to the last in order, except in man, thus through man, while man reaches from the innermost regions to the last. In man, the order of the whole creation is complete. In Adam, while he was in a state of integrity, the order was perfect, and at that time there was around him a perfect aura of angels. Something is absolutely perfect when it is perfect in each part of its order, at its own level, [all parts] harmonizing together, so that all are obedient to love, that is, to God the Messiah. It is otherwise when they do not harmonize: then the angels of God the Messiah can be called "very perfect," even though they do not reach through to the last in order; for imperfections increase step by step, and are the greatest in the last levels of the order.
[See WE 5181–83, concluding the explanation of Exod. 30:4.]
[See WE 5184, explaining Exod. 30:5.]
[191a.]   5185. That the combined activities of the angels are carried out by means of turning motions, almost perpetually circular [*cf. WE* 5179], and that they move back and forth, and therefore also by turnings,
[Ring; Form; Gyre]
[192a.]   *   as if they are speaking by means of turning motions, and thus conveying the words, that is, the commands, of God the Messiah—this I have observed sensately on many occasions. Therefore, choirs of angels in their activity are portrayed no otherwise than by "rings" [Exod. 30:4].
[Ring; Form; Gyre]
[See also WE 5186, treating further of "rings."]

[193a.] SPIRITUAL EXPERIENCES

[See WE 5242–44, discussing Exod. 30:17–21 in general.]

[193a.] 5245. Feelings bring about convictions, so that the mind believes to be true, and absolutely true, whatever moves it in regard to earthly matters. Enlightened knowledge, though, and resulting convictions in truly spiritual and heavenly matters, prepare the mind for the reception of heavenly feelings.

This is demonstrated by many things, including my daily experience, of which some went unnoticed at the time, and some was noticed. But everyone can prove it to himself by common sense, and even by experience. But a person rarely pays attention to this experience, because he or she is too taken up with earthly feelings, and unless these are removed, heavenly feelings never come to light. Yet when they are acknowledged to exist because of being told about, then they do appear in shadow, but this appearance is not so convincing as to actually bring on those feelings. For this reason, in order first to dispel those hatreds, i.e. the loves of self and of the world, God the Messiah makes use of other means— especially misfortunes, afflictions, temptations, etc. etc.[1]

[See WE 5246–49, concluding the general explanation of Exod. 30:17–21.]
[See WE 5276–87, explaining Exod. 32:1–35 in general, and 5288–5291, explaining verse 1 in particular.]

[194a.] 5292. These words were written in the presence of many of the Jews around me, and I do not doubt that Abraham also is present. For the Jews are striving for the same thing now as they were during life, as I can confirm by many instances, words, displays; but this is unnecessary. They will still turn everything into fantasy, when yet not the least bit of this is fantasy, but there has been ongoing conversation, as that of one person on earth with another, etc. etc., and this now for 15 months. That it is not fantasy, those may clearly know with whom I have meanwhile associated in Sweden, etc., and it may be evident from an historical account of my life, if the opportunity is given for writing it down.
[*Jews*]

---

[1] In the original, this portion of text [193a] is emphasized by the word *Obs.* written seven times in the margin.

[**195a.**] 5293. Just because a someone is permitted to speak with heavenly beings, with angels, with the dead as to the body, the person is not holy on that account, just as Jacob was not, Aaron was not, others were not merely because Jehovah had spoken with them. For we read that Jehovah spoke with Adam after the fall [Gen. 3:9], with Cain [4:9], even with the serpent [3:14], wherefore it can in no wise be inferred that such are holy above others. The fact that I have been granted to speak with angels, both good and evil, implies nothing holy about me, so that I cannot claim even the very least holiness on that account. But about these matters I will speak elsewhere, insofar as God the Messiah finds it fitting.
[Jews]

[See also WE 5294-97, concluding the explanation of Exod. 32:1 in particular.]

[See WE 5306-10, explaining Exod. 32:5-6.]

5311.   What they deserve for the breaking of a most holy covenant [verses 1–6] cannot be unknown to them. Nations that had done like things, had not entered into a sacred covenant, nor had they any knowledge of Jehovah, being in the midst of darkness, while this people was in full daylight, as is proven by many passages; and yet they condemn those nations to Tartarus, and raise themselves up onto the throne of God the Messiah. Let them reply, if it is they who were present [194a], for now there is silence! Nothing else

[**196a.**]   *   did they reply to me but "we cannot." Who these were around me, I do not know, but I think they were many.

5312. *Aaron himself, who later became the high priest, now performed those offices for the first time, but for the devil, whom he worshipped. Was he, then, not most unclean, even though the high priest? And that Jehovah God dwelt in the midst of their uncleanness, [see] Leviticus Chapter 16 verse 16.*

*   *Could not what was most unclean, then, portray what is most holy, and therefore could not a symbolic Church exist among those who could never be the chosen? Thus it was in no wise because of them, but because of their portrayal of the children of the True Israel, etc. etc.*[1]

---

[1] In the original, this last sentence is stressed by the word *Obs.* written twice in the margin.

[197a.] * This point they wished to refute, but to the passage in Leviticus, Chapter 16 verse 16, they could answer nothing.

5313. *The sentence, Jehovah Himself pronounced, namely, [Exod. 32:] verses 33 and 34, where these words [stand]: "But Jehovah said to Moses, 'Him who has sinned against Me, I will blot out of My book,'" verse 33. "'Nevertheless go, lead this people into the [...] which I said to you" (He does not say "land," but what this means, I do not know): "Behold, My angel will go before you; but in the day of My visitation I will visit punishment upon them for their sin,'" verse 34.*

[198a.] 5314. These words were written on the 8th day of July, 1746 (old calendar), on which day I also spoke with Abraham, who then charged me to write that in heaven, nothing whatever is done except through God the Messiah, Whom they worship.
[Abraham; Lord]

[See WE 5315–17, concluding the explanation of verses 5–6.]

5324. *[Exod. 32:] verse 8. "They have turned back suddenly from the way": that they did so suddenly is clear, for the sacred covenant had been ratified, etc., before Moses had ascended the mountain again.*

* [They turned back] *for a most trivial reason, [their wickedness] breaking out as though spontaneously, and as though they were being held by a bridle when kept to the worship of God the Messiah.*

[199a.] 5325. But I was asked by those who are around me—and that they were Jews, I was able to learn from many indications, without their own admission—I was asked why it had been foreseen by God the Messiah that they would fall, and seeing they were of this nature, why were they let into temptation?

I replied, in order that from being earthly people, they might be made spiritual. No other means has been provided so that people may be reformed or regenerated, which is taking place constantly in the person whom God the Messiah wills to draw to heaven. And they were tempted so that they themselves might see that they are of this nature, and thus inexcusable.

As to why it was permitted that they should actually fall, and thus be separated, I replied, because the worship of God the Messiah could not be commingled with the worship of the devil, which would have happened, had they retained the former in their minds. For this reason, those words [were permitted] to come true that are read in Leviticus Chapter 16 verse 16, that "the tent would dwell in the midst of their uncleanness." It is now added that they could in this way portray the True Israel, or the inner person, regardless of what quality they might be.
[Jews; Sin; Temptation]

[See 5382–86 up to this point, explaining Exod. 32:15.]
[200a.] * The things that happened to me now, and earlier, when I wrote about the Law delivered on Mount Sinai, are stupefying, and of such a nature that I dare not reveal them as yet [*cf.* 141a].[1]
[See the rest of WE 5386–90, concluding the explanation of this verse.]

[See WE 5392–5400, explaining Exod. 32:17.]
5401.   Such a war, or such a "voice of war," is heard in all kinds of camps, specifically in the spiritual and the heavenly person, in a society of such people, or the Church, in the world at large, even in heaven. For this kind of a war is going on continually between those who are self-righteous about their works
[201a.] * and those who ascribe righteousness to the Messiah Alone. They who are self-righteous turn all good into evil. Those who ascribe righteousness to God the Messiah, turn all evil into good. And this goes on continuously. Nor do evil spirits know that that war is engendered by the devil, who is invading, and that it is thus turned into peace by God the Messiah, Who is

---

[1] In the original this paragraph was emphasized by the word *Obs.* written in the margin. Above it the author had written and deleted:
> The things that have happened to me now and previously when I wrote about the Law delivered on Mount Sinai, as well as those portrayed to me today, the 11th of July, 1746 (old calendar), are stupefying, and so wicked, and of such a nature, that I dare not reveal them as yet.

[202a.] SPIRITUAL EXPERIENCES

defending and protecting the person, like a wall which the enemy tries to scale.[1]
[Good; Righteousness; Law; Evil]

* It is, therefore, the *"voice of war"* such as it has just been described, that is meant in the inward sense.

5402. *[Exod. 32:] verse 18. But now Moses replied, by whom is portrayed the Law in its outer aspects, as said before.*

* *But from experience of long duration, may it be allowed to speak of these matters, namely, about what is meant by this, Moses' reply.* Those who are for the outer Law, as has been said [WE 5400], are continually

[202a.] * attacking those who are for the inner law; that is to say, those who are for themselves and the world, and whatever arouses those loves, are constantly invading them in most diverse ways, as far as they are permitted by God the Messiah. And even though they succumb every time and are conquered, they still persist and do not give up; therefore, they say in their heart or suppose no differently than Moses does here, "It is not a voice crying out that there is victory, nor a voice crying out that the cause is lost."
[Outer (External); Inward; Law][2]

[203a.] 5403. As a result, then, the same thing takes place in a person who is fighting, as during temptations; the same thing in the Church, which is continually fighting, etc. For in the individual and in the Church is that battlefield, as it were, on which they wage the war.

[204a.] * From this also come so many schisms, etc. etc.

[205a.] * For in no other way is it possible for an earthly person to become spiritual and to be made new; this could never come about without such a war.

[206a.] 5404. Good spirits, however, while knowing very well that the victory will be granted to them, still cannot but defend themselves, and thus fight, since evil spirits are permitted to invade in this way.[3]
[Outer (External); Inward; Law]

---

[1] In the original this paragraph is emphasized by the word *Obs.* written twice in the margin.
[2] These also clearly refer to *WE* 5402, second paragraph.
[3] In the original is a notation written vertically up the margin of paragraphs [202a] to [206a], "These points are to be taken note of most exactly."

[207a.] * These, then, are secrets from heaven that explain very many passages of holy Scripture. Let only one be set forth, concerning Michael the Angel. He fought with the devil, and overcame him by the blood of the Lamb, Rev. Chap. [12:7,8,11], which will come to pass at the last day, when there will be judgment, that is, when God the Messiah shall come into glory. For this reason it is read also that that nation, or the people called Jacob, will not pass away before it shall see God the Messiah in His glory, etc. etc. [*cf.* Gen. 49:10, Num. 24:17].

[Outer (External); Inward; Law]

[208a.] 5405. On the last day also, the devil will know that he is to be overcome, and therefore one reads further in Revelation that he will burn with great wrath, and will come down to the earth, causing great commotion, etc. [12:12,17]. Before that, however, he does not know anything but that there is "neither victory, nor a lost cause"; for he is continually lusting, and his lust for power blinds him, as is usually the case in all those who seek self-glory.

5406. *"The voice of singing I hear," says Moses. Singing was customary at feasts, for we read, Exodus 15, verses 1 and 21, that they sang to Jehovah.*

[209a.] 5407. What power there is in singing when it is done from belief, I might show by many considerations, but here is not yet the place for it.

[210a.] 5408. So at this time those who were doing the dancing were singing, which is logical, because the devil wants to imitate exactly everything he knows that points to God the Messiah, for he is passing himself off as the Messiah. Therefore he guides the minds of those who are self-righteous in regard to works to await a Messiah who favors their passions. Hence the prediction about christs who are to come at the last day [Matt. 24:24].

[211a.] * The boasting of those who invade is here called "singing," for the wicked will glory for a time, and will

[212a.] SPIRITUAL EXPERIENCES

therefore sing, but for a short time, for their song will be turned into mourning [Amos 8:10].
[**212a.**] * What this song was, now follows.
[See also WE 5409–11, concluding the explanation of verse 18.]
[See WE 5412–14, explaining Exod. 32:19.]

5415. "It came to pass that Moses' anger grew hot, and he cast the tables out of his hand, and broke them below the mountain": that is, the inner Law was entirely wiped out, so that there was nothing of it with them; for it is broken, or made nothing, with those who adore themselves, etc.

5416. That [act] was inspired in Moses from heaven, so that this would be symbolized: for that deed is seen in this meaning in heaven, because there, the person is not looked upon as a person, but as the spiritual and heavenly quality that makes up the person. This is common in heaven, for they can never look at a person with the eyes as an inhabitant of the earth does, but look at the very inward qualities. Hence, they receive human beings according to those qualities from which they derive their humanity. This

[**213a.**] * is the reason why Moses is regarded as the Law, etc.

5417. Neither could Heaven bear that Moses should carry in his hand the Law, the work of God; thus his anger came from heaven, as did the fact that he broke the tables—and this, "below the mountain," thus portraying the outer Law, and everything that follows from it.[1]

[**214a.**] * For every feeling, even the least part of it, flows into us from above, in fact, every movement, because it originates from feeling. This I can corroborate by so many experiences that the volume would swell from just the examples, also [telling] how miraculous the inflow is into the human mind and will, and thus into our actions—so it would seem impossible for anyone to believe it, unless convinced by such an experience, etc. etc.
[Think, Thought; Inflow]

[See WE 5418, concluding the explanation of verse 19.]

[See WE 5431–32 up to this point, explaining Exod. 32:22.]
* For if heaven had then seen what [Aaron and the people] were like inwardly, and were speaking with them in the way they do

---

[1] In the original this paragraph is emphasized by the word *Obs.* written in the margin.

[**215a.**]   *   with me, whereby they are given to perceive all the thoughts of my heart—

*   *if this had been the case at that time, then anyone can judge that heaven could never have been with them, since even then, at heart they were worshipping idols, etc. Would not then, in the place of the angels of God the Messiah, the devil and his gang have taken over? To prevent this, many things which now follow took place.*

5433.   *But about these matters many particulars could be told, specifically, how an aura, or choirs of angels, is formed around a person so that nothing but their outer aspect may come, by a series of steps, to the innermost regions; and also, how [these choirs are separated] from the person's inner qualities, so that the person may be [outwardly] present in the choir of angels of God the Messiah. For no one can be inwardly in the choir of God the Messiah unless they are such that their inward qualities interact with the choir: and this state is brought about by God the Messiah; (besides many more particulars about which it was granted me to speak with*

[**216a.**]   *   the angels and spirits around me, and this was at the same time demonstrated to me by experience so diverse that it would be a very large undertaking to set it all forth.)[1]

If this were not so, mankind could never do anything but disturb heaven by its wickedness—something guarded against most wisely by God the Messiah, etc. etc. It now follows from this, that a superficial person who is wicked—even at heart an idolater, as this stock quite evidently was for the most part—can nonetheless portray holy qualities, especially when sanctified by things which to the innermost choir of angels, symbolize what is most holy, as though portraying God the Messiah, etc. etc. In this way, what is most holy is shown to heaven and as it were inspired.

[Interaction (Correspondence); Outer; Inward][2]

[See for the sake of context WE 5434–36, continuing the explanation of verse 22.]

5437.   *That outer holiness can also come over a wicked person may be quite well known from rituals that produce this effect. While an outer holiness can indeed seize the mind, especially when the*

---

[1] This sentence is emphasized in the original by the word *Obs.* written in the margin.
[2] These also clearly refer to the whole of *WE* 5433.

[217a.] SPIRITUAL EXPERIENCES

angels round about are moved, yet this is something separate from the person. But outer holiness arising from inner holiness is very different. About these matters I could make several observations also, but I do not

[217a.]   *   yet grasp them clearly; it may be allowed to make them at another time, if God the Messiah sees fit.

[See for the sake of context WE 5438, continuing the explanation of verse 22.]

5439.   *It is allowable for [outer holiness] to be called holy, for also the altar of whole burnt offering is called "holiness of holiness"[1] [Exod. 29:37], the altar of incense [30:10] "holy of holies"[2]; the oil also is called holy, the garments holy, and other such things. Where the holiness comes from may be evident from what was said above [WE 5433–34, 5437], namely, from the choir of angels, from the portrayal of the highest Deity, while the human mind is lifted up out of its own realm. Stupefaction then seizes the mind, flowing in from the properly human soul, which is not fallen. From this, now, a great many particulars can be deduced*

[218a.]   *   which regard man's salvation; but these are extremely secret.

[See WE 5455–59 up to this point, explaining Exod. 32:26.]

       *   And because, as said above [verse 14], God the Messiah was moved with compassion, for reasons spoken of above [WE 5333 ff., 5381], hence He wished now only to bring them into terror, that they might humble themselves, and acknowledge their sin.

[219a.]   5460.   For fright has the effect that one humbles oneself to the lowest level, prostrating oneself to the earth, and making oneself nothing; yet the fear has no other effect than to cause people to acknowledge their sin, for when they recover from the fear, they are of the same disposition as before. This is what fear accomplishes,

[Humbling; Fear]

[220a.]   *   as has also been actually shown, by the mercy of God the Messiah, in the case of certain spirits around me who had been so humbled by fear that they could not have been more humble, but straightway upon recovering were exactly as before. In their fear they did ac-

---

[1] *KJV* has "most holy."
[2] *KJV* has "most holy."

knowledge their sins, but beyond this acknowledgment there was nothing.
[Humbling; Fear]
[See also the rest of WE 5460–62, concluding the explanation of verse 26.]
[See WE 5463–65 up to this point, explaining Exod. 32:27.]
* But the fighting differs, depending upon the person's state. *In an earthly person, the devil conquers, and also, is conquered; while in a person after combat, that is, in the spiritual and the heavenly person, the devil is continually conquered.*

[**221a.**] 5466. These things have been displayed to me over a very long period by continual combats within myself, and later [by combats] outside of myself in the midst of which I was; so that if all that experience should be told, the volume would swell out.

[See WE 5467 up to this point, explaining Exod. 32:28.]
* *For the devil's gang are continually attacking, and trying to climb the wall, but they can never enter.*

[**222a.**] 5468. What it is to defend the wall can become clear by an understanding of our inward faculties. From early childhood, the human mind is subjected to outside assault, leading to an obedience of the earthly mind, and through that defense and combat is brought back to the truly spiritual form. So it subdues the enemy, but does not destroy him.

However, that the sons of Levi were allowed to kill their brothers, companions, and neighbors, was because they shared the same guilt, namely, of those who were sacrificing and worshipping. Thus they were like the others, Aaron, their head, being also of the tribe of Levi. Therefore it was allowed them to kill their own brothers, companions, neighbors, scarcely otherwise than as when God the Messiah punishes the wicked.

This is not done through good angels, who never punish or kill anyone, but defend themselves and subdue the enemy, that is, bind him, and hold him in bonds, with the constant intention of bringing him back to his senses. Heavenly love has this quality within it, that it never wishes anyone's damnation, that is, anyone's death: because they possess this quality from God the Messiah, Who rules them.

[223a.] 5469. Therefore, what is seen here is punishment rather than truly spiritual combat; for, whenever the devil's gang is allowed the opportunity, the one rushes upon the other; nor do they care if it be a brother, or a companion, or a neighbor, or even a son, as we read presently [verse 29].

[224a.] * Nevertheless, a spiritual combat is symbolically portrayed; for they were the sons of Levi, who were to be inaugurated into the priesthood—something that appears even more clearly from the words of the verse now following.

[See WE 5470–73, explaining Exod. 32:29.]

[225a.] 5474. When a person is paying attention only to the things that rush upon the senses, then the spirits [with the person] grasp nothing else but those things; and in order that this may take place without the participation of the person's inner qualities, the choir of angels is arranged in the way stated above [*WE* 5409, 5421, 5433, 5437; *SE* 216a], namely, so that the outer aspects are grasped by them, and are thus raised up. I have also experienced this in myself, that is, how they only grasp the outer aspects, apart from the inner ones; for they are at once touched by the outer aspects of an ordinary person, just as people on earth are. However, this could rarely happen in me except for the sake of demonstration and confirmation only, because inner elements were also among the outer ones at the same time, which I could clearly tell apart. Therefore, when holy subjects were being portrayed, then this was done near the tent of assembly and the ark, where a choir of angels was, this being the reason that at such times, all of the rites there were carried out so solemnly, lest any outer element should occur that would disturb.

Whether the angels of God the Messiah could be with this people in other places, must be doubted, except in the case of Moses, Joshua, and some others whose names are not on record here; as well as in the case of little children.

[Church; Outer; Inward; Order; Portrayal (Representation); Spirit]

[226a.] 5475. In the presence of the altar, the tabernacle, and other objects, all things that were present were raised up, and were so arranged by God the Messiah that a most holy display would come to the innermost region; thereby every means was supplied so that numberless ideas could be formed altogether according to the will of God the Messiah, thus portraying all righteousness, and all salvation, as well as the universal Kingdom of God the Messiah, with its infinite variety. That variety was bound to appear from the composition of all the elements, and of each in particular, since nothing could be so holy that it could not have been displayed in this manner. For one who grasps the idea of the rites and ceremonies in this Church, can obtain an idea of all the secrets pertaining to the true Christian Church.[1]
[Church; Outer; Inward; Order; Portrayal (Representation); Spirit]

[227a.] 5476. Now in the Church truly Christian are contained all and the least things in the Lord's Prayer; and what an infinitude of secrets it has within it, I was able to learn from those which were inspired into me day by day, with inexpressible variety, as I recited that prayer.
[Feeling (Affection); Church; Outer; Humbling; Inward; Prayer; Order; Portrayal (Representation); Spirit]

[228a.] 5477. In the Church truly Christian, that is, in an inner person, outer elements are entirely withdrawn from inner ones, so that what the eye sees or the ear hears, he does not take in, but is occupied inwardly, and so, all things go back to innermost regions. It is otherwise when outer sensations are present—then inner elements are somewhat troubled, unless a person is so trained that outer elements cause no confusion, but lead to corresponding inner ones.[2]

[229a.] 5478. Take, for example, "bread" in the Prayer of our Lord [Matt. 6:11, Luke 11:3]. When holy bread was displayed to them on the table, and also loaves upon the whole burnt offering, then, in the people's eyes, the holi-

---

[1] In the original this paragraph is emphasized by the word *Obs.* written twice in the margin.

[2] In the original this paragraph is emphasized by the word *Obs.* written twice in the margin.

[230a.] ness was in the bread, and from this a bread is portrayed extending to all the necessities of life, as well as to all spiritual food, and heavenly food, and finally, to God the Messiah, Who is the Heavenly Bread and the Manna. For this reason also, they obtained their heavenly bread day by day, so that only God the Messiah might be portrayed constantly in their food, and thus be all in all things.

The same thing also is imparted to the human mind in the Lord's Prayer; for just as [the meaning of] "bread" is extended also to all the necessities of earthly life, so by the inner person it is extended to all the necessities of spiritual and heavenly life. This, then, is the "daily Bread[1]."

[Feeling (Affection); Church; Outer; Humbling; Inward; Prayer; Order; Portrayal (Representation); Spirit]

[230a.] * From this it may also be evident how greatly the merely symbolic Jewish Church differed from the truly Christian Church, since it was such that the portrayals are not in the person, and raised up in that way, but only outside of the person.

[231a.] * When they are within a person, it is like being in the choir of angels, and then he or she is one and the same with the Church truly Christian, for that Church could see what is spiritual and heavenly portrayed in every single object, due to their connection by interaction.

[232a.] 5479. For the portrayal passes in this way from the outer to the innermost regions in the person, and thus the gate to heaven is opened, which is otherwise closed. And it is God the Messiah Who brings it about that there is nothing that is not raised up to Himself. This happens only through belief in God the Messiah Himself.

[233a.] * On the other hand, when the inner person passes over to the outer, as was the case in Moses, then it is not the innermost element that is operating, but a certain earthly element in which there is something spiritual; hence the shining of Moses' face [34:35]. The inner per-

---

[1] The original manuscript here has *Pater* instead of *Panis*.

son does not shine on the face, but most deeply within, as is clearly the case with the Word of God the Messiah.

[See WE 5495 up to this point, treating in general of Exod. 33:1–6.]
*   ....Therefore, what the "Mouth[1] of Jehovah" is [Num. 9:23] when there was a pillar, you may see explained earlier, namely, that it was a choir of angels who were taking up outer portrayals [see WE 5433, SE 216a, WE 5437, SE 225a].

[**234a.**]   5496. About the arrangements of angels for whatever use and purpose, with their immeasurably great diversity as to both rank and state in general and in particular, there are countless details, among which are those which I have disclosed above [225a]—namely, that they are arranged entirely according to whatever is in the person, in that manner, etc. etc. Therefore, something could be learned in a most general way from the form of their government, especially, their Ecclesiastical government.

[See WE 5497–5501, concluding the explanation of that portion.]

[See WE 5522 ff., explaining Exod. 33:5, especially 5525–27.]
[**235a.**]   *   But now some points about the choir of angels are being inspired differently—whether for the reason that this subject must be written about cautiously, or whether there had been an appeasement on their behalf, so that the Messiah's righteousness might be applied to them, etc. etc., [I do not know].

[See the rest of WE 5527 especially, as well as 5528–30, concluding the explanation of verse 5.]

[See WE 5582–85, explaining Exod. 33:11.]
[**236a.**]   5586. What was decreed—though not at that time, but from eternity—is not learned except from what happened, namely, that since no mortal can be saved without the inner law, that is, without belief in God the Messiah, and since this people, to whom the promise had been made, was such that they could not believe, therefore the Gospel was brought over to the gentiles.

[Abraham; Belief (Faith); Portrayal (Representation)]

---

[1] *KJV* and *NKJV* have "commandment."

[**237a.**] * But because the Jewish Church, in itself, must be one and the same with the Church truly Christian, as was the earliest or infant Church, therefore, so that that Church might be portrayed as an inner one, Abraham depicts a belief that makes one righteous.

The fact that belief was accounted to him because he had believed the promise concerning Isaac, who was to be the promised son [Gen. 15:4–6], could not have made Abraham righteous, unless at the same time he had believed that by the promised son was meant the Messiah, Who was to be born, and Who is the One Only promised Son.[1]

Neither could his obedience in being willing to sacrifice Isaac [Gen. 22:12] have made Abraham righteous, unless he had believed that the Messiah, here clearly figuratively portrayed, was the sacrifice for the whole human race. We do not read whether such a belief had been inspired into Abraham at the time. Nevertheless, Abraham does thus portray a belief that makes one righteous. See more on this subject above, paragraphs [*WE*] 5573–74.

[Abraham; Belief (Faith); Portrayal (Representation)]

[**238a.**] 5587. What has just been written here appeared to have been Divinely inspired; for the very words, although not dictated, were still perceptibly inspired. Other things which happened in connection with these words are many, and too holy to be revealed here; nevertheless, I solemnly declare that of these words, not the smallest one, or the least part of a word, comes from myself.

[Abraham; Belief (Faith); Portrayal (Representation)]

[**239a.**] 5588. (Reminder) I had a long conversation with Abraham, yesterday and today, to a point where he had become extremely indignant when it was shown to him that there is also such a thing as a symbolic belief, and that it did not make one righteous; for example, that believing the promise about Isaac, and obedience in sacrificing a son, does not make him righteous at all, without an inner sight of those symbolic events, [penetrating] to God the Messiah. This he deeply understood as demonstrated to him, nor was he able to oppose it, as they

---

[1] In the original this paragraph is emphasized by the word *Obs.* written twice in the margin.

have also confessed quite often; among very many other things.

Whether these matters are also to be inserted, I still do not at all know. I am waiting to see if consent is given by God the Messiah.
[Abraham; Belief (Faith); Portrayal (Representation)]

[See also WE 5589–91, continuing the explanation of verse 11.]

[240a.]   5592. That they feel at rest with self-righteousness on account of their own works, was demonstrated by an actual example in front of those spoken of above [239a], to the point that they could not at all deny it. But how this example was set forth, it would be too lengthy to describe. For in this matter, the case is the same in heaven among the souls who had lived in those Churches as when they lived on earth, because such as we are when we die, such we remain after death. This can be confirmed by so many particulars, that a large number of pages could have been filled in corroborating them.

[241a.]   5593. Just for this reason, I have been given by God the Messiah, from pure mercy, to learn what Abraham, what Jacob, and what Moses had been like, for in heaven they are just like they had been in life. Sometimes I was in doubt as to whether they were the same persons, or whether they had been depicted to me through others, as also happens. I spoke about this matter, and was allowed to investigate it in various ways, with the result that I have been led to believe that they were indeed the same persons; nor were they able to deny it, although they wished to do so for the reasons spoken of earlier [*cf.* 239a].
[Abraham; Church; Jacob; Moses; Portrayal (Representation)]

[See also for the sake of context WE 5594–5601, continuing the explanation of verse 11.]

5602. *Meanwhile, by the Divine mercy of God the Messiah, I have been enabled to learn how*

[242a.]   *   inner hearing and sight take place, differing in no way whatever from outer hearing and sight, except for the fact that no one else is at all aware of the matter. That hearing and that sight happens in such a variety of ways, and at different levels, even toward the innermost

[243a.] SPIRITUAL EXPERIENCES

one, that it would be too much if the testimonies of experiences were all recounted. Indeed, my sight penetrated to the innermost regions in such a way that those in the more inward ones were upset—as a result of which I was allowed to see the levels themselves; not to mention memorable occurrences of today, which are, in fact, being held back for the present, perhaps referring to Rev. Chap. 12 verse 7 ff.

But these took place as if above me, though in such a way that I could faintly observe them. How I was involved, I am unable to describe, but whether this was merely a portrayal of that war I cannot tell, for I was not permitted to inquire into such questions: the 18th day of July, 1746 (old calendar).[1] Later, I was also forced to be among them a little longer.

[243a.] 5603. As for the inward person in whom the way to heaven is being opened, all the inward faculties of such, distinctly and one after the other, are unclosed, to the point where they are able to be among the heavenly. This means that as to their earthly mind, they can be among those who are in the inward regions, as to the mind devoted to understanding among those in the more inward regions, and as to the soul, among those in innermost ones. Thus the door is opened again from the earthly paradise into the heavenly paradise.[2]

With the outer person, the case is different. Such grasp only those matters that come in from the outside, that is, through the outer senses, as well as through the earthly mind: so they can see angels, when it so pleases God the Messiah, with the eyes, and can hear them with the ears, but in an utterly upside-down manner; for in the earthly person, the workings of those [higher] faculties descend and are terminated in the world, whereas in the spiritual person, they are raised up, perceptibly, into heaven.

---

[1] In the original this sentence is emphasized by the word *Obs.* written in the margin four times, together with the notation, "Revelation Ch. 12, verse 7 and following."
[2] This and the next paragraph are emphasized in the original by the word *Obs.* written twice in the margin.

But these matters are such as cannot become known easily, without actual experience, and to describe them [thoroughly] would be a work of many sheets.

[See WE 5617, up to this point, in which Matt. 17:1–8 is discussed during the explanation of Exod. 33:13.]

5617. ....*By Jacob [Matt. 17:1]*[1], *however, the Church truly Christian [is meant], which*

[**244a.**] * should be clear to me from the things I have spoken about with Jacob.

[See also WE 5618–22, concluding the explanation of verse 13.]

[See WE 5643–50, explaining Exod. 34:1.]

[**245a.**] * How the inner Law condemns those who trust in the outer Law and in their own righteousness has, by the pure mercy of God the Messiah, been shown to me, for they were as if in hell and in inward torment when they heard the outer Law truly explained, and grasped its meaning.

The experience itself as to how this was shown would be long in the telling, but it is not allowed me to record it here, for many reasons that are very secret. From it I was enabled to come to a somewhat better conception of what hell is: for this was only a rather mild hell, and yet the torment was painful.

[Inward; Righteousness; Law]

[**246a.**] 5651. (Reminder: I was present when they were being convinced, and thus when the truth was penetrating; but when it was penetrating more deeply I was not allowed to be present, although I was still present in such a way as to be able to observe it.)

[Inward]

5652. But here it is most difficult to find out whether Jehovah wrote anew the ten words, or commandments of the decalogue, on the tables, for we read *[Exod. 34:]* verse 28, that *"he wrote upon the tables the words of the covenant, the ten words"* thus whether Moses wrote them with his own hand;[2]

---

[1] In the *KJV* this name is changed to *James*.
[2] See *WE* 5652, footnote 1.

[247a.] * for so it happened in my case, many times, that is, that I was writing, and my hand was being guided to the very words by a higher force, even to the point of feeling it, and sometimes quite clearly, so that I would then declare that these words are not from me, but from someone outside of me. Sometimes I was even given to know by which angel of God the Messiah they had thus been written.
[Hand; Write]
[See the rest of WE 5652–53, concluding the explanation of verse 1.]

5657. [Exod. 34:] verse 3. These words mean that at such a time no one should be together with Moses, that is, with those over whom he had been placed as leader and priest. For first the Jewish Church is to be judged by the Law. They received the Word of God the Messiah, and so they must be the first who will be judged. The Judgment, therefore, must begin with that house.
* For this reason it is here said "no man," that is, they who are from the earliest Church, etc., and neither "flock" nor "herd," by which are meant those of any other religion. Thus the judgment must begin with that house.
5658. [Not] "to feed in the vicinity of the mountain," means that they must not then be present, so that they do not see the judgment.
[248a.] * I could not help judging this to be the meaning of these words because of what happened today in heaven, when one person from that house, who represented the whole house, was cast out. But this took place as if above me, in a remarkable way. The 20th day of July, 1746 (old calendar).
5659. The judgment, of course, does not now follow at this point in the text, but still the same judgment continues as before, Chap. 32: verse 34. But now a new covenant is being contracted, as was the first one, the main point of which is that they should not worship any other God. But because they had even broken this covenant, they were sentenced to die in the desert, for they still wished to have other gods, as is seen in Num. Chapter 14: verse 4 and then the following verses.
* For God the Messiah now also prayed to Jehovah His Father [see John 17], as follows from verses 6 to 9 inclusive.

FROM *WE* TOME III [251a.]

[249a.] 5660. What it is to turn away the face, and thus to cause, or rather, to permit, the wicked to be punished by truth itself, which penetrates right to their more inward parts, causing torments almost like the torments of conscience, but more forceful—this also has been portrayed to me in an amazing manner. For I could not join in with them, and thereby they were drawn back; nor did I wish to prevent them, and while I appeared to wish to, this was taking place apart from me, yet still in such a way that I was observing these events in a most general manner, etc.

[See WE 5676–77, explaining Exod. 34:8.]

[250a.] 5678. That there are so many causes of a humbling, even if man is unaware of them, by the mercy of God the Messiah it has been granted me to learn. For I was allowed to calculate together with spirits, what all was present within one given feeling, and it thus came out incontestably that there are elements latent in what appears as a single feeling, about which a person does not even know, except when it is actually revealed to him. So now, in this first humbling [of Moses].

[Feeling (Affection); Humbling]
[See also the rest of WE 5678, concluding the explanation of this verse.]
[See WE 5679 up to this point, explaining Exod. 34:9.]

* Here [Moses] says "Lord," not "Jehovah," which shows clearly that he had to address his supplication to God the Messiah. As to whether he acknowledged Him, this may be doubted on the basis of some passages in the Word of God the Messiah,

[251a.] * as well as what it has been granted me, by the Divine mercy of God the Messiah, to learn, namely that he is still arrogant, trusting in himself, and therefore not esteemed, being one who worships the outer Law—I can only say this. Other matters regarding him, see elsewhere, and the passages may then be quoted—also, for example, who is meant by Moses and Elias when they are said to have appeared on the Mountain to God the Messiah [Matt. 17:3, Mark 9:4, Luke 9:30]. He is still aspiring to lead the people, etc.

[Moses]
[See also WE 5680–83, concluding the explanation of verse 9.]

[252a.] SPIRITUAL EXPERIENCES

[See WE 5741 up to this point, explaining Exod. 34:28.]

* It is read here that "he wrote the words of the covenant upon the tables," so it is evident that these were the words, as well as that Moses had written them, but an angel present with him had guided his hand, just as you may see attested to by myself in statements about certain writings [2a, 22a–27a, 78a, 247a]. For my hand [252a.] * was plainly being guided to the writing, to the point that the very words hardly appeared to be in my handwriting. For a long time, I could feel my hands, my fingers, my eyes, my feet, and my whole body, being controlled, which happened quite often, while at the same time I spoke about the matter with the heavenly beings. In fact, [this went] so far that [I would be led] into whatever gyres they wanted, even to a place unknown to me, or to my home, when I did not know the way, by streets unknown to me. If these experiences were to be recounted in detail, it would surely stun inexperienced minds exceedingly, which do not believe such things; but it is enough to tell of them in a general way and solemnly testify to them, etc.

[Control (Action); Body; Spirit]
[See the rest of WE 5741–43, concluding the explanation of verse 28.]

[See WE 5750-61, explaining Exod. 34:29.]

5762. It is most clear that those who are self-righteous wish to be judged by truth, that is, by the Law, but if they are judged by the Law, that they cannot but be condemned. What, then, brings restoration? Hence the Law condemns.[1] Now this was put to those of the stock of Eber, who [253a.] 5763. were with me, that is, to the dead who had risen, and they replied that they therefore seemed to be condemned, for they did not seem to themselves to have righteousness in them. But they thought that by grace what was unrighteous in them was pardoned, for they were declaring that only the one God exists, and this was also affirmed—but in three essences. But it was put to them, Whom did Melchisedek represent, to whom sacri-

---

[1] In the original this sentence is emphasized by the word *Obs.* written twice in the margin.

ficial victims were given [cf. Heb. 5:1, 6; 7:4]? To this they could give no reply. Further, they were asked, what did the sacrifices represent? And when they could still give no answer, the question was put to them, Whom did Isaac portray when he was made a sacrificial victim [Gen. 22:1–12]? But to this they kept silence, saying that it was unpleasant to them to hear these things. Comment: spiritual beings understand a person's speech just as the person is thinking, along with all his circumstances, differently than man does. And since this speaking was guided by the angels of God the Messiah, it was full [of meaning].
[Jews]

[See WE 5764 up to this point, explaining Exod. 34:30.]

* *For outer truth joined with inner is such that it terrifies earthly people, and it condemns them. This is supported by many instances in which earthly minded people shudder at truths that concern spiritual life or the life after death. For truth is entirely opposite to falsity, which is brought on by the loves of the world and of oneself, and because truth kills or destroys those loves, the earthly person is greatly upset by it.*

[**254a.**] * This can be confirmed by many instances. Truths that I expressed to some in the other life tormented them as if they were in hell. Thus they feared the truths so much, and the truths caused them such pain, that I was obliged to desist, etc.
[Faith; Truth]

[See also WE 5765–67, continuing the explanation of Exod. 34:30.]

5768. *It was this Light [see WE 5767] that was now radiating from the skin of Moses. As for how that Light is seen*

[**255a.**] * in the understanding part of the mind, this can be told on the basis of much experience. It simply cannot be described how tangible that light is, even though it is unknown to people on earth. It was this light, or this truth, that upset those who were hearing it so much that they were greatly tormented. Thus they realized that the punishment of hell must be that which results from truth stinging their consciences. But who were so upset by the truth, I am not free to tell at present. It happens in a

variety of ways, depending on the character acquired by each one during the life of the body.
[See also WE 5769–71, concluding the explanation of verse 30.]

5774.   *[Exod. 34:] verse 33. As for the "veil," it symbolizes shadow.*
*   This can be understood from what was said earlier about the closed door between the heavenly paradise and the earthly one [243a], and from very many other circumstances. I can also testify
[256a.]   *   that a veil being drawn away was displayed before me, and then I saw truth clearly in light; in fact, even my ocular vision became sharper, which amazed me.
[Eye; Veil]
[See WE 5775–76, concluding the explanation of Exod. 34:33.]

5777.   *[Exod. 34:] verse 34. What these words most deeply mean is not easy to explain. When anyone is granted to speak with those in the heaven of God the Messiah, a veil is pulled away, and a*
*   bright Light *comes into the mind. But when the person speaks with someone on earth, no such light is shining,*
[257a.]   *   so that he then appears just like another person, both in his conversation and in other respects. But as soon as he enters into heaven, the veil is taken away, and the Light comes. For the understanding part of the mind is able to be lifted up toward higher and heavenly regions, so it can look upwards, and also downwards, etc. etc.
[See also WE 5778, concluding the explanation of Exod. 34:34.]

5789.   *[Exod. 35:] verse 5, saying that "a Therumah to Jehovah should be taken" from them.*
*   A "Therumah to Jehovah" was spoken of above *[WE 4664–65, 5035–39]*, but here it is to be done over again.
[258a.]   *   For the things told earlier had arisen out of the dispute among spirits around me regarding the meaning of "Therumah" *[WE 5041, SE 175a–76a]*.
[For the connection, see the rest of WE 5789–96, continuing the explanation of Exod. 35:5.]

5797.   From this it is now understood what freedom is, especially in Divine worship.

* The greatest freedom comes from God the Messiah, and from that all Freedom is determined.

[259a.] * How free it is to be guided by God the Messiah, few are able to understand. But about these matters we will speak elsewhere, etc. etc.

[See also WE 5816, explaining Exod. 35:21.]

5817. As to freedom, the reader may see this discussed above *[WE 5797, SE 259a]*. But here two very distinct things are understood by the Angel of God the Messiah; for the whole order is complete when God the Messiah speaks, and when this either reaches the ears or comes into a literal form. This also,

[260a.] * by the Diving Mercy of God the Messiah, I was allowed to experience today, while praying His Prayer: the whole order was in it, or the meaning ascending and descending, from outermost to innermost. For it is in this way that a person on earth understands these words, whereas God the Messiah views every least one from the innermost to the outermost, so that in every least word there is an idea of creation, etc. etc.[1] About this, see above [227a–33a]. Thus the meaning is deduced in a way by the person praying, and this is that uplifting during prayer spoken of in those passages.

[Creation; Prayer; Order]

[See WE 5818–22, concluding the explanation of Exod. 35:21]
[See WE 5823–25 up to this point, explaining Exod. 35:22]

* So every effect *[of such gestures]* upon the choir of angels is likened to a "waving"[2], but what is taking place in the innermost regions is quite different from what is being portrayed down below.[3]

[261a.] 5826. So that these facts might be confirmed, it was portrayed how these matters stand. First, this whole verse was read, without my paying attention to it, and it was told that still the same effect was experienced on the spiritual plane.

---

[1] In the original this sentence is emphasized by the word *Obs.* written twice in the margin.
[2] The *KJV* has "offered an offering of gold," where the literal meaning is "waved a waving."
[3] In the original this paragraph is emphasized by the Word O*bs.* written twice in the margin.

[262a.]   This I could not grasp, except on the basis of other similar experiences in which things are drawn up and away from a person on earth, and the choir of angels links them in a way that they take on holiness before reaching God the Messiah. So each thing is turned into something holy; and this takes place in someone when everything, even evil, is turned to good. This I have been allowed to learn very well, from experience within myself, over a long period of time. So these are the "[gold] links"[1] [verse 22].

[262a.]   5827. But "wavings" were also shown in another way, as how the things portrayed by changes of their shape were turned into true images or shapes, so that evils and wrongs did not appear, but were removed so as to perish entirely and become nothing. Therefore, this is in agreement with the uplifting we read about in [Exod. 35:] verse 24, namely: "Every one that lifts a heave offering of silver or of brass." Hence, nothing reached God the Messiah but what is meant by "gold," that is, goodness, holiness, love.[2]

*   *But these matters are entirely mystical to those who do not understand what portrayals are all about. Such an infinity of secrets lie hidden in them that no one could comprehend it, etc. etc.*

[263a.]   5828. But the wavings occur in the inner person, having also a kind of reponse there, which comes from the angel who is acting upon him. For a truly inner person interacts completely with that angel, that is, with the angels who bring goodness into the person, all of whom God the Messiah rules from the highest, while at the same time ruling the soul of the person.

[264a.]   From this then it is clear how these words also relate to those of verse 21.

[See also WE 5832, explaining Exod. 35: 24.]

[265a.]   5833. When what is evil in a person is portrayed, a choir of angels raises it up and turns it into good, and thus into what

---

[1] *I.e.* "clasp, necklace, ring, and girdle" (Acton), or "bracelets, and earrings, and rings, and tablets" *(KJV),* said in *WE* 5823 to signify "all manner of links."

[2] This last sentence is emphasized in the original by the word *Obs.* written in the margin.

is holy. This is accomplished by means of various displays, which it is difficult to describe here. For there are tens of thousands of such portrayals, by whose help evils are turned into good—or what is profane is lifted up, and becomes holy. These displays I have at times
[*Good; Evil; Profane; Portrayal (Display, Representation); Holy*]

[**266a.**] * experienced, and today as well as yesterday I saw displays of that kind and was amazed at them. By means of them also I was shown what a "heave offering" is, and what a "Therumah of Jehovah."

[**267a.**] * An uplifting of this kind was needed among this people so that God the Messiah or the angel might be able to dwell in the midst of their uncleanness [Lev. 16:16].

5834. Consequently, "Therumah" was called by that people "Thrumah," meaning an offering (see [Exod.] Chap. 25, verse 2). But Thrumah or offering is applicable to the children of the true Israel, who are those that harmonize with the angelic choir—that is, whose inward parts, one after the other, harmonize with that choir.

5835. The evil spirits also, who rule evil people, lest they disturb those displays

[**268a.**] * are restrained in various ways and cast into bonds. From these bonds they are quite unable to escape, until the power to do so is given them.

But to tell about the ways in which evil spirits are cast into bonds or restrained would make a long story; suffice it to say that the angels of God the Messiah are given the power to bind and restrain them depending upon what they are up to.

[**269a.**] 5836. The purpose of the heave offering is that the evil spirit may be taken out of their midst, that he may no longer come and arouse evil.

[See WE 5837–38, concluding the explanation of Exod. 35:24.

[See also WE 5855, explaining Exod. 36:3.]

5856. *A state of non-freedom is never pleasing, for it takes away all that is delightful. This can be made quite clear by the love between married partners. Whatever is not shared by both in mutual love is not delightful and pleasant. And if there is even the least element of compulsion on the part of one or the other, or what appears as compulsion, to that degree the pleasantness becomes less; therefore it is the mutual love* between the partners that makes what is called freedom, *since acting from love is acting from freedom*.[1] From this we may infer regarding the heavenly marriage, which is the Kingdom of God the Messiah, that one who is without the love for God the Messiah above all things can never be given eternal happiness. Forcing anyone can never be joined with happiness, because it is not from the love of God the Messiah above all things.

[**270a.**] 5857. The above was shown to me so clearly in a dream in this night between the 27th and 28th of July, 1746 (old calendar) that nothing could be clearer. The spirits and angels who had been present, with whom I spoke about the dream after awakening, confirmed this same point.[2] But to tell the dream, together with all its circumstances, would be a large task, and besides, they cannot be appreciated so much by a person on earth as by the angels of God the Messiah.

[**271a.**] 5858. It is amazing, when one is engaged in conversation with spirits, how all of the surrounding circumstances are slipped in, so that the speech is very rich, expressing what cannot be said in conversation with man, or in writing, except by using many, many words.[3] For they follow one's thoughts in their every least detail, and understand them at once and all at the same time.

[See also WE 5859–66, concluding the explanation of Exod. 36:3.]

5867.   *[Exod. 36:] verse 4.* They are called "wise" who are filled with the Spirit of God the Messiah, mentioned above, verse 1, namely, Bazaleel, Oholiab, and the others (see the preceding Chapter and this Chapter, verse 2).

*   By these people are meant all servants and all the upright who are awaiting the Kingdom of God the Messiah, and the last day, and who are groaning, as we read of the creatures *[Rom. 8: 19–23]*. For they believe the last day to be at hand, thus the end of all work.

[**272a.**] 5868. In heaven, all the angels of God the Messiah are also ardently awaiting the last day; for they are thinking of nothing else.[4] This I can affirm by many experiences.

---

[1] In the original this sentence is emphasized by the word *Obs.* written twice in the margin.
[2] This sentence is emphasized in the original by the word *Obs.* written twice in the margin.
[3] This sentence is emphasized in the original by the word *Obs.* written twice in the margin.
[4] This sentence in the original is emphasized by the word *Obs.* written twice in the margin.

So this, too, is what is meant by the groaning of all creatures.
[Judgment]
[See also WE 5869–70, concluding the explanation of Exod. 36:4.]

[See WE 5873–76, to this point, explaining Joshua 1.]
*   ....*By an outward observance of the Law, they were able to inherit that land only, as they did, but never heaven.* **They observed the Law only outwardly.**

[**273a.**]   *   But that they now want to inherit heaven, in fact to seize it, I have learned very well from those who spoke with me. For they now maintain that the inheritance means heaven, not the land.
[Hereditary, Heredity; Jews; Land]
[See further up to WE 5880 the rest of the explanation of Joshua 1.]

[See WE 5903–04, explaining Joshua 8.]
5905.   The reason why ambushes were laid [v. 2, 9, 12]—but not as at Jericho in that it was put to ruin—is that enemies had to be punished by the same method they want to use, namely by setting traps; for this is a law of retaliation, which is Divine. So those at the last judgment who wished treacherously to lay snares for Israel, will fall by their own weapons. There would have been no need for these actions except to portray things that are to come. For who does not know that heaven has no need of traps?—unless that Law is a trap which decrees that such as a person is, so shall he be punished. A house that claims to be righteous by its own powers, such as the one and principal house of the Jewish people, is like that, wanting to set traps, and constantly trying to claim righteousness for its good deeds, and for its obedience.[1] This

[**274a.**]   *   can be illustrated by many instances, but it is not yet the time; for first there must be the house of Jericho, and then the house of Bethel. Compare Genesis Chap. 15:16,17,18, with what is said in this Chapter, then about the Amorites, Josh. Chap. 7:7, and what I have told earlier about Abraham [236a 41a]; then, the many dreadful things portrayed to me about him [*cf.*

---

[1] In the margin at this sentence is written "*What the House of God is*, as just above [WE 5903–04]."

[275a.] SPIRITUAL EXPERIENCES

115a–16a]. Also, that he portrayed himself about to slaughter his son [Gen. 22:10] so that he might become righteousness. But these things will be discussed at their proper time, for they must be handled prudently.
[Abraham]

[275a.] 5906. How horrible were the accusations and plots of that distinguished house against God the Messiah, which were displayed to me in heaven—and also those which came from them directed at myself—I could not ever express, because they would exceed all human belief.

That there had been such attempts since a long time ago, now exposed for the first time, I do not doubt: for they constantly want to justify themselves by their own righteousness, in many different ways. But because their attempts are so horrible, I would rather forget them than make them public.
[Abraham; Jacob]

[276a.] 5907. This house—which I do not yet wish to name—is such that he[1] wishes, aided by incredible cunning, and by various techniques, to make himself righteousness, as if thus to emulate God the Messiah, striving to possess the Kingdom of Heaven. It is therefore no wonder that here, Ai near Bethel was taken by ambush, since that person is here portrayed who, because he is deceitful, must be parried by a like deceit, this due simply to the law of retaliation and not to any other cause whatsoever. For he is as easily dashed down as the least thing on earth, etc. etc.
[Abraham; Jacob]

5908. About this people being called *"the house of God the Messiah,"* see the next Chapter 9: verse 23.

[See WE 5912–21, explaining Joshua 10.]

5922. Who is meant by *"the King of Jerusalem"* [verse 3] can be evident to some extent from what has been said before, namely, the one whom they worship as God, that is, who

[277a.] * wants to become Righteousness, and is therefore eager to gain the kingdom of God the Messiah, who was spoken of above, where something is said about

---

[1] Thus in the original Latin.

Abraham, paragraphs [274a–76a] etc.: **the distinguished one—**

[See WE 5923, discussing Joshua 11 in general.]

5924. How they will gather themselves together to do battle with those who belong to God the Messiah [verses 1–5] is clear from what happens in life. The evil always attack, but are conquered by the children of Israel—due to the fact that evil is turned by Him into good, which I have so many times been given by God

[**278a.**] * the Messiah to experience—and indeed, a great many other circumstances corroborate this. But the damnation of the evil is effected in a different way: namely, by conviction, causing continuous torture by their conscience. This was also displayed to me in a general manner. Moreover, there will be unspeakable torture of their conscience when they perpetually see the glory of God the Messiah, the happiness of the children of Israel, their own continual conviction and the consequent stirring up of everything they did during their lifetime. What an intensely deep pain there will be cannot be described.

5952. By the "Anakim" and the "three sons of Anak" *[Josh. 15: 14]* are meant the strongest enemies, whom God the Messiah Himself will drive out. Who these three enemies are, who were of this character,

[**279a.**] * I do not dare to say as yet, but the course of events will expose them. They are in fact well known, but people worship them.

[See WE 5987–90, discussing Joshua 24 in general.]

[**280a.**] 5991. What their gods are like [verse 23] has also, by the Divine Mercy of God the Messiah, been shown to me: boastful—especially those who want to become righteousness, and thus strive to possess that which is in God the Messiah: **but these matters must not yet be disclosed; perhaps.**

[Gods; Righteousness; Kingdom]

[See also the remainder of WE 5991.]

5999. *[Judg. 1:]* verse 8. "Jerusalem," the city of God, etc., is also, in the higher sense, the innermost **Kingdom of God the**

[281a.] SPIRITUAL EXPERIENCES

***Messiah**. Because the wicked have striven to take this city, and wanted to establish their own kingdom there, now therefore, in order that this might be atoned for, Jerusalem was "set on fire," and the men were "smitten with the edge of the sword." But with which edge of the sword, may be evident*
[**281a.**]   *   from what has been said above. The edge of the sword is truth, which penetrates to the innermost parts and torments [*cf.* 254a, 278a].

6005.   *[Judg. 1:] verse 19. "He drove out the mountain," that is, the arrogant, who were climbing up the mountain.*
  The "inhabitants of the valley" are the humble, "a chariot of iron" the earthly orientation that dominates in them, "iron" being the lowest plane of nature. Because of those who remained, the truth can stand firm. Truth on the earthly plane is "iron" or "a chariot of iron."
[**282a.**]   *   Perhaps these matters were portrayed by those who had been with me, who, although they were from that same people, were not like them, etc. etc.

6009.   *[Judg. 2:] verses 1 to 3.* This statement, that "they did not drive out the enemies," was made by the angel of Jehovah, because one of their orders was that they should put all their enemies under the curse.
  *   But that they did not do so, was permitted, not commanded. Therefore, because it was permitted, but quite differently commanded, they are reproached by the angel of Jehovah. The reason why the enemies could not be driven out was that if they had been, the people could no longer have been tempted as the true Israel. Without the presence of the evil, nothing introduces evil so that it may be turned into good. For man is evil from the root, and this evil is continually rising up. Without the presence of one who stirs it up, this evil is accounted to a person. Nor can the angels of God the Messiah be with anyone unless there is a fight, for that fight reforms the person. When the evil is stirred up, the wound is opened, and thus the person gets better and is reformed.
  These are the matters portrayed here, the reason for which will be said in the end of the Chap., verses 22 and 23, and in Chap. 3,

verses 1 and 2, see the notes[1]. *Evil otherwise stagnates in a person, so to speak, causing it to breathe forth rottenness. It clings also to the good in him, and is not separated from it without this kind of stirring up.*

[**283a.**] 6010. These are the matters which, by the Divine mercy of God the Messiah, it has been granted me to learn during a period of 16 months now. Otherwise they would have been mysteries to me, nor would I have been able easily to believe them.

6011. *But this people, because it wanted to inherit heaven as well, led by the devil, and so to invade the kingdom of God the Messiah, could not be corrected. For they supposed that this also was involved in the promise [Gen. 12:7]. This I was granted to learn from those who*

[**284a.**] * arose into the other life. Their arrogance is such that they wish to invade the Kingdom of God the Messiah at the least relaxation of restraints. Their attempts are frightful, but they all come to nothing, for the spirits of God the Messiah still constantly struggle against them. With His spirits, all evil is turned into good, but with them, all good is turned into evil, and so forth. For they are always conquered, yet they still persist.

[Gods; Righteousness; Kingdom]

[See also the rest of WE 6011 and 6012, concluding the explanation of Judg. 2:1–3.]

6022. *Whenever they are being delivered into the hands of their enemies, and deprived of their lands, etc. [Judg. 2], they portray a state of damnation. For then they represent the devil's gang, which is continually approaching and attacking, and continually being repulsed. Yet still they do not at all understand that the judgment is about to come, and that they are to be driven out of heaven. No matter how much they are taught, they still remain in their idolatry. At this point*

[**285a.**] * I could tell some amazing things, but I am not allowed to do so, except for one that concerns their character which they have brought with them from their life

---

[1] It is not clear what note or notes are referred to here and in *WE* 6023; perhaps to the notes written at the end of the tomes. See *Experientiae Spirituales*, Preface to Volume I, pp. xxx to xxxiii.

[286a.]   SPIRITUAL EXPERIENCES

in the world: that remains the same, and they wish to be worshipped as gods. I do not know that they adore other gods, but each and all adore themselves, etc. etc.
[Gods; Righteousness; Kingdom]

[See WE 6040, explaining Judg. 5:9.]
*   "Who showed themselves ready among the people, from a willing effort," as said above in verse 2, thus who were fighting: that the spirits of God the Messiah present themselves ready to fight with the evil after
[286a.]   *   death, and with the devil's gang, has been made known to me by long experience, lasting many months, by the Divine mercy of God the Messiah.
"To bless Jehovah" is to have faith in Him, etc. etc.

6042.   *[Judg. 5:]* verse 11. "Of them that drive the flocks between the watering places," are those who send the flocks to the pastures and to the waters, and protect them, lest they be fallen upon by wolves; thus they are the chief priests and leaders. Another translation[1] has "bowmen" instead of "them that drive the flocks between the watering places." One word is used having several meanings that are enclosed together within it. It is a characteristic of heavenly speech that the most carefully chosen words
[287a.]   *   are brought into use. For there can be nothing more skillful than the speech of angels of God the Messiah, who bring forth the most meaningful words, and where there are expressions involving several similar and concordant meanings, these are brought forth. This fact has often been made known to me when words were being examined for their content, etc. etc.
[Speak, Speech; Words, Expressions]
[See also the rest of WE 6042, concluding the explanation of Judg. 5:11.]

[See WE 6049, explaining Judg. 5:18.]
6050.   It must further be noted that these words are so involved, that the meaning cannot at all be unraveled from them unless this be done by the Divine mercy of God the Messiah. For it is heavenly language, which comes down in this way into the words—for in heaven,

---

[1] That is, Castellio: *disserite de sagittariorum inter aquaria strepitu:* "discuss the sound of the bowmen between the watering places."

all the names of persons and places symbolize spiritual and therefore heavenly matters. In heaven, such words do not exist, but there are universal subjects that are delineated by such terms as will complete the order.[1] However, the meaning is never understood except from the context.

[288a.]   6051. Last night I was spoken to in the heavenly manner, that is, by a speech encompassing universal subjects. I seemed to understand it at the time, while I was lying in bed, but presently, when my senses were fully awakened, I could not understand at all what had been spoken of.[2] For they were universal matters, and the language at the time was a universal one, such as that of the spirits of God the Messiah. See in the front of this book [WE 4002] the annotation concerning the speech of the heavenly.[3] August 3, 1746 (old calendar).
[Dream, Sleep]

[289a.]   *   Evil spirits, however, understand nothing whatsoever in this language, for they remain in outermost regions, being earthly minds. Only spiritual minds know it.[4]

[See also the rest of WE 6051, concluding the explanation of Judg. 5:18.]

6054.   *[Judg. 5:] verse 21*. About the "torrent[5] of Kishon," see the preceding Chap. 4: verse 13.
*   Here it is explained what the torrent of Kishon is, namely, a "torrent of overtaking," according to others, a "torrent of meetings"[6]. The "overtaking" is that they have different opinions about the Kingdom of God the Messiah than they should. This is called the "torrent of

---

[1] In the original, the second and third sentences of this paragraph are emphasized by the word *Obs.* written twice in the margin.
[2] This sentence is emphasized in the original by the word *Obs.* written twice in the margin.
[3] This annotation, found on page A1 of manuscript Tome III of *Explicatio in Verbo Veteris Testamenti*, says the following:
    It should be noted that there is no name, either of a person or of a place, written in the Divine Word, that does not enfold within it what looks toward belief, or toward God the Messiah, and His Kingdom. For earthly names are understood in heaven entirely differently than a person on earth could possibly be convinced of. For they symbolize matters which no one can explain, unless taught by God the Messiah, from His Word, etc. etc.
[4] This paragraph is emphasized in the original by the word *Obs.* written twice in the margin.
[5] The *KJV* has "river."
[6] I.e., Tremellius.

[290a.] SPIRITUAL EXPERIENCES

Kishon," because it overthrows them. For they think contrarily, and they do not wish to be taught.

[**290a.**] * This has become very well known to me from those who have spoken with me: they are never convinced of the truth. They always relapse into their error, no matter how often they have been convinced.
[Spirit; Truth]

[See the rest of WE 6054, concluding the explanation of Judg. 5:21.]
[See WE 6055, explaining Judg. 5:22.]

6056. "The clappings[1] of his mighty ones sounded out": for they clap, and they are happy, and indeed, the mighty ones, whom Deborah did not know; but an angel of God the Messiah was speaking. If she had known who
[**291a.**] * the mighty ones were, perhaps she would not have said those words. But she understood the mighty ones among the Canaanites.

[See WE 6057, explaining Judg. 5:23.]

6058. "Because they came not to the help of Jehovah, to the help of Jehovah in the strong ones": these words are likewise secrets
[**292a.**] * which cannot yet be disclosed. For there are some who almost want to confess on the side of God the Messiah, yet nod their assent silently or tacitly. For they look upon the others' wicked deeds, without intervening, when yet they are able to bring help. This is revealing of their character, etc. etc.
[Assent (Consent); Spirit]

[See WE 6060 up to this point, explaining Judg. 5:25.]

* "In a bowl of the magnificent[2], she brought butter": that is, milk fat. The bowl was a vessel that they used in sacrifices, so that what is meant is that everything involved in sacrifices was given to him. But he gave himself up to sleep, having no care, thinking there was peace, just like all who
[**293a.**] * trust in themselves and who wish to be righteous by their own power.

[See WE 6061 up to this point, explaining Judg. 5:26.]

---

[1] The *KJV* has "prancings."
[2] The *KJV* has "a lordly bowl."

	It is called also the *"workmen's hammer,"* that is, the *"peg."*[1]
	Therefore, the words now follow that she struck his head.
[294a.]	* These things were also portrayed to me, namely, how truth penetrates, as a peg penetrates the temples.

[See WE 6151, explaining I Sam. 26:19 in particular.]

6152. About what else is involved in David's taking away the spear of Saul in the midst of the people [verse 12], it has not yet been granted me to learn much. For all of the details portray how an enemy is to be conquered, or enemies in general. Specific and individual battles like this one occur, and from them, conclusions can be drawn regarding the general battle, and regarding the most general one, which will be waged at the last day. For every general principle has particulars like itself, and by a comparison of those particulars, one may learn what the general must be. This never fails. Several specific

[295a.] * battles in myself were portrayed, from which I could have drawn conclusions about the general one; but this was too much work. Let me just say this, that there are countless enemies, that is, as many as there are evil spirits—consequently, as many as there are people led by spirits. Yet these would have to be divided up more or less into their universal kinds, and then into their species, and species of species, and so according to their particular differences. All of these are conquered in their own way, in accordance with the general rule, that is, by the law of retaliation.[2]

[See also WE 6153, further discussing spiritual battles, and concluding the explanation of I Sam. 26.]

6155. Here [I Sam. 28] amazing things happen; specifically, that a woman of the python[3] or Apollo raised up Samuel.
 * However, it should be noted that Samuel was certainly not raised up from the dead by a medium, but that this was only a fallacy. It was someone else who was

---

[1] The *KJV* has "nail."
[2] In the original, almost every line of this and the preceding paragraph is emphasized by the word *Obs.*, written 14 times in the margin.
[3] The *KJV* has "a woman having a familiar spirit," while *NKJV* has "a medium."

[296a.] * raised up, representing Samuel. For whenever evil spirits, or their leader, are permitted, then they are able to impersonate whomsoever they wish, so skillfully—provided that person has been seen by and known to them—indeed, so cleverly, that not the least inflection of the voice, or anything that was natural to the person, is missing.

This I have been made to experience two or three times by certain spirits, who presented before me some people known to me during their lifetime, and I spoke with them for a long time. They were just like they had been during their life, yet I still doubted whether they were the same people, and I said as much to the spirits. So they are able to put on whatever person they are allowed, provided it had been an acquaintance. (But let us see how this may be set forth, as it should be told with prudence. For I do not know whether the spirits were good who were allowed to do this. Also, lest people doubt about those visions spoken of above.)
[People; Person]

6156. That it was not Samuel, is clear enough, because it was a medium woman who did it; also because we read in verse 13 that gods ascended, and in verse 14 that he asked whether it was Samuel.
[297a.] * It is so plain to me that it was not Samuel, but that he was depicted by some evil spirit, that nothing is more obvious.

6157. Evil spirits are also allowed to foretell things to come [cf. verse 19], but this comes from God the Messiah, through good spirits, who are allowed in such cases to control the speech of the evil spirits entirely at their will. This also it has been granted me
[298a.] * to learn, so often that I cannot count the instances, that is, that the evil spirits speak just exactly as the good spirits dictate. The evil ones, of course, do not know this at the time, but in my case, it was plainly indicated in various ways, at which they were very offended, for this was against their will.
[Portrayal (Representation); Spirit; Truth]
[See also the rest of WE 6157–61, concluding the explanation of I Sam. 28.]

[See WE 6244–46 up to this point, treating in general of Solomon's Temple, and in particular of I Kings 6:1.]

FROM *WE* TOME III [302a.]

*   *The angels nearest by only take in objects that appear before the eyes as magnificent,*

[299a.]   *   orderly, in good taste, harmonious. This I have gotten to know very well, for they have so often admired, with deep feeling, things of beauty that have come before my sight.

[Portrayal (Representation); Spiritual things; Spirit]

[300a.]   *   I have also come to know that these objects are transformed into spiritual, and heavenly ones. For by God the Messiah's Divine mercy, it has also been granted me to learn how readily they transformed everything confronting my outward, and then inward, sight, into something spiritual and heavenly, so that an entirely different meaning arose. It was just as if from an earthly paradise, a heavenly paradise arose, or as if from the ranks of nature in the world and in the body, or among its parts and organs, there was a heavenly order, which was only perceived when such things on the plane of nature were put before me and the angels nearest to me at that time.

[Outer; Portrayal (Representation); Spiritual things; Spirit]

[301a.]   6247. In fact, in some cases, even the very inward choir sometimes slipped in their light, causing me to see in the passages I was reading from the Word of God the Messiah, nothing but spiritual and heavenly matters, so that the literal meaning perished.

[Inward; Word]

[302a.]   *   From all this it is clear why there was now a temple, as there was earlier the tent of assembly [II Sam. 7:6].

[See also the rest of WE 6247, concluding the explanation of I Kings 6:1.]

[See WE 6251 up to this point, explaining I Kings 6:4.]

*   "*Windows in the house*" symbolize the same thing as do the eyes in man, namely inward sight, as well as very inward and innermost sight. These are the windows of man. "*Views*" here means sight, said to be "*narrow*"[1] because they were on the outside of the house, and could

---

[1] According to Schmidius: "And he made for the house windows giving narrow views." Castellio has: "He furnished the temple with windows which could be opened and closed."

[303a.] SPIRITUAL EXPERIENCES

thus be "opened and closed," agreeing with the idea they portray. These words
[303a.]   *   I have written as if by dictation from someone else, but I do not know whether this is right, except that the "windows of the house" symbolize the same thing as do the eyes, or sight, in man.
[Window; Eye]

6257.   [I Kings 6:] verse 11. As for Solomon, his life is described later on, and how he wandered away from the path of truth, on account of keeping so many wives, thus as many wives as gods, as will be seen later [I Kings 11:1–8]. Moreover, by the angels
[304a.]   *   who were around me, Solomon was portrayed as he is today among those living after death, namely, that he does not know anything spiritual, much less heavenly, but is so stupid that he does not know in the least what this house symbolizes, except that it had been so built to display splendor. Therefore, he is now among the stupid who before had been counted among the wise. His wisdom was also pictured as earthly, that is, a wisdom in earthly matters, and in civil ones relating to the life of society, but not in heavenly matters. This is the reason why it is compared to the wisdom of the magicians in Egypt, and of others who were learned only on the plane of nature, for such knowledge is also often called wisdom, as above, Ch. 4:29,30,31.
[Solomon; Wisdom]

[305a.]   6258. As for the enigmatic sayings which he spoke, and which he was able to explain [I Kings 4:32–33], this matter was shown to me earlier, when I spoke with him several times [68a]. He did not want to speak at all except by riddles put in such a way that he would utter half of his saying, then wanted the other to say it, and the rest would follow by guessing. So it was a broken conversation.

Beside these, there were also other kinds of riddles. I learned that he was able to guess at the missing segments, for he would suddenly be instructed by a spirit who was given to him, how he should fill in the blanks.

FROM *WE* TOME III [308a.]

But our dialogues, although frequent, soon ceased. For he was arrogant, and despised everything, as if he alone were wise, when yet he is anything but wise, that is, when it comes to spiritual and heavenly matters. He loved and strove after nothing but what meets the outer senses, and it was because of this that he so much glorified the delectable life of the body that he put on display. This can be seen from his wisdom, about which I cannot yet feel convinced as to whether it contained any wisdom.
[Solomon; Wisdom]

[306a.] 6259. He is one among earthly lives or minds who have no knowledge but that which comes with a character produced by earthly feelings. Those minds, such as he is, suppose that they are people on earth in their outer form, not knowing differently, even though they are spirits. And when questioned about the senses, whether they have eyes, or ears, or nostrils, or mouth, they reply, supposing that they possess a human face, that they have. Then, when told that they have no outer sight, nor smell, nor taste, thus that those organs would be of no use to them, they do not understand.

Questioning them further, I ask whether they know what faculties answer to those senses in spiritual beings, or whether they might possess types of senses adapted to receive whatever answers [on the spiritual plane to the objects of the outer senses]. But those earthly minds, of whom he was one, are unable to reply at all to these questions, being ignorant of any interaction of spiritual elements with those of nature.
[Interaction (Correspondence); Person on earth; Earthly (Natural); Portrayal (Representation); Spiritual things; Spirit]

[307a.] * It is different in the case of spiritual minds, who are spirits of God the Messiah. They understand that interaction well. In fact, the very inward spirits see and feel what is spiritual in things on the plane of nature; etc. etc.

[See WE 6318–19, explaining II Kings 19:28.]

[308a.] * Evil spirits, that is, their strong desires, and their reasoning, are restrained to the point where they cannot say a thing, no matter how they try, etc. etc. The

[309a.] same is true of man when he is being held in bonds that are spiritual, and various other restraints.
[See also the rest of WE 6319, concluding the explanation of this verse.]
[See WE 6322 up to the sign ⊖⊖, explaining II Kings 19:31.]

[**309a.**] 6327. ⊖⊖: The outward or outer person is the life of the body. The inward person is the life of the lower mind. The very inward person is the life of one's will, arising from the understanding, or the life of the understanding coming from the will. The innermost person is the life of one's soul. All these lives follow one after another. The last or outer life dies first, after that the inward life. Thus the very inward life remains, and the innermost. Then "the root is turned" and "it bears fruit" [II Kings 19:30].

Now these latter are meant by the "remains" or the "remnant" which "shall go forth out of Jerusalem" [verse 31], namely, those who are like the more inward person, whose will has been so far reshaped as to love and strive for nothing else than what pertains to God the Messiah and His Kingdom. These then must be the "remnant out of Jerusalem."
[Outer; Fruit; Inner; Hand; Root; Regeneration; Remains; Write]

[**310a.**] * The words that were written above were inspired into me by an angel who was with me, as I was able to perceive because of the light, and other signs. For the words came onto the paper of their own accord, and without dictation.
[Outer; Fruit; Inner; Hand; Root; Regeneration; Remains; Write]

II Kings Chap. 23

[**311a.**] 6328. In that chapter we read about how the Jews lived under the kings.

But Josiah was the only king whom God the Messiah loves. This is the reason why now, after
[Josiah king; Tear]

[**312a.**] * I read this chapter, tears ran from my eyes, for the reason, as I hear, that King Josiah is present here,[1] **and desires that these words be written, in his memory**: the 13th day of August, 1746 (old calendar). These words should be well noted.
[Josiah king; Tear]

---

[1] This portion of the sentence is further emphasized by the word *Obs.* written twice in the margin.

II Chronicles Chap. 18

6336. *The subject here is the prophets, and their methods of prophesying, as for instance, the one who had horns [verse 10], etc.—but who was a false prophet.*

* *Micah, however, said that he had seen God upon a throne, speaking with spirits and saying the words which Micah spoke [verses 18–20]. These things were thus portrayed to Micah, but with Jehovah God they could never happen in this manner. Rather they are the outermost portrayals among the choir of angels who were with Micah, It is in this way that decrees, and heavenly matters, are displayed in the outward regions. They can be compared to bodily gestures coming from an understanding in which the matter is entirely different than it is in the body. A great many*

[**313a.**] * displays of this kind are being shown [to me], but from them, a very inward meaning must be taken, and then an innermost one. Then such a display does not occur in them. The same is true now of words, which are similar and, so to speak, outermost portrayals of what is spiritual and heavenly, and for that reason, appear so disjoined—while the very inward and innermost meanings are most fittingly connected.

[See WE 6340–47 under the heading Lev. Chap. 1, treating of Exod. 40, "On the column of cloud and fire."]

6348. *(I still hear them saying that they had been in obscurity [cf. WE 6343]). But those who have been of such a character, are also such after death, like those who are now saying*

[**314a.**] * something. Even though everything has now been explained and unraveled for them, so that they now know everything which has been told about the sacrifices and rites, are they still in the same obscurity? So they do not grow wise. The same thing would also have happened to them [if they had been instructed during life][1]. For that was their character, and so they would surely have profaned the holy things at heart and would have mingled profanity with holiness, thus rushing into the harshest spiritual death of all.

---

[1] These words are supplied from the index entries.

To these words they replied that they do not wish to understand anything, that is, of these things that have been told.
[Church; Jews; Profane; Display (Representation)]
[See also WE 6349, concluding the explanation of Lev. 1.]

Leviticus Chap. 5

6356.   Here the subject is other sins, some of them not committed by error.

*   It should be noted here that a person was not allowed to sacrifice, before he had been convicted, or had himself confessed his sin. For when one is convicted, one admits the sin, and is ashamed of it. When it is admitted, one can be healed of it. So without some admission, either tacit or open, the sin is not forgiven.

This principle is derived from the fact that humankind is nothing but evil, for from their root, nothing but evil sprouts forth. This root is inborn, and thereafter springs up. For the human mind and will is first shaped by evil, consequently the root and its outgrowth, which forms new roots. Unless one admits these things, and believes that there is nothing good in us, the sin can never be forgiven, nor thus we ourselves be reformed. This has been proven to me so many times

[**315a.**]   *   by the spirits who are around me—that is, that there is nothing but evil in mankind, in our thought, etc.—that I am able to declare it from actual experience. Therefore, if God the Messiah should desert anyone for even one moment, that evil rooted in them would break out into act, etc. etc.

[Lord; Hereditary, Heredity; Evil]

[See WE 6377, explaining Lev. 6:28.]

[**316a.**]   6378.   It is wonderful how physical elements constantly reach outwards or downwards, while spiritual ones are lifted upwards. Then the physical elements are separated from the spiritual, which reach out towards heavenly ones and are lifted up, while the latter or the bodily elements become dull, as if they were nothing.

However, when a physical element is active and when it reaches out, as said, outwards or downwards, then what is spiritual ceases its activity. This I can confirm by much experience in regard to these matters in myself. For example, when I spoke with heavenly beings, the loftier the subjects were, and the more spiritual, so to speak, the more the keenness of my outer senses, especially of my sight, was dulled, and passed away—even though I did not notice this except upon reflection. Also the reverse was true. But this experience will, if God the Messiah deems it fitting, be brought forward elsewhere.[1]

From this the conclusion follows that the physical elements [in a person] must necessarily die, so that the spiritual elements may be lifted up, away from earthly ones, to heavenly ones—and that this must take place both in every particular in regard to bodily loves, and also as a whole. For without death, no one can ascend into heaven.

[Outer; Inward]

[See also WE 6379, concluding the explanation of Lev. 6:28.]

[See WE 6405–08, explaining Lev. 11 in general.]

6409.   But in these details, secrets lie hidden regarding spiritual and heavenly matters, which would be too much to explain at this point. There are animals and birds of light, and there are [**317a.**] *   [animals and] birds of darkness. This is a known fact, which I have learned from many circumstances. But this matter is more fully illustrated in the books of the prophets, where such creatures frequently occur, especially in visions, which are heavenly and spiritual portrayals, materialized in this way.

[See WE 6415–17, explaining Lev. 13 in general.]

6418.   This is something that goes with the portrayal *[of spiritual matters]*, or with the symbolic Church, for the angels were permitted to punish with leprosy a wholly profane person, or one who tried to mix together holy things with profane ones, and then to cast him outside of the camp.

[**318a.**]   *   How angels are able to inflict on us, in any of our parts, every kind of illness and pain, I could tell on the basis of so many experiential examples, that no one

---

[1] In the original this portion is emphasized by the word *Obs.* written twice in the margin.

could raise any doubt in the matter; but because these instances savor of miracles, I wish to forbear.
[Pain; Illness]
[See also the rest of WE 6418, concluding the explanation of Lev. 13.]

[See WE 6438 up to this point, explaining Lev. 13:47.]
*   This happened, that is, that leprosy penetrated into the clothing in this way, and into the wall [Lev. 14:37], as a sign that the people should beware of profaning holy things, and of wanting, from being an earthly person, to become, by one's own effort, a spiritual one, or from being an outer person, to become an inner one,
*   and so, of one's own undertaking, to strive to possess heaven, or dominion in heaven, and the heavenly priesthood itself. For they were of that character, that they would lay claim to this also. This is evident enough
[**319a.**]   *   from those who are living after death, with whom I have spent much time, and spoken with. They are striving for nothing but dominion in heaven, and I said to them that they must have no other leader but the devil, who likewise strives to possess heaven. For to wish to climb up, from idol worship, from no belief in God the Messiah, from denial or in fact crucifixion of Him in their hearts, into heaven—this could not be attempted under the leadership of any other than the devil, who has such aspirations.
[Gods; Rule (Kingdom); Spirit]
[See also WE 6439–40, concluding the explanation of Lev. 13:47.]

[See WE 6625 up to this point, explaining Lev. 24:10.]
*   But here, under the theme of "the son of a man of Egypt struggling with a son of Israel" the subject is those who will be cast down.
*   For the wicked struggle with the sons of Israel, and indeed, concerning God the Messiah, Whom they then also blaspheme, in plain words as well as in their heart. This is evident enough to me
[**320a.**]   *   from experience, for the wicked after death, especially those from the people of Israel and Judah, both openly and tacitly blaspheme Him. About the

struggles I dare not tell, because they are profane; nor can I bear to speak of the fights.
[Jews]

[See also the rest of WE 6625, concluding the explanation of Lev. 24:10.]

[See WE 6652, explaining Lev. 25:20.]

* During life, people are anxious about what they shall eat, what they shall put on, and other things *[Matt. 6:25]*. But those who have the Kingdom of God the Messiah within them, are given daily *[what they need]*, and even more so, those who are in the Kingdom of God the Messiah. For they will have no worry, they will live in the greatest peace. Something new, with endless variety, will be given them each hour. For they will be like the spirits, ([1]who, if it is allowed, may then be described, namely, that they are unaware of time, and therefore do not worry about things to come, but are given *[whatever they need]* every minute; as well as more particulars from the descrip-

[321a.] * tion of spirits, which, if God the Messiah finds it fitting, can be reported at this point.

[See the rest of WE 6652, concluding the explanation of Lev. 25:20.]

6665. *[Lev. 26:]* verse 7. Also the Church, and her battle, are concerned, when the subject is the Kingdom of God the Messiah.

* Therefore, in the Church, where there is a continual battle, they must chase the enemy, that is, the devil and his gang, or evil spirits, who are the enemy, since they hold all in hatred who belong to God the Messiah.

[322a.] * For they are continually trying to attack those who belong to God the Messiah, nor do they ever refrain, as long as they are permitted to be present. About them, so much could be told, that I would run out of pages. They are more poisonous and sly than anyone of mortals could imagine—as I have quite often been allowed by God the Messiah to experience.
[Jews]

[See the rest of WE 6665, concluding the explanation of Lev. 26:7.]

---

[1] A vertical stroke and colon at this point in the ms. seems to mark where the indent, thus paragraph [321a], actually begins.

[323a.] SPIRITUAL EXPERIENCES

[See WE 6671 up to this point, explaining Lev. 26:13.]
*   "They would go upright" answers to the words that they will not be under "a yoke." So they would no longer look downwards, to the worldly and bodily objectives to which they had bowed down, or which they had worshipped;
*   but they will be raised up on high, and will behold heaven. To "walk upright" is to be lifted up; for a child of the true Israel is raised up, that is, all its thought is uplifted and withdrawn from mankind on earth toward heaven, and toward God the Messiah, and consequently, altogether separated from the body. This has happened to me so
[323a.]   *   often, that I am unable to number the times.

[See WE 6674 up to this point, explaining Lev. 26:17.]
[324a.]   *   For just as God the Messiah loves all the people in the universe, so the devil hates them all. He is indeed agreeable as long as he has no power to harm, but as soon as he is permitted to act, he tries to wipe out the whole human race, even his own worshippers. This is the reason, as soon as the people had become idolatrous, and were therefore put to death, why a large part of the camp perished [Exod. 32:27–28].[1]

So also they perished by pestilence at the time of David [II Sam. 24:15], etc. These things happen at once, when the devil is granted the power. It is an inevitable consequence, and the truth of it so well proven to me that I am able to affirm it beyond anything else. For if God the Messiah withdraws His hand
[Lord; Little child, Innocence; Spirit]
[325a.]   *   even in the slightest degree, they at once attempt to bring the human race to destruction, even harmless little children. This I have also told them several times, and they were not able to give me any reply at all.
[Lord; Little child, Innocence; Spirit]
6701.   [Lev. 27:] verse 20. He can also "sell [the field] to another [man]," can give himself over to another as a servant. For whether it is said "sell the field," that is, the sowing, or "sell oneself," it amounts to the same thing.
[326a.]   *   For in heaven there are some who boast that they have become righteous by their own deeds—whose

---

[1] This portion in the original is emphasized by the word *Obs.* written twice in the margin.

FROM *WE* TOME III [330a.]

names as yet must be kept quiet. To these, there are some spirits who devote themselves, acknowledging them as their lord, and such a one is now meant by a "[another] man."[1] So they go aside from God the Messiah, into the service of another. About the condition of spirits in heaven many particulars could be told, but
[Gods; Righteousness]

[327a.]   *   since they are for the most part unbelievable, it is better to pass by, than to record, matters that evade belief. There are, indeed, those who want to become righteousness, equal to the Messiah. That is why this wicked ritual of sacrificing their own children to Molech also became prevalent on earth, even if it was done in a different way.

These spirits, then, are meant by the man to whom the person who sanctifies [his field] sells himself.
[Gods; Righteousness]

*   *For in this way he entirely deprives himself of those things which are in it, that is, which are meant in the spiritual sense by the sowing, so that they can never again become his. Therefore we read that "it shall not be redeemed anymore."*

[See WE 6712–18 up to this point, explaining Num. 2:1–17.]

[328a.]   **These classes regard those who shall be at the right hand.**
[See also WE 6719–24, explaining Num. 2:18–24.]

6725.   But here much more is involved than can ever be set forth, as, for instance, that

[329a.]   *   the Jews, or descendants of Jacob, want to claim heaven for themselves alone, and indeed, to be in the first place, etc. etc.

Thus far it concerns those who shall be at the left hand, or in the third class.
[Jews]

[See WE 6726–33 up to this point, explaining Num. 2:25–31.]

[330a.]   **Those who shall come in the last place.**
[See also WE 6734–35, concluding the explanation of Num. 2.]

[See WE 6764, explaining Num. 4:2–4.]

---

[1] This sentence is emphasized in the original by the word *Obs.* written twice in the margin.

[331a.] SPIRITUAL EXPERIENCES

6765. *As for their ages, from 30 to 50 years, it is said clearly in verse 3 that they were those who "were fit for military service, and thus for doing work in the tabernacle of meeting."* But spiritual warfare is here meant, that is, the battle with the devil, as takes place in the Church militant. That only those are fit for battle who are within the range of 50 to 30 years, is quite obvious from the human state. For it is at that time that a person begins to make use of the understanding and to put willful urges into order, thus doing battle with elements streaming in from the earthly mind, namely, with perverse desires and longings, thus with the devil, who arouses them. For it is none other than the devil who arouses

[331a.] * the passions of the lower mind, and inherited evils. This to me is a firmly established truth, for I have experienced it now most clearly for almost 16 months. In fact, I have experienced it so clearly that by the pure Mercy of God the Messiah, I was granted to learn in detail how they aroused them, and which evils they aroused, and I was also permitted to reprove them aloud for doing so. They likewise were allowed to speak with me, to reply to questions, even to pour forth their poisons, thus also to fight verbally. But these cases are so copious that I would run out of pages.

Therefore, I can testify that there is not even the very least evil, among those that creep up from the body and its nature into the mind, which is not aroused by evil demons. I have been oppressed by such a multitude of them, over such a long period of time, that anyone would be amazed. Nevertheless, they could do nothing whatsoever, except grow angry, swell up, try—but every evil was turned into good, etc. etc.
[Passion (Desire); Evil; Spirit]
[See also WE 6766–67, concluding the explanation of Num. 4:2–4.]

[See WE 6804–14, explaining Num. 6:1–21 in general.]
[332a.] 6815. In order to uncover the secrets of this cooperation [i.e. of the outer faculties with the inner ones, *WE 6805 ff.*], one must be aware of the following fact regarding the perfect person, Who the Messiah Alone was: Into the spiritual regions of His Mind, not only inward elements of nature were drawn up, but even outward elements of nature, such as takes place in the body so that life con-

148

tinues (as in the lung, the heart, the liver, the spleen, the brain—but these facts should not be mentioned, because they are as yet unfamiliar, and would therefore be more confusing than enlightening).

At the same time that ideas are rushing in from the memory or lower mind, they are also rushing in from the senses into the understanding, and from the blood into its will. Only in the perfect person do the elements coming from bodily sensations, etc., cause the person continuance of life and constant purification.

In the imperfect person, however, if those latter elements should rush in at the same time, they would bring on death, thus extinguishing the person's life. This is the reason why physical elements can in no wise be admitted, but must come to rest, as long as inner elements are active, and the reverse. These facts I have also been allowed, by the Divine
[Outer; Inward]

[**333a.**] * mercy of God the Messiah, to learn from personal experience, through conversation and inward displays, since I have been so long among heavenly beings. For I could not be among them as long as physical elements were active at the same time, because then it was as if [my mind] were closed toward heaven, and to any association with them. But I have not yet been allowed to observe various circumstances in regard to these matters.
[Outer; Inward]

[See also WE 6816–18, concluding the explanation of Num. 6:1–21.]

[See WE 6861–62, explaining Num. 6:26.]

[**334a.**] 6863. Something of peace it was granted me, by the Divine mercy of God the Messiah, to experience, but I solemnly swear that no tongue could ever give expression to it. For it is a combination of all kinds of happiness, together with the highest life, devoid of the life that arises from strong desires, bodily enjoyments, worry, anxiety about things to come. It is being in the bosom of God.
[Peace]

[See WE 6877, explaining Num. 7:9.]

6878. This passage is not understood unless one understands something about the human mind. For it is shared by inward and outward elements, or those which are above and those which are

[335a.] SPIRITUAL EXPERIENCES

beneath. It is like a crossroads, where there is lodging for those elements which come down from above, and those which are drawn up from beneath.
6879. *Those which are holy come down from above, or rather, speaking according to the actual fact, are drawn up by God the Messiah, or raised upwards. This I have so clearly*
[335a.] experienced for a long time, that nothing is clearer, in fact, hardly anything is more tangible.

* *Then at the same time those elements are raised up from the lower mind which are to be combined with those in the thinking mind and its will. These will compose what are, to be sure, called spiritual elements, but are in fact matters of understanding. For truths of nature are combined with spiritual truths in such a way that they take on almost the appearance of daybreak, or of a rainbow, understood in a spiritual sense.*

[336a.] 6880. So those elements are now raised upwards that are good and holy, for a force to do this comes from the fountain of all goodness, like a spiritual attraction. This I have felt clearly by a general sensation, and then at those moments what is

[Nature, Earthly (Natural); Weight; Spiritual things]

[337a.] * merely of nature mixed in is separated. This is what then weighs down, and is likened to a weight, and it can never be raised upwards, but falls down, like dust on worldly objects, and so the person is purified, etc. etc.

[Nature, Earthly (Natural); Weight; Spiritual things]

[338a.] 6881. Moreover, it is very difficult to express heavenly matters, which in turn contain spiritual ones, these again putting on earthly features, all combined in agreement with laws of succession. For when the mind is absorbed in the displays of heavenly matters, one understands at the time what they are, but as soon as nature is allowed to enter the mind, the understanding of them is dispelled, and it cannot be recalled.

So that which is heavenly is ineffable, as I have also experienced by the Divine mercy of God the Messiah; for heavenly matters enfold inexpressible things. But when they are in the mind of one who inspires prophets, they must necessarily be adapted to worldly

circumstances.[1] Then words fall into place so remarkably, that from the meaning of the words by themselves in outer form, they can hardly be grasped. Yet in the very inward meaning, and still more in the innermost meaning, there is a most beautiful pattern, concordant with all the laws of order.
[Nature, Earthly (Natural); Weight; Spiritual things]

[339a.] 6882. So in the present case, the words, "which the Kohathites carried upon the shoulder, because theirs was the service of the sanctuary[2]," involve what has been told, besides countless other matters that are inexpressible.
[Nature, Earthly (Natural); Weight; Spiritual things]

6883. *It should be especially noted that by the classes of the Levites here are meant those differences in the priestly Kingdom spoken of in the description of them in [Num.] Chap. 3 [see WE 6736 ff.].*

[340a.] 6884. To continue with the above subject, an angel who inspires words in a prophet or in those who speak inspired words, as he here inspired them in Moses, is in spiritual elements only, and thence works into the mind of him who is being inspired, arousing thought. By means of thought, the [spiritual elements] fall into words in the usual way. They are words such as the prophet has in him, thus within his grasp, and in the shape they have to him. This is the reason why the style of each of the prophets is so different, all depending upon the type of discernment previously acquired. But this, I, who am inspired, can solemnly affirm, that there is not the least bit of a word, not even a jot, that is not inspired, although there is some variation according to the natural bents of the one who brings forth the words. But in spite of this, there is not even a jot that is not inspired.
[Inspiration; Prophet]

[341a.] 6885. Now this is how the songs were inspired, spoken of in the books of Moses [Exod. 15, Deut. 32], of the Judges (if I am not mistaken) [Judg. 5], in the Psalms which David sang, who also observed this, and in the

---

[1] In the original this sentence is emphasized by the Word *Obs.* written twice in the margin.
[2] *KJV* has "sanctuary," *NKJV* "holy things."

[341a.] SPIRITUAL EXPERIENCES

prophets [Lam. 1–5]. But where we read that Jehovah spoke, this was done aloud, as mentioned earlier [4a, 83a, 114a]. For a live voice is like that of a person speaking from various distances, both from afar and from nearby, so that one can tell where it comes from (this is so well known to me that nothing is more familiar), even from a tower, from the sky[1], or from overhead, etc. So it is no wonder we read that Moses heard the sound [of a voice] from a bush [Exod 3:4], from the mountain [Exod. 19:3], from the mercy seat between the cherubim [Num. 7:89].

But the fact that He spoke in a way that bystanders also heard, as He did from Mount Sinai, I cannot yet explain from experience. For although the voice is almost as clear and loud as a person talking to himself—for it can be heard even when others are talking—still it does not come through the air into the ear from the outside, but comes into the ear from the inside. For this reason it is not heard by a bystander, even though some spirits believed that their voices were being heard by those present, because when I spoke with those people, the spirits heard my words almost in the same way as they heard those of the people speaking with me. The same was true of my speaking with the spirits, for it also went out as if in sounds. But the subject of speech with spirits, if God the Messiah deems it fitting, will be discussed elsewhere.
[*Speak, Speech*]

[See WE 6889–90, explaining Num. 7:13.]
6891. Now the understanding is developed from truths, and every truth flows in from the feeling that shapes it—for understanding is born of feelings, and [a person] has only so much [of truth] from feeling in the understanding, as there is of feeling [in the person]. (This must be put more clearly.) Therefore, an understanding devoid of feeling is not a holy understanding. For if I should understand everything, or possess all spiritual knowledge in heaven and on earth, and it is devoid of love, or charity [cf. I Cor. 12:2], the understanding or higher knowledge is of no use whatsoever. There-

---

[1] J.F.I. Tafel read the word *coelo*, "sky," as *colle*, "hill."

fore, as much as an understanding has from love, so much it is holy. It is love that sanctifies.

Now this is why those vessels were filled with "mincha"[1], which symbolizes love. But the mincha was made of "fine flour mixed with oil," which symbolize elements that can hardly be described, and can only be

6892.   vaguely understood. The understanding is of such a nature that while it is developing, it again and again sows seeds, from which truths are born anew. So truths are arranged in order, over and over again, like trees of paradise, and like a cultivated field, for development goes on uninterruptedly. Hence it is now said "fine flour mixed with oil," for the flour is finely ground and made into mincha. So they are those elements that pass from the understanding into the will, which is ruled by feeling. But these matters, as said before, cannot but appear vague. Yet matters that

[342a.]   *   are almost ineffable are able to be portrayed in an abstract form, and come down into words, while that ineffable matter is nevertheless couched within the words, etc. etc.; see the discussion in the indented portion above [337a–41a].

[See WE 6904 up to this point, explaining Num. 8:1–3.]

6905.   However, when the ritual is not performed with lamps, confirmation is nevertheless portrayed by means of flames, such as have appeared to me, by the Divine mercy

[343a.]   *   of God the Messiah, very often, and indeed, with a diversity of size, color and brightness. Scarcely a day has passed in some months, while I was writing a certain small work, that a flame did not appear, as vividly as the flame of the fireplace. It was then a sign of approval, and this was before the time when spirits began to speak with me aloud.

[Flame]

[See also the rest of WE 6905–07, concluding the explanation of Num. 8:1–3.]

7005.   [Num. 11:] verse 9: "when the dew came down on the camp in the night, the Manna came down on it." That it came down at night means when man does not know it, as God the Messiah says,

---

[1] NKJV has "fine flour mixed with oil."

[344a.] SPIRITUAL EXPERIENCES

"The wind blows where it wishes, and one cannot tell where it comes from, and whither it blows" [John 3:8]. This is what "at night," when a person is asleep, symbolizes. The "dew" falls in the morning, at the first dawn, when a person is in the sleep nearest to wakefulness, and usually awakens. "Dew" symbolizes the heavenly blessing that comes down around the time of just waking up. So on the dew, the Manna came down, that is to say, the love of God the Messiah.

[344a.] 7006. That this is the meaning of these words, was revealed to me in a remarkable way. Without revelation such words cannot possibly be understood. It was dictated, but in an amazing way in my thought, and my thinking was guided to an understanding of these words, and was firmly concentrated upon the individual words by a mental image, as if being held by a heavenly force. So this revelation took place consciously. We will speak elsewhere about other kinds of revelation, which are many, if God the Messiah sees fit.

Revelation is also accomplished in another way, when the thought is visibly lit up by a certain light, and the writing is so guided that not even the smallest word can be written differently. But at times this happens rather unconsciously, at others so consciously that the finger is borne along in writing by a higher force, so that if it wished to write something different, it could not possibly do so. And this kind takes place not only together with an understanding of the subject, but also, as has happened in varying ways once or twice, without any understanding—so that I did not know the series of subject matter until after it had been written down. But this only occurred very rarely, and only for the purpose of informing me that revelations have also been made in this way. Those sheets were deleted, however, because God the Messiah did not will that it be done in this way.

Neither is it allowed them to dictate anything aloud, even though I have been spoken to aloud for such a long time, almost continuously. But when it was being written, they kept quiet.

These matters will, if God the Messiah deems it fitting, be spoken of more fully elsewhere, so that people

may know what revelations were once like in times past, in the earliest Church, then in the representative Church, and finally in the symbolic one. From this they can learn that there is not even a jot in the Books of Moses, of the prophets and of David that was not inspired; and therefore, that heavenly matters are inwardly contained under the shapes of the earthly elements expressing them, which belong to the letter.
[Inspiration; Prophet]

[See WE 7022, explaining Num. 11:16–17.]
7023.   *First it should be known that by "spirit" here [Num. 11:17], as by angel, many are meant. One spirit is mentioned because there is agreement. For spirits are arranged around a person, at the will of God the Messiah, in a way that they are absolutely taken to be one—in fact, so much so, that sometimes the speech of many seems like that of one person, when yet they are speaking together with amazing harmony and unison. How these*
[345a.]   7024.   *and many other phenomena work cannot so easily be described, because they are wonders. For it is as if a society makes up one person, and thus the whole society is acting and speaking as one person, so that hardly anyone, unless instructed by God the Messiah, can tell that they are many. This is the heavenly form, or the form of heavenly beings, imaging God the Messiah's Kingdom. But this kind of harmony among many is not possible except among the angels or spirits of God the Messiah.*

Although much more could be told here, this is enough to illustrate the fact that by the spirit of Moses is meant a multitude, which is thus divisible into many. But a different spirit was around Joshua, as we read earlier[1], *and therefore it was he who would bring those who had formerly been little children into the land of Canaan.*
[Form; Kingdom; Society; One (Unity)]

[346a.]   7025.   *When many are speaking at the same time, there is a certain most beautiful harmony, a very lovely kind of wave-like movement toward oneness, because of the*

---

[1] This may refer to Num. 27:18; see Acton, *The Word Explained* 7024, footnote 3.

agreement. At such times they also possess much more force of action and speech, as I have, by the Divine mercy of God the Messiah, experienced on several occasions, together with a deep happiness. The beauty itself of the melodic progression, ending up in unity, was also shown to me in an amazing way, and it was stunning, beyond all description.
[Form; Kingdom; Society; One (Unity)]

[See also WE 7028–31, continuing the explanation of Num. 11:16–17.]

7032. Meanwhile God the Messiah governs every person, even if surrounded by evil spirits—which subject you may see discussed earlier [315a, 325a]. For if God the Messiah should interrupt His control even for a moment, the person would at once perish. This I have learned, by the Divine mercy of God the Messiah, from so much [347a.] * experience, that nothing could be truer. But how the spirits are arranged, cannot be explained; for this takes place with ineffable variation, depending upon the genius of each person, and, of course, depending upon their state, both their permanent state and the changing one.
[Lord; Order; Universe]

7105. *[Num. 13:] verse 21.* These places were toward the south, for we read in the very next verse, as previously [verse 17], "and they went up by the south," thus coming gradually into light, that is, into a spiritual knowledge of how things are in detail. So the "wilderness of Zin" is a state like shade, for which reason it is called a desert, but it is morning shade; while Rehob is daybreak, or the morning light. Even "to Hamath," finally "to Hebron," as follows [verse 22], means where there is noonday light.

But all this has regard only to spiritual knowledge, or the light of such knowledge, when a person is as described earlier [WE 7096]. Even the enemy has this light in that heaven, but it is entirely outside of him. For they admit that they know how things are, and even that they believe the spiritual knowledge,
[348a.] * but say that they still cannot act accordingly. As long as they are in this state of mind, which God the Messiah brings upon them by [arousing] various feelings, then it is as if their earth-bound soul becomes quiet, and does not function. But as soon as they come into a different

state, nearer to their normal one, they backslide, harboring nothing but enmity, etc. etc.

7120.   [Num. 13:] verse 29. Those are called "Amalekites" who are in the light of spiritual knowledge about God the Messiah and His Kingdom. Therefore, they are said "to dwell in the south"; while those absorbed in their own longings arising from the love of themselves and of the world and called demons, are "the Hittite, the Jebusite and the Amorite."

7121.   For they are even gifted with a cunning nature that one would never believe possible, seizing upon anything whatever that a person is thinking, and

[349a.]   *   transforming it into something evil, and this in an instant. Some do this with such slyness, and with such a poisonous skill, that they at first appear as good angels. They are the worst kind, deceiving those off guard with tricks that one could never have thought possible, unless taught by God the Messiah. These are the Hittites, who had formerly dwelt at Hebron and were friendly to Abraham [Gen. 23]. They wish to make themselves righteousness and completely assume the guise of God the Messiah, and thus wish to be worshipped; yet they are the worst of demons. Next after them follow the Jebusites, then the Amorites, who are less harmful, acting not with cunning but only with malice. These are said to "dwell on the mountain," because they are demons.

[Feeling (Affection); Think, Thought; Trick (Deceit); Evil]
[See also WE 7122–23, concluding the explanation of Num. 13:29.]

[See WE 7127, explaining Num. 13:32.]

7128.   Now they no longer say that it is a land flowing with milk and honey, but a "land that devours its own inhabitants." For there is such a great multitude of them that they almost fill up that earthly region [WE 7127]—something that is also apparent from what a multitude of earthly people there is. Furthermore, it is also called a land that devours its own inhabitants because the one devours the other. For as soon as there is

[350a.]   *   even the slightest provocation for inflicting harm upon one another, immediately the one rushes against the other, and they tear at each other, exactly as

[351a.] SPIRITUAL EXPERIENCES

such mobs on earth. These do seem unified while plotting evil, and mobilize in camps; but as soon as the question of plunder arises, and occasion for doing harm, one rushes at the other. For inwardly, they hate each other, and only outwardly do they support their comrades. If comrade should see comrade inwardly, he would not see anything but plunderings—in fact, hatred against his companions. This hatred, however, does not break out as long as they are keeping company in pursuit of their plunderings, etc. There is an unbelievably great assortment of such in that earthly region; so it is "a multitude, which devours the land."

7129. They are said to be "men of stature" because they appear large, that is, to those whom they terrify. For they imagine they are large, because they strive to gain nothing less than the universe, and the power. And whenever they overcome someone, they believe it happened of their own powers, and they swell up over it, being most deeply ignorant of the fact that they have no powers whatsoever, except what is given, for reasons which the Word of God the Messiah speaks of. Such as the powers are, such also is the stature; for stature consists of powers. They are portrayed as giants because they all want, for various reasons, to be like people

[351a.] * on earth, even though they are spirits, etc. etc.

[See WE 7182, explaining Num. 14:40.]

[352a.] 7183. It is similar now, at the last time. For now this earthly-minded people and those like it—trusting in their own works, and thinking that heaven has been promised to them, while formerly they had believed only that the land was promised to them—now they maintain, now that they are in the lower heaven, that heaven has been promised to them. For the situation they are in governs them and directs their strivings toward any opportunity that situation has to offer. Yet during their life, they had not wanted to understand anything at all about the Heaven of God the Messiah. That this people is now going up into the mountain,
[Jews]

[353a.] 7184. and, due to their inborn character, wish to go up into heaven, to this I can testify; and that they think the

Kingdom of God the Messiah, which they had not believed in, belongs to them, and therefore try by vain attempts to seize it. Therefore they say here, "Let us go up to the place of which Jehovah has spoken[1]."
[Jews]

7185. *It is added that they say, "for we have sinned." They acknowledge their wicked deeds, namely, that they had been*
[354a.] * idolaters, and that they had so often sinned. This they can in no way deny, because they say it has been written down by Moses. But still they do not leave off thinking that the whole Heaven belongs to them, in fact, they do not want to let hardly anyone in but their own. They worship Abraham, and Jacob, and also Moses, unaware that it is the gods they had kept in their hearts that control them and goad them on. In a word, they are constantly in revolt.
[Jews]

7187. *[Num. 14:] verse 43: "but the Amalekite and the Canaanite are there in front of you," that is, they are in them. As for what is meant by the Amalekite and the Canaanite, see above [349a, WE 7120–22, 7122, 7166]. They bear that enemy in themselves, thus "in front of them"; for they had been in the highest light of miracles, see verse 11. They are the enemy spoken of in verse 42 just before this.*

Thus they shall "fall by iron," iron being a weapon, but also called iron is anything which pertains to the body, and which fights them, and kills them. For copper is the earthly mind, while iron is the body. So they fall by their own arms. Their state of mind is such that when their reins are let go the slightest bit, or when they are given the freedom, they at once rush
[355a.] * the one against the other, altogether unable to spare either a companion or even a little child, panting for the death of all. Nor can it be otherwise, because it is their nature to pursue everyone with hatred, spontaneously. In fact, they are even divided amongst themselves. They do indeed love their own people, and yet do not love them, everything in them being at odds. This is spir-

---

[1] *KJV* has "promised"; the Latin is *loquutus est*.

[356a.] itual death to anyone. For unity in oneself is also unity among one's own, because they are ruled by God the Messiah. This is life.
[Jews; Hatred]
[See also WE 7188, concluding the explanation of Num. 14:43.]

[See WE 7260, explaining Num. 16:36–39.]
7262. It is also depicted here how that heaven, where the devil had been let in together with evil spirits, then becomes the heaven of those reasoning minds—those earthly minds that have a reasoning soul—when the devil has been cast down or swallowed up by the earth, etc. Meanwhile, if
[356a.]   *   it is allowed to mention it, there are wonderful things happening in that heaven—specifically this, that those minds, even though they are truly rational, can still be aroused with various desires; so it is very difficult, as long as this is being permitted to happen, to tell them from evil spirits. This also is depicted by the congregation, etc. etc.

[See WE 7300–01, explaining Num. 19 in general.]
7302. The heifer was to be burned to ashes, and this outside of the camp. This means that those elements should be wiped out, that is, those desires which wish to take over, thus the life must be taken from them. That the ashes from it were unclean, is clear from the fact that the priest would be unclean, and should wash his clothes, and touch water so as to rinse away his uncleanness. For this reason, that "ash" symbolizes the earthly filth thus wiped away, as if reduced to ashes. Very many por-
[357a.]   7303. trayals of this kind exist among the angels. For their contemplations are based upon such displays; and they are so difficult to explain when they appear to someone, that I have very often wondered why such things occurred. But when they are presented before the angels of God the Messiah, then earthly elements are removed from them, and they are understood in a spiritual way, etc. etc.
   These rituals were performed on account of the portrayal just spoken of, especially those which now follow.

7304.   However, the ashes of this heifer, which were unclean, mixed with water, were to be sprinkled upon him who had touched a dead person. This reflects the fact that what is unclean must be wiped away by what is equally unclean, as happens in nature. By way of illustration, take the fact that [the effect of] a scorpion sting, and of snakebites, is taken away by their ashes or dust, etc. It is similar in regard to spiritual matters. But that unclean spirits carry away

[**358a.**]   *   uncleanness, cannot but be a very hidden matter, for experience alone can bear witness to such facts. For evil spirits are made use of to arouse evils in man, and in this way the evils are not only recognized, but also acknowledged. Before this, they are not taken away. But it is evil or damned spirits who then take these evils into themselves, or swallow them up, and so the person is freed of them. This, of course, is what also occurs during struggles and temptations, but the person is then not at all aware that it is happening.

Through the Divine mercy of God the Messiah, I am able to bear witness of this phenomenon, from long experience; for I have frequently spoken with certain spirits about it, whenever it occurred. And often I was driven to great indignation that such unclean spirits were stirring up so many evils that lay hidden within my nature. But I learned that without them, there was no medicine; for this is the way the wounds must be opened up, and healed.

This, then, is why unclean ashes could remove the dead things in a person, etc. etc. Therefore, when one believes that one is most unclean, because of such a character, then he is in the best state of mind—and the reverse, which I have also learned by experience, as I can testify.

[Evil; Spirit]

[See WE 7320–26, explaining Num. 20:1–21.]

7327.   But what is meant here [verses 14–21] in the spiritual sense by the land of Edom, is plain from the sequence of events, namely, that the people had undergone their temptations, and thus portrayed the Messiah, Who Alone overcame temptations by Himself. The children of Israel must also all undergo temptations, yet they all

[359a.] SPIRITUAL EXPERIENCES

give in. It is God the Messiah Alone Who upholds us, and Who conquers for us. This I have very clearly experienced in myself,
[**359a.**]   *   because up to this point, I have had to undergo temptations similar to these in a certain spiritual sense. As for me—and I was allowed to mark this well—I could not but yield in all of them. For having been brought to a certain point, I myself had succumbed, but was nevertheless lifted up by God the Messiah. The temptations led, I think, to a good outcome, but I could clearly see that by ourselves we cannot possibly endure temptations, not even the least one of them. Therefore it is the work of God the Messiah Alone that a person is upheld in temptations.
[*Temptation*]
[*See also WE 7328–31, concluding the explanation of Num. 20.*]

[*See WE 7345, beginning the explanation of Num. 22.*]
7346.   *This attempt of the devil is depicted by the king of Moab, Balak, son of Zippor. Moab you may see discussed earlier [WE 7343], particularly that he was born from a daughter of Lot in a drunken state, by a wicked adultery [Gen. 19:33,37]. We are instructed further in what follows, about what Moab was like.*
     So in Balak son of Zippor, as chief person, Moab is depicted, and the devil appears. For he was a worshipper of Baal, thus an idolater to the extreme.
7347.   *Further regarding the attempts of the devil: they are so wicked and so dreadful*
[**360a.**]   *   that they cannot possibly be described. His extremely deceitful tricks are so unspeakable that it is inconceivable to those on earth. For nothing whatever of evil can exist that he does not call forth in people, in order to lead them astray. Therefore, unless one is under the protection of God the Messiah, one cannot possibly escape, even for the slightest instant, from falling headlong into damnation.
     But these attempts, many of which I am familiar with from experience, it is better to give over to deep oblivion than to make public before men; for they cannot but do harm to all minds. Through them I have learned this, that if God the Messiah had not delivered me from these extreme temptations, which I believe I never could

have endured, I would have fallen right into damnation. But to this deliverance not the least thing could my own powers contribute, and they would have hurled me headlong into damnation, had not God the Messiah been present with His help.

[Trick (Deceit); Spirit; Temptation]

[See also WE 7348–51, continuing the explanation of Num. 22.]

7352.   Further particulars regarding the speaking donkey *[verse 28]* may be seen in what follows. In advance, it should just be stated that a donkey can never speak, as it is contrary to all Divine order. What really happens is that a person with whom angels

[**361a.**]   *   are speaking, and in fact, from within, cannot hear otherwise, when it pleases God the Messiah, than that either a beast or an inanimate object is speaking. For the sound that the beast or inanimate object emits combines with the words being dictated inwardly to the person. This has been proven to me several times so vividly, that I was hearing the very hoofs of the horse, the very whinnies, even the blows of hammers, as if they were speaking the same words that were being said to me inwardly, so that I could absolutely not perceive it differently.

About this phenomenon, I spoke with the angels around me, and then I was shown that the donkey's speaking with Balaam was of this kind, the words so closely sticking to the sound, so to speak, that they cannot be separated by the hearing. I even thought that bystanders were hearing them in the same way, because it was an external sound that carried them into the ears.

We do not read here that Balaam knew about this, yet it does not say that he was surprised that the donkey had spoken to him, for he answered it as he would a human being. From this one may conclude that he was used to such phenomena also.

[Speak, Speech; Hoof]

7353.   But these historical words about the donkey also contain secrets concerning present events, for the same kind of portrayals are being given at this day. They therefore involve secrets that were under investigation at those times, etc.

[*See WE 7359, explaining Num. 22:14–20.*]

7360. What this now portrays can be learned from the fact that [Balak] wanted Balaam, who was then a man of divinity, to curse that nation which portrays those now arriving at the end of all their temptations. It is like what is done [to them] by the Word of God the Messiah, that is, by those who teach the Word of God the Messiah, saying that they are nevertheless cursed, so that they come into despair of salvation. This is generally the ultimate trick of the devil. They also bring up many passages to support it, to the effect that they cannot become righteous by their own power, consequently that they are therefore condemned—as if, since they can obtain no merit by their own effort, they are therefore without any hope of salvation. This has been said to me many times

[362a.]   *   by evil spirits, and so often that it even made me feel sick, until they were forced to be silent, etc.

[363a.]   7381. [Num. 23:] verses 25–30, inclusive. Here [verses 18–24] [Balaam] is describing that people, as it is now told [verse 24]. Therefore [Balak] says that he had neither blessed them, nor cursed them, but had extolled them with praises. Yet beneath these words also there lurks deceit. But he insists yet a third time, hoping that the Spirit of God the Messiah would part from Balaam, which it would if he could bring him to cursing [Jacob], even though his curse would have had no power whatever, since it would not be the angel of God the Messiah speaking through him.

ᵐThus even those of good character are deceived by self-profit, etc.ⁿ

But lest the devil have any reason for saying that the man who was given the power to curse and to bless had nevertheless done his bidding, therefore it was made to happen, that he tempted him so many times. In the next Chap., 24 verse 2, it is therefore said that "the spirit of God came upon him"—obviously so that he would not speak from any other source. The devil

>   draws all things to himself and to his own side. If there is
>   even the least little word which he thinks to contain
>   something contrary to the truth, he at once seizes upon it
>   and condemns the person. This, too, I have experienced
>   several times, by the Divine mercy of God the Messiah.
>   Indeed, he pours passions into people, then thoughts, and
>   persuasions, etc., when he is permitted to, and immedi-

ately attributes them to the person as being his or her own; in short, the things he attempts to do are very wicked.

[Accuse; Condemn, Damnation; Falsity; Evil; Spirit]

7382. Now, however, he wished to lead him to "another place," where he would not see that people in the wilderness, that is, in the state of mind that it now portrayed, so that he would not see them dwelling or camping, arranged according to what they portray, as explained earlier *[WE 6712 ff.]*, as appears from the next Chap., verses 1 and 2—but so that he would see them without clarity, consequently apart from what they portrayed, "from the top of Peor, that looketh toward Jeshimon[1]," thus from their idolatry. For Peor was where the idol of Baal stood, Chap. 25:3, so that [from there] he would see their idolatry. Therefore he says, verse 27, "Perhaps it will be right in the eyes of God that you may curse them for me from there." As for what is foretold about them on account of their idolatry, see Chap. 24 at the end *[WE 7403–04]*.

Thus he wanted to trick him. In his extreme wickedness he becomes so insane that no one could ever be more insane. For even though he has learned a thousand times that an angel of God the Messiah cannot possibly be fooled, yet he continually persists. So he lives completely in the dark about this matter, in that he surely sees, but does not want to see at all. This is his nature, which is constantly urging him on.

He also convinces himself that he is the one who can do all things, and even though he sees thousands and thousands of times that he cannot do the least thing, yet he can never be removed from that fantasy that he can do all things, and that he will possess heaven.

He also thinks that he can do all things from his own power, even though he knows by experience that he cannot even set a tiny feather in motion, without being permitted. Nevertheless, he swells up, continually inflated with these arrogant attitudes.

There is so much more of the same kind that one has to laugh at him as insane. He is extremely shrewd in plotting—for he is permitted to do this for

---

[1] *KJV* has "Jeshimon", but *NKJV* "wasteland."

[364a.] SPIRITUAL EXPERIENCES

numerous reasons, especially on account of the temptations into which those on earth must be led in order to be regenerated. He is permitted also so that he may thereby swallow up the actual evil in them [*cf.* 258a]. For no other nutriments are given him, and the rottener the carcass, the more ardently does he seek it and the more eagerly does he devour it.
[*Power; Spirit*]

7386.   [Num. 24:] verses 3 and 4. *Here Balaam is described in his character as an oracle, or how he conveyed the responses of God the Messiah. For it is known that responses used to be given in different ways, such as by dreams, by visions in the dark; also, with the eyes closed, entirely like daytime visions; by an actual voice, from within and from without; further, by other means spoken of elsewhere [WE 1144, SE 3a, 15a–16a, 42a–44a, 114a, 341a].*

Here Balaam is described, that is, his eyes being opened so that he saw the angels of God the Messiah as in daylight, as others also had done; for this was not rare at the time of the earliest Church. Thus angels appeared to Abraham, to Sarai, to Lot, in fact, even to evil people, as angels did to the inhabitants of Sodom [Gen. 19:4–11]; also (if I am not mistaken) to the servant of Elisha [II Kings 6:17]. That Elijah and Elisha belonged to this group is credible from what is told of them.

But however clearly an angel may appear before the eyes, it is nevertheless a vision, coming from within. Therefore we read here first of all, "the utterance of the man whose eyes are opened," then also later, "who falls down, with eyes opened wide"[1]. *That Balaam was one of these, see [Num.] Chap. 22: verse 31 and also in another place, where it says that God came to Balaam, etc. [verse 9]. Nor can anyone boast of the fact that he has seen angels, just as Abraham could not, and others. For very many evil people have seen an Angel, even the worst, like the inhabitants of Sodom; in fact, it is even said of the Donkey in the Chapter cited above, verses 25 and 27. Therefore, this vision is an illusion of the inner sight; for*

---

[1] KJV has "falling *into a trance*, but having his eyes open."

thus something meets the eyes, as if coming from without, which is actually inwardly in the earthly mind.
          But different

[**365a.**]   7387. is the vision that comes when the eyes are closed during full wakefulness, in which it is just as if things were seen in broad daylight.

          Indeed, still another kind of vision exists, which comes in a state midway between sleep and wakefulness. For at that time one thinks one is wide awake, because all one's senses are active. But there is also another kind between the time of sleeping and the time of awakening, when we are in the process of waking up, and have not yet shaken off the sleep from our eyes. This is the sweetest kind, for then heaven is working into our rational mind with the utmost calm, but imparting understanding.

          Again another is the vision in dreams, which varies.

          But in addition, there is a very inward vision, and this is the properly human kind, which does not appear as in light, but as in shade; but still, this vision is connected with the more inward powers.

          There are, in fact, many other kinds of vision, which cannot possibly be described. The above have only been described in a general way, because I am able, from the much experience granted to me by the Divine mercy of God the Messiah, to bear witness of them. For some kinds have been shown to me so often, with so many objects, in a state of full wakefulness, that if I should describe only the hundredth part of them, those would be amazed who do not believe that visions have been given, and thus revelations: not to mention conversations, which have now been going on for almost a year and a half.
    [See, Vision]

[See also WE 1388–89, concluding the explanation of Num. 24:3–4.]

7426.   *[Num. 27:] verse 12 to the end. Moses and Aaron as heads, together with the people, portrayed the Church of God the Messiah, which is in constant combat, and as a matter of fact, those who gave in during the combats. On this account they could not por-*

[366a.] SPIRITUAL EXPERIENCES

tray those who would enter into the Kingdom of the Heavens of God the Messiah. But then another was to be set over them, namely, Joshua, who together with Caleb and the minors and little children as well, had not given in so as not to be able to portray it.

Now, therefore, when the Land of Canaan was in sight, Moses was ordered "to go up onto mount Abarim," the mountain of crossings where one crosses over into the Kingdom of God the Messiah, "and to see the land." Moses was such that he could not enter, as can be clear from the words in verse 14, namely, that together with Aaron, "he had rebelled, and had not hallowed God the Messiah." See above, Ch. 20: verses 8 to 13, where the waters there are called "Meribah," while here in a broader sense, they are called "Kadesh."

About Moses, much could
[366a.]   *   be told as to what he is like, and how he is still continually rebelling in the other life, however much he knows and sees the Kingdom of God the Messiah, because such particulars have been portrayed to me. But I am not allowed to set forth any more of them, except for the fact that the same attitude remains in him. Meanwhile, he is the head of those who give in in temptations, or who worship the Law in its outward form. What the inner person is, he does not want to understand, although he does understand, but the love of self strives against it. See Deut. Ch. 2, verses 48 to the end, where these points are very clearly expressed. For Moses was their Head, because the people had been given to Moses, as it is said here and there, just as the Levites had been given to Aaron. Therefore, while these two portrayed the heads, the people portrayed the body; so the body could not be separated from the Head, for together they portray all who yield in temptations.
[Law; Moses; Temptation]
[See also WE 7428–30, concluding the explanation of Num. 27.]

7504.   [Deut. 32:] verse 43. These words are likewise congruent with those that John said in Revelation Ch. 12, verses 10, 11, 12. The entire song now builds up to this climax, namely, that because the people of Jacob and his posterity has become worse from generation to generation, and because it has become the devil's gang, it will be cast down, and then the gentiles, the people of God the Messiah, shall sing. Thus *"He will provide atonement for His land,"*[1] *that is, for heaven, in the lower part of which that gang now is, having been admitted there. About the state of that nation in that lower heaven so-called, much could be said, as that they are to be disbanded, and that those people are*

[367a.] * meant who had lived in light, and yet had embraced idol worship in broad daylight, and who worship the devil; and who are trying to subject heaven to themselves and so, are continually rebelling against God the Messiah [*WE* 5311–12, *SE* 196a, 101a *and the paragraph preceding it*, 273a, 284a, 319a–20a, 353a–54a]. But these matters are too lengthy to be set forth here.

7506. *[Deut. 32:] verse 48 to the end. The subject here is the death of Moses, while previously, in Num. Ch. 20, it was the death of Aaron. What Moses had been like you may see described earlier [WE 3338–40, 3382, 3473 ff., SE 80a, 86a, 241a, 251a, WE 5679, 7038–39]. What his life was like is now described by his death, namely, that when tempted, he yielded, and this not only once, as we have observed [WE 3479, SE 90a, the paragraph preceding SE 101a, WE 7021, 7426, SE 366a]. But he was in that state when dying that is described here—and that state remains after death—namely, that he shall see the Heaven of God the Messiah across from him, but shall not go there. The same thing is symbolized also by "mount Abarim, or Nebo, in the land of Moab." What Moab stands for may be seen above [WE 7343, 7346, SE 360a]. For Moab was born from a daughter of Lot, while the father was drunken. From this, as well as many other references, the land of Moab reflects the character of trusting in its own powers, and worshiping the Law in its outward form. On a mountain of that land Moses died; for mountains symbolize the peaks of that wickedness. Their gods or idols were even called rocks or mountains; see this Chap. 32, verse 31.*

[368a.] 7507. How these matters stand in heaven could be told in many accounts, for so many things have been displayed to me on this subject that I cannot possibly recount them even in part. Let the readers know, however, that these words are truths, and symbolize things

---

[1] Thus *NKJV,* while KJV has "will be merciful unto His land."

which are taking place in this last day. It is his character to mingle holy things with profane, and to rebel constantly against God the Messiah, as he did at the waters of Meribah [Num. 20:11–12]; and to consider righteousness to consist in outward acts. He wants the people Jacob to be the Priesthood, or the only one to possess heaven, of which he eagerly seeks to be king. Nevertheless, he has been admitted into the lowest heaven, where he looks across at Canaan, that is, the heaven of God the Messiah. But that he will not come to it, I am able to know quite certainly from all that has been shown to me and, of course, from the things he has done and said, which are enough to fill many pages.

In the text it is clear that he rebelled against God the Messiah, so that it was his own fault, which he twice before had cast upon the people (saying that he would not see the land of Canaan because of the people's transgression [Deut. 1:37, 4:21]), when yet it was he who had struck the Rock [Num. 20:9–11] without praying or speaking solemnly to it, as commanded.

As for the expression, "gathered unto his people," it was a ceremonial formality to say this; for we read the same words elsewhere about the wicked (look up the passages, I do not remember where they are).

When he urged the people to live according to the precepts of the Law, it was from inspiration, so they were not his own sayings. For, as everyone knows, it is an entirely different thing to teach, [which can be done] by anyone whatever, [than it is to live], etc. etc.

[Law; Moses; Temptation]

[See WE 7516, explaining Deut. 33:9.]

7517.   But it is characteristic of the prophetical style to imply a great deal that does not appear in the words, and therefore it is so succinct that unless it is supplemented, the meaning cannot be drawn out of it. Many things are implied when the angels of God the Messiah speak through someone, as I can [369a.]   *   testify, for then there are very many ideas in the mind that do not come into words; hence the concise style, especially when some words have to be inserted that contain a double meaning.

[Speak, Speech; Prophet; Word; Words, Expressions]
[See also WE 7518–19, concluding the explanation of Deut. 33:9.]

[Paragraphs from *The Word of the Old Testament Explained*, Volume IV (Is. 1:1 to Jer. 50:3), unnumbered by the author, but paginated from 1 to 106, numbered by A. Acton from 7567 to 8263]

7665.   [Is. 14:] verse 9. By hell is meant all the infernal multitude, whose leader is the devil, which likewise has been cast down. For we read in the next verse, "Have you also become as weak as we, have you become like us?" By the "king of Babylon" here [verse 4] is therefore meant the devil in particular. Hell includes all those who call themselves kings and princes of the universe, thus all the arrogant. Now follows in a series how all these address their leader,

[**370a.**]   7666.   [Is. 14:] verse 10. namely, that he had become weak, and yet they had placed their hope in him on account of his boasting. For everyone in hell recognizes his own leader, whom they style prince, for they

call themselves lord of the universe, even Jehovah, and also the holy spirit, and to the extent that the power is left to any one of them, he rises up more and more. But because that power is not given except to a few, therefore they recognize those as their princes and kings. Those eminencies claim to worship Jehovah, but such insanity is effused by some of them as to call themselves God of the universe, and therefore they are waging war with those who worship God the Messiah.

But I would be giving amazing accounts if I told about these eminencies, who are there so that there will be as many kinds and as many species of spirits as there are characters and minds of men, etc. It is these, therefore, who are now addressing the devil, knowing now that he had tricked them.

[Gods; Character (Genius); Jehovah; Hatred; Spirit]

7687.   [Is. 16:] verse 2. *The ford of the Arnon was the border of Moab,* see the many passages in the **Collection**[1].

From here up to verse 6 follows an exhortation to those who place righteousness in the law in its outward form, that they should take refuge in the Righteousness of God the Messiah. But verses 1 and 5 speak quite openly of God the Messiah, that He

---

[1] See *The Word Explained*, Appendix, under *Arnon*.

Himself became Righteousness, and thus bore our sins [John 1:29]; therefore they should now repent. They are here called *"a wandering bird,"* meaning that they think aimlessly, nor do they know what they want without being of two minds, persisting in the question whether it is so.

[**371a.**] This even happened just now, that doubts were clinging to them about [meanings drawn] from the Law that were round about me. But that this is what is meant, and not the destruction of Moab in the proper sense, can be clearly concluded from the particulars. For without these meanings, there would be no sense to all the words of this prophet in this passage, which otherwise, in its literal meaning, is so vague that no one can draw anything from it.

The ford of Arnon is toward the wilderness, where is "the lamb of the ruler of the land from the rock[1] toward the wilderness, to the mount of the daughter of Zion" [verse 1]. The "lamb of the ruler of the land" in the highest sense is God the Messiah, Who is the Lamb of God, the same as the Lamb of the Ruler of the land, Which Lamb *"takes away the sins of the world" [John 1:29].*[2]

[**372a.**] 7693. [Is. 16:] verse 12. "When Moab sees himself so completely conquered that he is wearied upon his high place" (for being an idolater, he sacrificed upon high places), "then he will come to the Sanctuary to pray or to implore, but he will not be able." This is what happens to those who convince themselves very deeply, even to the point of taking on principles from which they cannot afterwards go back. When proven wrong, being wearied by the truth, they wish to pray, but because the nature they have acquired from their principles resists this, they cannot. This is clear from much evidence, which I cannot publish—that is, that those who have been steeped in principles and have derived a nature from them, so that they are steeped in love of self, and from that in self-righteousness, cannot pray even if they want to. Outside of themselves they see the truth, but within them there is something that fights against it.

[Prayer]

---

[1] *KJV* has "...to the ruler of the land from Sela...."
[2] This paragraph is emphasized in the original by the word *Obs.* written twice in the margin.

7743. ....[Is. 22:] *verse 19. This follows from the same cause, and in agreement with the prediction, namely, that he will be pulled down and cast out, which is meant by "pulling him down from his position."*

[**373a.**] Much more about what these words stand for in heaven, where there are eminencies and overseers [*see* 370a], can indeed be told (as concerning Abraham, Moses, and others) about whom, **however, silence must be kept at this point**). For they are gradually being moved down from their place; and the degree of descent is proportionate to the degree of ascent, etc. They likewise portrayed the treasurers and overseers of the king's house [verse 15], and consequently the fathers of the Church.

[**374a.**] **7758.** ....[Is. 24:] *verse 8. All spiritual and heavenly joy will also cease.* Inner joys of a different kind are described here, and different causes that arouse joys which cease when the causes cease. What heavenly joys are nobody can know but one who has learned it by the Divine mercy of God the Messiah. And because I have had this experience now over a period of time, I can only declare that they are ineffable, and that if they were to be expressed even as to the least part (for they are indescribable), no human being not having had the experience could believe it. Nothing whatever occurs that is not joined with that ineffable joy, in a thousand variations, etc. etc.

[*Joy*]

7759. *Verse 9. A comparison is drawn with the joy of the inhabitants of the earth.* For the fact that the joys of the world are completely bitter to those who are tormented by a bad conscience, may be well known to many, as also to those who are in mourning, and even more to those mourning spiritually. What a bitterness of spirit there can be in the midst of outward joy, I have also learned from experience, because

[**375a.**] I was also smitten over a long period of time by that kind of sorrow, and neither can it be described. But this matter (if it pleases God the Messiah) will be spoken of in the description of my temptation.[1]

[376a.] *Isaiah 26*

7769. Both this chapter and other contemporary prophetical writings show quite transparently that there is much content lacking verbal expression, which is nevertheless implicit in the words. The reason for this is that a spirit speaking contemplates inwardly very much that cannot be expressed by words, which then all comes down into similar expressions, though differently with one prophet than with another.[2]

I can testify how much there is in a mental image, when one is engaged in spiritual thought and the resulting speech, which, however can never be expressed; and if it were, little would be expressed in many words, for often one mental image requires an entire exposition. For this reason, the words contained in the prophetical writings can never be explained by any spirit, nor by anyone on earth, but only by God the Messiah, Who spoke them through angels.

[Speak, Speech; Prophet; Word; Words, Expressions]

7770. Therefore, because words come forth in such a wonderful way for the purpose that some meaning may emerge, one interpreter adds connecting words differently than another. Consequently, just as many meanings can result in one little verse as the number of translating interpreters. But from its innermost content, then also from the connection of what precedes it with what follows it, the meaning or sense of the letter becomes apparent.[3]

[377a.] 7776. ....[Is. 26: verse] 13. As for the "other lords," they have dominion when God the Messiah slackens the reins; but they have dominion only to the extent that the reins are slackened, and not one whit beyond that, as I am able to affirm and testify from

---

[1] This probably refers to the missing paragraph 66.
[2] This sentence is emphasized in the original by the word *Obs.* written twice in the margin.
[3] This paragraph is emphasized in the original by the word *Obs.* written twice in the margin.

such manifold experience, that it would fill up many pages. I was allowed to observe the very intervals of their domination, and how they were unable to go the least step further, as even the evil spirits could observe. In fact, I have spoken with them many times about this same matter, for it has been granted me, by the Divine mercy of God the Messiah, to speak without any danger with spirits of diverse characters who had been given the power to operate in, and as it were to dominate [me].

I could tell very many things well worth recording that sometimes happened on these occasions, but for the time being it is enough to say that they persuade themselves that they are acting on their own power, and thus think they are in control of themselves. And they are held in this opinion for several reasons, for such spirits do not want to be convinced to the contrary. Yet I can solemnly swear that they have not the least particle of power, but are only instrumental means, employed so that people may be punished, tempted, and thereby reformed; for without these spirits as instruments, man cannot be reformed by temptations. In fact, they then swallow up a person's evils, for they carry the evils away in themselves, etc. etc.

[Evil; Permission; Power]

That God the Messiah does all works, is said in verse 12; and here, that "by Him Alone they make mention of His Name," that is, call upon His Name. For no one can call upon the Lord except through God the Messiah, etc.

[**378a.**] 7777. ....[Is. 26:] verse 14. "The dead," that is, the damned, do not live, that is, they do not come alive again and dominate any more. The "Rephaim"[1] are their chiefs, for they are like eminencies, as you may see discussed before [370a, 373a], having those who worship them as

> their greatest, as their Deity, some this one, some another one, but most, the one they had worshipped during their life, just as very many worship Abraham, Isaac no one I have heard of, Jacob also many, but not with

---

[1] *KJV* translates this word "deceased."

such great honor, Moses also, and so forth, who are the chiefs of those from among the Jews.

But others have different eminencies, so the papists will worship their own saints as Deities, and therefore cannot but perish, together with certain of their deities—specifically, the ones who accept that adoration and thus want to be worshipped. (See what has been told elsewhere about Peter [13a, 67a]). Such is their condition in heaven. Similar spirits are meant when the "Rephaim" are spoken of; do see the *Collection*[1] in regard to the *Rephaim*. They are also meant by those whom Joshua drove out from Hebron [Josh. 10:36–37], also called the *Anakim* [11:21].

^mLook up to see whether Rephaim means "devoid of life," as another interpreter has it.[2n]

[Gods; Guardian spirit; Spirit]

"To visit them" is to judge them, and thus expel them. The day of visitation is the day of judgment. That they are cast down, and thus "wiped out from their memory," may be seen above [cf. WE 5923 ff.].

[**379a.**] 7780. ....[Is. 26:] verses 17 [and 18] treat further of their affliction and temptation. "To bring forth wind"—look at the Text to see whether it is like the pain of colic. They were afflicted to the point of despair, even until "there was no deliverance in the earth." The complaint is that "the inhabitants of the world have not fallen," for in the next verse the response is given that "the Rephaim shall fall."[3]

Temptations are continued to the limit of a person's endurance, as I can confirm from experience, even until there is no hope left; but afterwards comes help. One reason why temptation is carried so far is so that we may learn what we are like in temptations, if God the Messiah does not uplift us, and so that we may acknowledge the mercy of God the Messiah. These things I have experienced very often in a wonderful way.

[Despair; Temptation]

---

[1] See *The Word Explained*, Appendix, under *Rephaim*.
[2] Tremellius: *expertes vitae non resurgent*. See Acton's footnotes to *The Word Explained* 7777.
[3] *KJV* has "the earth shall cast out the dead"; see previous footnote.

[380a.] SPIRITUAL EXPERIENCES

Now, therefore, uplifting follows; for temptation, as is well known, goes on even until the death of the body in the case of martyrs, etc. etc.

[**380a.**]　7784.　[Is. 26:] verse 20. The comforting continues of those who are in [this] life. For "to hide themselves for a little moment, to enter their chambers," while a person is living in the body, is to enter within oneself, and meditate, and "shut the door," that is, not let in anything which distracts one into what is contrary, delaying, "until the anger is past." For temptation is very much like an anger of God the Messiah, when yet there is by no means anger, but love, so that the person may thereby be regenerated.

The words likewise concern those who are to rise again after the life of the body. For them, the chamber is the grave, the door to which is closed, and it is a "little moment" from one's death until the last judgment. For to those who are in heaven, there is not time such as there is to those in the life of the body. That for them there cannot be any such thing as time, may be clear

from many considerations, for they do not, like those in the body, ponder about the future, and deduce things to come from things past, thus measuring intervals of time as mankind. Neither do they feel the anxiety and the concerns which also prompt people to keep track of time.

Such is the state they are in, so that it is a little [moment] for them from the time of their death to the last judgment, even if they should live for several thousand years. If you ask them where they have been for so long a time, they do not know; whether they are about to do something, whether they are going somewhere else, this they do not know, either, being altogether dependent upon the will of God the Messiah. However, one can hardly tell the difference between their state of life in the present and the state of life of people on earth.

But the description of their life and of the difference between the life of spirits, or those living after the death of the body, and the life of people in the body, will, if God the Messiah deems it fitting, be continued elsewhere, as the occasion arises. In the meantime, [suffice it to say that] the state of those who are in the Heaven of God the Messiah is a most happy one. They

have no anxiety, because no recollection of the past nor concern for the future, and most important, none for the present. But the state of the unhappy will be continual distress in time present, one grief perpetually leading to another, etc.
[Happiness; Future; Past; Time]

[**381a.**]   *Isaiah 33*
7828.   Verse 1. **Against the devil and his gang, that he attacks the Church**
        Verse 1. The "plunderer"[1] is the devil, and his gang, each member of the gang plundering in his own way. "You who deal treacherously" is also the devil, his gang being not only his spirits, but also people on earth. He provokes the Church, that is, those from the Church, without any reason, only because of a vicious character. For those who are from the Church of God the Messiah, in the heavens and on the earth, are not attacking him, but seeking in various ways to bend his gang toward goodness, but he is still eager to ravage and kill the innocent, and even little children. This is plain to me,
        by the Divine mercy of God the Messiah, from such manifold experience, that I can declare it on the grounds of lengthy experience alone, as I have been with so many different spirits who have attacked me in numerous ways, and indeed, without reason, etc. etc.
[Good; Evil; Spirit]
        But in the end, "they will be plundered." Here the prophet is repeating the same words, for the law of retaliation reigns: *as anyone does, so it shall be done to him.* This is the cause of many events with the people of Jacob, as, for instance, that they had to attack the enemy by lying in ambush *[see WE 5905]*, etc. etc.

7863.   From the above *[WE 7854–62]*, it is evident that this whole Chapter *[Is. 40]* concerns God the Messiah and His Coming, which is described *[verses 1–11]*.
[**382a.**]   Moreover, if it should be permitted to confirm all these matters from experience, namely, that God the Messiah Alone is Wisdom *[verses 12–14]*, that He has all Power in heaven and on the earth *[verses 15–24]*, that He

---
[1] *KJV* has "that spoilest," A. Acton, "waster," for the Latin *vastans*.

knows all things most deeply [verses 25–28] and is the Only One who imparts a life of belief [verse 29 to the end]—if all these points should now be confirmed by the experience I have acquired by the Divine mercy of God the Messiah, it would fill very many pages.
[Lord; Power; Wisdom; Life]

7867.   ....[Is. 41:] verse 20. *Here is described wisdom and faith, or the spiritual together with the heavenly quality that will be imparted to them—consequently, the belief that God the Messiah Alone has done this. The primary point of wisdom and faith is that we should believe we are nothing in ourselves, but everything in God the Messiah.*

[383a.] There is no power whatsoever in spirits, and thus neither in people on earth, although they may think themselves to have some powers. This was the subject of a conversation I had today with spirits. There were many of them around me, speaking with me, and among them some who thought they had some powers of their own. They even confessed seeing that they had none, for spirits do see this, even if they do not acknowledge it. But the angels of God the Messiah not only see it, but also acknowledge and thus see it inwardly and understand it. Those who think otherwise see it experientially, thus outside of themselves. The 7th day of November, 1746 (old calendar).
[Power]

[See also WE 7874, explaining Is. 42:6.]

7875.   [Is. 42:] verse 7. *These following words result from the fact that [God the Messiah] became the Light. For Light could by no means have been imparted to human minds if the Messiah had not become Righteousness, and thus if Heaven had not been opened again. For without the Righteousness of the Messiah, heavenly light cannot possibly penetrate, but only the shade of night. For this reason it is here said, "to open blind eyes." Then again, without the Messiah having become Righteousness, all mortals, even the angels, [would be bound]—as can be shown plainly enough*

[384a.] and corroborated by experience, even as to methods— that is, they *would be held as captives by the devil. From that captivity they were freed only by the Messiah, for which reason it is said, "to bring out from the prison him who is bound"*[1]. *The like is meant by the words, "from the prison house, those sitting in darkness." The prison is connected with the "pit" in Ch. 24:22.*

7883. ....*[Is. 42:] verse 25. In the innermost sense of this verse, the people of God is meant, and that they were punished in this way; but the punishment did not go so far that [this people] perished. For it soon follows, in the first verse of the next Chapter, that they were rescued and brought back, or redeemed. But in the highest sense, the Messiah is meant, and that He endured all the anger of Jehovah, and thus suffered for the human race. This also comes out clearly in the words of the next verse.*

[385a.] When certain spirits having a nature-bound soul were saying just now that they understood these words differently, they received the reply that whose who have a nature-bound soul cannot but understand these words of the prophet in an earthly way. On the other hand, those who have a spiritual, heavenly soul, understand them in a spiritual and heavenly way, for they do not understand earthly matters any other way, etc.
[Inward; Letter; Earthly (Natural); Word]

7924. ....*[Is. 46:] verse 1. The works of the Law are compared to idols,* "Bel" *being an idol that is said to be bowed down; likewise* "Nebo," *but look at the Text to see whether or not it is* "idol," *as another interpreter has it.*[2] *They are compared to beasts and cattle that sink down under their burdens.*

[386a.] Verse 2. Here likewise, they are called "stooped" and "bowed down," and it is said that "their soul goes into captivity," or "into servitude," for they are slaves.

According to the letter here and elsewhere, the subject seems to be nothing else but their idols, or idolatry. But through the description of their idols everything is reflected which they idolize. Idols are all the things they worship and love, whether outside of people, or within them, that turn them away from the love of God. These are beyond number, for there are kinds and species of them.

---

[1] *KJV* has "the prisoners."
[2] That is, Tremellius, but in a footnote.

[387a.] SPIRITUAL EXPERIENCES

Here, the works of the Law are reflected. These they worship, and consider they are saved by doing them, etc. It is the prophetical style to depict such things by many comparisons, which are symbolic portrayals. For the angels of God the Messiah understand earthly matters, and everything that confronts the senses [of the body], spiritually. Therefore, prophetical speech is a kind of heavenly Language,

but one which is not understood by any but those who are truly spiritual and heavenly, that is, who let themselves be led by God the Messiah. This Language is inexpressible as it is produced by the angels among themselves; but because men must be taught from heaven, the speech comes down into expressions like these, which are not understandable except to heavenly guardian spirits taught by God the Messiah. Otherwise, what would it mean that "Bel is bowed down, Nebo is stooped," etc. etc.? Other spirits, however, do not understand this language, savoring only what is portrayed in an earthly manner, which sometimes takes place in insane ways.

About this heavenly speech that lies concealed within prophetical discourse, I spoke today with certain spirits of earthly character, and it was compared with the angelic Language, which they hardly understood. In itself it is a language that must be learned like any other language. For by their symbolism, entirely different and, indeed, more inward and higher things are to be understood than earthly minds grasp, etc. etc.

[Prophet; Symbolic Portrayal (Representation)]

[387a.] 7932. [Is. 47:] verse 8. [The daughter of Babel] is again called "delicate one"[1] [as in verse 1], because it appears to them as more beautiful than any other doctrine. She boasts that there is no other as beautiful as she. Thus she boasts that she is above all in the universe, and goes so far as to exclude all others from the kingdom of Heaven.

That such is the arrogance of the Jews, I have heard quite often from those who have spoken with me

---

[1] *KJV* has "given to pleasures" in verse 8, but "delicate" in verse 1.

who had been of the Jews. They boast that they alone will occupy heaven, excluding all the rest, whom, in fact, they hold in deadly hatred; and if they had the power, they would want to admit none of them. All others they regard as the damned. But they hardly tolerate anyone of their own, except in that certain case where it has to do with eminence, and they are then worshipped, etc.

[Jews]

"Not to be a widow" and "not bereaved [of children]" means that she would last to eternity.

[**388a.**] 7934. [Is. 47:] verse 10. [The daughter of Babel] calls it the highest "wisdom and knowledge" when they wrongly interpret the Word of God the Messiah and apply to themselves whatever is written about Zion and Jerusalem, as well as wanting themselves to be meant wherever Israel is named in a good sense. All other passages which are against them they explain in a distorted way. No matter how they have lived, even though engaged in extreme idolatry from the beginning to the end, still they maintain that the promise was made to them. They did not remember the covenant and that they had broken it time after time, and that they were to be entirely rooted out when they rendered the covenant null and void, as Moses so often declares to them, as do the prophets.

They say these words in their heart, as we read just before [verse 8], that "there is no one else besides" them. Moreover, they also say amongst themselves that they worship Jehovah the Creator of the universe, but they do not want to know that there can never be any approach to Him except through His Only Begotten Son, Who is prefigured in every ritual and sacrifice of their Church. And because they do not have faith in the Only Begotten of Jehovah, they therefore cannot possibly be admitted to Jehovah. This is also the reason that they almost continually fell into idolatry and worshipped idols, to which they ascribed all power, in fact, even the creation of the universe, and also called the idol Jehovah, as appears plainly enough in Exod. 32:5.

[Church; Jews; Symbolic Portrayal (Representation)]

[389a.] SPIRITUAL EXPERIENCES

[389a.] *Isaiah 53*
7968. Verse 1 to the end. **A most clear prophecy about the Messiah, that He would come in the appearance of a Servant, despised and afflicted, and would die for the sins of the human Race.** This prophecy is so clear that
> while I was reading it, the spirits around me, who were from the Jewish religion, were completely silent, and could make no objections whatever. They were even afraid that it might be read in front of them a second time, and thus they were convinced. And it is strange, but from shame and from an inborn hostility, they had not wanted to be convinced, as I could see clearly.

[Jews]

[390a.] 8037. [Is. 65:] verse 25. What is described here is that sins will no longer condemn them, since there is no damnation for those who are in God the Messiah. For the Righteousness of God the Messiah is accounted to them, and then the guilts of original sin, and many more guilts coming from acts of life, cannot rise up and defile a person, for as soon as they rise up, they are immediately bent to what is good, and thus taken away. Those sins and evil feelings that remain rooted are meant by the "Wolf," the "lion," the "serpent" which shall lie hidden in the dust. Thus they shall not do any evil, because they cannot; for God the Messiah is leading them, etc. etc. These points could be confirmed by so many experiences that they would fill very many
> pages. For by the Divine mercy of God the Messiah, experiences over a period of so many months now have made it very clear to me that evil feelings, aroused and awakened from a hereditary root, and a new root implanted by acts of life, have been turned immediately into good; etc.

[Condemn, Damnation; Evil]

[391a.] 8080. [Jer. 5:] verse 6. There are evil spirits, symbolized here by wild animals, who are around
> us; and when the person is the kind who no longer has any belief, they distort and so to speak tear up anything which might once more instill belief, thus all the articles

of faith, or creeds. For then not any thought at all can come to mind which is not thus torn apart.

This I can solemnly swear to on the basis of many experiences. For such as one is, so one is treated by spirits, until they have so distorted all beliefs that there is no sanity left. Thus they extinguish all light, turning it into frightening darkness, in which one lives together with one's own evil spirits.

This condition grows successively worse in us the more we think we understand things, and the more abundant our knowledge of nature is, thus in the learned of the world more than others, to the extent of their knowledge. For evil spirits arouse more and distort more in a person regarded as learned than in anyone else, and then more firmly fix those distorted ideas, and thereby thicken the shadows so much that the person is almost beyond hope. For all the deeply inhering knots must be untied, and all parts of the shadow dispelled. If they are not dispelled, they remain within as if they were part of the character one has developed from one's own understanding, to the point of conviction.

To this I can solemnly swear on the basis of much experience, namely, that spirits are constantly trying to do this, and that they call forth even the tiniest doubts that have crept in from infancy on, endeavoring to distort [all beliefs]. But in the case of the elect, this takes place, as it does during temptations, for the purpose of dispelling the doubts one by one. Therefore, if the learned and the philosophers are to be brought back onto the path, this must be done by sharper and deeper temptation than exists with those who are not learned, etc. etc.

I am therefore convinced that we must most humbly beseech God the Messiah that we may not come into temptations, that is, into the kind in which we doubt the Word of God the Messiah, etc.

[Educated, Learned, Doctrine; Belief (Faith); Light; Distort (Pervert); Truth]

[**392a.**] 8084. [Jer. 5:] verses 15, 16. It is the devil's gang, or evil spirits around a person, who, because we are unaware of them and what they are like, cause us to identify them as thoughts, instead. For human beings believe their thoughts are under their own control. Therefore, any who do not want to believe that spirits arouse their thoughts, and their feelings, may if they so wish, believe that their thinking does this. But then it is worse with a person, for in this way we make ourselves to blame, etc. etc.

Those evil spirits are "like an open tomb," that is, like hell, which rushes in around us. And they are "mighty men" indeed, for they do not allow the least thought to slip in, derived from faith in God the Messiah, that they do not instantly seize upon, and distort—and, as said, "all" of them. They notice [anything coming from faith] in the very least, as in the greatest [thoughts],

> for they are full of hatred, so that the least ray of truth distresses them, and they distort it. I have had manifold experience in this matter, etc.

[Light; Truth]

[**393a.**]   8109.   ....[Jer. 7:] verse 23. It is here told what was commanded them, namely, that "they should walk in the way which was commanded them," that is, in the way of truth, about which see [what has been said] above in many places.

Verse 24. But they did not want to understand this, but "hardened their heart," and at this day also they harden it, as is known, so "they are going backward," that is, towards hell. It was shown earlier that the way along which they who are distorted walk is backwards [*cf.* WE 2967 *ff.*, SE 61a, 62a]. For upwards is toward heaven,

> and no one can raise themselves upwards, but God the Messiah raises them, that is, all their thoughts, and the contents of the thoughts, to Himself. This can be established on the basis of so much actual experience, that it would fill many pages. Soon, however, when He releases the thoughts, then they fall backwards of themselves, and indeed, into the world, etc.

[Think, Thought; Belief (Faith)]

8113.   ....[Jer. 7:] verse 33. The "carcass" is spiritual death, "for the bird of the heavens" is for their atrocious fantasies; likewise "for the beast of the earth." And, in fact, this death will not pass away. A like expression occurs in Abraham's vision, Gen. Ch. 15, [verse 11], namely, that the birds of the heavens came down on the

carcasses and would eat them, and it was then allowed Abraham to drive them away. But afterwards, thick darkness arose, and it was not seen what was done with the carcasses. This also has happened, as I can
[**394a.**] confirm *by the displays I have seen before, and saw today: the 20th and 21st day of Nov. 1746 (old calendar).*
^{m}How [the guilt] still remains on their hands for wanting to merit righteousness by sacrificing their children, has also previously been seen by me.^{n}

8118. [Jer. 8:] verses 4 to 7. **There is no liberation from hell, because they remain in their wickedness.**
8119. Verse 4. These are words of grief, and of mercy; for God the Messiah has mercy on all, both in this life, and in the other life. He does not will the death of anyone, but that they may live. This is just why it is here asked "whether they will never return."
Verse 5. Here is the quite gentle reply, filled with the grief of mercy, namely, that "they refuse to return."
[**395a.**] *Verse 6. For when the opportunity to return is given them, just as it is here, they persist in their former words, just "as the horse rushes into the battle."*
8120. This I can likewise aver on the basis of many experiences. For while they are being held in bonds,
they keep silent; but they constantly injected into my mind everything that was exhaling from them, like vapors, which I could smell so plainly that nothing could be plainer. For I was allowed to find out, not only that it was they who were pouring in that exhalation, but I was also given to know who they were; for as soon as I turned my mind in their direction, they were pictured before me, and were chastised. And as long as the chastisement lasted, they would stop; but afterwards they still persisted, and did not cease until they had been cast out.
I could feel so vividly that they were being cast out, as if by a delicate sensation during that whole time—when they were being driven out, and others when they simply went away, sometimes [others] when they were coming. Moreover, they also made their presence evident to me by other indications; for it was sometimes allowed them to completely draw toward themselves, so

[396a.]   SPIRITUAL EXPERIENCES

> to speak, and then to occupy, the aura of my thoughts—and to do this so firmly and harshly that it almost pulled away my brain. I could never have been freed from this but by the Divine mercy of God the Messiah. Then at once I could actually feel my state change. But if I were to recount all those particulars, they would be too many to set forth in detail, etc. etc.

[Spirit]
[**396a.**]   8121.   Verse 7. For they live in an entirely contrary order of life, so that their minds are not like birds, yet are here compared to birds because birds symbolize thoughts, each one according to its kind. Each bird in this verse has its own explanation. For they are led by their feelings, which are inborn and occur in accordance with an order. But with these people it is the opposite order. This, too, I told them once, namely, that birds portray the kingdom of God the Messiah,

> and this was also demonstrated by many instances, as also do animals and the vegetation of the earth, wherein depictions of the Kingdom of God are most apparent. For nothing can be lasting that is not a portrayal of the Kingdom of God the Messiah.
>
> This was indeed shown to them quite vividly, because my thought, which was in the form of speech, was almost of the kind that enabled me actually to portray these matters in a spiritual way, as spirits do, which also surprised them. They fully acknowledged that those things did portray the Kingdom of God the Messiah; for they could not contradict the truth. So then they were also shown that only the kind of people on earth and spirits who do not let themselves be led by God the Messiah, do not portray the Kingdom of God the Messiah, but on the contrary, that they represent the kingdom of the devil, and thus the lower regions, not the higher.

[Bird; Kingdom; Portrayal (Representation)]

[**397a.**]   8134.   ....[Jer. 10:] verse 5. Therefore, people, "be not afraid," because they can do nothing that they are not allowed to do for the sake of mankind's punishments and temptations. For while they are being allowed to punish or tempt, they think that power to be their own, and to come from their own planning, because they are allowed to act in this way. But really, when one is allowed to learn of their attempts, and their plans, even their thoughts, as I have been granted by the Divine mercy of God the Messiah to learn, one really cannot help laughing at how they think that everything is due to themselves, and even convince themselves of it, and cannot bear to be told that they are dead, and can achieve nothing whatsoever with all their imagined foresight—even when they are shown clearly that they cannot say, much less do, anything whatever from themselves. This has also very often been granted me to show them vividly, but after some indignation, they at once forget the experience and return to that ridiculous imagination that they know and can do, some of them, everything.

These words that I am now writing are also now in their midst, and they are becoming very indignant. But whenever it pleases God the Messiah, the ability to speak, to think, to act, is taken from them so obviously that it cannot possibly be denied. And after a while they are given permission, and then, to the extent of that permission, they become enraged. It is evil spirits I am speaking of.

[Prudence; Spirit]

[**398a.**]   8178.   [Jer. 19:] verse 15. This is a summing up of what has preceded. "To stiffen the neck" is to behave stubbornly. How stubborn they are is known from their hatred, as well as from many other circumstances I could bring forward. They do not allow any truth to enter in without at once extinguishing it,

just as happened to me. While, through His Mercy, I was contemplating the more inward parts of the Word of God the Messiah, they were then continually trying to destroy them. It was even quite often permitted that I should not be able to make out any coherence or connection, right to the end; so I was obliged to struggle with those spirits in various ways. The particulars are too abundant to be told even in many pages.

[Understanding, Understand; Light]

[399a.]   8181.   **The subject here [Jer. 20] is the persecution of the faithful, and their captivity in the temple; and, at the same time, the pronouncement of the destruction of those who are persecuting the faithful, and holding them captive; finally, the extreme captivity of the faithful, or their being sent down as if into hell.**

           8182.   Here many examples can be brought up, confirming how the devil's gang persecutes those who receive faith, and in how many different ways, and holds them captive so that they can hardly think about God the Messiah; and how they are thus pressed down, even to hell. This is also portrayed in several ways, but these particulars are too numerous.

[Captive, Captivity]

[See WE 8199–8202, explaining Jer. 23 verses 1 to 8.]

[**400a.**]   8203.   Certain spirits who were around me just now could not help understanding these words, and that God the Messiah is meant, as some of them even said. For this reason they also tried to draw my mind away from this point, but they did not succeed, as I also told them. For they were of the descendants of Jacob. 1747, the 23rd day of February (old calendar).

[Jews]

8211.   *[Jer. 23:] verse 17. So speak all those who blot out faith by means of philosophy; for faith should go into knowledge, and acquire knowledge, to serve as its body, and thus as a fulcrum for the understanding; for without objects of memory, a person can hardly understand anything. But when philosophy acts as the soul, and the faith of truth as the body, so that one's faith is developed from philosophy as from the body, when it ought to be from the soul, the order is turned entirely upside-down, and so everything is distorted. Thus the heart is hardened, and they think "no evil shall come." They are in mere darkness and cold in respect to what is truly spiritual and heavenly. For a bodily soul, which philosophy thus becomes, cannot bring on anything but darkness and coldness.*

[**401a.**]   8212.   This, too, I am able to affirm by quite a lot of experience. For when knowledge, and matters of memory, which are exceedingly limited, wished to go into spiritual matters and more or less store them up, then I would immediately fall into doubts, and if these had not been removed by God the Messiah in His infinite mercy, I would have fallen headlong into the thickest darkness, into doubts and denials.

For particulars can never enter into universals. Lower things must be contemplated from what is higher, thus from its watchtowers, and never the other way around. The more universal principles, which come together to form truths, are introduced by none other than God the Messiah. For all truths, however many there may be, focus upon belief in God the Messiah, and they do so by a varied interrelation. Truths of nature likewise focus upon it, for earthly things are depictions of spiritual and heavenly realities.
[Philosophy]

[**402a.**]   8236.   ....[Jer. 30:] verse 7. "The day is great" because the human race is preserved and saved. "Jacob" here is the Messiah, so it is added, "he shall be saved out of it"; but see the text. Verse 8. Here that appears even more clearly, because the "yoke," that is, eternal death, "is broken" from on Him, and thus "the bonds have been burst," so that they should no longer have to serve the hellish gang, nor the evils within themselves. For the righteousness of the Messiah is accounted to them, and the evil removed so as not to appear, even though it remains. This is noticed the moment we are left to ourselves, however faithful we may be. This could be corroborated by much experience, for if we are left even the least bit to act from self and from our inborn desires, we at once fall into evil. Thus that accounting [of righteousness] is accompanied by a continual uplifting and almost separation from evil, causing us to suppose that we are faithful, when yet just the opposite is the case.
[Evil; Sin]

[At the end, after the explanation of Jer. 50:1–13:]
[**403a.**]   8263.   There are those who are called Babel in several senses, as well as those who are the worst Baals of all, and there are many degrees of them. This was made plain to me by companies of hellish spirits, who violently

[403a.] SPIRITUAL EXPERIENCES

attacked me while I was writing these and the earlier paragraphs, pouring such black poisons into my thoughts, and if possible, also into my feelings, that they can never be described. The 9th day of February, 1747.
[Baals; Babel; Spirit]

FROM THE *SE* INDEX 8.

[**This second section of threshold materials is a reconstruction of the lost text of *Spiritual Experiences*, paragraphs 1 to 148$^{1}/_{3}$, from the indexes and the "Bath Fragment."**]

1. Spirits are only tools or instruments of life, yet serviceable for certain purposes. *[Tools (Organs); Spirit]*

2. Spirits are bondservants, the more inwardly evil, the more insane. What use they serve. *[Tools (Organs); Spirit]*

3. The spirits that have been placed next to someone take to themselves the person's knowledge and memory, and this causes them to think they are that person. Still, each one possesses its own desires, thus its own nature, and cannot take on the person's desires or nature. *[Knowledge; Memory; Spirit; Person on earth; Nature]*

4. Spirits play the part of anyone a human holds in great respect, and say they are that person, because they want to be revered under the guise of such. They especially want to be taken for the holy spirit. *[Holy; Spirit; Gods; God]*

5. About the portrayal among spirits of various things on earth, which arises from things they saw while living in the body. *[Portrayal (Representation)]*

6. *[The index also refers to no. 3.]* Spirits put on a human's knowledge and memory, thinking them to be their own; but they do not influence a person's mental images except through feelings, from which mental images originate. *[Spirit; Knowledge]*

7. Spirits bring on dreams, and when the person is sleeping, they dream the same. *[Dream, Sleep]*

7$^{1}/_{2}$. The things seen and portrayed in a dream were grasped in the dream, but were inexpressible after I awoke, both as to what kind of things they were and where they came from. *[Dream, Sleep]*

8. Dreams coming from angels are entirely different— beautiful, enjoyable, informative, predictive. *[Dream, Sleep]*

9. SPIRITUAL EXPERIENCES

9. About Solomon, what he was like, and about his wisdom [cf. 68a]. *[Solomon; Wisdom]*

10. About speech and association with spirits—several facts. *[Association; Speak, Speech; Spirit]*

11. There is no permission [of evil] except for the sake of a good purpose. *[Permission]*

12. *[The index also refers to no. 15.]*
A kind of permission [of evil] is apparent among spirits, even among evil ones. *[Permission]*

13. I was given the power to seemingly permit, in several ways. *[Permission]*

14.

15. *[The index refers also to nos. 12 and 16.]*
Permission takes place through many intermediaries. *[Angel; Lord; Intermediary; Permission; Truth]*

16. *[The index refers also to no. 15.]*
Truths, however, flow in from the Lord directly, even if through angels. *[Angel; Lord; Intermediary; Truth]*

17. [There was] communication with spirits by means of inward thought. *[Think, Thought; Inward]*
A spirit attempting to do evil becomes upset by being looked at. *[Spirit]*

18. Spirits gladly speak with people, provided the person does not ponder about their nature—and they cannot bear it if spirits coming from elsewhere speak with the person. One spirit is not aware of the presence of another. When they are not being spoken with, spirits do not know otherwise than that they are the people [they are with]. *[Spirit; Speak, Speech; Nature; Person on earth]*

19. The spirits nearest by did not understand, nor do they understand today, the inward meaning of the Lord's Word, and there-

fore neither did the prophets of old. The secrets contained within it are expressed by means of symbolic portrayals. See *Prophet*. *[Inward; Prophet; Word]*

20. During the praying of the Lord's prayer, the threefold meaning was perceived as a threefold life. *[Prayer; Life]*

21. Earthly spirits think they are people on earth, furnished with bodies, and therefore want to be regarded as such. However, it is not the body that makes the human being, but the mind, or understanding and will: so good spirits and angels are human beings. *[Spirit; Person on earth; Body; Understanding, Understand; Will; Mind]*

22. The human mind is null, when a person is born, but it is formed by things of this world. Therefore it must necessarily be reformed in order to become spiritual. *[Mind; Regeneration; Spiritual things]*

23. Spirits are held in bonds in many different ways, not knowing that they are being so held, and when they are released, they think they are acting from their own power and do not know how they are being restrained.*[Bond; Power]*
   Spirits were led by me to speak in such a way that they did not know otherwise than that they were speaking from themselves. *[Speak, Speech]*
   They speak and act according to their own nature. *[Nature]*
   About Permission. *[Permission]*

24. Spirits become insane when they think, speak and act out of their own fantasy, and they consider insanity to be intelligence and wisdom. *[Insanity; Wisdom; Fantasy]*

25. Wisdom is to look and strive toward purposes pertaining to the Kingdom of the Lord: so the Lord Alone is Wisdom. Purposes tending in that direction are numerous beyond estimation, and they are arranged in order of priority. See *Purpose*. *[Purpose (End), Kingdom; Lord; Wisdom]*

SPIRITUAL EXPERIENCES

26.   The human soul is purpose. If it looks and strives toward nature, the soul is earthly. *[Soul; Purpose (End); Nature]*

27.   *[The index refers also to nos. 39, 40.]*
Evil spirits are much more insane than beasts because by means of reason they act against order [*cf.* 18a].[1] *[Beast; Insanity; Order]*

28.   About inward spirits whose belief is based on understanding: they cannot stand being called instruments of life. They are meant by Gad.[2] *[Belief (Faith); Implements; Gad]*

29.   By evil spirits who are not living in order, delights also can be produced, so that they are "the delights of a king," or Asher [Gen. 49:20].[3] *[Spirit; Pleasure; Asher]*
I could not think even the least thing, but what flowed in from the Lord. *[Thought, Think; Inflow]*

[THE "BATH FRAGMENT":][4]
....Also distinguished into heavens, according to their different kinds of mental belief, are the angels who govern inward human thoughts: for people have around them an inward, and a very inward, heaven—even an innermost one. I also was enabled by the mercy of God the Messiah actually to share my thoughts for a while with those who were in the heaven of understanding—or rather, to have contact with them through my thoughts and, by intermediaries, to speak with them. I was even allowed to purify my thoughts to the point where I directly touched those who were in the heaven of belief based on understanding. Then I saw that it was they who are meant by "Gad" in a more inward sense. For even though they know, and are therefore able to believe, that God the Messiah Alone rules them through the Holy Spirit, and that they only had power when they were directly enlivened—still they were upset and wanted at first to cause a commotion, but after some contention with me, they quieted down.
Moreover, I was also allowed today, by the Divine mercy of God the Messiah, actually to experience the fact that spirits, even

---

[1] See *Experientiae Spirituales*, Vol. I, p. xxxi, locus 1.
[2] See *Experientiae Spirituales*, Vol. I, p. xxxii, locus 17.
[3] See preceding footnote.
[4] See *Experientiae Spirituales*, Vol. I, p. xxxiii.

if they are evil, that is, in upside-down order, are also able to give "the delights of a King" [Gen. 49:20]. These, when they are in that state, are meant in an outward sense by "Asher," for they were able to produce harmonious pleasures, performing services to the inward heaven, or inward person.

These are the matters that are hidden here, and more could be said about them: 1747, the 8th day of February, on which day I was allowed to note something in the margin about the blessings of the sons of Jacob, chapter 49 of Genesis.[1]

30.   Differences of speech revealed who they were, and where. *[Speak, Speech; Spirit]*

30½.   *[The index refers also to nos. 32–35.]*
     Combats were seen, as if of a last judgment, p. 11.[2]

[Combat]

31.   [I spoke] with the Apostles, saying that by them, just as by the Tribes [of Israel], are symbolized the essentials of faith, or of the Church; that they were not to sit upon thrones and to judge the universe [Matt. 19:28, Luke 22:30]; that they form a synod. *[Apostles; Church; Faith (Belief); Tribes; Judgment]*

32.   *[The index refers also to nos. 30½, 33–35.]*
     An effigy of a last judgment, illustrating the words told in the book of Revelation, that they will be cast down onto the earth [*cf.* 12:9]; and how the casting down will take place at that time. *[Judgment]*

---

[1] See *Experientiae Spirituales*, Vol. VI, Appendix E.
    In the upper left hand corner of page 62 of Swedenborg's *Schmidius Bible* is the annotation, "About *Gad* and *Asher*, see *Experiences*, Tome III at the end." In the lower right hand corner are his annotations on Gen. 49:19–20, which read:
> Vers. 19.) Gad is the righteousness of the more inward person, thus of faith through understanding, in that we think we are our own, not believing we are controlled by God the Messiah in the least details, as is usual with everyone lacking Divine experience. They are the fruits of faith by understanding, thus "he whom a troop tramps upon." He "tramps upon the heel" when it is Jacob, in almost the same sense as [the prophecy] that nature tramps upon the heel, Gen. [3:15?].
> Vers. 20.) Asher is blessedness that is the result of loves, or Issachar, in the more inward meaning, and in the inward meaning.

[2] The pages containing the missing paragraphs were numbered by the author from 1 to 63.

33. [*The index refers also to nos. 30½, 32, 34–35.*]
The deceitful were cast down out of heaven. See also page 11 there, no. 30½.[1] *[Deceit; Judgment]*

34, 35. [*The index only refers to these under* Judgment *(no. 33).*]

36.

37, 38. Regeneration takes place in every individual case in the same way as it does collectively, namely in the Church, in the world of spirits, in heaven: there is a continual combat of inner elements with outward ones, thus of the Lord's angels with the spirits controlling the person's outer elements. This happens in different ways, depending on the nature of each individual, and their various states. See also *Temptation*. *[Regeneration; Combat]*

39, 40. [*The index refers also to no. 27.*]
Humankind is viler than the beast, not knowing on their own the laws of order and of society, but having to learn them, and even then, they grasp at falsities as if they were truths, unlike beasts. For this reason, they must be regenerated [*cf.* 141a]. See also no. 27.[2] *[Regeneration; Society; Beast; Order]*

41. What Peace is, and that Peace has countlessly many aspects. Calmness [on an outer plane] corresponds to it. *[Peace]*

42. Enlightened knowledge from the Word prepares the way for belief; and what else it accomplishes. *[Enlightened knowledge (Cognitions); Word]*

43.

44, 45, 46. The inward parts of the Word are most beautiful, but the outward sometimes ugly—an assertion that is supported by the comparison of the inner and outer figure, structure and form of a human being, and can also be illustrated by optical projections.[3] See *Word*. *[Word; Inward]*

---

[1] See footnote to 30½.
[2] See *Experientiae Spirituales*, Vol. I, p. xxxi, loca 10, 12.
[3] *Cf.* 2164.

FROM THE *SE* INDEX 54.

47.   *[The index also refers to nos. 48, 50.]*
Mankind has been given the ability to command evil spirits, not to be commanded by them.[1] *[Person on earth; Spirit]*

48.   *[The index refers also to nos. 47, 50.]*
Spirits and demons control a person's reasoning power through feelings. See also *Understanding*. *[Feeling (Affection); Understanding; Reason, Rational; Spirit]*

49.

50.   *[The index refers to this under* Person on earth *and* Spirit *(no. 47).]*

51.   I spoke about the bodies of the angels, what shape they have. *[Body]*

52.   What the Kingdom of the Lord within a person is: the feeling and looking is focussed upon the Lord, through belief. From this there is salvation. *[Kingdom; Salvation, Savior; Belief (Faith)]*

53.   What the kingdom of the devil is: the looking is focussed upon oneself, and if upon what is outside of self, yet it is reflected back toward oneself. From this there is death. *[Love; Devil; Die, Dead; Kingdom]*

54.   A proposition put to spirits: whether Demons are able to do anything contrary to what they desire; for they say that they want what they desire. It was answered that they are not able. See also *Love, Feeling*.[2] *[Desire; Power; Will]*
A proposition put to spirits: whether Pure Love is able to will anything but the salvation of all. It was answered that it is Pure Love Alone Who wills, and it is the Salvation of all that He wills. See also *Freedom*.[3] *[Salvation, Savior; Will; Love]*

---

[1] See *Experientiae Spirituales*, Vol. I, p. xxxi, locus 14.
[2] See *Experientiae Spirituales*, Vol. I, p. xxxi, locus 11.
[3] See *Experientiae Spirituales*, Vol. I, p. xxxi, locus 11. See also *The Word Explained* 5336 and footnote.

55. A kind of vision in a seemingly wakeful state, which state was unknown to me before. Perhaps this kind of vision is what the prophets had. What I saw. *[Prophet; See, Vision].*

56. Twice in a wakeful vision, I walked along a road, in the spirit, [experiencing] something like what is read about Stephen [Acts 7:55-6], that he was led by the spirit. *[See, Vision; Spirit; Road]*

57. What peace is: a reflection on peace, and on what things disturb it. *[Peace]*

58. From curiosity spirits want to know everything, so that they also inquisitively arouse all and the least things in a person's memory, and this process cannot be stopped. *[Curiosity; Person on earth; Memory]*

Spirits think that they are people on earth in every respect. *[Person on earth; Spirit]*

(In the margin.) Evil spirits do not want good people to be spoken well of; and they do not want good people around; and they are not aware of the presence of another spirit.

(In the margin.) Spirits take it very hard that they are controlled by a person on earth. *[Spirit; Person on earth]*

(In the margin.) Evil spirits do not want anything to be revealed about themselves. *[Spirit]*

59. Spirits eagerly call forth things that agree with their native character. Spirits want to be parted [from a person] when they come across things that go against their nature. *[Nature; Spirit]*

60. Truth is whatever looks to the Kingdom of the Lord, so that truths are all the means that look, tend and lead to it. But when it comes to means, circumstances make each case different. *[Kingdom; Circumstance; Truth]*

61. A certain spirit, from an idea persisting with him, suddenly denies the resurrection. *[Resurrection]*

62. All people and all things in the world and in heaven, with unlimited variety, are instrumental means [leading] toward the prime and final goal, that is, the Kingdom of the Lord, thus [they are] for the sake of the Lord. *[Goal (End); Kingdom; Lord]*

63. Abraham's faithlessness was transplanted into Jacob and his descendants.[1] *[Abraham; Jacob]*

64. In how many different ways spirits flow through feelings and thoughts into a person, from feeling into thought, and the other way around. *[Feeling (Affection)]*

65. It is different when they are speaking with people. *[Feeling (Affection); Thought, Think; Speak, Speech]*

66. My lamentation regarding temptations [*cf.* 133a, 375a].[2] *[Temptation]*

67. The fact that the Lord controls the universe can be evident from the government of all things in the body by the hierarchy of minds; also, from the development of a tree and of a plant from the seed. *[Lord; Universe]*

68. Spirits with me who did not know I could speak with spirits were pleased [to think] that spirits control people, and that they are the person [they are with]. But they were displeased that the person replied, and was investigating their character, and controlled them. *[Spirit; Person on earth]*

69. In every least particle of love of self and of the world is concealed the ambition of possessing the universe, thus hatred against the Lord. See also *Feeling*, and *Desire* and *Will*. *[Hatred; Love]*

70. Horror-provoking visions and displays brought on by evil spirits. *[Display (Representation); See, Vision]*

---

[1] See *Experientiae Spirituales*, Vol. I, p. xxxii, loca 15, 16.
[2] See *Experientiae Spirituales*, Vol. I, p. xxxi, loca 9, 13.

71. It was shown by a vivid series of experiences, how the Lord governs the thoughts, and that people are unable to think differently [from what is ordained], however much they suppose that they can. See *Thought*. *[Thought, Think; Inflow]*

72. When my thoughts were focussed on the world, they carried me down like weights, and my inward thoughts seemed to be erased, and then I seemed to be governing myself. It was shown, however, that this was not true. *[Weight; Thought, Think]*

73. Thoughts were streaming into my mind imperceptibly, and my actions were being governed by spirits. The spirits were stirred with feeling when my thought was directed toward them. *[Inflow; Thought, Think; Spirit; Action]*

I could tell spirits apart by their speech. *[Spirit; Speak, Speech]*

74. Spirits were aroused to speaking by my looking at them by an inward gaze. *[Looking; Speak, Speech]*

75. *[The index refers also to no. 90.]*
While I was in a most sweet sleep, some spirits were very severely assailed, thinking it was done by me, when yet I knew nothing about it.[1] *[Dream, Sleep]*

76.

77. The cunning and malice of some spirits, when they are allowed to pour in desires and persuasions, is beyond description. They can hardly be recognized for what they are, except from their motive. *[Malice; Motive (End); Persuasion; Deceit]*

There are simple spirits who speak and think hardly anything of themselves, but from others, such being their nature. *[Thought, Think; Simple; Speak, Speech]*

Cunning and evilly disposed spirits more easily lead astray learned people and sharp philosophers than they do others, because with them, they are able to slip in more falsities. *[Learned; Philosophy]*

---

[1] *Cf. Arcana Coelestia* 1983.

Even the most cunning and wicked spirits have no power. *[Power]*

78. Spirits and angels do not have a memory born from and next to the physical senses, but an inward one, which is rather a nature, or character. A sense-based memory they have from the person they are present with. *[Character; Memory; Nature; Person on earth]*

79. Symbolic displays by good spirits and angels, which are of a wide variety and a source of much pleasure, regard the Kingdom of the Lord. *[Kingdom; Display (Representation)]*
Symbolic displays by evil spirits concern the kingdom of the devil. *[Devil; Display (Representation)]*

80. The spirits with me could tell that they were not people on earth, and this by our speaking to each other, and by our separation, and by instruction. The process of being separated, I was sometimes allowed to experience quite keenly. *[Spirit; Person on earth; Speak, Speech]*

81. While I was praying the Lord's Prayer, my hands were folded and unfolded by a manifest force. Also, the words seemed to be lifted up, and mental glimpses of the contents imparted *[cf.* 128a]*.*[1] *[Hands; Prayer; Words, Expressions; Glimpse (Look)]*

82. (1) A person on earth is a spirit clothed with a body. *[Body; Person on earth; Spirit]*
(2) Spirits are not strong in sense-based memory, nor are angels. *[Memory]*
[(3) *is not referred to in the index.*]
(4) When I was in company of spirits, not as one of them, but as an earthly human, I was unable by my own effort to bring up anything from my memory. *[Memory; Associate]*
(5) A person on earth cannot live without being governed by means of spirits; for which reason the Lord, Who rules spirits, rules the whole human Race. *[Lord; Person on earth; Spirit]*

---

[1] See *Experientiae Spirituales*, Vol. I, p. xxxi, locus 8.

(6) If the Lord were to slacken His control for a moment, immediately mankind would be cast headlong into insanities and a most hideous death. *[Insanity; Die, Dead; Lord]*

83. The sensitivities of the father and the mother are born with and in the offspring. But the father's are inward sensitivities, so that they develop after a longer period of time; while the mother's are outward sensitivities, so that they develop within a shorter period of time [*cf.* 37a].[1] *Father; Hereditary, Heredity; Mother]*

84. From concord there is Light, from discord shadow. *[Harmony; Ignorance; Light]*

85. How spirits raise up mental images out of a person's memory, which fall into words of speech. *[Mental image (Idea); Speak, Speech; Memory; Words, expressions]*

Spirits quickly steal away and hide the things [in a person's memory that] they are averse to. *[Memory; Ignorance; Spirit]*

Spirits speak as hastily [as possible], and sometimes more quickly than people on earth, and in fact, with the usual rhythms [*cf.* 54a]. See *Gyre* and *Choir* and *Form*.[2] *[Rhythm; Speak, Speech]*

86. About choirs of spirits and angels, and their harmonies, unity, forms, whirling and back and forth movements in speaking and acting, which image the beauty of things heavenly and spiritual. Also, about the heightening of happiness from many united into heavenly forms by the Lord. See also *Rhythm, Gyre, Form, Choir, Unity, Agreement, Love, Society.* *[Angel; Choir; Whirling (Gyre); Form; Unity; Harmony; Speak, Speech; Happiness; Lord]*

About Choirs of spirits and angels, which are small images of the kingdom of the Lord, see *Form* [*cf.* 63a].[3] *[Spirit]*

87. Heavenly pleasure perceived by me, together with speech, also accompanied by an anxiousness to feel the pleasures more keenly; see also *Joy* and *Happiness*. *[Pleasure; Joy]*

---

[1] See *Experientiae Spirituales*, Vol. I, p. xxxi, locus 3.
[2] See *Experientiae Spirituales*, Vol. I, p. xxxi, locus 5.
[3] See *Experientiae Spirituales*, Vol. I, p. xxxi, locus 6.

88. Dreams were introduced by evil spirits and were obstructed by good spirits, which I heard the spirits admitting after I awoke. *[Dream, Sleep]*

89. A dream appeared to spirits not to be a dream, but something carried out in wakefulness, and they would hardly believe [it was a dream] before it was proven. This also shows what the life of spirits in connection with people on earth is like. *[Person on earth; Spirit; Dream, Sleep]*

90. *[The index refers to this number under* Dream, Sleep *(no. 75).]*

91. There are not the least traces of thoughts and feelings a person can perceive, which inward spirits do not perceive more clearly. *[Feeling (Affection); Thought, Think]*

92. *[The index also refers to no. 93.]*
Several experiences showing that spirits present with other people do not, as they do with me, see through the people's eyes nor hear through their ears, but that they have portrayed inwardly objects of sight and speech, which affect them according to their nature. See *Hear, See.* *[Hear; See, Vision; Ear; Eye]*

Spirits do not see through the eyes and hear through the ears, like they do with me, in those to whom [the spiritual world] has not been opened, see *See.* *[Spirit; Person on earth]*

How things were when for the first time it had been opened in me, and how greatly surprised the spirits were; and what their state was like when I was in human company; and other matters. See *Hear.* *[Hear; See, Vision; Company (Association)]*

93. *[The index refers also to no. 92.]*
Without humankind, order is not complete. The Lord Alone is most perfect order, that is, Order. *[Lord; Person on earth; Order]*

94. How spirits of the inward world communicate with spirits of the outward world [of spirits]: there is an inflow that is hardly perceptible and expressible. *[Correspondence; Inflow]*

95. A perception of the calmness of peace, with its delights and diversity [*see* 41]. *[Peace; Calmness]*

96. Evil spirits continually strive to cast people down into fatal hazards, thus to bring harm upon them, and this comes from the spirits whether they know it or not. But good spirits and angels, [acting] from the Lord, strive continually to rescue people. *[Spirit; Danger; Die, Dead]*

97. About little children and those innocent like them: lower spirits are controlled through them by the Lord—both the lower spirits' powers, and their fantasies. *[Little child; Innocence; Fantasy; Power]*

98. Of Loves, there are kinds and species, from which come all and the least things of a person's life. These loves derive primarily from a certain prevailing love that is present in every other love and also determines the person's nature after death. *[Love; Nature]*

99. The inward level of meaning in the Word cannot be seen at all unless the meaning of the letter is almost blotted out. This applies also in other things, as in philosophical material, when the mind dwells on the words by themselves, as on trivialities; or when a person is absorbed in outer and physical objects. A like principle applies when it comes to the *more* inward level of meaning. See also *Knowledge, Wisdom, Learned, Preach.* *[Word; Inward; Philosophy; Outer]*

When the mind dwells on the words by themselves, the inward meaning does not show itself. See *Inward.* *[Words, Expressions]*

100. *[The index refers also to nos. 101 and 101½.]*
Demons and evil spirits arouse and bring out in a person the things that agree with their own nature. They skillfully take away words, and the meaning of words. *[Nature; Spirit; Words, Expressions]*

101. *[The index refers also to nos. 100 and 101½.]*
Demons and evil spirits arouse for some evil purpose whatever agrees with themselves in a word or in a mental image
/acquired and put together from various sources *[Mental image (Idea); Evil; Good; Words, Expressions]*
/originating within different groups *[Nature]*
/gathered during bodily life *[Spirit]*

101½. *[The index refers also to nos. 100 and 101.]*
Good spirits and angels, [acting] from the Lord, divert

their efforts and bend them toward good, or else make a reply. *[Spirit; Evil; Good]*

102. Evil spirits call everything that is true and good evil. *[Good; Evil; Truth]*
It is customary for spirits to call me "underlig."[1] *[Wonderful]*

103. Very many symbolic displays have appeared to me, when my eyes were closed, and also some of the inward kind. *[Display (Representation); See, Vision]*

104. Spirits are brought into company with each other, according to their own nature and character, to the point where they are societies. See also *Form*. *[Spirit; Nature; Society (Consociation); Character; Person on earth]*
Evil spirits want especially to control people, and when this is not allowed, after fighting over them, they go away. *[Person on earth]*

105. Spirits and demons induce desires together with conviction, and this so diligently, that people do not know otherwise than that it comes from themselves. Sometimes they bring on a persuasion such as they themselves are not subject to, for the purpose of leading the person astray. *[Desire]*
Spirits and demons induce desires along with conviction, and this so diligently, that I scarcely knew otherwise than that it came from myself. Sometimes they brought on a conviction such as they themselves did not hold, for the purpose of leading [me] astray. *[Conviction (Persuasion)]*

106, 107, 108, 109.

110. The ancient Church people beheld in physical objects spiritual and heavenly things, and therefore they were in company with spirits and angels. Today, when it is not even known or believed that there is any interaction [between earthly and heavenly things],

---

[1] Swedish for "wonderful," "amazing," "strange."

111. SPIRITUAL EXPERIENCES

that has completely changed. *[Church; Spirit; Angel; Interaction (Correspondence)]*

111.

112. *[The index refers also to no. 113.]*
Riches should be valued according to the use to which they are put; similarly sciences, philosophy, and gifts of talent. *[Science (Knowledge); Riches; Higher knowledge (Cognitions); Use]*

113. Also, [wealth of] higher knowledge about spiritual matters, from the Word. See also *Philosophy*. *[Knowledge; Use; Wealth; Higher knowledge (Cognitions)]*

114. By the names in the Word, realities are symbolized—this illustrated by examples. See *Word*. *[Name; Word]*

115. I have seen the inward parts of the Word almost apart from the literal meaning. *[Inward; Word]*

116. Spirits have read through my eyes the things I wrote. Also they have written by my hand, as well as dictated words aloud. *[Write; Hand]*

117.

118. *[The index refers also to no. 119.]*
Spirits said that the Lord governs the universe. *[Universe; Lord]*

119. *[The index refers also to no. 118.]*
What the speech of spirits with me is like. *[Speak, Speech]*

120. The spirits present with a person are like the person, well-informed in one who is well-informed, uncultivated in one who is uncultivated: for they are unable to arouse in the person any but those characteristics which agree with their own nature [*see* 100]. *[Person on earth; Spirit; Nature]*

121. *[The index refers also to no. 138.]*
Spirits arouse anything whatever in a person's life—past

events, any of the things done in his or her life, or things thought. *[Memory]*

122. Spirits bring with them from life in the body an unwillingness to have their thoughts exposed—something which they greatly resist. *[Thought, Think]*

123. Many spirits are around a person, the one not knowing the other. Each one supposes that he is that person. They come, they go away—but from where, to whom, and from whom, they do not know, believing they have come on their own, that they have always been there, and always will be. *[Spirit; Person on earth]*

124. Truth and goodness are instilled [into a person] by the Lord through angels and good spirits, which is really repugnant to evil spirits, so that they want to withdraw. Therefore, truth is commonly aroused by them as well. But with anyone who is the kind to be moved by truths, good spirits are associated. *[Spirit; Truth]*

Spirits arouse feelings especially, and from these, thoughts, speech, and acts. *[Thought, Think; Feeling (Affection)]*

[A person's] nature is improved by means of temptations and combats. *[Temptation]*

125. Several groups of evil spirits, convinced of certain truths, were nevertheless afterwards just like they had been before. *[Nature; Spirit; Truth]*

126. Spirits who say there is one creator of the universe, and will not acknowledge the Lord, when yet they are Christians, are evil and deceitful to the same degree that they depart from the acknowledgment of the Lord; nor do they let themselves be led to [Him]. *[Lord; Evil; Deceit]*

127. Evil spirits hold people in murderous hatred, and they strive for nothing but their destruction, except when they imagine themselves to be the person [they are with]. *[Person on earth (Man); Hatred]*

128. How miserable the state of [evil] spirits would be if all in the universe were not ruled by the Lord, can be clear from the fact that they get their life's pleasure from torturing others, whomsoever they can. See also *Grief*. *[Torture; Lord; Pleasure]*

129. A person's spirit is in a more perfect state when separated from the body to which it had been attached. *[Spirit; Body; Person on earth; Soul]*

130. I was allowed, with all the senses of the body, to be in the company of spirits. *[Spirit; Sense]*

131. I was enabled to perceive the spirits' characters by an inward sense, so that they could not fool me. *[Nature; Sense]*

132. Certain spirits are most deceitful. They are sirens. The kinds and species and differences among them are countless. *[Deceit]*

133. *[This is also referred to in no. 127.]*
Every evil spirit has the urge to be lord over others, and some, to be lords of the universe; so they are stupid, and one is easily controlled by another. Every one of them wants to subject someone on earth to himself as a most lowly slave. Consequently, if the Lord were not in complete control, people [on earth], possessed [by spirits], would instantly perish. See *Gods*. *[Gods; Lord; Bond; Person on earth; Slave]*

134. I saw and read writings and the words of the writings, as clearly as if in daylight, with my eyes closed. *[See, Vision; Write]*

135, 136.

137. Spirits are certainly substances, and these substances, forms. The activities of these [spirit-substances] are variations in form, and changes in orientation. These [activities] are the source of thoughts and feelings. See *Substance*. *[Substance; Orientation (State); Form; Feeling; Thought, Think; Spirit]*

138. *[This is also referred to in no. 121.]*

FROM THE *SE* INDEX 145.

139. Spirits were amazed that mankind lives in such ignorance about their own soul and about the individual human faculties that constitute their life. *[Mankind (Person on earth); Soul; Ignorance]*

140. *[The index refers also to no. 295:3.]*
What the Book of life is: all and the least things thought, said, and done are inscribed upon a person's nature, so that nothing so miniscule can be imagined that is not in it. *[Book; Words, Expressions; Thought, Think; Nature]*

141. The speech of the heavenly beings among themselves is incomprehensible, and contains more within it in an instant than can be unfolded on many pages. *[Angel; Speak, Speech]*

142. The speech of spirits with people on earth is in their own vernacular, or in other languages which the person is practiced in, not in their own, which they do not know at all. They prefer familiar and clear words that obviously follow from their mental images falling into words. They are not heard by anyone but the person being spoken with, even in the midst of company. See *Speech*. *[Speak, Speech; Words, Expressions; Mental image; Language]*

143. Many spirits collectively who are being led along by love of self and of the world, not having been withdrawn from these loves by the Lord, are called the devil. Of these there is a very great multitude. Love of self, see *Arrogance* [*cf.* 97a].[1] *[Love; Devil]*

144. Another bond [*see* 23] is that many spirits are not able to think and act differently from each other. Sometimes this happens when they are under some leader. In this way, one is controlled by another, and many by one. *[Leader; Society; Bond]*

145. All are ruled by the Lord, all the human race through spirits; indeed, [it is led] toward the final goal by way of intermediate ones. *[Person on earth; Goal (End); Spirit; Lord]*

---

[1] See *Experientiae Spirituales*, Vol. I, p. xxxi, locus 7.

146. I experienced with my senses as witness that I had thought nothing at all from myself, but that everything had been inspired and imparted. *[Thought, Think; Sense]*

147. A conversation with Jews about eternal life. They expect it to be full of joy, at first like sleep, then the very happiest of all states. When asked whether they wanted to share life with their fellows, or be by themselves, they said, In a large society together with their leaders. Asked whether they wanted to live with the others as they [really] are inwardly, they said they did not know what the inner person is. But then it was told that in the other life they would live with their companions as they are inwardly, and thus (since they well know each other's inward character and also know that of their leaders) that they would live in disharmony, hatred and unhappiness, they finally revealed that they were awaiting the Messiah, Who would unite them [cf. 51a]. See Jews.[1] *[Jews; Inward; Society; Lord]*

148. The bad things that happen to a person are all and each one from evil spirits, even if not deliberately, because it is their nature [to inflict harm]. *[Bad (Evil); Spirit]*

148½. Evil spirits inspire feelings together with conviction, especially [in people] who trust in themselves and ascribe everything to their own judgment; for these credit themselves for everything and think themselves most wise, when yet their wisdom is insanity. For wisdom should be judged by the end [in view], but these are guiding themselves toward an end which is hell. See also *Knowledge, Philosophy, Learned, Preach*. *[Wisdom; Conviction; End; Hell]*

Sometimes those who think themselves the wisest are the most insane. See *Wisdom*. *[Insanity]*

148⅓. Evil spirits believe especially that they are the holy spirit and that the Lord can do nothing without them. But they were asked from whom they go forth, whether it was not from some god of the heathens, baal or some other. *[Holy; Spirit; Gods]*

---

[1] See *Experientiae Spirituales*, Vol. I, p. xxxi, locus 4.

FROM THE *BIBLE INDEX* [148¹/₆.]

[This third section of threshold materials consists of three annotations found in front of the *Bible Index of Isaiah and Jeremiah* and apparently belonging to *Spiritual Experiences*.]

[148¹/₄.] The speech of the ancient Church was like an earthly paradise from which they discerned the heavenly one. The speech of the Prophets is like this, for by what one reads there, spiritual and heavenly matters are to be understood. But in the course of time, that heavenly paradise was changed into a merely worldly and earthly one. At the coming of God the Messiah, the gate from the earthly paradise to the heavenly one was opened; and at His Coming into glory, it is to be opened again. [1747][1]

[148¹/₅.] For one who is being regenerated, matters of understanding come first; for one who has been regenerated, matters of the will come first. A person is formed by the world through ambitions, and the resulting education, but is [then] formed anew through the understanding, so that the will may be reformed. This takes place by means of matters of understanding and, at the same time, things heavenly entering into them, bringing Charity, and thus a [new] character.

[148¹/₆.] 1747, the 7th day of August (old calendar): a change of state in me, [introducing me] into the heavenly Kingdom, in figure.[2]

---

[1] The year 1747 is deleted in the manuscript.
[2] In this passage the translator takes *in imagine* to refer to Swedenborg's projected image in that Kingdom as a man, while actually still living in the world.

149. SPIRITUAL EXPERIENCES

[**This first section of experiences extracted from volumes of the** *Index Biblicus*, **containing paragraphs 149 to 205, was originally written at the end of the** *Bible Index of Isaiah and Jeremiah*.]

About the Terror of those who have led a corrupt life

149. It was observed that among spirits, the instructed who had corrupted their way are, more than others, extremely frightened and tremble at the judgment of truth, so that they give up hope then and there, while others do not. Indeed, they resort to more humble prayers than others, and they do not know where to hide. But still, the moment they recover from their fright, they return to the former arrogance and pride, thinking themselves to be the only ones in the whole of heaven, as I today found out. 1747, the 9th day of October (old calendar).

About the native Character of the descendants of Jacob

150. For quite a while, the descendants of Jacob who are in the other life, and who act in character, depicted to me what they had been and what they are like, namely, that in every dangerous situation, they yield, are very fearful and despairing, humbling themselves even to the dust; but the moment the dangerous condition is past, they return to their character and are haughty, scorning all in the universe in comparison with themselves. Moreover, just to acquire earthly and worldly possessions, they resort to any means, even deceptive supplications, and very many other devices.

About the Jews, what they are like

151. Just as they were described by Jeremiah, so the Jews indeed are in the other life; their character exactly matches the description. This was shown to me by much experience, for very many of them who, by God the Messiah's Divine Mercy, were round about me, spoke with me after having been let into torments. But they were still insane, so there seems to be hardly any remedy for them except, as I told them, to be woodcutters and water carriers, like the people spoken of in the Book of Joshua [9:27]. 1747, the 12th of October (old calendar).

FROM THE *BIBLE INDEX*

There was one who was with me for a while who could still grasp more inward matters, and was quite amazed (I was told that he was Nicodemus). He was able to understand that they were true, but, after staying and conversing with me for some time, either he withdrew, or else was amongst the spirits who are not speaking. The 11th day of October, 1747 (old calendar).

About the collective [energy] field of spirits

152. It is certainly difficult to understand what the collective field of spirits is, and what their impact upon human minds is, without being informed how spirits are differentiated most distinctly into kinds and species, and how their energy, which creates that field, responds to, and thus guides, every single thought and mental image in a human being.

[The relation of human minds to] the collective field of spirits is no different from that of the air, which is the grosser atmosphere and related to hearing, compared to the ether or purer atmosphere related to sight; or the dense clouds around the earth compared to the clear and serene region up above.

1) The [energy] field of spirits is now so corrupted, that whatever flows from the more inward heaven into their realm, which constitutes the third heaven[1], becomes so distorted that whatever [is communicated] does not become known at all, but all and the least messages stream into human minds with an entirely opposite content.

2) Such is that field at this day, and so it has been growing and is growing toward the last day, when it will be dispersed. But in most ancient times, it was not so. It is also because of this field that revelations cannot come forth today as they did in ancient times, except by an extraordinary way, and that there is no such communication with the heavens as there once was.

3) For a period of some hours I was shown how the collective field operates into human minds, and in fact, when it was allowed, how I was not in the least able to stop them from taking away my thought, and from prevailing—such is the strength of that field today, when spirits are given the power to act.

---

[1] *I.e.*, in descending order.

4) The whole field utterly opposes the angels' endeavors; and the power of the angels, who all belong to God the Messiah, is increased so that they are able to overcome.

5) Astounding things would emerge if I should tell what filthy objects they portray when they are allowed to work by fantasies—which I would rather pass by, because it would be shocking to tell; they are nothing less than filthy.

6) Angels of the third level[1] can also be in that same realm, and because they are governed by the heaven of angels, they cannot be hurt at all.

7) A fact I have found noteworthy was that at times, I have heard a spirit speaking with me, and he was abruptly removed. Now I have been allowed to learn that he was snatched away by the collective field, that is, compelled to speak in accord with the field's action. I observed still more things that have slipped from my memory: for that field takes away whatever truth and goodness they find to be the most unpleasant. But if God the Messiah sees fit, [I will speak] more fully elsewhere about this collective field, in general and in details. 1747, the 14th day of September (old calendar).

8) The collective field can be compared with the ethereal atmosphere, in that this conveys to the eye the individual objects, like those on streets and in the countryside, in all the details of their forms and shapes—indeed, to a thousand eyes at the same time, or even tens of thousands—and in this way, to each of a person's thoughts, reasonings and fantasies individually. [The comparison is valid,] for [the collective field] lies inside of nature.

About the persistence of evil spirits in bringing evil upon people

153. From experience I have learned several times that spirits do not ever abstain from, but very obstinately persist in doing evil to people on earth, so that whenever the opportunity offers itself to them, they cling to someone for many days, and indeed continuously, without interruption and without stopping. This fact was proven to me lucidly several times. For they brought on pains in various parts of my body—now in the feet, so that I could hardly walk, now in the dorsal nerves so that I could hardly stand up, but fell over; likewise in parts of my head. They did this so unyieldingly, that

---

[1] *I.e.*, third in a descending order.

the pain and other effects lasted for quite a while, and without interruption.

That these things were brought on by evil spirits, I was taught plainly enough by the ones who spoke with me: for alternately, the pains were allayed and worsened—and really suddenly. From the conversation with them, and from the changes etc., it became quite clear to me [where they came from]. To recount the experiences in detail would be too much.

About evil spirits: they are able to lie down and feed together with believers, according to Is. 11:6,7,8,9[1]

154. Today again I was shown by actual experience how the evil, in fact, the worst ones of the devil's gang, could be present and make the greatest effort to destroy my beliefs. But even though they labored very intensely, [their attempts] were utterly devoid of any force or power. So they were shown to me actually lying down together and being fed. And they were fed, too, for then they even got to hear the points of faith [enumerated]. 1747, 19 August (old calendar).

In Isaiah 11:6,7,8,9,[2] it is expressed symbolically how evil things can be in us and yet not harm us—and thus that one need not be at all afraid on account of evils perpetrated when one is in the Hand of God the Messiah. The case is similar in the Church, and also in the Heavenly Kingdom today, and later, when evil spirits will learn—but these are secrets, to be told prudently.

About Speech and the understanding of things, with Angels

155. 1) I have spoken with spirits around me about the speech of angels and their understanding of matters which the spirits are extremely interested in knowing about. Having been taught by experience, I said that the angels' speech cannot be perceptible to us, because it contains countless elements almost simultaneously, which would have to be unfolded extensively in a sequence and in many roundabout ways; and that it is not portrayable to us except by forms virtually beyond our grasp and my powers of description, whirling

---

[1] The manuscript has verses 4,5,6,7.
[2] The original has 4,5,6,7.

around together in gyrating motions, following the varying pattern of more inward forms. About these forms as they were shown to me, I have spoken elsewhere [191a–92a].

2) Meanwhile, there is a form of speech, or of very many speaking at the same time, which, when it falls into the lower orb, does not appear the same, but sometimes quite different, for the most part turning into pictorial symbolism like that of the Prophets, which consequently more inwardly contains heavenly, and therefore hidden, matters. There is a reactive understanding with the angels, that is, arising from these symbolic displays, which, when exhibited through our mental images, are transformed into heavenly subjects that angels can understand, so that the earthly paradise can pass over into the heavenly one.

3) It was also shown to me how angels, from facts of nature alone properly joined together, have understood a series of very lofty, heavenly matters. Yet this cannot happen with the angels except through the mercy of God the Messiah. 1747, the 21st of August (old calendar).

4) Such gyrating motions I have sometimes been able, by the Divine mercy of God the Messiah, to feel come over me vividly, and I was able to gather therefrom that myriads of such more inward mental images could compose one material one, we may call it[1], in which such a countless number of elements are contained that a person in the world could never believe it, much less comprehend it. In every more inward mental image, in its turn, [are contained countless elements], but in an incalculably greater degree of perfection.

Now this form, and consequently the influence of God the Messiah through angels, and from them through spirits, upon human minds, becomes disturbed when a person lives in a contrary order, especially when one wants to go into the mysteries of religion by means of knowledge that has been called up by the love of self and the world, and therefore by cupidity. From this there arises a confusion or disturbance like that among the Babylonians building the tower, when their lips were confounded [Gen. 11:4–9],[2]

5) affirming the absence of God the Messiah from humanity, even though all things are nevertheless ordered in such a way

---

[1] The meaning is not that "material" is the wrong term, but it is being used in the sense of "an idea with man in the material world." —tr.
[2] This paragraph and the first half of the next is emphasized in the original by the word *Obs.* written four times in the margin.

that they may be restored to a semblance of some heavenly form. This can take place in countlessly many ways. For no matter what abstruseness, entanglement, jumble, comes to exist in the lower realm or world, it can nevertheless be brought back to order by God the Messiah; otherwise mankind would perish and not be able to understand anything. On this account there is still a spiritual influence enabling them to exercise their reason. The door from the heavenly Paradise to the earthly one is said to be opened when one is acting from what is higher, that is, according to order—which also is "to turn the face toward." *About the Babylonic confounding [of the lip] and the opening of the heavenly Paradise.*

About the Three classes of angels

156. Angels of the first class are to be called Heavenly; they are governed directly by God the Messiah through Love; they have a lofty Understanding of goodness, and of its truth. Angels of the second class are to be called truly Spiritual; they are governed by God the Messiah indirectly through heavenly angels. Angels of the third class are to be called feelings or Goodnesses; they are governed through heavenly angels, as well as spiritual ones, thus indirectly by God the Messiah; for their intelligence and wisdom is not of that quality that they can be governed directly. The rest are called Spirits, among whom there is immeasurably great diversity.

Angels ascend according to their perfection and are therefore to be called higher and lower; or if they are being introduced [into heaven], then they are to be called inward, very inward, and innermost. Now these are symbolized by Jacob, Isaac, and Abraham; and also by Egypt, Assyria, and Israel in Is. 19:25.

About the disturbance of my understanding due to the dissension of spirits

157. Sometimes spirits were granted the opportunity or freedom to disagree about some matter, to the point that one held a different opinion than the other. This very readily happens when there is a slight slackening [of bonds] and freeing [from constraints]. Then instantly, my mind becomes so confused that I understand almost nothing of what lies hidden in the more inward level of meaning [of the Word]. It is as if darkness comes over the understanding and blots out the light.

I have experienced this several times, with great indignation. For sometimes spirits reasoning together—who can be called "reasonings," but want to be hailed as angels of understanding—are given the opportunity to dispute among themselves. From this, a like turmoil arises among lower spirits that utterly confuses the mind and utterly deprives it of the light of truth.

This is a severe trial, when the mind is concentrated on the necessity of thinking—demanded by one's conscience, which I could not resist—and at the same time one seems to lose all patience, and one's mind is anguished by the fear of overlooking that obligation. 1747, 22 August (old calendar).

This takes place also for the reason that the spirits centered on understanding want to be distinguished from reasoning ones, thus to be called angels, when yet they also are spirits, and really the least intelligent when they are left to themselves. Therefore angels are spirits, and in fact, not good when left to themselves; but they are angels when they let themselves be governed by God the Messiah. About this fact I spoke with them today, but they were very indignant—and so, it was proven to them by an actual experience.

A mental image in the understanding comes forth from and consists of a multitude of mental images

158. Today I was allowed by the Mercy of God the Messiah to learn by actual experience that the ideas of truth and goodness in our understanding, individually, actually come forth from—and indeed one after the other—and consist of, a multitude of the mental images of those who are [called] angels of understanding.

So there is a configuration of harmonizing ones when truth flows in, and of disharmonious ones when any confusion arises. The intermediate stages, from agreement to disagreement, are immeasurably numerous. These shapes are composed by God the Messiah Alone, entirely according to the spiritual condition a person has come into.

Therefore, not even the least, or any element of human thought about religious truths and goodness originates from us. Rather, when anyone is allowed for a short time to have something flow in from what is in their memory, then this instantly disturbs and

FROM THE *BIBLE INDEX* 159.

confuses the mental image, like it does when spirits are permitted to argue about something, etc. etc. [*see* 157]. 1747, 23 August (old calendar).

That constant disagreement was wearying my mind; while agreement makes it vigorous and lively—something I have experienced several times before.

In general, about the spirits' normal power of communication with people on earth

159. This morning it was clearly shown to me how spirits operate into us, that is, how God the Messiah leads people on earth by means of spirits and angels. In full wakefulness, I was occupied with a thought that had previously been familiar to me—so much so that I was more or less talking to myself about a certain matter, with fairly vivid mental imagery—and I continued in this thought. (So I was in about the same state as formerly, when spirits did not speak with me, as also now there was a similar state when I was writing these things, and normally is when I am speaking with friends in company, like at the table, and when I am writing letters.)

In any case, in order that I might learn how things really stand in regard to that communication with mankind (because at times I have doubted about this, since no sense can perceive the spirits', much less the angels', operations themselves, and still less those of God the Messiah through angels and thus through spirits, indirectly and directly), after I had been for some time in the state as though I were without spirits around me, suddenly this state changed, and spirits began to address me and, with the consent of God the Messiah, began to tell me what state they had been in when I seemed to be by myself in that thought.

They said they did not know that it was not they who were doing the thinking, believing that they were meditating amongst themselves in that way, and seemingly speaking—so the ones nearest by really believed it was they who were thinking the thought, but the ones farther off less so, and those still farther away less again, but still, even they were to some degree in that kind of state, but with a difference depending on the distance, or what is the same thing, depending on the relationship of the subject of thought to the spirits concerned.

160. When I asked afterwards whether there were few or many of them, I then realized from the way they spoke and answered that there were very many of them. But then on further inquiry, I realized that with a person who separates the inner sense from the outer, there are very many present, who prompt this;[1] whereas with someone who is led only by the senses of the body, and whose thought is captured by everything that comes along and does not dwell very long on any one of them with his inner sight, there are very few [spirits], so that they are led for the most part by a certain general vital force from spirits, although the spirits are nevertheless there, because every person is being led by God the Messiah toward the final goal.

161. I have been informed further, that spirits, demons, angels, are thoroughly differentiated from each other according to kinds and species countless in number, and that each category is together, enjoying their own happiness and pleasure, which are very different in each case. These they pass on to people on earth by way of symbolic displays, at every wish and permission of God the Messiah, so as to perform for them an appropriate work. It is for this reason that mention is made here and there in the Word of God the Messiah of places that were holy, good angels being in delightful places, ponds[2], lovely fields where there are also clear and flowing waters, but the evil spirits in swamps and unpleasant places.

162. What also seemed amazing to me was that I have gotten to know places like these, where I even spoke with them, and have been able to speak with them again as if they were present, although I was a hundred miles away, for distance amounts to nothing; but this happens only insofar as God the Messiah grants it.

About this fact I have spoken from time to time with spirits, and have proven it to them by means of human sight, which likewise sees objects at a very great distance apart from distance, like the Sun, Moon, stars. So why should there not be communica-

---

[1] The index entry at *Spiritus* reads: "There are many spirits with one who thinks separately from the objects of the senses; and fewer with one who thinks only from the objects of the senses. The latter are ruled by a more general influence." Thus, in the original, instead of *internum ab interno*, the intended words were *internum ab externo*.

[2] The ms. has *lucanis*, probably for *lacunis*, "lagoons," but A.W. Acton translates the word as "sunlit groves."

tion with spirits, who are on a deeper plane than that grosser nature where the sight [of the eye] is? So there is communication of even the most distant angels and spirits with humanity. Their being present with me was a sensory illusion; for something like a presence results when spirits are taking part in someone's thought, that is, those spirits who as intermediates and from closest by are to help carry out the matters which God the Messiah wills and permits to be done. These [words were written] on the 24th day of August, 1747 (old calendar).

163. About the general vital force by which brute animals are governed, and also those human beings, to a degree, who live a life like that of the brutes, you may see spoken elsewhere [167]. But still, there are no human beings who do not have their own spirits around them. They are few [in some cases, *cf.* 160], because there is not a great deal of communication with them.

About the usual state of spirits when they are with
people on earth

164. I have sometimes pondered what the state of spirits was like when they are together with a person living an everyday life; for even I have doubted at times that there were spirits and angels around people as they are with me, for the simple reason that I did not sense them, being persuaded also by the commonplace reason that I did not see them.

And indeed I noticed that usually, their state when left to themselves, as they are when the person [they are with] is sleeping, was dream-like in various ways, whereas when the person was awake, it altered, but still differing entirely from their state when with me spoken of elsewhere [207]: I mean that when some person was speaking or interacting with me, they were instrumental means, in such a way that they were not aware of what they heard or saw, as they admitted. Immediately after the verbal exchange, when I reflected inwardly into my spirit, then they seemed to come to themselves, and to realize that they were lives by themselves, separate and separable from people.

165. The conditions of spirits are many, and they will be discussed elsewhere if God the sees fit. Here only these two states ought to be mentioned: [1] That in which very many together constitute one form, and act conjointly, as though they were one person; and likewise then speak as one. Thus do the angels portray the kingdom of God the Messiah in its least form. I have been allowed from time to time to see this and even, clearly, the activity of their [collective] form. [2] Then there is the other state, in which they are removed from people on earth and are consequently in a dream-like condition, like the state of a person asleep. 1747, the 24th[1] day of August.

A demonstration of the effect of envy with the evil, or the hellish gang, when they see the happiness of the blessed

166. After a troubled sleep, near first awakening, there was shown a vision, so lovely—of green, laurel-like wreathes wound together in a long, double strand with space between them, in a most beautiful arrangement, being linked together and at the same time free to move—that the vision cannot be adequately described on account of its beauty and the feeling of blessedness streaming forth from harmony. The vision was quite visible even to evil spirits.

There followed afterwards another vision, even more beautiful and, as I may surmise, most especially lovely because joined with heavenly happiness; but it was not more than rather obscurely visible. There were little children playing heavenly games that no words can describe. These things were exceedingly touching, but they could not be clearly observable and perceptible except to angels in the innermost regions. These things [I saw] in a state of wakefulness.

Afterwards I spoke about these visions with the spirits, who admitted that they too, like myself, had seen the first vision clearly, but not the second, which they also intensely wished that they had seen. As a result, an indignation rose up in them and gradually after that, envy; and this their envy I was also allowed to perceive by feeling it, so that nothing would escape me that might be educational. Their envy was such as to cause them not only extreme annoyance, but even very deep grief, for the simple reason that they had not seen that second vision clearly like the former one. After-

---

[1] The manuscript has the 2nd.

wards they were led along by different kinds of envy, until they seemed to ache at heart, as the saying goes.

While they were in that state, I spoke about their envy and said among other things, that they could be content because they had seen the first vision, and that they would have been able to see the second one also, if only they had been of upright character. This caused more anger, which in turn increased the envy, to the point where they afterwards could not bear even the recollection of it without being stricken with grief.

I am unable to describe the changes that occurred, one after the other, for the purpose of actually showing what kind of envy, and consequent grief, is in store for the wicked; nor can their torments from that one source be described. For I felt that envy not as my own, but as theirs. At given stages that the different types of envy passed through, I spoke with the spirits, but I was unable to comfort them in any way.

From all this I was able to learn in some measure what the state of the wicked will be like, specifically in regard to envy, when they see the blessedness of the upright. Many things happened that I could not retain in my memory. Nor did those spirits want them to be revealed, as is usually the case, on which account they are even permitted to snatch away the remembrance of certain matters. 1747, the 25th, 26th days of July[1].

About the life of brute Animals

167. About the life of brute animals I spoke with angels, and I said that they are ruled by a kind of general vital force, which is the life of demons and spirits. For demons and spirits are arranged in classes, and by kinds and classes they are kept in their order and in their suborder. Now because they are forms of energy, a general life emanates from them that is actually concordant with the diverse powers and abilities brute animals possess. This is true of every other form of energy: it spreads itself out and builds up a field, which may be called a field of energy, and extends itself in the finer regions of nature to a great, in fact immeasurable distance.

Every demon and spirit has their own field of energy, as has been demonstrated to me in many ways, as also do all collec-

---

[1] Probably for August

tively have one. The field of energy agrees with the rank in which they are, and unless that order were maintained by God the Messiah, every single life form on earth would perish, in fact the whole heaven would be thrown into confusion.

This is the reason why animals live according to their own nature, and do not deviate from it, and why the various kinds of animals are aroused by different physical objects, and by changes in the condition of either blood[1]. Man, however, and evil spirits, because they live a life contrary to nature, must absolutely be ruled by God the Messiah through angels of various classes, and also by spirits who are given greater power to operate with a person who is let into temptations. And unless people on earth were ruled by God the Messiah through angels and spirits, the part of their mind devoted to understanding could by no means be opened, or instructed, for we are born without understanding, and the understanding develops in the course of time. It is different in the case of brute animals.

The education of little children in heaven

168. But as for little children, they are governed by angels, and this at first by means of a general vital force, and afterwards by a more particular one, as their mind develops in reason and understanding. However, little ones who die in their early infancy, who have as yet no understanding, and as yet no acquired character, these after the death of the body are trained in heaven among angels—and about this development and education, there is much to tell, but the matter has not yet been revealed to me in such a way that I am able to speak about it from sufficiently lucid experience.

About the most High God and creator of the universe as seen by those who do not acknowledge God the Messiah as the Mediator

169. I spoke with spirits about whether any can acknowledge the Supreme Jehovah, Parent of our Savior, as the supreme Creator, who do not acknowledge God the Messiah, and who are carried away by cupidity into wrong living; and then it came to me quite vividly that they cannot acknowledge any other as the creator of the

---

[1] Probably referring to the "spirits" and the "serum," see 962.

universe except some entirely earthly God, who boasts himself to be the supreme one—thus some demon speaking grandiose words.

That this kind of demons do exist, I have learned from actual experience with some who supposed and boasted themselves to be the creators of the universe, and in this way were deceiving many. But it would be too much to describe their boastful words, and the many things perpetrated by them. I will only mention this, that after I had almost come to believe they were as great [as they claimed], they were then thrown down at my feet, and in speaking with me said so much drivel, that I really could not keep from laughing.

So demons of this kind are gods whom those adore who, led astray by cupidity, live in an upside-down order, and then have joined company with those who acknowledge nature as the creator of all things; for they find it impossible, due to the darkness of their understanding and the grossness of their character, to penetrate beyond nature. These things were written in the presence of spirits. 1747, 24th of August.

ᵐNow this is why the pagans acknowledged and adored so many gods, who all symbolized things in nature, and those who had sunk the lowest, idols, but others, different human beings who once lived; etc. etc.ⁿ

On the Punishment of pride, i.e. of trust in oneself

170. From actual experience I was allowed by God the Messiah's mercy to learn how self-trust is punished by the pain of dejection. There was deep grief, unceasing lamentation, accompanied by near despair of any salvation. But I did observe that in the midst of the grieving and lamenting, hope of salvation was constantly present, which softened the pain.

Otherwise, pride is also suppressed by a seemingly spontaneous submission, causing a person to desire nothing but lowly things—but this is a gift of God the Messiah. 1747, the 24th day of August (old calendar).

A continual compassion also attended me. I distinctly perceived at the time that an evil spirit was attacking, and that God the Messiah was ever assisting by inspiring hope of salvation.[1]

---

[1] In the original this portion is emphasized by the word *Obs.* written twice in the margin.

178.   SPIRITUAL EXPERIENCES

About the life of man after death

After the death of the body, [a person's] life remains such as it developed during the life of the body. But knowledge and the like recede that were only instrumental to the person's development. It is the character itself that remains, which is the essence of a life.

About the food and drink of spirits

178.[1]   Everyone can understand that spirits and angels do not indulge in earthly food and drink; nevertheless, they do want and crave to be reinvigorated. But their food and drink is spiritual, that is, they are always eager to know whatever is happening, and are almost never satisfied. The heavenly angels' food is love, and at the same time understanding of truth and goodness, which they enjoy exceedingly.

The food of spirits, who are to be called feelings [156], are many types of feelings, all according to their character; and their eagerness to know things is their drink.[2] For there is nothing they are not eager to know, whether it is their business or not. It is for this reason also, that in the Word of God the Messiah, wisdom is called heavenly food, and understanding, drink.

About the End of the World

179.   So easy it is for Jehovah God to destroy the whole human race, and everything living on earth—and indeed, instantly, and by fire or hellish pains! For there are evil spirits who very closely surround the nature-bound person, and arouse his or her life; and as soon as they are given the power to act, the person is instantly tormented by a kind of spiritual fire, and dies, perishing in a moment, when God the Messiah does not, out of mercy, firmly hold all things, down to the very least, in order.

This is so true, and I can affirm it so certainly, that I am permitted to swear to it most emphatically. For I have observed it very frequently, and indeed, through experience so real that there can

---

[1] Paragraphs 171 to 177 are lacking in the manuscript.
[2] Meaning no doubt their thirst.

never be any, not even the least doubt. This is the "Terror," and also the "fire," by which the world is to perish [*cf.* Is. 33:14–18][1], if it does not repent, and also [the meaning of the words] "that the seas will roar," "the Sun and Moon will lose their light," etc. 1747, the 27th day of August (old calendar).

About spirits of different kinds, and their plays

180. This past night I also observed that there were spirits who presented dreams, and that their life was dreams, while a person is sleeping. When several persons are dreamt of, each spirit plays the role of one person—a fact that I openly discovered upon awakening, for then I spoke quite a while with those who were acting the part of this or that person.

The evil spirits' fantasies are foreboding and cruel, as they delight in treating people cruelly. So that I would realize this, their savageness continued for a long time after I awoke, and they could not desist from it.

181. Even now I am permitted to watch certain kinds of spirits, such as those who are fascinated by measurements and related matters, who by nature seem to be allured to studies of the Geometric sciences. Their imaginings, displayed to me, dwelt upon those studies, so as to correlate them all in a remarkable way with the category of measurements. They did not appear to me as evil.

There was another kind of spirits who were boastful of themselves, yet who were not so bad, etc. etc., actually being only feelings [156, 178], who touch a person with a certain delightful pleasure—and if evil, are to be called Sirens.

182. The different species of Feelings as they are called, when together, speak some below, some above the person, by a method of almost a pulsation. By their positions they seem to be distinguished from each other.

183. The simple speak very simply, but still pleasingly, for good simplicity is in itself pleasing.

---

[1] See also 189.

184.   There are of the lower sort a great multitude, who have little belief and enlightened knowledge by which what is spiritual and heavenly could develop in their character. These are to be of service in providing force, strength, stability, endurance.

How a person on earth is withdrawn from the company of angels

185.   Sometimes I have lapsed into thoughts about worldly matters and the associated worries, and each time I would sink away from the company of spirits. I discovered the reason: the corresponding more inward elements were being separated and my mind was becoming absorbed in outward ones only, without interaction.

This is the reason why the children of the ancient Church spoke throughout their life with angels, and had continuous association with them: because in outer things, the interacting inner ones were portrayed to them. But when people pay attention only to outer things, then they are removed from open association with the angels and are governed by spirits, who in turn are ruled by angels.

Then such a person is indeed governed by God the Messiah, in all things down to the very least details—but in a permitting manner; and in this way, all are protected from evil spirits, every single moment.

186.   Whether the angels know what is now going on in the world, I cannot say for sure; for what comes through spirits to the angels is changed to such a degree that there is not even a resemblance—which is, of course, so that they will not be disturbed in their heavenly joys. For there is an interaction between all things, which can turn [what comes to them] into pleasures [*see* 29].

By means of various interactions, in fact, when God the Messiah so guides all and the least details, very clear, pleasing displays can be drawn forth, so to speak, out of extremely confused and disturbed mental imageries of a person individually, and of many at the same time. This can also be confirmed by experience, for when the mind is generally absorbed in pleasing things, then everything that comes up turns into an aspect of that pleasure.

About spirits when apart, and when together

187.   For the most part, spirits act in company with many of the same species. With me also they have many times spoken in company—a fact I was enabled to perceive plainly. But besides this, there are spirits apart, seemingly speaking on their own, but who are apart for the purpose of taking in and, let us say, collecting the reasonings of others—in fact, of many species belonging to their own kind—and then of speaking with me.

When these spirits seemed to have departed from me, they fell back to their own species in order to pursue a compatible life with them. The diverse species are distinguishable by many indications. They are also differentiated by the sounds of their speech and, when they are conversing and doing things together, by a characteristic murmuring noise. 1747, the 28th day of August (old calendar).

About angels and spirits in general

188. Angels are distinguished from spirits in this principal respect, that spirits bend everything whatsoever that is thought of, or that presents itself, toward evil; while angels turn each and everything toward good. There are also intermediate spirits, who are almost exclusively devoted to understanding things; and through them, for the most part, the fantasies of spirits communicate with the very pleasurable mental imagery of the angels. But this takes place through angelic spirits based on understanding, for there are two kinds of spirits of understanding. The good ones are distinguished from the evil only by faith. 1747, the 28th day of August (old calendar).

About the extreme passion of evil demons and spirits for destroying and tormenting humanity

189. Today when I was extracting the passages contained in Is. 34 about a universal destruction, evil demons and spirits could not restrain the desire to exaggerate them and to unleash their fury, and their state of cruelty was so intense that they grieved that the universe was not being destroyed. Then each of them [wanted to vent his fury] on the other, to the point of wanting nothing to be left, and barely himself. For that desire originates from an inner self-hatred. 1747, the 29th day of August (old calendar).

Spirits had not heard or understood the thoughts

190. Today I was allowed to write something about the inner and outer person when very many spirits were present, as I clearly realized by sense. But afterwards I was told by one of them that he had understood nothing of what had been thought and written. I was thus taught by experience that spirits could not perceive any but such things as agreed with them, and that all understanding of the matters at hand would be cut off from them when it so pleases God the Messiah. 1747, the 31st day of August (old calendar).

About the character of people in the other life

191. People in the other life are not the same as in the life of the body, for now they are not able to pretend, to say one thing and do another, and, making use of the mental intellect, to put on goodness when they are evil. The character pertaining to the will now remains, while matters pertaining to the understanding that have not been branded upon one's character, pass away. So no one is able to pretend to be a different kind of person than they are in their will, thus in the way they live.

There are even deceptive spirits who are able to put on the appearance of angels; but they are the worst, and the cunning ingrained in their character is nevertheless exposed. Few such spirits have been admitted to me, for they must be kept far away from the company of others so that others may not be contaminated, and for many more reasons. 1747, the 31st day of August (old calendar).

About various kinds of symbolic depictions made by Spirits

192. When the physical senses are withdrawn from the inner parts so that the inner parts can operate and stand forth—something that occurs at this day in very few—then mental imagery of a different kind than the usual seems to open up.

1) One kind occurs when one is allowed to *sense* and *become aware of* the workings of spirits, not so much by an inner sight, as by a sense that accompanies dim sight; likewise also their presence one by one, as well as their approach and departure, not to mention other phenomena. In this kind of imagery, which, by the merciful consent of God the Messiah, I have been following now for almost three years, I have sensed and become aware of so many

facts, particularly regarding the workings of spirits, that they could never be described without filling volumes. However, this one noteworthy fact I would like to relate: that evil spirits continually try by this kind of fantasy to stir up hostilities among themselves, and when it is permitted, they may simply fantasize their companions into different kinds of animals, like different kinds of snakes, for example; and their companions, so depicted, cannot free themselves from that illusion before the permission is withdrawn.

So [spirits can be turned] into different kinds of animals, merely by being portrayed as such; and this is the reason why they speak of the devil and others in the fables of the ancients as having been turned into so many forms of animals, and why in the Word of God the Messiah [spirits] are also portrayed symbolically, as by serpents, dragons, wolves, etc., all depending on the desires and the stages of the desires they are in.

2) As to the second kind of imagery, the things that appear to the mind of those who have been allowed to separate outer things from the inner, are portrayals just as alive—with closed eyes, but fully awake—as [those seen] in bright dreams, and sometimes as [those seen] in broad daylight. In fact, at such times, a kind of morning Light usually appears, with a flaming fire, and in that light as well as apart from it, various objects [are seen], such as people and things, as if in broad daylight. And all the while, there is usually conversation going on with the spirits depicting all this.

3) The third kind of imagery is as actual as when one is wide awake and accompanied by complete sensation, so that there is no noticeable difference. But in me, this kind emerged at a time when, and as long as, [my] inward person was separated from [my] outer.

4) There is also another condition of active or live imagery, which should specifically be called the vision of the prophets, when all the least spiritual objects are portrayed by the kind of subject matter that is contained in the letter, or literal level of meaning, of the [books of the] prophets.

5) I have been allowed to see also finer and purer things portrayed, but to me in this state they were rather imperceptible, yet in it the objects were somewhat perceptible to me, but not to spirits.

[m]That the ancients, especially the children of the ancient Church, were in that state and thus saw various symbolic displays by spirits and angels, can be conclusively ascertained from very many sources; but this state no longer occurs, for numerous reasons.[n]

SPIRITUAL EXPERIENCES

192.

Conjugations — I or פָּקַד [*to visit*]

In I or פָּקַד, both in the active and in the passive, the point prevails in the first syllable, that is, פ

— also ו in the active,

— The passive is נִפְקַד.

In II, or הִפְקִיד, פ prevails without the point

— then (יִ) in the active, and ה with ֲ in the passive without (יִ). The passive is הָפְקַד.

In III, פִּקֵּד, the point prevails in both syllables ק and פ.

— In the passive ֻ prevails, as in פֻּקַד.

In IV הִתְפַּקֵּד, the ת prevails, with points in both syllables

— it is called the reciprocal conjugation, for it is *to visit each other*.

Conjugation II or נָגַשׁ [*to approach*]

In the Ist or נָגַשׁ, the (נ) is absorbed, and then ג has a point

— in the passive or נֻגַּשׁ, the (נ) is retained, and in the ג there is a point

— also in the (נ).

In the IInd or הִגִּישׁ the (נ) has been absorbed, and the ג has a point

— in the passive the (נ) has been absorbed, and everywhere there is a (ֻ) as in הֻגַּשׁ, with a point.

In the IIIrd or נִגַּשׁ, the נ is kept, but with a point in the ג

— in the passive likewise, with ֻ under the נ, as in נֻגַּשׁ.

FROM THE *BIBLE INDEX*

In IV or הִתְנַגֵּשׁ: as above, everywhere with the (נ).

Conjugation III or יָשַׁב [*to dwell*]

In I or יָשַׁב, in the active just like with נָגַשׁ, the (י) is absorbed like the (נ) above.

—In the passive for (י) ו is substituted, as in נוֹשַׁב, and the ו or ו is kept everywhere.

In II or הוֹשִׁיב, there is everywhere a ו, with an added (י ִ).

In III or יֵשֵׁב the (י) is kept everywhere, with a point in the שׁ

—in the passive under the י is ֶ , as in יֵשֵׁב, the י and the point in שׁ are kept.

Conjugation IV or מָצָא [*to find*]

In I or מָצָא, there is a ו as in פקד, except in the future, where there is אֶמְצָא.

— In the passive there is a point in the מ.

In II or הִמְצִיא, י ִ prevails without a point in the מ

— in the passive ה with ֻ as in הִפְקִיד, or הָפְקַד.

In III or מִצֵּא, the point prevails in צ, as in פִּקֵּד.

— In the passive there is ֻ under the מ.

Conjugation V or גָּלָה [*to reveal*]

I or גָּלָה: in the active and passive like מָצָא.

II or הִגְלָה; here י ִ does not occur as it does in the previous cases.

192. SPIRITUAL EXPERIENCES

III or גָּלָה, is recognized by a point in the ג and in the ל.

— likewise the passive by a point in the ג and ל, and also by the ְ , as in גֻּלָה.

IV or הִתְגַּלָה, as elsewhere.

Conjugation VI, or סָבַב [to turn about]

In the Ist or סָבַב, the prevails, as in פָּקַד

— but not in the passive or נָסַב; here a point is in the ס.

In the IInd or הֵסֵב, as usual but without י and without a point in the ס.

— In the passive הוּסַב, the ו prevails throughout.

In the IIIrd or סוֹבֵב, the וֹ prevails with double בב

— likewise in the passive.

In IV or הִסְתּוֹבֵב, as usual, with ס placed before the ת.

Conjugation the VIIth or קָם [to arise]

In the Ist or קָם, the ו prevails, as in קוּם.

— In the passive also, the ו prevails, with a point in the ק.

In II or הֵקִים, (יִ) prevails.

— In the passive (יִ) turns into (וּ), as in הוּקַם.

In III or קוֹמֵם, double מם prevails, and also וֹ

— likewise in the passive.

In IV or הִהְקוֹמֵם, as usual.

FROM THE *BIBLE INDEX*   194.

About the permission given to evil spirits, and about how they are restrained or withheld; they are less than nothing

193. In the course of much and daily experience, I have noticed that evil spirits were able to carry out or exercise their malice at one time a lot, at another little. The reason for this was today disclosed to me more clearly than formerly, namely, that to the extent that their restraints are slackened or loosened by God the Messiah [working] through angels, they carry on in evil ways; but to the extent that angels are active, their bonds seem to be tightened, that is, their power of action is taken away, so that finally they can do nothing, and do not even know what they were about to do.

It is as if the amount of slackening and tightening of their bonds were being precisely and exactly weighed, as on a scale, depending upon what degree of liberty God the Messiah wills that the person [they are with] be let into. It is such an exact balancing that it cannot be described on account of the countless number of different cases.

Likewise, when they are permitted to speak in a condition of slackened bonds, they say horrible and filthy things, whereas in the condition of tightened or so to speak pulled in reins, or [restricted] freedom, they speak from themselves, or from others. When from others, which also occurs with immensely great diversity, then they say things they do not want to say, such as truths contrary to their character—or else, they simply do not know what they are saying. 1747, the 2nd day of September (old calendar).

From all this it follows that they are nothing, or less than a nothing.

Spirits and angels suppose that they are acting and speaking from themselves, even though they do so from others

194. I have also very often observed that spirits or angels acting or speaking with me supposed they were doing so from themselves, when yet it came from others more inward, and still more inward than themselves, who were also given the power to slacken and to tighten the restraints governing the will and the mouth, spoken of above [193]. When I had observed this and told them about it, they were indignant for a little while, but still could not but acknowledge it.

195. SPIRITUAL EXPERIENCES

From this we may conclude that there are intermediary functions in a continuous chain, distributed in an incomprehensible manner by God the Messiah, consequently also intermediary stages of permissions in succession, which always increase in proportion to evil intent as the descent is made toward evil spirits.

It follows from all this that the permissions of higher angels look to better goals than those of lower ones, in descending order; and that a permission granted directly by God the Messiah, is for the sake of the best or final goal, namely the Heavenly Kingdom, in regard to humanity, and thereby the glory of Jehovah. 1747, the 2nd day of September (old calendar).

195. Another reason why it became quite clear to me that there are intermediary stages of permissions in succession, is that I myself have been allowed several times to permit spirits to speak, and this, taking into account the fact I pointed out earlier, that they were led by their own nature and could not refrain from so speaking—although they were indignant later that they were permitted to do these things, because in this way their character was exposed.

The states of human minds are portrayed symbolically by seasonal changes, such as by rains, in the morning

196. Matters of the spirit are frequently portrayed symbolically by those of nature, as by clouds of diverse density and color, by clear weather, by storms, winds and calms, by hail storms, also rains of different kinds. Now since symbolic portrayals of such matters are extremely familiar to us also, as figurative comparisons of the same, obviously very many spiritual conditions answer to these phenomena of nature.

About the setting in order of evil and ungodly spirits

197. That spirits are arranged by kinds and species into classes has, I believe, been said before [161], and, in regard to any given society in particular, so arranged that in their midst are the worst, such as those who had knowingly departed from and obscured the light of truth. Going outward, those closer to the circumference are better by degrees, and at the periphery are those who, though similar to the rest, had not known better.

This arrangement is made by God the Messiah, so that the worst ones are surrounded and restrained, for they are unable to act or to speak except as a group. According to the judgment of God the Messiah, the spirits toward the outside are allowed to speak or to do—many as one, so it is the collective speech of many—things that are not too harmful, in times of temptation; and the spirits toward the inside, too, as in times of inward temptations. 1747, the 4th day of September (old calendar).

All spirits and people on earth are held in bonds

198. Something I have very often noticed was that all spirits were held in bonds, that is, in the kinds of restraints that withheld them from breaking out into lusts and passions—each species of spirits in a bond different from that of another. And to the extent that they are given the liberty, they rush into lusts and passions beyond measure, unless held in suitable restraints by God the Messiah. Likewise also the angels, for each one of them, like people on earth, is evil to the core.

Today I also found out that one spirit, when his bond was loosened, flew up on high, and wanted to go still higher, and if he had been allowed to fly forth in pursuit of his lust, I do not doubt but that he would have burst, or else fallen to nothing. For a spirit, like a person in the world, if given the liberty to break away and follow the impulse of his lust, does not abstain from the ardor of his passion until he bursts. 1747, the 5th day of September (old calendar).

About the working of spirits and angels in regard to human thoughts

199. Experience has confirmed that if the spirits through whom a person's lower thoughts or material mental imagery is governed, were not thinking together with and being held in the same thought the person is thinking or speaking—that person would not be able to think at all, but from a turmoil of differing thoughts among spirits, would be plunged into the greatest darkness and would not be able to understand anything, even in everyday matters.

As for the angels, however, especially the very inward and innermost ones, they seem to be able to think together with humans on earth, because they are in a higher realm, from which their thoughts can flow into human minds without distracting, still less confusing them. For one mental image of human thought can be composed of almost immeasurably numerous mental images of the heavenly angels, and besides, the angels' thoughts are harmonious and unanimous, thus in no way distracting. They are therefore exceedingly delighted when a person on earth becomes a believer, for then they can stream into his or her thoughts with heavenly joy. This is why it was said by [God the Messiah][1] that the angels greatly rejoice over a person who repents [Luke 15:7,10], that is, a person who accepts the faith. 1747, the 5th day of September (old calendar).

Much of the inward content of the Word of God the Messiah cannot be learned from the experience of the present human race, but from that of the ancient human race, and of spirits

200. One comes across very many things in the Word of God the Messiah, both in the Old and the New Testament, which cannot but appear as unintelligible. But this is because the human race living today has completely changed from the race that lived in the ancient Church, and afterwards in the earliest [Christian] Church. If they had been living today, they would have been able to know very well [what those things meant] from experience and by means of revelation [given] to them.

It can also be learned better by observing the condition of the spirits and human souls now filling up the lowest realm of the heavens. This is the reason why I am being permitted to bring in experiences from them, too, about things almost erased from human memory today, and in this way to make up for the ignorance.

These words [were written] in the presence of spirits, who became indignant that their experience was being taken, 1747, the 15th of September (old calendar), such as what is meant by *being drunk*, by *blushing*, and the like.

---

[1] In the original, there is a space in place of these words, which were first supplied by Dr. J.F.I. Tafel.

A filthy odor

201. When religious truths and goodness are being broken down and thereby blocked off, then this is depicted by filthy odors, like that of a swamp, or of a corpse; so also if this is being done for the sake of one's pleasures. Therefore a similar offensive and filthy odor presented itself to me, when my eyes were closed, at nighttime.

About the devil's Extreme Wickedness

202. That he could be so wicked as to be able to tempt the Messiah most deeply, I have wondered at within myself! But I have heard from heaven that because [the devil] was created into a state of perfection, and fell from it, such wickedness as was in him cannot ever be imagined; and because Adam had been infected by that wickedness, he was cast out of the paradise, and the way to the tree of life was put under guard [Gen. 3:24]; for he is able to corrupt every human being, except the Messiah Alone. But now he is kept in bonds; only his gang is let out, which is therefore meant by "the devil," as he is called. 1747, the 23rd day of September (old calendar).

About the condition in which spirits and angels perceive things that are in the body and in the world

203. The condition of angels and spirits in people on earth is such that they cannot perceive any of the things that are in the lower realms, except in those persons to whom the gate into heaven has been opened. Such a person can devote himself to inner matters, when the senses have been withdrawn from outer ones.

The reason why the angels and spirits in this case do perceive things is that they then more or less attract perceptions, and the person on earth passes these on to them by consciously mirroring the things, as if inviting them to perceive the surroundings. This has been verified by numerous instances.

So angels and spirits perceive nothing whatever from humans, except insofar as they are given that ability by God the Messiah. As for the reflecting that enables them to perceive, much would have to be told about it. 1747, the 4th day of October (old calendar).

204. SPIRITUAL EXPERIENCES

About the gentiles, or the uninformed: they come into the Heavenly Kingdom more easily than the informed

204. Today I was shown by actual experience how gentiles with an evil character more easily embrace the faith and practice charity than those who have been instructed. Gentiles somewhat evil in character were [present] for quite a while and stirred up many evil things; but they did this for the reason that they had been unable to hear and understand what had been said and talked about. I judged them to be evil spirits, but later, when the light of understanding was given them by the mercy of God the Messiah so that they would understand like the informed, they began to speak, and very devoutly, calling upon the mercy of God the Messiah, and displaying heartfelt charity toward the others; so they were allowed to join them.

They behaved so kindly and so intelligently and wisely, that I could not but marvel; while on the other hand, the informed were indignant at their being admitted into heaven. Thus those they had judged to be spirits were changed into angels.

About the persecution of those same ones this last night and the evening before, I cannot say anything except that there were persecutions and lamentations. I can testify that there were persecutions of the devout gentiles by the informed. 1747, the 6th day of October. This also confirms [the prophecy] that from Arabia would come those who would strike the instructed with shame, as we read in Chapter 66 of Isaiah. Obs.: When the light of understanding is taken from them, then they are evil, which they complained about vehemently; whereas when the light of understanding is dawning, then they quickly change, and are good and affectionate; it is different with the informed.

About the deceptions of the senses in all things: unless they are dispelled, truth can never appear

205. Angels were very amazed that people of the present time, even those reputed to be learned, do not grasp the fact that the human being is composed of three distinct faculties—in addition to the body, which will die—that actually relate to so many heavens of angels. And they were also surprised that people still do not know that a human being's life does not at all belong to the person, but that all life is poured in by God the Messiah.

In other words, people are under such great shadows and deceptions, that they can hardly believe otherwise than that the eye sees of itself, thus that the mind within feels of itself, and that the human intellect understands of itself—when yet a lower entity [is governed] by one higher than itself, and all [are governed] by the Highest, thus by God the Messiah. It is only instrumental functions that human beings have [from Him], by which they are individuated, as everyone can understand.

Therefore, if we do not dispel these fallacies, we can never be said to abide in truth. To have faith, it is necessary that one believe truth; this opens up the way to God the Messiah, Who is Truth Itself.

Therefore they are also greatly amazed—since human beings do not perceive by sense even the most nearby causes behind the objects of nature [and yet believe they are there]—that they should be unwilling to believe in the spiritual, heavenly and Divine realities that are remote, remoter and remotest, unless they perceive them with the eyes, and practically feel them. 1747, October 9th.

SPIRITUAL EXPERIENCES

[**This second section of experiences extracted from volumes of the *Bible Index*, containing paragraphs 206 to 972½, was originally written at the end of the *Bible Index of the Prophetical Books*.**]

Abraham does not know us, as we read [Is. 63:16], and the angels do not know us

206. For a long time I believed that the innermost and very inward angels knew what I was doing and thinking, since I thought it was their doing that the evil plans and deceptions of lying spirits were constantly being restrained. But when I was allowed on several occasions, by the Divine Mercy of God the Messiah, to speak with others who were bringing down the thinking of those angels to me, it was told by them that those angels did not know at all what I was doing or seeing, as did the spirits closest by, but that they were nevertheless continually reacting against the endeavors and acts of evil spirits, or of their aura, which they sensed most keenly, but did not know from what cause or from what person [it arose]. So it is only God the Messiah, Who acts through His angels, Who sees and knows every least thing, and Who therefore directs human endeavors. Now this is what is meant by the words, "Abraham does not know us." Today by means of a certain abstract thought, something ascended to the angels which moved them. They were surprised, and then spoke with me through others. 1747, the 13th day of October (old calendar).

Nor do the angels want to know what is going on on earth, because they are aware that everything has gone to corruption and ruin; wherefore they desire that the Kingdom of God the Messiah may come, hoping that communication may thus be opened up between them and mankind.

About the normal state of spirits with people on earth [164]

207. Spirits around or in people who do not speak with them or reflect upon them, do not at all believe they are those people they are present with, but only that they are people, and that they live like them. For every spirit believes himself to be a person on earth, and is indignant if told otherwise. In fact, they think they have ears, eyes and senses such as people on earth, and when I told and showed them that this cannot be the case, for several reasons, it displeased them.

1) But because I was able, by certain reflections granted to me by God the Messiah's mercy, and several other methods, to give them the feeling that they had use of bodily senses, I came to the conclusion that this idea does remain with them after the death of the body, and that the more inward aspects of a person do not know otherwise than that they are a human being, for into the image [of the more inward person] the body was formed [in the first place]. By means of muscles, the body acts in unison with the will, as is well known, whence comes the abiding idea of body.

2) Today also I was shown that spirits could be present and speak with me, as well as perceive my thoughts—and nevertheless see nothing that I did. So I was almost sent back into my former state; then I could feel nothing whatever of their operation as I usually could, except so little that I could hardly tell the difference between this and the ordinary state. 1747, the 13th day of October (old calendar).

Things that spirits most especially shrink from, such as sharp articles, and certain kinds of animals

208. There are some things which spirits most especially shrink from, as when anything like sharp, pointed articles were imaged in my mind, immediately then, as if aroused, they would start to make trouble. I believe this was due to the fact that things of this nature cannot be conveyed and portrayed to the angels; for earthly figures are those that are comparatively sharp, while heavenly forms begin from what is circular. There are certain kinds of animals also which they very much abhor for the same reason, such as those, I suppose—I am still not sure about this—which are forbidden in the books of Moses and considered as profane.

About a Spiritual property on the plane of nature, and the fact that religious truths can be preached by an earthly-minded person

209. What we are calling a spiritual property on the plane of nature is that element within the light of nature that gives people the ability to reason in general, even about spiritual and heavenly matters, and about religious truth, and also to preach and persuade regarding them, even if it is an earthly-minded person. It should be noted that [with such,] these are matters of the memory, which are brought forth by a native perspicuity, and this from various motives and desires, both short and long range.

The spiritual property that endows an earthly person with the ability to reason is something spiritual that does not have the heavenly within it, because if it had, then it would come forth from what is heavenly, thus from the geniune source, that is from Love, thus from God the Messiah. However, one may think of this spiritual element as being encompassed by the heavenly, because without the heavenly element, no ability to reason can exist.

About general fields arising from everything in the Kingdom of God the Messiah

210. Nothing more amazing and unbelievable can be told than that there are seemingly general realms or fields of those properties which constitute God the Messiah's Kingdom, that interact with those in human minds, both the more inward and the inward, which are in the Kingdom of God the Messiah. These fields cannot be described, but the matter could be illustrated by a comparison.

In general, there are higher and lower heavenly, as well as spiritual, fields. The lowest realm has been ruined as long as it is allowed for evil spirits to inhabit it, and this field still rises up even to the rational realm, and disturbs it.

Today, by the mercy of God the Messiah, I was placed in that rational field in such a way that the reasoning part of me was in harmony with that realm, which was therefore not disturbed as at other times. Then the spirits in it felt oppressed, saying that they could not live in it, as a bird in an atmosphere where there is no air, but [only] ether, or as a fish in air, but wanted to flee away. This tells me that when the Kingdom of God the Messiah comes, then evil spirits are necessarily cast out, for they are almost unable to draw breath in it, as just said. 1747, 20 October (old calendar).

When I was praying, especially the Lord's prayer, I was received into that realm, which enabled me to view the more inward content of that prayer.

All those heavenly and spiritual realms look to the Kingdom of God the Messiah, because they are from God the Messiah,

Who is the Kingdom of God. It follows from all this that there must surely be a general realm, in order for there to be individual ones, which cannot exist except in community; and that all individual things relate back to collective ones, which in turn guide the individual ones—ultimately into the order they themselves are in. Otherwise individual elements must necessarily be cast out of the community. These are rules known to Philosophy, and universally valid.

211. There are also realms of evil spirits which are to be called hellish ones, because they will be turned into hellish ones on the last day of judgment—these realms or fields rise up in proportion to the increases of human wickedness, or in proportion to the destruction of belief on the earth. Therefore, since they have risen so high at this day that they are suffocating or extinguishing all truth and belief, it necessarily follows that the Kingdom of God the Messiah will come shortly—otherwise no flesh can be saved [Matt. 24:22], and hardly anyone of the human race be regenerated.

212. As for the individual realms which constitute the collective ones, each angel, and each spirit, make their own realm, that has its own changing conditions. From the individual ones, a collective realm is thus formed by God the Messiah, which He does by arranging the angels and spirits by kinds and species, or classes, as if in tribes. Whether there are as many realms of angels, and as many contrary realms, as the tribes of Israel and Jacob, is still a question in my mind.

213. From this it can also be quite clear how everything is dependent upon the Providence of God the Messiah, which guides the collective, and all individual things toward the best end. And the fact that in the lower realms, so many incongruities are encountered, which are attributed to luck, is also for the sake of the best outcome, for a variety of reasons.

About the gentiles or uninformed, and the informed, in heaven

214. Strangely enough, the gentiles in heaven are still in a kind of captivity, though not grievous, arranged in orders and levels; and when they were sometimes liberated, they were well-mannered, and easily received the faith, [confessing it] both by mouth and by heart. The informed, however, still seem to be floating up above, but are not in captivity (for what reason I have not yet been told) even though they are stubborn, and deny the faith with the mouth and the heart. But it has been told to me that there will be a turnabout, namely, that the gentiles are to be released from their captivity, and that the informed who have not received the faith are to be cast into bonds. 1747, the 21st day of October (old calendar).

About the diversity of desires, feelings and longings

215. All my longings, both for eating and for drinking, with their varieties, and those of all my senses, also for going places, for travelling, however many their kinds and species, were for a long time being controlled, changed and varied by spirits and angels—so plainly, that nothing could be more obvious, as they say—and this I experienced over an extended period of months and years.

The conclusion clearly emerging from this is, that all longings whatsoever that exist and govern the life and thought, originate solely from spirits and angels, when God the Messiah so permits, empowers and wills. 1747, 22 October (old calendar). There have been [both] slow changes, and sudden ones; and in order to confirm [the fact], I spoke with the spirits who had been permitted to do these things; and I spoke about that diversity, etc. etc.

My understanding, especially of more inward matters, was taken away

216. To this also I can solemnly testify, that my understanding of especially more inward things has so frequently and conspicuously been taken from me, altered, and thus changed, that I cannot keep count of the times. Experiences so numerous are reason enough to conclude that one cannot understand anything, especially when it comes to more inward matters of religion, except what God the Messiah permits, grants, and mercifully gives one to understand.

At times it has come to such a dispute and scolding of those spirits who were openly removing my understanding of more inward things, changing it into a different one, that I am not allowed to describe it. Written 1747, 22 October (old calendar).

*Evil spirits are ever trying to act against order,
even though they are aware that they
are not in the least able to*

217. Early in the morning there was a kind of spiritual conflict, namely of spirits who wanted very badly to attack me, and indeed, with all their strength, but it was as if I had been removed. Although I was aware of their attempts in an extraordinary way, I did not hear their speech, but it was as though a field were withholding me from their attempts. I was surprised at their stubbornness, and the fact that they could not pause, but only stubbornly keep on striving, though in vain; and I was also surprised that they could not accomplish anything whatever, or have influence upon me.

It was a state such as I cannot at all describe; but it seemed to me that if they had then succeeded, they would have completely overpowered me. I likewise noticed at the time that it was an inward collective realm or field into which I had been raised—I do not know whether those spirits were in the same one. I also observed at the time that there was not the least thing that did not come through the guidance of God the Messiah and His compassion toward me; also, that a spirit could not do even the most minute thing except by permission. 1747, the 22nd day of October (old calendar).

*Many of the good are held in capitivity, while the evil
are enjoying freedom, in the other life
About the State of disbelievers at the time
of the last judgment*[1]

218. How good souls are still being held in captivity has been made known to me so openly that nothing could be clearer. I was allowed to undergo it, and at the same time to speak with them; likewise, to learn that they are sometimes granted freedom and seemingly a reprieve from captivity. I cannot describe that experience, how perceptibly I underwent it, and for days at a time; also how they were raised up out of captivity and restored to a certain freedom, and again drifted back, one after another, into captivity. Then too, from their description, how those who are in hell were tormented, and

---

[1] This second heading in the original is emphasized by the word *Observe* written and underlined in the margin.

what hatred reigns there, causing one to persecute another, even unto death.

Meanwhile others, who are ungodly and extremely profane, are still enjoying freedom. The reason for this has been revealed to me, which is that unless those spirits enjoyed freedom, the human race, whose faith has now been devastated, would not be able to live in such bodily and earthly pleasure, and sensual pleasures, as they do, but would be in continual misery and torment of conscience. For if good [spirits] and angels ruled in that lowest heaven, they could not but infest mortals with continual torment of the conscience; and this, for many reasons, is not allowed as yet, while the devastation process still goes on.

But at the time of the last judgment, the upright who have lived in ignorance, called by the prophets "the gentiles," are to be released from their captivity, and evil spirits to be thrust down into harsh captivity and hell, as the prophets foretell in many passages. Then there will come upon mortals leading an ungodly life, and also upon those like them in the other life, the anxiety about which God the Messiah speaks [Himself][1], as well as through the prophets. 1747, the 24th day of October (old calendar).

I have spoken about these matters with those who are in captivity, and those who are in freedom. Those in captivity take consolation, thus have hope. Many of those who flit about freely have no care, believing that this is not true.

I seemed to be given the ability to communicate heavenly pleasure to upright souls in captivity

219. Since many years ago it has been granted to me to clearly sensate heavenly pleasures in different ways, and so many of them and in such a variety of ways, that I cannot in the least describe those pleasures. They were of a kind that a person on earth could never believe or understand, if I should attempt to describe them.

In any case, today, by the mercy of God the Messiah, heavenly pleasures were given to me, not expressible, which I was then allowed to transfer—as if they were from me, when yet they were not from me—to souls in captivity, who said they were able to feel those pleasures, and from them they also received consolation.

---

[1] Possibly a reference to Matt. 24:15, Mark 13:14, Luke 21:20.

Moreover, they are called birds[1]—which is a great comfort to them—because of the way they rise up from captivity into a kind of freedom, both of speaking and of understanding, of perceiving, speaking and seeing; nor can I describe their pleasure, even though I am being allowed to perceive it tangibly. 1747, the 24th day of October (old calendar).

An image of the last judgment depicted
About the torment, and finally setting free of the unhappy
A dispute about mercy

220. This night when I awoke, many things were exhibited to me that are rather hard for me to describe. There appeared a kind of revolt by spirits, for I plainly saw that many who were in the last heaven were being thrust down, and many who were in captivity were rising up. But what was granted to me to see very clearly was that the unhappy ones who for a long time had been in harsh captivity were striving, many at a time, with those who were in freedom in the last heaven and who wanted in fact to deprive them of mercy, thus all hope of salvation.

This dispute continued by day, until I awoke. They complained greatly, with much anxiety, and this over and over again, that the others wanted to take away mercy, and that then it would be over with them. For they had been undergoing severe punishment, so that they wanted nothing more than to lose their life completely. The only hope brought to them by God the Messiah was that they were able to think there was still mercy; and when the wicked ones having freedom wanted to take even this away, their anxiety was doubled, and they were falling into despair.

As regards the strife itself, how they disputed about mercy, it is not an easy thing to describe, for the displays like these of spirits evade description. Therefore, when they had complained most bitterly about that injustice, that is, that their only comfort—that there would be mercy—was being taken away from them, finally the hope dawned upon them that they would not lose the mercy promised to them. I was even able to feel to a degree within myself an emotion of mercy, not as my own, but as belonging to the heavens, and thus to God the Messiah. Finally I saw these spirits who had

---

[1] J.F.I. Tafel read "sheep" (*oves*) for "birds" (*aves*).

been in such anxiety wonderfully liberated, by a kind of ascending, which likewise cannot well be described. Afterwards I spoke with them, and being very kind, they are now among the happy. 1747, in the night between 27 and 28 October (old calendar).

At the time, I was shown on several occasions that they were almost deprived of mercy—it came very close—so that they were brought to the extreme of distress and [fear of] eternal death, before being liberated. But it was told to me that they had led an evil life.

About the happy state of infants

221. This morning before I arose, I came into a calm state and remained in it for some time; and I spoke with someone during that time about this state—for it was extremely calm, and approached closely to peace. But that it was not the peace I had previously felt, was because my attention was always being draw to other matters, and specifically to a pain which certain spirits caused me in the region of the loins and had now held me in for a second day—and things of that kind.

I spoke with him about that happy state of infants, who were said to live in that pleasurable state. I also spoke about that state [of calm]. The spirits who were round about and able to hear the speaking, but not be in that same state, thought I had been transferred to a different place, because they were not able to grasp anything at all as before, except the sound and its effects. Thence arose a discussion of place, and we were taught by the experience that [a place there] is not a specific location—even though many at the same time can be in one place—but that it is a state belonging to a given realm, if you will, into which one can be brought, in whatever place one may be.

The 3 solar atmospheres operate in the earthly mind, not in the very inward mind; but God the Messiah in the very inward and the innermost mind is the Sun

222. There are four earthly fields emanating from the sun. The [aerial] atmosphere that makes hearing possible is well known.

A purer atmosphere separate from the aerial one is what produces seeing, or sights, by wonderful reflections of all objects. How far this atmosphere penetrates into the earthly mind, or whether it presents material ideas, as they are called, or fantasies and mental images, is not yet so clear—but it seems probable from many considerations. This, then, must be the first atmosphere that governs in the earthly mind.[1]

A second atmosphere, still purer than the ether[2], is the one that produces the powers of magnets, which govern not only in relation to the magnet in particular, but also to the earth as a whole. But how far-reaching these forces are, it is not our job to describe. This atmosphere produces the structure of the whole terraqueous globe according to the poles of the world, and many more phenomena concerned with magnetic elevations and inclinations known to the world. In the earthly mind, it seems to produce reasonings, which must also contain what is spiritual in order to be alive, just as the sight and any other sense must, in order to perceive.

The purest ethereal atmosphere is that universal one in the whole world, which manifests itself in the reasonings of the same mind, whence that mind is said to be earthly. Its inward workings when corrupt are called reasonings, and when in accordance with order, simply reason, which is the outward aspect of thinking, accountable to the spiritual influence.

These atmospheres pertain to the sun, and can be called solar atmospheres, and thus pertaining to nature.

As regards the very inward mind, however, in it there is no such thing, that is, what is of nature, but what is spiritual, and in the innermost mind, what is heavenly, both of which are produced by God the Messiah Alone, and are alive; and if realms are to be given names, these should be called spiritual and heavenly ones.

This morning an angel and I speaking together discussed this subject, and so I became convinced. 1747, the 27th day of October (old calendar).

All things down to the very least in the innermost and very inward heaven that reach the inward and outward one, where there are hellish demons, are turned into evil

223.   For a long time, and more than a year now, I have very frequently and, in fact, daily experienced that almost everything

---

[1] *I.e.,* what is elsewhere called "ether." See *True Christian Religion* 32, *Last Judgment (Posthumous)* 31, *Coronis* 17.
[2] *I.e.,* what is elsewhere called "aura." See the references in the preceding footnote.

coming out of the very inward heaven, which I had also been allowed by the mercy of God the Messiah to perceive, was turned into the contrary, and thus into evil; and it surprised me for a long time, how they were able so suddenly to find those opposite and contrary things. But finally I was given to understand that those demons who at this day still inhabit the last heaven, or hover about there, especially those who inhabit hell, turn what is good into a contrary and thus responding evil, as well as turning what is true into a responding falsity. Turning truth into falsity is typical of the last heaven, and in fact they did this so suddenly and skilfully that I could not but marvel.

I was also given to learn that they did not even know what was being done in the very inward heaven, but nevertheless corrupted it into the opposite, so that there was [in that last heaven] a sort of conversion of all goodness into evil, like the inward heaven's [conversion] of truths into falsity—as happened today: while I was reading [the word] "Chaldeans," they suddenly turned it into "Jews," which was the contrary. 1747, the 27th day of October (old calendar).

All evil, even accidental, comes from hell

224. From things that have been said, it is already clear that all evils, even accidental ones that the hellish demons are not aware of, nevertheless break forth from them. For the innermost and very inward Heaven, acting as means or intermediaries, dispose and administer those things which are foreseen and provided by God the Messiah. Now because they dispose and administer the things conducive to the salvation of the human race so foreseen and provided, therefore with people on earth who trust in themselves, these are turned immediately into evils, even accidental ones. So there is not even the very smallest evil thing that happens to a person, that does not originate from hell.

I have spoken several times about these matters with demons of the inward heaven, and sometimes they would say that a thing could not have happened, because they were unaware of it, and at other times they so obviously did things they could not deny, that they openly admitted having done them. 1747, the 27th day of October (old calendar).

FROM THE *BIBLE INDEX*

The worst demons, or furies, are shut up in hell, and they cannot be released from there without the human race being destroyed

225. No one can possibly conceive how harmful that gang is that is kept bound up in hell. Some of them who had been slightly loosed, attacked me so hard, and so very cunningly and sharply, that I would never have been able to believe such poisons could ever exist. This is why that gang is kept bound up in such a way that they cannot as much as open their mouth to, much less attack, anyone except the very worst kind for whom there is no more hope, or when someone aroused with murderous hatred is committing criminal acts. Unless this hellish gang were held in bonds almost like chains by God the Messiah, the human race would perish.

But their bond is loosened, as far as it is permitted, when a person on earth falls into a fury. I have experienced that fury several times previously, this being permitted for the purpose of enabling me to tell about it.

When I had written these things, the reins of those furies were very slightly slackened, which so alarmed the spirits in the last or earthly heaven, that they openly made known their terror, and then wanted to resort to supplications to God the Messiah. From this it can be evident how grotesque the faces must be of those earthly minded spirits who hover about in the earthly heaven [218, 223]. 1747, the 28th day of October (old calendar).

A conversation with spirits and angels about the indeterminable, about philosophy, about fallacy

226. When new angels had arrived, a conversation with them was arranged, and after I had shown them the things that came before my eyes, such as urban scenes, and more, the conversation focussed on the diversity of auras and states of mind in the heavens, i.e. that they were indeterminably numerous, which was also proved; also, that all variations of state of mind are from differences of love in the people concerned.

There was then a discussion about the indeterminable, namely: 1) That indeterminables can never exist except from the infinite. 2) That indeterminables regarded in themselves are images of the infinite. 3) When they said they were being instructed in things they had not known before, it was answered that they are not being taught by me, but by themselves—which was a paradox to them. But it was explained in this way: one imbibes philosophical knowledge by oneself and by the working of one's own mind, and when we have learned it and reduced it into rules, we are not aware that it is something from within, and in fact, indeterminably more perfect [than if from without]. And because man is ruled through angels and spirits, I therefore must have these things through them [and not myself]. Hence we can now conclude how poor and what a nothing philosophy is, because of which people are nevertheless acclaimed as learned—when yet any young boy whatever is much more learned of himself, or in himself. 4) So it was shown that in many areas, the same fallacy exists. 1747, the 29th day of October (old calendar).

About miracles: they accomplish nothing where there is no faith

227. I spoke with a certain angel, and the subject of miracles also came up, [namely,] that they accomplish nothing whatever in disbelievers, being like a wind that touches, and is dispelled. For there is nothing within such persons to which [the miracles] relate. The descendents of Jacob were such [disbelievers] right after the exit from Egypt, near the sea of Suph[1]; and also later, when they had crossed over the sea.

Certain spirits said that miracles were what they wanted to see so that they would believe, and they received the reply, yes, but belief is on the inside, and takes root in the inner parts of a person; it does not care for miracles, it despises them, but in those who do not have faith, miracles can never produce any root.

These and similar matters are better and more fully grasped when discussed with spirits, who see the entire meaning, together with the antecedents and consequents; also, the meaning is reinforced by a kind of symbolic display and imagery, which is a form of angelic speech. 1747, the 30th day of October (old calendar).

---

[1] *I.e.*, the Red Sea.

About the state of the damned in hell

228. In the night between the 29th and 30th of October (old calendar), 1747, I had a dream from which I awoke again and again, for evil spirits were attacking me from everywhere to the point where I was unable to continue sleeping. After a number of awakenings, when I was finally fully awake, I was being shaken throughout my whole body, and I plainly saw a kind of column surrounding me. I was able to perceive it by sense.

As I was waiting [to find out] what would come of this—I judged that I was being defended in this way from evil spirits—I could feel that tangible column becoming successively larger. The thought crept in that this was the "brazen wall," as it is called [Jer. 1:18, 15:20], which defends believers against the attack of evil spirits. Therefore, when there continued to be this column or wall around me, which could not but consist of angels in whose midst was God the Messiah, Who is the "Brazen Wall," then I realized the reason for it, namely that I was being let down to the unhappy in hell, in order to see their condition and then report to the world, especially to the incredulous or unbelieving person, that there is a hell—and not only that there is a hell, but also what their state is like, though I really cannot describe it satisfactorily. I heard lamentations, and indeed, such as this: "Oh God, oh God, may Jesus Christ have mercy, may Jesus Christ have mercy!" That, which was the first thing to draw my attention, went on for some time.

After this, while I was in hell, and actually in the body as I am today, one of those miserable people was allowed to speak with me, which also continued for a rather long time, but I am not able to recount the conversation—only this at present, that they were complaining about those spirits at liberty, or those furies [218, 223] who are still being lodged in the third heaven[1], saying it is they who are tormenting them, for it is their passion to torment people, and any spirit whatever. In short, their torments are unspeakable. But I was allowed to encourage them with some hope, so that they would not wholly despair (for they were saying that they believed the torment would be eternal), telling them that God the Messiah is merciful, and we read in His Word that "those bound in the pit" are to be released [Zach. 9:11, Ps. 40:2, Is. 51:14], where "the pit" means hell. This I

---

[1] *I.e.* the third in descending order.

also heard confirmed from above so that they might have some comfort, which they then said they did feel.

Something still more wonderful—I testify to you that you may believe it, for it is true—is that God the Messiah, moved by innermost mercy, appeared to them out of Heaven, and indeed, as it was told to me, in glory. Even I was able to discern it, although not as clearly as the unhappy spirits. They made it known that they had received much consolation from this occurrence. It is now being said to me in my ear that the angels also have comforted them and will continue to comfort them. Moreover, I also want you to believe this one thing that I know to be true because I observed it: many of them were raised up from hell and torment, into heaven, where they are living today; and to one of them, who had suffered the greatest torment, it seemed that God the Messiah embraced and kissed him. Afterwards also, many freed from hell were raised into heaven. In the night between 29 and 30 October (old calendar), 1747.

About the fear in the spirits who are still free

229. Very much could be told about the spirits who are as yet free, and are producing all the evils and falsities in the human race. They appear sometimes as though they were insane, for so far as they are permitted, they act and speak without any reason. But when it was pointed out to them that they were still humans, and that they therefore could be rational, and were asked whether they saw that they are wild animals, not humans—then an ability to look upon themselves was given them by God the Messiah, and they acknowledged themselves to be like wild animals of the forest, and worse.

But they nevertheless soon returned to their insanities, until it was proven to them that they could never accomplish anything, and that they would be more unhappy than the rest. When this was shown to them by a spiritual method, then such a fear seized them that they fell to their knees. But quite obviously, the moment the fear is gone, they return to their own nature. 1747, the 28th day of October (old calendar).

About the state of prostitute souls

230. In the night between the 30th and 31st of October, female spirits were allowed to come to me—or I was admitted into the realms composed of them—who, having no serious belief, had lived a loose and whorish life in the world. They consisted, as I was able to make out, of the kind of women who drift about, and do not pursue any other life than one of prostitution, not caring about legitimate marriages. So they are little or not at all concerned [to know] what the inner person is, and what belief is, and consequently, [such knowledge] could have little affect on their character.

These realms, as they may be called, or societies, were divided up into kinds and species. With certain ones of them I was allowed to converse, so that I might know what kind of life they live after death. Their life was like insanity, devoid of reason, not to mention of understanding. I was wondering whether there were insane women in the other life, but I was told that the souls of these were [insane], not knowing anything of beauty or modesty. Such women corrupt everything having to do with true marriage love, especially by bending it toward free love. The number of such is very great. They lead an unhappy life, for they no longer know what pleasure is, such as there is in the other life. 1747, in the night between the 30th and 31st of October (old calendar).

From sadness and insanity, there are pleasures of intelligence in the other life

231. I saw an amazing thing in mental imagery, after having observed those female spirits [230], that is, when I was grieving at the existence of such in the other life whom I judged would be of no use. There was a remarkable symbolic display during an interval of some time, portraying how insanity, blended in various ways, would still gently and sweetly touch the mind.

So that I might perceive this better, there was also present an element of understanding, something like an eye, which was observing, and considered this as pure insanity. But by an amazing interweaving, so to speak, something was being portrayed all the while that resembled lace, meaning that it could be converted to something beautiful in appearance. But that eye of understanding prevented me from being touched by any pleasure, about which I complained, and indeed there was someone who was looking on these things, indignant that I was apparently being moved by insanities thus intertwined, and I realized that if that element of understanding had not been there, I could have been quite moved, and in fact by a new pleasure I had not experienced before in this way.

Therefore, while I was considering further what would become of those unhappy, seemingly insane souls in the other life, and what use they might be to themselves and others—because nothing is ever permitted by God the Messiah apart from the goal of use in His Kingdom—I finally realized that as a consequence of the influence of such souls as these, pleasures could be produced similar to those that flow into innocents and wonderfully affect them. It is of course through the Divine omnipotence that they are arranged like wonderful interlacing patterns of such a kind that from them, pleasures can be woven together and touch blessed minds, especially young children, and thus innocents.

So from insanities, even the saddest and most unpleasant ones, God the Messiah disposing, gladness and pleasures can be produced and grow as if by germinating, just like an abundant crop of standing corn out of the dust of the ground. I was also allowed to get from angels of God the Messiah the feeling of a kind of gladness, from the fact that even such states of actual unhappiness and unpleasantness could be useful, together with the hope that those among these women who are being enlightened in matters of belief in God the Messiah, might also be able to feel pleasures from a different source, composed of things opposite, or the little eyes of understanding. 1747, the 29th day of October (old calendar).

[m]These things have been described to some extent, so that some kind of a portrayal of spirits and angels may be discerned.[n]

The punishment of witches

232. It appeared to me in sleep that some witch was using her witchcraft for the purpose of taking away true love, and thus of weakening a person. When I awoke, the witch appeared, who, being recognized, was handed over for due punishment. That punishment was horrible—I could never have imagined that such a punishment exists. I was told that it occurred when angels simply inquired into her wicked deeds. And in fact it was such that she gradually melted away into horrible snakes or worms, and wholly vanished into them. So she was cast out of sight. 1747, 3 November (old calendar).

FROM THE *BIBLE INDEX* 235.

About displays

233. It is customary with some to present displays especially of holy things, and to make dramatizations of sacred subjects. Dramatizations of this type are not allowable, because the image of them remains after death and by the profane is turned into profane portrayals. For the level of their character determines the subject matter of the portrayals in the least details, so that when the character is corrupt, it follows that the rest of the contents, or the individual details, reflect that, and take on a melancholy and profane countenance.

However, displays of this kind are turned in a different direction by those who are of an upright character, and are innocent, which I experienced tonight while in a wakeful state. For little children, together with innocent souls, softly portrayed the Messiah let down into the tomb, but never did they show the Messiah, but another, in a way that one could know from a afar that the Messiah was being represented; then also how, after the resurrection, He descended to those bound in the pit, and loosed the captives there, and led them with Him to heaven; and that He was joined to His Divine Essence. But as I have said, these things were portrayed so softly, and so devoutly, that they were not in the least allowed to think of God the Messiah except thus as if from afar, so that it would be in no way frightening, as are the dramatizations on earth.[1] 1747, the 1st day of November (old calendar).

234. Moreover, while He was in the tomb, for a short time they portrayed something watery being softly let in, to represent life returning, during which time it was in a gentle wave-like motion. By this they were expressing symbolically, although from afar, as said already, the spiritual life in Baptism.

235. When they were portraying the descent to those below, they most beautifully depicted delicate tiny cords let down by them, by which they wanted to raise up God the Messiah from thence, and by which they also wanted to depict the loving longings they were gifted with by God the Messiah to be able to do this, as they are now

---

[1] "Apparently a reference to the so-called Miracle, Mystery, or Passion Plays common in the Middle Ages"—A.W. Acton.

dictating to me. 1747, the 1st day of November (old calendar), after getting out of bed.[1]

236. It was also told me from within that God the Messiah allows very many things of these and similar things in the world, for the reason that upright souls and innocents who had been brought up with such displays during their life, persist in them. For they only perceive harmless things therein. 1747, the 1st day of November (old calendar).

In a single human thought there are myriads
of feelings and the like
About the Cherubs

237. I was today engaged in a tacit conversation with heavenly beings, and it was given me to grasp clearly with understanding that in one human thought, myriads of myriads of influences from the heavens converge. In thoughts that are empty and earthly, the influences of spirits, or those who are in the third heaven[2], converge, but in those that are spiritual and heavenly, the angels' influences, so that God the Messiah arranges human thoughts by means of spirits and angels, with a variety that is great beyond calculation. Wherefore spiritual and heavenly thoughts, which embrace the truths of religion within them, move [the minds of] the whole angelic heaven, when God the Messiah so disposes.

238. Empty thoughts cannot rise up higher than to the third heaven[3], for there are Cherubim, as they are called [*cf.* Gen. 3:24], who keep guard, and who turn those things which are false and evil into truth and goodness, and at last into innocencies, of which the innermost heaven consists. 1747, the 3rd day of November (old calendar).

What true belief is, how it touches the heavens
of God the Messiah

239. From the above it can be evident what true belief is, and what effect it has, namely that it touches the heaven of God the Mes-

---
[1] *Cf. Arcana Coelestia* 2299, *Heaven and Hell* 335, *Marriage Love* 412.
[2] *I.e.*, the last, or third in descending order.
[3] See preceding footnote.

siah, that is, the angels, and reaches even to the heaven of innocence, and if it is an innocent believing, even passes into that heaven itself, and thus to God the Messiah. 1747, the 3rd day of November (old calendar).

There are Sirens also in the last heaven

240. The worst female spirits of all are those who can be called Sirens, for they mask their wrongdoing with a veil of innocence, with so much cunning that anyone would be taken in if the deception were not exposed by God the Messiah. Such a one was she who was described a page back on November 3rd under the heading, *The punishment of a witch* [232]. Anything whatever that can be found in a person that they can bring out, they do bring out for the purpose of invalidating truth, so one must beware lest anything false enter [the mind], except to be refuted.

About very inward things, or the form of very inward things[1], *which can never be broken through, but withstands every assault, and emerges ever firmer: differently from an inward form, and still more, from lower earthly forms*
m*What the spiritual is without the heavenly: it is broken*n

241. 1) I was in thought about forms and in fact about that of very inward things, which is the spiritual form. It is of such a nature that it withstands every assault.

The properties of that spiritual form are: that it can be reduced by anxieties and pressures into all possible, thus an infinite number, of forms; it can be attached to all forms whatsoever in a lower region, and really be hardly troubled by them at all (however much those inhabiting the lower realm may think it is [troubled], because they reason from self[2]); and it becomes all the firmer, the more stress it comes under. Each one of an immeasurably great number comes together and unites for the protection of the other; for there is nothing in a community that is not protected by the individual, in fact most individual components—even up to an immeasurably great, indeed infinite number—and thus held fast forever, so that it can never be harmed.

---

[1] The manuscript has *interiorum*, but the context calls for *intimiorum*.
[2] That is, from the point of view of self-love, which *would* be troubled.

241.

And many of the things deduced logically from the stability of that form, may also be deduced in regard to its perfection. Collectively it protects the individual component, and every individual component joins together in support of the community; and it is a fact that the more this form yields, or is yielding, or in other words, the softer it is, the more firmly it stands—for then what is innermost, both universally and in the individual parts, which is its universal element, joins in, and so on, etc., etc. [m]And that there is nothing so irrational, that it is not traced back to something rational, thus which does not have a place in the immeasurably great number of finite elements, i.e. in the infinite—that is in God the Messiah.[n]

2) These were my thoughts this morning on the subject of forms; and the angels of the very inward heaven, and of the innermost one, received [them] I believe, but as applied to heaven as a whole and the angels' modes of resistance, stability, patience, and other like qualities, which are spiritual and heavenly; and so they confirmed these things by a voice that reached me, saying they were amazed that such a thought had ever been able to come into a human mind. So when human minds know truths, then from the mercy of God the Messiah, this passes over to the very inward and the innermost heavens.

3) It is entirely different in the case of falsities, even in natural science, for which the learned world today is so avidly grasping that hardly anyone knows what is true and what is good, either in matters of natural science or of morality—as a result of which, communication with the very inward, and thus with the innermost heaven, is being taken away.

When I was writing these things, [I noticed that] earthly words are not adequate, because they contain more of the earthly element in my mind than could be removed so as to reveal what is spiritual more clearly.

4) However, it is a different matter when it comes to the inward form[1], which contains that earthly element that was bruised [*cf.* Gen. 3:15]: this form communicates so closely with the lower earthly forms, or forms that have become imperfect, that they can easily be broken—and the more earthly they are, the more easily. All

---

[1] See the footnote to the heading of this article.

its perpetuity comes from the very inward form, whose perpetuity in turn comes from the innermost, and thus from God the Messiah.

In fact, the spiritual element itself, without the innermost filling it up, so to speak, is broken. This I have learned in many ways, and indeed, by wonderful symbolic displays, as well as experiences. This is the spiritual element that dominates in man today and creates the impression of being more inward, when it is only inward. Therefore it is called thinking, but it is [mere] reasoning; for anything rational is accompanied by the true spiritual inwardly within it, and this in turn by the heavenly within it [*cf.* 209]. 1747, the 6th day of November (old calendar).

It is a spiritual paradox that in human beings, especially in their inner parts, there is nothing but a fluid stream, like the spirit outside of the person

242. It cannot but seem paradoxical to everyone that in the most minute human fibres, there is nothing solid, or fixed together, and thus at rest; for if it were fixed together, or thereby standing still, it would be exceedingly breakable and would most quickly perish, because not attachable to anything. But in the inner regions, not even the least part of a part of a part, even unto the more and the most inward spiritual substances, is at rest, but they are most fluid, as in spirits and angels.

Only physical elements can be said to be fixed together—but not in the way that the fallacy of sight and touch leads one to believe: for the less something is concretized or approaches solidity, the more durable it is. This is apparent from many examples, as in old age, when the parts begin to harden and become more solid—thus to all appearances, more firm—whereas they are then more fragile, and more susceptible to deterioration.

From these considerations it therefore follows that man is a spirit, also while living in the body, and that the coherence of the individual parts depends upon their being yielding, and thus upon their being at the disposal of very inward and most inward elements, and through both of these, of God the Messiah. 1747, the 6th day of November (old calendar).

243. SPIRITUAL EXPERIENCES

About the sea roaring at the time of the last judgment

243. This night I seemed to be crossing a turbulent sea by boat, and soon, when half awake, I saw that sea, so black, with the waves surging up so high, that it would strike anyone with terror. That turbulence in the sea also seemed to be increasing. The waves at first heaved from left to right, then again toward the shore where I was. There were some people on an island or a rock, who were rescued.

When I awoke more fully, I plainly perceived for some time a commotion, with a feeling, as on other occasions, that I was surrounded by spirits, who were rising up. And as I heard, they were the bound from the pit, who, by the mercy of God the Messiah, had been loosed or set free at this place. There were a lot of them, as I could make out from the noise and other telling sensations; and it was also said that the Seas roaring at the last day or time, denote these and similar events [*cf.* Jer. 51:55, Luke 21:25].

The liberation of the bound from the pit is like the coming of the unborn babe to the mouth of the womb in a woman about to give birth

244. A heavenly secret I have been instructed about several times, is that those who had been bound in the pit, or purged, of whom the prophets spoke so many times, are not set free from thence until their punishment or chastening has been completed. When this is completed, liberation ensues like [the delivery] with a woman in labor, in the sense that there is a certain necessity which can no longer be resisted, urging them to struggle forth, and to be set free from slavery.

But in this connection very many things come to mind about the condition of those who are being purged, or punished—regarding [the nature of] their chastening and punishment, and the state of liberty into which they struggle, and the modes by which they are set free—which would fill many pages, but which I do not think would really increase belief.

Heavenly states are of such a nature that if they were laid bare to anyone living in the world, they would not be believed, but would drive them crazy. This is due to the incredulity of those who want to believe nothing but what they understand, and [yet] are not able to understand the causes in nature that lie nearest to their physical senses. How then could they understand spiritual and heavenly things so remote, in fact the most remote, from the senses which they nevertheless want to use to investigate them? 1747, 12 November (old calendar).

About spirits who distort holy things by "plastering with untempered mortar" [Ezek. 13:10–15]

245. Today again, I was shown how the worst spirits distort holy things, namely that they bring holy things to bear as if they were their own, and as it were plaster them over, and bring them in this form to human consciousness; consequently, innocent people can easily be persuaded that the very inward holy things come from those spirits, when yet it is mere "untempered mortar," as described in Ezekiel [13:10].

At first I considered that the sensation of very inward things originated from them, but afterwards, when better informed, I was allowed to expose their deceptions to them through conversation and symbolic depiction. This angered them, especially the fact that from something evil a perception of goodness can result, and one of truth from something false. Along these lines the clay *wall* [v.10] was also explained. 1747, the 12th day of November (old calendar).

They imagine they are good and holy when they are declaring their vows, like the dragon now and then, when yet inwardly they harbor malice, although in that state they do not know it.

About a supplication by certain of the Jews for the mercy of God the Messiah

246. When the sixteenth chapter of Ezekiel was being explained, where the whoredom of the Church of Jacob's descendants is treated of, some of the Jews who said they had been from the sect of the Pharisees, when they had given their attention for some time to the inward meaning of the words, were so moved by truth that they devoutly implored the mercy of God the Messiah, confessing their sins. 1747, the 13th day of November (old calendar).

The extreme cruelty of some who nevertheless profess mercy and holiness with the mouth

247. Something so very cruel was depicted to me this night, that anyone would shudder if he should get even a slight notion of it.

Therefore I want to spare chaste eyes and ears an account of the details. They were proclaiming the mercy of God the Messiah, which they arrogated to themselves alone. For some quite trivial reason, as I explained to them, they seemed to want to lay a most cruel hand upon innocence itself, for the sake of revenge (but in the manner of spirits, who believe that what they conjure up by fantasy is really there). So they were occupied with an act entirely opposite to mercy, but whether they have any mercy, and charity, anyone can judge, since they themselves committed an act contrary to mercy and charity, just for the sake of vengeance against innocence—not against wickedness, or with a good motive.

When the last Heaven is not controlled by angels, those who are there burn with anger and are malicious to the utmost degree

248. I also experienced today that whenever in the last heaven, and below it, evil spirits are not controlled through angels by God the Messiah, they are so malicious and burn with such anger that it cannot be adequately described. For this reason, there is always a controlling presence of angels and a consequent calming effect, adapted to a person's state or his orientation with respect to the final goal. 1747, the 19th day of November (old calendar).

Natural sciences, or the sciences of natural phenomena, at this day are still like the last heaven, which distorts truths into falsities

249. I conversed today with the spirits and angels around me on a variety of topics, and afterwards about the sciences, or the wisdom of this age. It is incapable of serving as a basis for spiritual truths, much less for heavenly truths, but is like the last heaven, which distorts the truths coming down to it from heaven into the opposite. For today, whatever is taught by the sciences about the natural causes of observable things, like those in the human body, such as the senses, or whatever they contribute to a knowledge of the soul and related matters, is full of false hypotheses, in which not even one truth comes to view—in fact, the way is even closed by them to the point where it is not allowable to reach out the thoughts beyond grossest Nature. Therefore spiritual and heavenly things are considered to be nothing.

Since this is the kind of basis into which spiritual truths are coming down, they are necessarily stopped and prevented from entering, for there is no natural truth there to receive, connect with, and confirm them, but it either completely repels them, or distorts them into the opposite.

Hence one may conclude of what use scientific truths, or truths unearthed through the sciences, could be. 1747, 14 November (old calendar).

250. When I say "of use," I mean for those who study scientific matters with the attitude that they cannot believe anything without them; besides its use in schools, where nothing but such material is propounded and taught by philosophers, even by those who are committed to the priestly office. It is also of use because this kind of knowledge is a challenge to youth, promoting their ambitions. An additional use is that by its means, spiritual things let down from heaven are not so readily distorted, so as to blind their minds and lead them unconsciously into a wavering belief or no belief.

Because the world today is considered to be scholarly and does not want to believe anything but what it understands, therefore with people of this character, what is spiritual can scarcely function effectively unless the existing false and lying basis is either completely broken up and perishes, or is converted into a basis consisting of natural truths.

What these people will be like after death, those of them who possess some discrimination can conclude from the fact that life after death is a continuation of the life of the body, and that distortions of this kind, which are falsities in spiritual matters and concealments [of truth], when specific and individual memories pass away [after death], overlay [the mind] with a sort of crust, and thus virtually corrupt the core, or character [see 245]. So they cannot but become most stupid, and thus the wiser they were in the body, the more stupid [they become] (in fact, more stupid than those who had not learned anything whatever of the sciences), because of having imposed the sciences upon the exploration of spiritual matters. 1747, 14 November (old calendar).

The whole of nature in general and in its parts symbolically portrays the properties of heavenly and spiritual things
*ᵐManmade things are of small value compared to those of nature*ⁿ

251. I was conversing with spirits and angels about the things that come to sight in nature, and which no one reflects upon as being like images of things heavenly and spiritual—for example, the way a plant or tree is born and grows from its seed. The life-giving sap of the plant or tree is drawn up through the bark and rind, to be distributed throughout its mid and central parts, just as spiritual elements must go back to heavenly ones. Then also, all and the least of its parts regard the fruit as their goal, that is, the renewal and thus perpetuation of life. Likewise, in every fruit, even those surrounded by hard crusts within which the kernels lie concealed, there are coverings or surfaces of various kinds one within another, through which the juice is conveyed to its inward and innermost parts until the fruit is ripe.

These things depict similar processes in a person who is being regenerated. The coverings depict earthly elements, matters of knowledge and reason, as well as matters of the understanding which are spiritual elements; and, as from a general plane diverging into an infinite number of pathways, they can go back and be distributed to all and the least parts in the innermost recesses. The resulting perpetuity in such things [of nature] corresponds to eternity in a human being's life. It is similar with all things down to the very least in the animate kingdom, in the human body, and in its smaller and least parts. 1747, the 15th day of November (old calendar).

252. It is also remarkable that mankind has not yet rightly observed that all things whatever which are manmade, or artificial, such as statues, pictures or countless other things, may be beautiful in outermost appearance and even regarded as very precious, when yet inwardly they are composed like clay and mud. It is only the surface that the sight of the eye admires.

But those things which grow from seeds begin from within and grow up or advance toward the outside; these are not only beautiful to see, but even the more beautiful, the more inwardly they are viewed.

It is similar in a person's life: those things which begin from the outside, or start with the human, are comparable to what is artificial, the outer surface of which people value and admire, while what is within is completely worthless; but things that are fashioned by God the Messiah from most deeply within are to be likened to those in nature that are beautiful from their innermost parts. This, then, is what God the Messiah says, that all of Solomon's magnificence cannot be compared to a tiny lilly, which is nevertheless little valued [Matt. 6:28–30, Luke 12:27–28]. 1747, the 15th day of November (old calendar).

Spirits also, like people on earth, acquire many habits reflexively

253. Besides other experiences, it has also been observed that evil spirits, who are ever intent upon doing evil to us, also acquire the habit of bringing evil upon people unwittingly. For example, whenever they hear a carriage, or the sound of a carriage, then unconsciously, as if unaware of it, they attempt to force me toward the carriage—among other things also that stream suddenly into their minds, solely from habit; but it is needless to recount the experiences.

(Today also, and previously, I found out that the dragon was learning deceptions that he had not practiced before, and was therefore severely punished, lest they add to his [evil] nature.)[1]

To one human thought, thousands, in fact a myriad, of spirits and angels contribute, all of whom God the Messiah arranges in order and governs

254. This cannot but appear as a paradox to a person on earth, who supposes that a thought is a simple unit, and not formed from tens of thousands of components. But even though it can be demonstrated by very many things in nature—[as] that to one action, thousands in fact myriads of muscles, as well as of the tiniest fibres all the way from the brain to the action, contribute, or, that throughout nature, myriads of rays contribute to the formation of one single object, as also to the propagation of growing things—still it appears as a paradox that something similar applies to a person's thoughts, and feelings, because the operation and influence of spirits and angels upon human minds has not been attested by experience.

---

[1] This postscript was probably written at the end of August, 1748, about which see 2967–68.

But from experience, through the mercy of God the Messiah, I am able to say that thousands of spirits and angels contribute, even though only a few are very close by. I am unable to explain the experiences, but can only say that this fact has been shown to me on several occasions, by sight and also by sense. I have even perceived their operations, somewhat obscurely, but so tangibly that I can affirm the matter with certainty. I perceived them both by sensation and from the murmur, in different ways and at different times, but their situations and states vary, according to the good pleasure of God the Messiah. And this will not be strange to any educated person if he only rightly compares the things in nature with those which must be in the heavens. 1747, the 19th day of November (old calendar).

Like [the experience when] one spoke, and there was shown a bright cloud round about, so that I might see how much flowed in, also [how much] from his speech.

About the very inward Realm, and about Cherubs

255. When I was brought into thoughts about how the very inward and innermost angels influence human minds, and was reflecting that they do so in an imperceptible manner, being in the realm of the very beginning points of human thought, consequently in a like realm of mental imagery or depiction, which is imperceptible (such an imperceptibility must be the plane proper to thoughts)— while I was pondering on these matters, then I was given from the mercy of God the Messiah to sense a gentle kind of turning motion overhead, into which I later even seemed to be raised up, or which enfolded my thoughts. At the first sensation, when I was not yet in it, it was like the turning motion of a soft cloud settling down, and it was said that this can be called "the Cherubs," to whom "wheels" are ascribed [Ezek.1:9,10] on account of that turning motion. After this, that field encompassed me, and I experienced a great calmness. The last heaven, in which I had been previously, was below me, and in fact, at my feet and below the feet. There I heard someone speaking, but as if out of the lowest place, complaining that I had been raised up away from them, and that therefore he did not want to live.

When I was later thinking about the very inward realm, which must as yet be called strictly "cherubic" and in which realm I am while writing these things, I am able to understand not only why wheels, but also why four faces, were ascribed to them [Ezek. 1:10], i.e. "of a lion, of a man, of an eagle"—namely: "that of a lion," because of its strength [extending] into the lower realm, or last heaven, for it holds that in proper order, otherwise it would fall to pieces; "the face of a human," because the very inward person, to which this realm properly relates, is "human" —the kind of thought we have pertains merely to the inward person, which in turn is governed by the very inward realm [*see* 241:4]); "the face of an eagle," because it rises up high above the realm in which our perception or sense-based understanding lies. "The face of an ox" is omitted, and afterwards by Ezekiel "the face of a cherub" is named in the first place [10:14], because then he understood that it was the cherub to whom three faces were being ascribed. 1747, the 20th day of November (old calendar).

Belief in God the Messiah joins the very innermost or deepest things with the very outermost

256. When I was in the cherubic realm [255], I was given to understand that the angels there do not know what is going on in the last heaven, unless, by the mercy of God the Messiah and by the presence of God the Messiah Himself through belief, communication is effected with those in that last heaven, thus enabling [the angels in the cherubic realm] to become aware of and to perceive it.

I have been permitted to understand this fact, due to the mercy of God the Messiah. For except when I was concentrating my inner gaze upon God the Messiah Alone, I received word from them that then they knew nothing about what was going on in the realm below them, and about what I was thinking.

Therefore, belief in God the Messiah, [coming] from Him through the innermost and the very inward heaven into the realm of humankind, is the very thing that joins and associates all things together, from the Most High even down to the most low.

Without belief in God the Messiah, inward elements would be torn away from the more inward ones, and would therefore perish. 1747, the 20th day of November (old calendar).

257. Self-procured belief, however, or a believing one seeks to impose upon oneself, is not worth anything, but only a belief inspired, given, as if poured in, by God the Messiah. For a faith procured for oneself from one's own imaginings, is only illusion, and does not ascend.

But here there should come several observations, such as how a person can know that belief has been given by God the Messiah; and very many other points.

I was raised up into the very inward realm, as often as I prayed our Lord's prayer, though in differing ways

258. Whenever I was praying our Lord's prayer, morning and evening, almost every time I was raised up, in different ways, into the very inward realm, and in fact [this raising up,] together with the change, was so perceptible that nothing could have been more so. This [has been occurring] now for more than two years.

Explanations of the more inward contents of the Prayer were inspired at these times, with a great deal of variety. But when the prayer was finished, I was let back into my normal environment.

Very many of those bound in the pit are ascending, and therefore the last time is at hand
About the place of the lower ones

259. This night at a time of wakefulness, also by the mercy of God the Messiah, I was enabled to learn that very many of those bound in the pit [*see* 228, 244] are now being borne upward by God the Messiah, that is, from the pit (which is below the last Heaven), otherwise called the place of the lower ones.

The ascent lasted for quite a long time, which leads to the conclusion that there were very many. And that it was the believers who were being raised up, was also shown—by spirits of gold, small ones in effigy. From this one may conclude that the last time is now at hand. Therefore, let those on earth be watchful! 1747, the 20th day of November (old calendar).

About the man not invited to the banquet, and not dressed in a wedding garment, who was cast out [Matt. 22:11–14]

260. Today a certain evil spirit appeared to me who thought that he had risen up into the very inward heaven, because he had lifted himself very high overhead and wanted to stir up trouble there by diverting belief from God the Messiah and transferring it to himself. Thus he wanted to exalt himself even unto God the Messiah,

FROM THE *BIBLE INDEX* 262.

and claim His power to himself—not knowing that he was only in the last heaven, where evil spirits are still dwelling. This fact was shown to him pictorially, but to no avail; for he went on with his wickedness.

But because this person was an evil spirit, he had to be dealt with by means of symbolic displays, or mental imagery. Therefore, truth was wrapped around him symbolically, whereupon he was cast out, and he shouted that he was being greatly afflicted, begging to be released from that place.

This is what must be suffered by those who contemplate arrogating to themselves power over the faith [of others]—especially when this effort is the result of more than mere simplicity. 1747, the 20th day of November (old calendar). In his distress he said that he had been instigated to doing this by the diabolical gang.

About the liberation of those who are bound in the pit; then,
What is meant by the pain of a woman in labor

261. Some of those who are bound in the pit are not set free before they arrive at the utmost of despair, that is, until they have paid the last of the debt [*cf.* Matt. 5:26]. This is also called the pain of a woman in labor, and the arrival [of the unborn babe] at the mouth of the womb [*see* 244].

There are realms of calmness, which are to be called auras
of ignorance, in the third heaven

262. This morning I was guided into several realms, so to speak, of the third heaven[1], and in fact to its innermost region (for each heaven has its innermost, very inward, and inward parts) where spirits were said to sojourn who are recently delivered from the pit. There was *calmness*, and nothing sad was noticeable; so that here is the calmness that in the inward degree corresponds to *peace* in the innermost regions [41]. Afterwards, surrounded by something like a column, I was guided into other auras, so to speak, of the inward Heaven, and indeed, to the heaven of ignorance (every heaven is distinguishable into its heavens), where not a sound was heard, but it was calm.

---

[1] *I.e.,* in descending order.

ᵐThese are the habitations or mansions about which God the Messiah [spoke] [John 14:2], which are here called auras[1].ⁿ

Finally [I was conducted] to another heaven of ignorance, consisting of the kind of people who are unconcerned about heresies, and who neither affirm nor deny anything, saying that every person fosters his own opinion. Yet here it was not so calm. It was as if someone wanted to smash the wall with an axe, and someone said that he feared that person might finally strike him.

These heavens are separate, and well guarded, so nothing in the heavens is disarranged, except as to appearance in the inward heaven—which is no longer to be called the inward, but the lower heaven.[2] There abides a gang of lower spirits above hell who carry on licentiously. 1747, the 21st day of November (old calendar).—Obs. The heaven of *ignorance* in the inward heaven interacts with that of *Innocence* in the very inward and innermost heavens.[3]

About the teachability of spirits, and about magic

263.   Besides the many experiences I have had one after another over a long period, I have also today learned through some unique ones that spirits are teachable, and in fact avidly seize upon things that are beyond imagination; also, that the Egyptians' magic on the plane of nature resulted from this fact. For there are very many spirits who try to utter such things, but because it is abominable and profane to do so, their mouth is immediately closed up, and they are cast out from the society. Since they are abominable pests to societies there, they are kept in a place where they are no longer able to communicate their magical powers to others. They are only given access to me for the purpose of temptation. 1747, 23 November (old calendar).

264.   There are also spirits who are unceasingly intent upon things contrary to truths and goodness, seeking to distort them in ways so evasive of our consciousness, that if we were told we would hardly be able to believe it. This has surprised me at times, when I noticed truths and goodness being thus compromised by spirits.

---

[1] The Latin word is *sphaerae*.
[2] Nevertheless, the author continues to call it the inward heaven for some time.
[3] This sentence is emphasized by the words *Obs. Obs.* written in the margin.

But these spirits conceal themselves more than others and are more invisible, so that I was at the point of believing they could not be found. Still, they were found, and some of them were punished and cast out, the punishment being of a kind to fit their criminal attempts. 1747, 23 November (old calendar).

Spirits are being transferred into the very inward heavens, and are becoming angels

265. Today it was granted me to observe that spirits become angels, and that they are transferred into the very inward heavens, and thus seem to disappear from spirits. For they do not speak after this as they did before, except through the spirits who are serving them and whom they control, and who, when they realized this, were indignant. 1747, the 23rd day of November (old calendar).

There is a group of spirits, some of whom are in a person's head, and some outside, and these interact

266. At times I have observed, when certain spirits were outside [of me] and also speaking with me, and when they were thus holding me captive so that I could not get away from them, which has happened to me several times, then at the same time they also had their auxiliary spirits or troops in the head, either within or outside the brain. It was granted me to observe this by manifest experience, for when those outside with whom I was speaking were cast down, then the ones in the head flowed out, and indeed with a sound like something going out, and being pushed out, through the ear. It was evident that there were many, from the fact that now and then ten, twenty, more or less, seemed to be drawn out in this way by those who were outside and with whom they were as if bound together in society.

It can also be inferred from this how a person is kept bound by an evil band of spirits, and that they are within as well as outside of the person, thus closing off the operation of angels. Nevertheless, the angels' operation slips in in a wonderful way like a more inward activity within an action, and so, the person is given to understand what is true and good, although with difficulty. 1747, the 24th day of November (old calendar).

267.   SPIRITUAL EXPERIENCES

Spirits who are sent to a person on earth think
they are the person to whom they come

267. Certain spirits, by ascending, came to me, saying that they had been with me from the beginning, thus that they were the ones who have spoken with me from the start. When I became indignant and rebuked them, because I did not recognize them, they finally admitted that they had just come for the first time, but that they put on, so to speak, everything of the person, so that they think they had been with him or her from the beginning.

It is amazing, but a spirit puts on in a moment a person's characteristics, knowledge, language, and the like, just as if he had possessed them from the beginning. About this subject I have conversed with spirits also from time to time. 1747, the 24th day of November (old calendar).

Human souls are transferred into heavenly joy,
to see the glory of God the Messiah

268. Today I witnessed two people I had known in life and with whom I had been speaking—after the conversation had turned to the subject of heavenly joy, and the fact that the delight of talking with a person after death was nothing compared to the joy in the heavens— transferred into the very inward heaven, into some habitation of it. From there they spoke with me, now as if from a higher place, while it was only from a more inward one. They testified that such joy is unspeakable, and that compared to it, earthly and worldly delights are nothing. 1747, the 24th day of November (old calendar).

About witchcraft, magical arts, fortunetelling
and the like—where they originated

269.   1)   It has been shown me by experience that some of the spirits thought they could do anything in heaven and on earth, if only they were taught by symbolic displays involving divine matters, and brought these into practice, thinking they would have the same result as if they were divine. It is unnecessary to describe the displays themselves. [*See* 233.]

This is at first allowed for a number of reasons, especially because of ignorance, when such things are learned by those who in simplicity believe them to have a miraculous power. But afterwards they are corrupted by desires to practice them in the pursuit of profit and self-glory; then the goal immediately perishes, and they become like fallen leaves, or like shells without kernels, which drop of their own accord, and perish. All this was portrayed to me in a sequence, which it would take too long to describe. 1747, the 27th day of November.

2) At this day, those who engage in such practices have been put down, and spirits of this kind are held in bonds. Several times, when somewhat loosed from these bonds, they wanted to persuade me to learn similar arts, but due to the mercy of God the Messiah, it was in vain, so they were returned to their bonds, where they must necessarily undergo a considerable change, through torments comparable to either fire or decay.

The Egyptian magicians were of this kind, because they distorted the symbolic depictions of the ancient Church and thereby practiced magical arts, probably countless in number—but all of which were like shells without the kernels, or leaves that fall off when the sap is gone, even though they may outwardly appear bright with varied colors for a short time.

Equivalent to such magical arts, therefore, are those qualities in which people seem to shine, such as their own good judgment, and the like, by which they imagine themselves to be in control of everything. Likewise, science and philosophy, by which people believe they control spiritual and heavenly matters, are like fortunetelling and witchcraft. Therefore these are to be understood at the present day by witchcraft and the like, and by Egyptian wisdom, etc. 1747, the 27th day of November.

The environments where souls are after death interact with the parts and members of the human body

270. From actual and quite sensate experience, I have learned that the auras, as they are called [262], where human souls abide after the death of the body, interrelate entirely with the human members; specifically, the heavenly domain with a person's head, but the lower ones with the loins, and the lowest with the feet. For this reason, when I was let down once again into the lower place without the angelic column around me [228], then it was granted me to perceive sensorially that the lower place, where there were souls, corresponded to the feet, so that the lowest place must correspond to the soles of the feet, or to the region under the soles—which, however, I was unable to perceive because I was not let down that deeply.

But also by the Mercy of God the Messiah, it was granted me to feel that the souls were emerging from the lower places and thus coming into the last heaven (in the lower place I spoke with them, also when they were rising up), and that they also gave expression to their gladness at being delivered from their bonds, and from the pit. 1747, the 28th day of November.

The lower place of damnation is extremely cold, and their life at that time had been miserable

271. Those who had been in a certain lower place were many, who are so cold that they seem to themselves obliged to acquire heat through labor, and the cutting of wood; for this kind of fantasy stays with them, and they do not know but that it is real, supposing that this work will make them not only warm, but also deserving of salvation. The cold is comparable to cold in the teeth.

Now these are the ones who are represented by the wood-cutters [Deut. 29:11, Josh. 9:23–27]. Who they are that are being held in such an extremely cold prison, may be concluded from [the nature of] their loves in the life of the body, namely, that they had then been cold, not instructed at an early age in any true love, but only enticed by bodily pleasures contrary to true love. So perhaps one may infer that they had come more from the crowd of gentiles, but on this I am not so well informed. These people were exceedingly glad to come into the day, and to see the light, which also shows that they had been in darkness. No one can describe how miserable these crowds are. 1747, the 28th day of November.

About a certain one let down into the lower place, who was finally raised up

272. A certain one who had been let down into the lower place was finally being raised up, but on the way he labored very hard and struggled with the greatest exertion and labor to ascend, but for a long time it was in vain. From this, I was able to infer that an ascent and raising up comes through God the Messiah, Who Alone releases the miserable from the pit, and elevates and bears them into the heavens.

I spoke with this person while he was laboring, and after he was allowed to emerge from the place of the lower ones; so the truth of this has been witnessed to by actual experience. 1747, the 27th or 28th of November.

*Continuation about those who were raised up
from among the wood-cutters in the cold place*

273. With those who were raised up from the cold place, I spoke later on. Many were also raised up afterwards, and, as they say, into the light. Actually, they are people who have been selfrighteous about good deeds, and have attributed to them the power of salvation. As for the righteousness or merit of God the Messiah, they have regarded it only as a kind of example, which they should follow, not [aware] that He Alone became righteousness for the sake of all.

After they were elevated, they came into a higher habitation, and were there instructed about the reason why they were kept in that cold place and in continuous labor; and there they seemed to themselves to be clothed in shining white garments, for so it appeared to them, because thus the imagery of their lives follows from their acquired character. They were also instructed in other matters about which they avidly received teaching, though something still persists with them at the beginning from their former fantasy, of which they say they desire most eagerly to rid themselves. These words were written in their presence. 1747, the 29th day of November.

*About the habitation of those who live devoutly, but only
acknowledge the one God, not knowing that God
the Messiah is God over the Universe*

274. This morning in full wakefulness, while I was being brought by the mercy of God the Messiah through many habitations, I was also led down among those who had not known that God the Messiah was the God of the Universe, but had still led a devout life. Among them it was really calm; the rest I am not given to remember.

But these also were raised up to a higher habitation, where they were taught, and thus given to feel inward joy, although the notion persisted with them that they had come into a beautiful city, and into beautiful dwellings, besides other places. 1747, the 29th day of November.

Even in the inward heaven[1] there are habitations for those who believe they are living in a kind of earthly paradise

275. I was also guided to one habitation that is even in the inward heaven, which habitation can be called that of the blessed; for they have such a blessed and pleasant life of imagery, that they seem to themselves to be in paradise and to be enjoying delights like those of an earthly paradise, together with manifold gladness. It was granted me to see a glimpse of their garden, not from very close by. 1747, the 29th day of November.

One kind of habitation, where they were being amused by being led around in a circle

276. Also shown was the dwelling of some, where something like a wheel coming down from on high was led around in a circle, and it was said that those were entrenched in this fantasy who care for nothing but things that are different, and run about in search of them, and from them derive their only amusement. 1747, the 29th day of November.

A turbulent sea with great waves was seen

277. When by the mercy of God the Messiah I was being conducted through several habitations of the inward heaven[2], it was also granted me to see, not nearby, a great sea, swelling with huge breakers that dashed against some unseen shore.
It was told that such are the fantasies of those who want to be great in the world and to innovate all things, and in this way acquire glory for themselves.
Thus it is the swelling of their mind that produces this kind of a fantasy. 1747, the 29th day of November. [*Cf.* 243.]

---

[1] See 262, footnote.
[2] See 262, footnote.

The arrangement of the habitations

278. It was also granted me to reflect on the arrangement or situation of the habitations of the inward heaven[1], and it struck me that there was a precise order, so that they formed a figure by which the one habitation faced and enclosed the other, but which I was unable to understand. For from above, I also heard spirits speaking whom I thought to be among the lower ones. So their situation is not determined by height alone, but also by some incomprehensible arrangement.

The arrangement of the glands in the brain would seem to be able to cast some light on this matter, if investigated; for in the individual human being are such things as interrelate, both as to situation and as to arrangement, with those in the universal human being. 1747, the 29th day of November.

Why the heavenly field, vortices and habitations correspond to the parts of a human being

279. The reason why the parts of a human being interact with the heavens and its habitations, and lower things are felt under the feet—and in fact as coldness, according to the experiences adduced previously [271]—is that God the Messiah, as Human, fills the universe, so that the things in the universe interact with Him. Therefore Heaven is God the Messiah Himself, because He is all in all things, and thus the heavenly field, vortices and habitations correspond to Him and His parts. 1747, the 29th day of November. Otherwise, Heaven and the universe could not go on.

The habitation of many, where they think they are building cities and giving them away free

280. Early in the morning I was guided into one habitation of the inward heaven[2] where imagery of a manifold variety prevails, and, in fact, to those spoken of before [274] who had been raised up into a higher habitation. Here they now seem to themselves to build cities, and to give them to others, and even to hide something secret

---

[1] See 262, footnote.
[2] See 262, footnote.

in the city which they want no one to discover, lest it be done violence.

There is a kind of innocence about them, and for this reason they are even protected by little children. I stayed with them for a long time, and I could not but love their life, [which was] similar to a sweet sleep. 1747, the 30th day of November. They are all childlike, and do not know anything of evil, being also in a state of ignorance.

*About my conversation with Abraham, Jacob,
the Apostles, and many more of the ancient time*

281. For many weeks I was in conversation with the Apostles, with Abraham, with Jacob, Moses, Aaron, Sarah the wife of Abraham, Leah, Rachel. At the time, I could believe no differently than that I had been speaking with them; but afterwards, being taught by experience, I was able to deduce that they were spirits who impersonated them in the inward heaven[1], and even believed they must be the same people. For the angels in the very inward heaven can speak with people on earth through spirits of the inward heaven—thus this is done indirectly—but these spirits impersonate them, and are able in so doing to show what those [angels] had been like in the first period after the death of the body. It is different when they appear to a person in the very inward heaven, [thus directly,] which is done by a lofty portrayal. 1747, the 1st day of December.[2]

These things came today into my thought, but whether this is the way these matters really stand, I am unable to find out as yet for certain.

*The worst of the devil's gang cannot exercise even the least
power on those who trust in God the Messiah*

282. One was let out of the lowest hell, about whom see the next page [284–87], who trusted in himself and his own power to overturn everything, even to the point where he thought he could displace boulders. So he was permitted to exert all his strength and power against me, but he was not able to inflict upon me even the very least of the evil he had brought to bear—not even upon my

---

[1] See 262, footnote.
[2] The manuscript has *die 31 Nov.*

thought, except something vaguely. At this he was astonished, and afterwards he sank away. 1747, the 1st day of December.

*I arrived in one habitation where heat
occupied my feet and loins*

283. While by the mercy of God the Messiah I was being guided through several habitations of the inward heaven[1], I was also led through a habitation where heat at once occupied my feet and loins, and then I was told that here the kind of women were who had indulged in a life of bodily pleasure, but had nevertheless desired children; one of them even seemed to me to be pregnant.

This habitation is therefore quite unlike one in which women were who had had no desire for children, where I had felt no heat.

The conclusion follows that these women, even though they had indulged in pleasures, still had not extinguished the natural desire of love, which is to procreate offspring.

About hell and the hellish gang

284. After midnight I awoke twice, and was having a vivid vision of what was going on in the spiritual realm around me, and there was someone let out of the lowest hell accompanied by some also infernal gang that seemed to be carried about in a kind of circle under the feet, around which they were marching in search of [something]. It was innocents they were looking for, and this with all cunning and eagerness. At length that gang, after seeming to themselves to walk a complete circle and to have sought in vain, finally thought they had come upon an innocent, whom they seemed to themselves in fantasy to treat in dreadful ways, inflicting ceaseless blows and lacerations.

Finally they also approached me and wanted to transfer me from one place to another, as one of them said, and then to corrupt me with their deceits, but by the mercy of God the Messiah, I was kept safe. Still, I perceived how subtly they were able to distort my thinking, through a most remarkable influence that bent whatever was good in a different direction, replacing it with something like

---

[1] See 262, footnote.

poison. For the very evil character of those in hell is such that although they do not know what goodness is, they nevertheless sense its presence by means of their contrary character, and corrupt it in a moment.

285. Another noteworthy thing is how fantasy deceives them. For when they have been let out [of hell], they think they are walking around some circle, and trampling the universe beneath their feet, imagining themselves to be the greatest gods. Moreover, the hellish place is portrayed to them as a tub with a covering, and a little globe nearby on a kind of pyramidal base, on which they believe the universe to rest, which they look at, and which they control.

By their fantasy, I seemed to be let into such a tub, where a state prevails such as can never be described; for hell is too harsh ever to admit of description. But from mercy, it was not God the Messiah's good pleasure that I should be let down into it, because of the dreadful and wicked things there.

286. Further, I was told afterwards from heaven that those abide there who have so little left [of what is human] that they remain there for centuries, and that there are people there who have been there already for twenty centuries. I was also told that there is no one there today from among those who perished at the time of the flood (these were released from that dreadful hellish vat), and who have been created anew.

286½. Later, when I was arising from bed, that devil [282, 284] was amazed that I lived on the earth. These things I saw in full wakefulness, accompanied by conscious thought, as well as speech; so that this is the untarnished truth. 1747, the 1st day of December.

287. The lowest hellish gang, therefore, consists of those who act most cunningly, and in fact almost unnoticeably, upon human minds, so that [their activity] is nothing but deception and venom, and indeed, diametrically opposed to mercy, and to innocence.

About heavenly joy

288. Today some of those who were around me and spoke with me—both acquaintances and people unknown to me—were raised up into the very inward heaven, and they told me through messengers that the happiness is such that it can never be uttered by the mouth or perceived by the mind [of anyone below]. Then it was also granted them to guide my hand while I was writing these things, so that it would be as if they were telling and writing them.

But before they had been raised up into the very inward heaven, a certain one who had departed the life of the body not long before, seemed to me to have to shed his outermost parts, or the earthly element that was still clinging. This can never be allowed to enter into the very inward heaven; but those enveloped with the earthly element are able, by the mercy of God the Messiah, to live in the last heaven, also among the blessed. About their condition, see the things reported here and there above [cf. 220, 262].

Happiness does not consist in the kind of symbolic displays, seen by the eye, that exist in the inward heaven[1], but in the kind which the tongue can never utter, and which the mind in the body can never contemplate. Thus Paul, who was caught up into the innermost or third heaven [2 Cor. 12:2–4], must have been divested for the time of both the body and the earthly mind—which is [effected] by the omnipotence of God the Messiah.

2]   Some others supposed that they also had been raised up to that heaven, but because they had not been divested of bodily and earthly elements, they were raised only toward the outer court of the very inward heaven; even they were proclaiming the blessedness [they felt].

Meanwhile, I spoke with several about the state of those who were raised up into the very inward heaven, saying that when they returned to their earthly mind, they would be unable to express the happiness, the reason being that the earthly elements of the mind as it were hide it from their sight, because those elements dominate in spirits of the last heaven, no differently than those of the body and the senses do in bodily life.

Some spirits also who were unwilling to attach faith to these things were then also raised up toward the outer court of the very inward heaven, and they exclaimed aloud that they had never seen nor could ever have imagined anything more beautiful, and more delightful. 1747, the 2nd day of December.

---

[1] See 262, footnote.

289. SPIRITUAL EXPERIENCES

*About the harmony among angels, even so far as
a speaking of many in unison*

289. By prolonged experience this morning, through the mercy of God the Messiah I was shown that angels cannot live together in blessedness unless they are the kind that can speak and act together. Blessedness consists in unanimity and harmony, whereby many, even very many, consider themselves to be a one. For from many agreeing together, or a harmony of many, comes a oneness, which results in blessedness and happiness and, from a shared feeling of happiness, a doubled and tripled happiness.

289½. As for their speech, today by a lengthy experience I was shown many at the same time speaking, thinking and understanding together, as is usual in the heavens.

I was also shown that when there is anyone among them who thinks by himself, or who wants to say anything more [than the rest] due to some kind of love, or to a habit formed because of a given love; or if others who are not similar are brought into their company—especially when they are not yet prepared by a purging process, and initiated—then that discordancy among the many is at once quite clearly felt, so that it can never fail to be found out who of the spirits is at variance. So that spirit is dissociated in some way, depending upon the nature of his dissent, until such a time as he is prepared, and becomes accustomed to joining in, and to taking an active part himself in creating heavenly harmony.

Therefore it is unanimity coming from the love of society, this in turn coming from the love of God the Messiah, which makes what is heavenly. 1747, the 3rd day of December.

*Souls after death see their own parents, children, friends,
and experience from this an innermost gladness*

290. That souls after death see each other, and join in conversation, and even think it is just as if they were together on earth—in the beginning, that is, before they have been well initiated in spiritual matters—to this I can testify, as well as to the fact that they experience an innermost gladness, provided there had been a mutual love between them in the life of the body. 1747, the 3rd day of December.

FROM THE *BIBLE INDEX*

The power of the devil is mere illusion, and thus boasting, and he can be cast out by one innocent, and then be tormented by himself

291. It happened that one of the hellish gang came up to me stealthily and worked deceitfully. To expose this, he was sought out, and found, and then he spoke many boastful words about his power; he had even been invisible. When I had spoken with him for a little while, saying that he possessed no power but what it was permitted him to have, then he was allowed to exercise his powers, and when he had tried in vain to do so, he admitted that he had been able to accomplish nothing whatsoever here. And after he was told that one little child alone could cast him down, one of the smaller innocents was sent to him, who only approached him and, as it seemed to me, circled around him; and because of this he was overcome by such great anguish that he cried out and implored that the innocent might leave him, because he was feeling so oppressed and anguished that he could not describe it. 1747, the 3rd day of December.

There is a diabolic gang who boast that they are the Messiah and perform miracles

292. He with his gang, who was permitted to enter into me, in order to practice their arts more effectively also attempted to perform miracles in front of those who were with me in the other life, both acquaintances and unknown people not very long deceased, and others, and they really thought they were performing them even though they were only illusions. For they seemed to themselves to be let down into the depths of the earth, from where they were nevertheless able to speak with me, thus as though they were hidden or absent, which seemed miraculous, as if he could turn the universe around or upside-down, as such magicians imagine they can do.

This kept on for quite a long time, and when I was inquiring into his character, he replied that he was the Messiah, and indeed he thought he was, and was eager to aver it quite definitely, but I did not want to hear it.

Thus [the saying] of God the Messiah comes true, that those would come who would call themselves the Messiah, and would do miracles [Matt. 24:24]. 1747, the 3rd day of December.

293. SPIRITUAL EXPERIENCES

From the inward heaven[1], angels are being transferred to the very inward heaven, where there is peace and joy such as no one can utter

293. Today, from early morning until noon, I was among and spoke with those who had been in the inward heaven and had been transferred into the very inward heaven [cf. 265]. A conversation was able to be carried on with them, but through an intermediary angel, who told me this, namely, that he had now been made a sort of medium to establish communication from me to them.

They said that there was joy, and peace, such as a person could never feel even the least bit in mortal life, and which was eternally changing. In order that I might feel this happiness to some degree, an *Angel* came to me. Other happy ones surrounded the Angel, and they approached toward me, and then, only from its proximity, the joy and happiness so penetrated my innermost parts and, as they say, the deepest marrows, that I would not have been able to sustain it, without almost dissolving from innermost joy. 1747, the 4th day of December.

In the other life man and wife can indeed converse with each other, but yet not remain together; the same applies also to brothers, sisters, friends

294. It was said before [290] that in the other life, Fathers, mothers, brothers and friends can converse, but nevertheless they are separated of their own will, because earthly associations hold them back from striving for heavenly things. Besides, on such occasions the things they had thought are brought to view, which cannot [but] draw them downward to worldly matters, and cause annoyances in various ways. 1747, the 4th day of December.

The state of souls after death in regard to memory

295. Spirits believe, as do souls after the death of the body, that they utilize all of the kind of memory they had in the life of the body. But by a revealing experience today, like some earlier ones, I have learned—and spoken with souls and spirits about the same mat-

---

[1] See 262, footnote.

ter, who were obliged to admit it—that they have no memory of personal matters, but a more inward memory that pertains to character, on which all and the least things are inscribed that they had ever thought in the life of the body and that they had done. One might say that knowledge more or less occupies the surface, and everything related to feelings constitutes the core.

1) To souls and spirits who were able to speak from their character making use of the knowledge within me, it could by no means appear otherwise than that they had retained all remembrance of their bodily life. They put on that knowledge as if it were theirs, so that they could not know otherwise than that my memory was theirs. This happened in one way with those I had known in life, in another with those I had not known. This is obvious from the single fact, to which I bear witness, that all spirits when they came to me were able to speak in my vernacular tongue, no matter where they had been born, not knowing but that it was their language and that they had been born into it. About their own language they knew nothing whatever.

2) Their character takes the place of memory, so that they loathe, or love, truths or goodness, as if by some keen scent. For as soon as anything comes along that is not agreeable to their character, they bend it off toward things that soothe their character. They do this so skilfully and amazingly that they do not know but that they are acting from the memory.

Moreover, they can even converse among themselves on a variety of subjects from things in a person [they are with]—which is also amazing, although I did not hear [the discussion]—and then likewise, not know otherwise, than that they are speaking from their own former memory. Certain acquaintances were surprised at this, but still could not but acknowledge the truth of it.

But it must be understood that all things, even the very least, are so governed by God the Messiah that they cannot take out of anyone's memory any but those things that can serve a use. Thus it is wonderful the way all things and each detail are governed.

3) Nor should there be any doubt but that each and every detail inscribed on [the memory] during the life of the body can also be brought forth and shown to them, as I have experienced myself most lucidly. The smallest details are brought out, and even in their own point of time, and I could not in any way prevent it. To recount the particular experiences would be a needlessly lengthy undertaking. 1747, the 4th day of December.

Spirits think they are bodied people

296.   From a great deal of experience I have learned that spirits and also [newly arrived] souls after death thought, in fact believed, that they were in the life of the body, and indeed, with such conviction that they were extremely surprised when they were told [the truth] and were able to know it [themselves] from the fact that they could be transferred, as well as other experiments [showing] that they were spirits without bones and flesh; nor could they learn [in any other way] that they were dead as to the life of the body. 1747, the 4th day of December.

Those who are raised up from the lower part of the earth, or pit, by God the Messiah, into the inward heaven[1], also into the very inward one, are allotted their own places and habitations in a most precise manner

297.   I was amazed how thousands, perhaps tens of thousands, were raised up by God the Messiah out of the pit, or lower parts of the earth, and especially how all of them were able to be allotted their own places in the heavens. Finally today, I learned that the greatest part of them seem to themselves to be transported in carriages or coaches, and to be driven around to various places, to test whether this or that place is suitable, that is, whether the person is in harmony with the souls who are there. If not, as happens in most cases, they are carried about until they find agreement, and thus rest, namely among souls who harmonize with their own character. Nor is there ever any soul raised up by God the Messiah who does not find his or her own rest, and thus a companionship with others harmonious with his or her own character.

     This travelling from place to place can take a rather long time for some, but there is no anxiety; for in the meantime they are also being adapted, and perfected, so as to be able to live within a heavenly society.

298.   Moreover, the heavenly female inhabitants of any one habitation can feel and see at once whether someone is concordant with their character and thus able as a part to contribute to their hap-

---

[1] See 262, footnote.

piness—and this so accurately, that nothing could be more so. They can even [discern] in which place in the habitation, or with which people someone can be compatible—and all of this, as to each and every detail, by the arrangement, and under the indirect and direct auspices of God the Messiah, Who is All in all things.

299. I was raised up also into a habitation of the very inward heaven where, by the mercy, and under the direct and miraculous auspices of God the Messiah, I was able to abide for a while, and at the same time speak with the angels, who sensed most sharply that someone was present. For they are extremely happy about newcomers, and want most eagerly for a newcomer to become one of them. But from that keen perception, they at once know and sense whether that person is able to live among them. If not, they are sad, and still make every effort to initiate the soul, but when there is not concord, they separate themselves. Then the soul is again allowed to be transported around in carriages, which I have not only heard, but also seen; and I have been with them in the carriages, and afterwards conversed with them at some length.

From these circumstances in the inward and very inward heaven, one can see how things are with those who are quickened immediately after the life of the body, namely, that "they walk through dry places, and seek rest" [Matt. 12:43, Luke 11:24]. 1747, the 5th day of December.

No one at all among mortals can go up out of the grave, except through God the Messiah

300. It is the infrangible truth, and thoroughly corroborated by experience, that no one of humankind can be aroused out of their grave, still less be raised from the lower parts of the earth into the heavens, that is, into the inward[1], the very inward and the innermost one, except through God the Messiah—which also it was granted me to learn from plain experience. In order that I might know it, I was allowed to feel it by a certain kind of drawing up or pulling up, which I can hardly describe. So it is in the whole of heaven; for God the Messiah, Who has all power in the heavens and on earth [Matt. 28:18], most intensely and deeply burns with the love and mercy to

---

[1] See 262, footnote.

save the whole human race, His Love and His mercy being of such force, because He is omnipotent. 1747, the 5th day of December.

In the very inward heaven, the pleasure and happiness is unutterable

301. By the mercy of God the Messiah, I was raised up into the very inward heaven, as told [293, 299], and spoke with the angels. It was granted me there, only by the mercy of God the Messiah, to be in their company for a little while, which miracle was due to the way in which the angels around me were arranged.

In this way I was taught about the matters previously related, and thus I could feel, even though very faintly, what it is like, and that without heavenly harmony and an agreement of characters, and without having attained the [necessary] state through the purging process, it is impossible for anyone to live among them.

Such joys as these also arise from the most delicate, and humanly imperceptible, or sublime, mental imagery, that makes it an entirely heavenly paradise, with absolute and inexpressible joy in endless variation. For the displays are so alive as to surpass, by leagues beyond number, any that a person on earth is able to picture to himself, or even think up. Such joy results from mutual love, and from the sentiment of all, that none want to be their own, but each individual fervently desires from deepest affection to belong to all. But the words are lacking, to be able to express these matters. 1747, the 5th day of December.

About the life after death of those who are continually engaged in studies, and who think they make them wise

302. I was guided today into one habitation in which I had surely been before, but without knowing at the time whose habitation it was. It is like a broad field on which are many chariots and arsenals. Where the chariots and horses are, there are many people who seem to be walking or riding in chariots hither and thither; and when I inquired who they were, one of them, approaching me, inquired about those alive [in the world] who are highly educated, asking which ones had achieved fame above the rest. Then I mentioned two or three whom I knew. But I was informed by the angels with me that those pass their life in that place who are much occupied with studies, but who are nevertheless of sound reason and do not impose the philosophy of their mind on heavenly things. 1747, the 5th day of December.

Those who are the innermost are as bases and as multiple centers, like the stars in the heavens, to which all other things relate, as to their centers

303. That the Kingdom of God the Messiah is most perfect order, and perfection itself, and consequently form itself, can be evident to anyone. So because it is most perfect form, it must also have its centers, or its bases, spiritually understood. Those who are innermost and most of all under the mercy of God the Messiah, are such centers—likened to the stars of the heavens [Dan. 12:3], in which there is a reflection of the Kingdom of God the Messiah, as there is in all and the least things of nature.

But the arrangement among these centers I cannot find out, still less describe, because this goes beyond the human understanding, which is deeply ignorant of heavenly forms. 1747, the 5th day of December.

When the human mind is absorbed in worldly concerns, it is as though it is let down, and falls from the heavens

304. I have also learned through Experience, when I was being led around in the heavens here and there, which took place during a time of wakefulness, that when I lapsed into thoughts about worldly matters, then what I had seen in the heavenly habitation at once disappeared. So those who let their thoughts drop into the world, fall from the heavens. 1747, the 5th day of December.

Centers and bases, which are like stars of the heavens, are very numerous in each heaven

305. There are many centers and bases in each heaven, and by means of them, direct communications exist between the heavens, and with God the Messiah. They are in a cery calm state, and cannot be compared to anything more aptly than to the ganglia in the human body and to the nodes in the brain, into which countless tissues run, and where they are as it were renewed, and thus the things around them are put into order to accord with the purposes present in the first substances[1]. Therefore everything is arranged in a most perfect order and a most perfect form by God the Messiah Alone. 1747, the 5th day of December.

People rise again not long after the death of the body

306. Today I spoke with someone I had known in the life of the body, who recognized himself from his image, as that of a living person, raised up in my mind's eye; also from some other things displayed mentally that he recognized—and this after a period of about 5 months from when he had died. Of course, he did not know or remember much at first, because spirits had not been attached to him; but after spirits had been attached to him, he came back into a seemingly complete understanding and recollection. 1747, the 5th day of December.

About some who were raised up into the very inward heaven

307. Today again two were raised up into a certain forecourt of the very inward heaven, and from there they spoke with me, saying in a loud voice that the eye had never seen, nor could the mind ever grasp, such things! I even felt the happiness itself in me for a time, as well as a sort of waft of pleasure felt in the very inward heaven by one who had been transferred there, and who cried out, saying that he could not bear the joy, if he were not let down; but being surrounded by angels of God the Messiah, he was able to stay there [*cf.* 293]. 1747, the 5th day of December.

One of them, guided into certain habitations of the very inward heaven, cried out, saying that he was feeling an unceasing variation of delights, accompanied by a very deep sense of joy.

Someone was also raised up with them as an angelic companion, but he said that he noticed nothing of the kind; so that apparent height does not accomplish anything, but only the inward and more inward qualities of heaven.

But those two were only at the outskirts of the very inward heaven, because, not having been dead for very long, they

---

[1] *fines in principiis*, perhaps comparable to seeds which are beginning substances containing every future stage in potency.

were still not prepared to enter more inwardly. They cried out again, saying there are countless different kinds of delights, so many that no language could ever give expression to them. They really wanted to describe the very wonderful harmony, but could not. They seemed to themselves to have been caught up into the third heaven, but it was only the forecourt of the very inward heaven, as I am now being told. 1747, the 5th day of December.

They who are being conducted to their own habitations seem to be transported by carriage

308. Today for the third time, I learned from experience that those who are being conducted to their own habitations, as was told before [297-99], believe they are being driven by carriage and thus being carried about as if by labyrinthine routes. For they go back and forth, so that they may arrive at that habitation where there are those of almost the same character. With these they stay, until God the Messiah mercifully sees fit to take them away from there and move them to some better habitation. I spoke with some who were in a carriage, and they said that they do not know otherwise than that they are being driven. 1747, the 5th day of December.

About the perception of angels, and also that of souls, in the other life

309. In the habitations of the very inward heaven, there is such a keen perception, or recognition by perception, that when a soul or angel of a different kind or genus, or else of a different species, is present, then in a miraculous way they either turn away, or they are moved by the harmony. It is by this method that they who are being driven around in the more inward heaven are admitted; and while they are passing through the changes between many states, then by a remarkable inward sense it becomes known, more and more, whether, and in what way, they are discordant. So they are either held off a little, or else they are brought in at a place where the disagreement is not so noticeable, with the result that the heavenly form of that particular species [of angel] is shaped within that genus and is thus continually perfected, even to such a degree of perfection that anything more perfect is inconceivable. 1747, the 6th day of December.

310. These things just written were shown to me by much actual experience. For I was conducted into habitations of the very inward heaven, and I came into one of them where I could even sense, without being told by the angels, at one moment that there was discordance, but at another that there was harmony. This was because there were changes in my state [of mind], as well as the workings of certain [spirits] present, which mixed in and varied the perception.

311. A similar thing obtains in the inward heaven[1], but with a great difference when it comes to the kinds of perception. But here there are so many things that language can never articulate, because there is nothing that is not ineffable, and inexpressible!

312. Moreover, there is also another kind of inner sense which could be called that of the understanding, although it is also unconscious. By this we are led for the most part during the life of the body, when we sense—because of what we have been taught from the Word of God the Messiah—what opposes [the Word] as if from conscience, and thus when we refrain from doing it, even if the loves of self and of the world may urge us to.

Those can be admitted into the very inward heaven's habitations who have recently come from the life of the body, but still in a different way

313. Some were also admitted into the very inward heaven, with whom I had spoken and whom I had known, who had deceased only several months before, and some a few years before. These also were admitted into certain habitations of the very inward heaven, that they might see heavenly glory there [*cf.* 268], and perceive it by sense, as well as hear it. But because they could not yet be in such a state that they could remain there, they were therefore encircled by an angelic field by which all discordance is taken away, so that the angels of that habitation could not be harmed or troubled thereby. 1747, the 6th day of December.

---

[1] See 262, footnote.

*Heavenly happiness is ineffable, and the very deepest happiness
of a person on earth experiencing heavenly joy, does not
equal even the least happiness of the angels*

314. Today a number of those who were in heaven were longing to learn what heavenly joy is, and it was therefore granted them, by the mercy of God the Messiah, to feel heavenly joy to the deepest degree possible for them—even to the degree where they could not bear any more. They were actually of diverse character, so that the joy of one of them reached its deepest level (as he also acknowledged), but still was not as great a heavenly joy as some had.

From this experience they were allowed to learn how great heavenly happiness is, and what heavenly joy is like, since their very deepest did not even come up to the least of the angels.

What the deepest joy of some of them was like, it was granted me by the mercy of God the Messiah to feel in myself and thereby, to learn that those joys that were their deepest, were among the lesser joys. And what is amazing, the deepest joy of one of them, who declared it to be the very highest and the most heavenly, was actually nothing but coldness, which I was likewise allowed to feel plainly.

So that they could bear those heavenly joys (as they supposed them to be, because they were their deepest ones), it had been provided by God the Messiah that they should be surrounded by an angelic field, lest they perish, and be dissolved. 1747, the 7th day of December.

*A person's thoughts and mental images become so plainly visible
in the heavens, and those who are there can so plainly
see them streaming toward the person and causing
him to speak, that one could not imagine
anything more obvious*

315. There was one soul surrounded by evil spirits who, as far as I can judge, had never believed differently than that each and every thing he thought and did was from himself. Then something happened to show clearly to the souls and spirits standing around him, how such a soul is led, and that he says and speaks nothing whatever but what flows in through the spirits around him, unseen by him: one little word only was spoken, and it became visible as is usual in the spiritual heaven; and it was heard how the word that was let down rolled around among the spirits and thus came to all those who were speaking. So the soul in the middle imagined he was speaking from himself, nor could he tell otherwise, he now declares.

Presently it was granted him to speak his thoughts in a similar way, but more quickly, so as to show how plainly they can be seen and heard in still more inward regions. The speaking went quickly, just as when a person is thinking—only a little more slowly. It happened in the same way, but then one could see that this encircled soul could not tell otherwise than that it was he who was thinking and speaking. 1747, the 8th day of December.

Evil spirits can even enter into heaven,
thus be among the heavenly

316. By actual experience I learned that evil spirits from the devil's gang can also enter into heaven and be among those who are there and, as they believe, can do this by means of tricks that they think up—something I was also granted to hear. For they thought that I did not understand their intrigues, but I was enabled to hear and see them.

Their plotting was about a way by which they imagined they could safely enter. One method they turned down, another they seemed to themselves to discover, by which, in fact, they did ascend.

This I perceived also by sense; but as I had been taught previously [307, 314], they are then surrounded by a spiritual field, which makes them unable to tell otherwise than that they are now in heavenly joy, because of being in heaven. But these are cases of permission, and the angels of that heaven are not aware at the time that such spirits are there. But if any one of those spirits were deprived of the spiritual field adapted to each one's state of mind—and also changing at every moment—then the angels even from very far off would not be able to bear their approach, much less that they should enter, because it causes such coldness that they could never be together. This coldness it was also granted me to be conscious of and to feel plainly. 1747, the 18th day of December.

FROM THE *BIBLE INDEX* 318.

About the permission given to spirits to bring evils upon mankind and upon [newly arrived] souls

317. By the mercy of God the Messiah, it was granted me to sense to a certain extent how permissions take place, enabling evil spirits to bring evils upon people on earth and souls, even to induce falsities of doctrine and evils of life, and so to corrupt them. For all are led in accordance with their character, which is evil rooted in by heredity and augmented by one's own deeds. And when people are being led by their character—so that it would break them and inflict spiritual harm upon them if they were turned in a different direction—then there are spirits having a similar character and passion, who want to [lead them]. Therefore, they then go to work, and this is called permission.

But here so many secrets come together, that the matter cannot be explained in a few words. 1747, the 8th day of December.

The cunning of the devil in distorting truths and goodness cannot be adequately expressed

318. Now from actual experience I have also learned that the cunning of the diabolic gang is so great that they could even corrupt the heavenly, if it were possible. For I was surrounded by very many of the devil's deceitful and pernicious gang, which, together with others in heaven collaborating with them, was distorting all thoughts from the Word of God the Messiah at that time. Indeed, they were able in an instant to seize from my mind truths that I understood; and they were turning them so skilfully into falsities, that the heavenly beings who were at some distance from that place began to be upset, until they could bear it no longer, thinking that even they had been able to be corrupted. This I was enabled to realize from their weeping and complaining.

So the cunning of the devil, who is held bound in hell, is such that he imagines himself able to corrupt even the heavenly, who, even though they are most safe, are nevertheless fearful.

That I was surrounded by such a diabolic gang, I was not only given to hear from the heavenly ones but also [to know] because of a clear sensation that came over me—of cool wind, whenever they were gathering together, and again, of a coldness that touched me; likewise by a vague sensation when they were in action, that is, when they were distorting truths into falsities, as well as by a loud voice scolding them, and from their replies. I heard it also from those who were then around me, who were saying that during this time they had been in hell, and had seen most dreadful things, and toward the end realized that they had been close to me. For hell is not in one place, but everywhere, as is heaven, too—in fact all the heavens, and God the Messiah. 1747, the 8th day of December.

Souls of the dead do not at all know otherwise, than that they are in their bodily life, only undergoing various changing conditions in it

319. I have spoken with many of those deceased or departed from the life of the body, both known and unknown to me, about whom I can tell these things—but from rather much experience, because gathered from many sources.

The souls had scarcely believed otherwise than that they were in the life of the body and that they were thinking in the same way and at first, especially [about] the things that touched them most closely and deeply and seemed to draw them toward desire and action.

1. As on previous occasions, many of those who are around me today acknowledge this, and now the ones who realize that they are in the other life are amazed.

As for their condition, they have their states, of which there are many changes only between their deepest sleep and their highest wakefulness. They acknowledge, and I have also learned this from experience, that they have a waking state similar to what they had in the life of the body, and in fact, even much more perfect for the reason that they are able to grasp and see the inward content of speech and of mental images.

2. From this, their highest state of wakefulness, they are also carried into a sleeping state, just like a person in the world when he sinks gradually from a waking state into one of sleep, even into the kind of sleep in which he would dream dreams—and thus is borne from one state into another.

There are also states of sleeping as if one were awake, in which I also have been—and so I have learned these and the above matters from experience—and in which they do not seem to themselves to be asleep, but awake, because they are speaking with a companion or with companions about one thing and another while in this state as they do when dreaming[1]. This can be grasped by a person who has been allowed to experience a transition from wakefulness, through several states of very gentle sleep, and then into a deep sleep, all accompanied by varying patterns of mental imagery.

So the things I have here told about souls, I can affirm so positively, that they should never occasion any doubt.

320. Their sleeping state is when they come into or are in the same conditions as when they were living [in the world] and do not know otherwise but that they are still so living. When they are in this state, they suppose it to be their waking state; but it is, or begins to be, the waking state, when they realize that they are in the other life, and not in the life of the body or of the world. 1747, the 9th day of December.

321. They so easily slip from the one state into the other, that it happens in an instant. But all and the least things happen by the mercy and disposition of God the Messiah.

Only the Love, therefore the Mercy, of God the Messiah, brings about and accomplishes Man's resurrection after death, and his being brought to heavenly dwellings

322. By the Divine mercy of God the Messiah it has also been granted me to learn, and in fact by an experience today, that the Love, consequently the Mercy of God the Messiah toward the human race—in willing to save all and each and draw them from hell into heaven (for love has a power in it that cannot but express itself by a drawing action) and thus join them to Himself in countless different ways—is the one and only cause of man's resurrection. By that same mercy, all and the least things are held together in a heavenly arrangement and form, according to which they come forth in succession [in time], and are kept together [in eternity]. 1747, the 9th day of December.

---

[1] The manuscript has *in somno* "asleep," but *in somnio*, "while dreaming," must have been intended.

323. SPIRITUAL EXPERIENCES

*Spirits can smell odors, and those odors correspond to
the spiritual life of [the deceased persons]*

323. It is also amazing in regard to the dead after [earthly] life, that when it is so permitted, it can be clearly and perceptibly smelled what someone is like who has died; and when they had lived an evil life, then such an offensive odor is smelled from the corpse, that the spirits cannot stand approaching them. They have told me that it is an odor like that of a most stinking corpse, and that the differences between such odors or stenches are like those between spiritual qualities of their life. A stench of this kind has many times arisen near me, especially that of a decaying mouse, which corresponds with greed in its countlessly diverse forms.

These facts lead me to the conclusion that by the sign put upon Cain, an odor of this kind is meant, so intense that he could wander nowhere, without being driven away [Gen. 4:14,15]. For a similar thing happens in the other life, as I have been shown by much actual experience.

But such an odor is removed from everyone when they are brought to their own habitations, for if it were then present, they could not be received anywhere and stay. So they are admitted into habitations by being perceived in a different way, through the disposition of God the Messiah Alone. 1747, the 9th day of December.

*The states of man's life as to spiritual things are also
portrayed in the other life as cold and heat*

324. By actual and oft repeated experience, I have also been shown that those who have lived a life devoted to the body, or to the loves of the world and of self with their many states, degrees and varieties, are cold entities. In fact, they are so cold, that on repeated occasions they numbed my various members with coldness, then also with cold blasts like wind, when they came near, as tangibly as if there were a wind—but likewise by heat, when they are also given permission to counterfeit heat. These states likewise are countlessly diverse; but they too are removed, except in certain cases, even until [some] are raised up into heaven, about whom [I spoke] earlier [297, 309]. 1747, the 9th day of December.

The diabolic gang are not only utterly powerless, but can even realize it is true, and admit and acknowledge it —even as if it were not against their will to do so

325. This I learned today from experience, that even spirits of the diabolic gang who are otherwise most stupid in matters of true belief, were nevertheless forced to admit that they knew it was true they could do nothing from themselves. They fully acknowledged this, and in fact, not [just] with the mouth, but even from a certain conviction. Afterwards, however, they were ashamed. 1747, the 9th day of December.

Human souls, even angels, can be transferred into the condition of their earthly mind, thus into their yearning desires, and then also be examined, revealing what they are like when left to themselves [see 372]

326. Today, as previously [157], I was shown by actual experience that the human ability to understand can seemingly be taken away [from people], leaving them their native discernment and still as much and such ability to understand as nature allots to make them human. And I learned from actual experience that the souls of the dead in that state are then devils, and commit crimes like a devil, which was also shown by extensive experience.

In fact, it was even shown that angels can be reduced to that same state, revealing what kind of a person each one had been as to the will. For then it is as if the will, which is reined in in the world by one's ambitions, as well as by the civil law, is set free. However, God the Messiah does not permit a saint to act so freely that he sees his own infernal qualities. 1747, the 10th day of December.

To one who is in God the Messiah, nothing can be harmful

327. By plain experience, I have learned that the curse of the wicked, or the devil's curse and all his other devices, cannot in the least harm or touch those who are in the Hand of God the Messiah, that is, in God the Messiah.

This was shown me by a curse being read, and turned by devils into a display, with the intent of applying it to some devout person; but the power was granted to me to have the depiction of that curse turn around toward me. While others shuddered at it, it was even permitted to enter into my mouth and inner parts, because of the confidence that nothing of this kind, thus nothing of the devil's curse, can hurt or even touch those who are in God the Messiah.

Today also, obsessed by the devil's gang when he was practicing his cunning tricks upon me in vain, I was finally distanced from the incessant, combined curses that were being aimed at my heart. For several hours they kept coming, so aimed; but at the time I was really unable to feel the curses except by perceptible heart-palpitations, as well as by a certain feeling in the inward parts of my body arising from them. They even slipped into my thoughts their wish that I despair of life—as if they can achieve anything by that—but still nothing whatever can harm or even touch [me]. 1747, the 11th day of December.[1]

Love is the very power that brings about
the resurrection of the dead

328. It has been shown before [300, 322] that the Love of God the Messiah toward the whole human race is the sole cause of the resurrection of spirits from their graves, for there is a kind of drawing up by this power.

That there is a kind of drawing up, I have learned from actual experience, both previously and today, by feeling a kind of drawing up of my head; besides other things that this is not the place to bring up. 1747, the 10th day of December.

Everything whatsoever that meets the eyes, no matter how diverse,
is nevertheless enlivened by God the Messiah to be turned
into lovely pleasures, and series of pleasures

329. When I was walking in the street, I was looking at different objects with my eyes, which, because of their diversity, no one would ever guess could be transformed, and thus enlivened to become a continuous series of pleasures. Then I heard from angels that these things had come through to them as an uninterrupted variation of pleasures, and this from objects they could not see at all; and so I was able to understand [this phenomenon], because there is

---

[1] The manuscript has *die 11 Dec.* for this passage probably written on the 10th.

nothing in the world that is not a reflection of the Kingdom of God the Messiah. 1747, 10 December.

Wood-cutters in the other life receive comfort

330. The wood-cutters in the other life were spoken of before [271], namely, that they labor continually. But at the time when I was there, what I did not see was that there sometimes appears to them a lamb with a baby lamb, who tell them to wait yet a little while, and that God the Messiah shortly would come. From this they receive comfort. 1747, 13 December.

The beginning of jealousy that is seen in little children is most sweet

331. From an experience today, I learned that the apparent envy in little children toward other little children when in rivalry over the mother, arises from a most pleasant beginning, and from love, thus through heaven. For while I was being kept in thought about envy in little children, it was said to me aloud from heaven that they felt a heavenly sweetness, which varied according to the individuals.

From this one can conclude that the very passions and desires in a person all come from a heavenly starting point, and from Love Itself, therefore through heaven; but that on the way, outside of heaven, they are turned by spirits into something opposite, likewise by each person as receiver [they are qualified] by his or her essential form, and its variations with their changing states of mind.

332. It is similar to the way philosophic truths, which are in themselves truths[1], in each receiver or person, by application, are bent toward evil, or toward agreement with their desires. For people are apt to justify their desires by such truths, even to the point of convincing themselves.

Similarly also [they bend] the truths of the Word. From this heresies arise, and the attitudes that result from them, such as the condemnation of all who do not agree. 1747, the 11th day of December.

---

[1] The manuscript has *varietates*, where *veritates* is most likely intended, which we, like A.W. Acton, have taken to be the correct reading. There is a faint correction of the first -*a*- into an -*e*-, possibly done by the author, possibly by Chastanier.

333.   SPIRITUAL EXPERIENCES

Souls of the dead carry with them from the world the character of the body

333.   Souls of the dead carry with them from the body all of its characteristics—even to the point that they think they are in the body, dressed in clothes, and so on—and also its desires, such as an appetite for eating, and so on, so that the characteristics of the body are inscribed upon the souls.

The nature which they carry with them from the world and the body, they keep, but in the course of time it passes over into a kind of oblivion, so that they think they have put it off altogether, especially when they have become angels—this for the reason that they have been gifted with the ability to receive the mercy of God the Messiah. Then because of their accepting that ability, their former nature seems to be erased from memory, when nevertheless it remains.

For if it should please God the Messiah to take back His gift, and to place the angel back in his former life, then that soul becomes exactly as it had been before, when leaving the body—so every soul can be told that they lose nothing, and that nothing has been taken from them—but then they become wild animals and devils. 1747, the 11th day of December.

The story of Joseph portrays both comings of God the Messiah

334.   Today, when some of those who had died were together and carrying on a discussion in which Joseph was mentioned, an angel from heaven informed them that Joseph portrayed both the comings of God the Messiah. Then they declared that they recognized all and the least particulars [told to them] to be so true, that there was no doubt about it. 1747, the 13th day of December.

When the Psalms of David were read, they had such power in heaven, that some heavenly [angels] were struck with amazement

335.   Several psalms of David were read, and indeed, in such a way that the inward and more inward levels of meaning were conveyed, by the mercy of God the Messiah, to the perception of certain heavenly [angels]. They were so struck with amazement as to declare aloud that they had never believed such things [were in them]—as did also those who were dead in the life after death, because the Word had similarly affected them.

In order that the difference could be observed, the meaning of the Word was brought to them just about as it had been in their lifetime when the same things were read, and this was so different that they had seen in it hardly any heavenly life at all.

From this one may infer what kind of power there is in the Word, when God the Messiah mercifully enlivens it; and what kind when the letter is as if dead, as it is when read by the dead. 1747, the 13th day of December.

When enlightened knowledge of spiritual and heavenly matters, which is pure truth, is [embraced] by belief and thought in a human mind, it can delightfully move the whole heaven of angels

336. Today I was taught by the mercy of God the Messiah that just the thoughts of heavenly truths move the angels, and thus the whole of heaven, in an ineffable manner. For the angelic heaven is on the path of truth, because there cannot possibly be a truth but that it leads to God the Messiah through belief, this being the source of the angels' pleasure and even happiness.

For those are angels who take delight together in the happiness of all and long for the salvation of all, for this is the property of mercy, and of love, and of pleasure and happiness, and it results in a sharing of happiness throughout the whole of heaven.

I was taught these things by some who had felt that heavenly pleasure, at a moment when I was thinking heavenly truths: they then, as if awakened from a peaceful sleep, got a sense of their pleasantness, and gave witness to this and confirmed it to me aloud. [Psalm 4.][1] 1747, 4 December.

---

[1] Written and partly deleted in the original, this annotation perhaps refers to verses 7 and 8.

Angels think they are doing everything, down to the least details, from themselves, but still have an inner sense, and thus an awareness, that nothing is theirs

337. It is remarkable that some never want to believe that God the Messiah rules all things, such as spirits who are not so bad, as well as all evil spirits. Yet even angels imagine no otherwise than that they are acting and speaking, and they think this is from themselves. For God the Messiah has so arranged all and the least things, that He wills nothing to be His own and all to belong to the angels. This may seem amazing to everyone without experience in the matter, yet it is the very truth, as the angelic heaven testifies by noticeable agreement. 1747, the 14th day of December.

The intellectual activity of some consists of nought but mere offenses

338. It was foretold in the Word that offenses would come [Matt. 18:7, Luke 17:1], and indeed against the faith, or the truths of religion, which all regard God the Messiah. For [the truth] that He became a human being, spoke as a human being, and many similar ones, the earthly mind can never believe; therefore, even if one professes belief, yet still, on consulting the earthly mind, one falls into doubt and then into unspoken denial. The same process follows in regard to particular matters of belief, with the consequence, that the person's mental life consists of nothing but offenses.
Therefore, Only God the Messiah knows whether the life of people who completely deny God the Messiah, even to the point of blaspheming [Him], when they had been taught to do so from childhood, is worse than the life of those who had thought themselves well versed in the doctrine of faith, and had professed it, [and yet entertain such offenses]. 1747, the 14th day of December.

About Mohammed, and the Mohammedans

339. Because certain ones of the dead at the entrance to heaven drew away angrily in search of a different heaven, so they thought, where someone other than God the Messiah reigned, finally they imagined they had found another heaven, one where Mohammed reigned (no doubt they had talked to Mohammedans who had died some years before). When they were about to show this heaven to others whom they wanted to lead away, it appeared to me as if another so-called heaven in the depth was being opened, from which I could hear them speaking. I was then informed that they were Mohammedans who imagined they were coming there to their own heaven, to stay there. After I had spoken with them for a while, God the Messiah appeared to them in glory, through an Angel, whereupon they fell on their faces in devout adoration.

After this Mohammed was quickly raised up from there, and was present with me and spoke with me at length; and I can bear witness that when he had been instructed about God the Messiah, he spoke kindly—and more kindly than many Christians (I could feel that he was speaking as he was thinking), and he instructed those who were in the depth that he could do nothing whatever from himself, and that he realized that he was no God, but a simple man, and that certain spirits had chanced to speak with him. He also wants to be instructed in the doctrine of true faith.

I even showed him the city of Amsterdam and the Town Hall there[1] from two sides, as well as inside, and he was amazed at the great number of marble works. He is now also present and affirms this fact. 1747, the 14th day of December.

340. The Mohammedans also declared that when they were listening to the more inward contents of the Word and heavenly truths, they had slipped into a heavenly happiness; and now as I am writing these words, they are bending forward upon their faces and adoring the God of the Universe, Who is Jesus Christ, saying that they were grasping this also by a heavenly method. This will be spoken about elsewhere [342]. 1747, the 14th day of December.

As soon as causes or means are detected, or they believe they have found them out for themselves, belief perishes

341. Several times it has been observed that belief passes away as soon as they know, or think they know, a cause.

---

[1] *I.e.,* the *Stadhuis.*

Those spirits could not but acknowledge this, who had doubted about the power of God the Messiah when they arrived at a certain cause [of something]—such as that it took place by means of angels, or by means of heaven.

Therefore it was shown them that this would happen without those means, because God the Messiah is all in everything, and all-powerful. Nevertheless, when they have once or twice become aware of the causes, the thought sticks in their mind that there is yet another mediating cause, which lies hidden; and in this way also, belief perishes. This is also the reason why, as soon as they imagine they have discovered the cause of a certain thing, they reject [the very idea of] belief[1]. Therefore, belief is also destroyed by human philosophy, because they want to investigate the cause of everything there is by their own method and by their own philosophy. 1747, the 14th day of December.

Souls of the dead are brought by many means to recognize that God the Messiah is the Lord of the Universe

342. Souls of the dead such as the Mohammedans, who have come among the rest, and others who had inwardly doubted about God the Messiah for the reason, spoken of before [338], that nothing but offenses had filled their outer mind, are brought to recognize that God the Messiah is the Lord of the Universe. This is done both by vivid instruction adapted to each one's grasp, and by their being transferred into heavenly happiness—as they imagine it. They may see a great variety of the loveliest pleasure gardens, so delightful to them that they decide they have arrived in the heavenly paradise; for this [idea] is inspired into human minds.

But later, they are taught that this is not true heavenly happiness, so they likewise are allowed to experience their deepest possible states of joy, until they declare that this innermost joy is out of sight and out of reach to any human sense. Then they are also brought into their deepest possible state of peace, in which they again declare that nothing of it could ever be expressed. Finally they are brought into a state of innocence, the deepest possible one for them, even to the limit of their ability to feel.

---

[1] That is, they believe only what they have discovered.

This is done so that they may learn to tell what is truly good, what is truly spiritual and heavenly, that is, what is Divine; for true happiness, true peace, true innocence, are entirely Divine. Afterwards they come into these states, in differing ways, depending upon each one's life; for they are guided more and more towards heavenly regions, according to the character of each one. 1747, 14 December.

The state of temptation and purging:
God the Messiah tempts no one

343. I was also shown by actual experience how temptations are caused by inner torments of distress, and at the same time, inward grief; likewise, how they long when they are in that state to know what should be believed, and how that [thought] keeps coming up that they [act] from themselves, and they therefore want to claim some merit for undergoing temptations, and thus enter heaven—as well as other thoughts I could not observe.

In addition, [I was shown] what their thinking was like at the time—as that everything they had heard and seen was of little value, empty, almost untrue—to which thoughts their conscience more or less assented. Thus it was allowed to observe how they were when emerging from that state—in short, they could not but think that God the Messiah permits temptations, which still involves [the idea] that He tempts. 1747, the 15th day of December.

About Mohammed

344. A seemingly separate heaven was displayed, where the worshippers of Mohammed were, but there were only spirits there, not angels. Those spirits, when they heard what was being said in this heaven[1], requested that they too might come up and speak. When they came, they spoke so sensibly and prudently, and also with such pleasing ingenuity, that the spirits of the Christians' heaven felt ashamed. Then communication was also opened up, so that they could speak together, and being questioned about Mohammed, they replied that they acknowledged Mohammed, not knowing any better,

---

[1] *I.e.,* the heaven of Christians.

but that they only wanted to worship the One God creator of heaven and earth.

Then Mohammed, with the wave-like gesture of that heaven, for there were many of them, answered them, saying that he could do nothing from himself, not even speak, but that he realized he had no power from himself, and that there was only one single [God]. This he testified before the spirits, and so he was raised up from there, and he worshipped the Most High God—none other than God the Messiah. 1747, 14 Dec.

345. Mohammed told that the spirits who were in the heaven where he was were everywhere decreasing in number, and that he did not know why they were leaving; but he was informed that they were being withdrawn into the angelic heaven, and they are there being instructed in the teachings of the faith, and besides this, that all their little children were in the heavens.

346. Mohammed also said that he knew no otherwise than that he was living on earth. For the condition of all in the other life is such that even though they are informed about specific facts, as that they are not living in the body, yet immediately afterwards, they forget it; for they are not gifted with a memory of things of this kind, for reasons of necessity. Also the spirits around him said they believed they were living on earth.

Only the little children of Mohammedans come immediately into heaven, but not the boys and girls

347. When a concern arose in my mind about the little children of Mohammedans, whether their boys and girls of a few years old will be taken away to the heaven of God the Messiah, I was told that their little children are raised up, but that boys and girls 10 years of age, more or less—depending upon education, ability, character— are not at once elevated into heaven, but are transferred among their spirits, and then gradually perfected and raised up. What I have also heard said is that they did not know where many of them had gone whom they had known before, and I realized that the reason, [namely] that boys and girls cannot be raised up quickly enough to avoid being firmly indoctrinated in heathenism. 1747, 15 December.

FROM THE *BIBLE INDEX*

The heaven of God the Messiah consists in a variety of all

348. The subjects themselves, or angels, must exist in a countlessly great diversity of forms, a variety that is arranged by kinds and species, both by individual [angels] and individual habitations, similar in all ways, likewise at every level. Only from variety is there a harmony of the kind where all believe that they are as if a one. From this, or from the beauty of harmony, comes happiness, in countless variety, and this to eternity. These things were said in a gathering of innumerable souls, spirits and angels, and I heard no one dissenting. 1747, 15 December.

349. They likewise agree that a universal entity [can] in no wise be universal but by virtue of its most single parts, consequently that there can in no wise be a universal Providence that does not extend to the very least details.

All things, even the least, can be demonstrated in heaven in full light

350. It might appear remarkable, but I am told that many spiritual and heavenly matters can be demonstrated, as if in noonday light, to the souls around me today. Now they are saying that they see the character of a person, and things of that kind—how much someone possesses of good and evil, of falsity and truth—altogether as if in daylight, within the person. They also [see] what someone had been like, and is now like in various states. I wanted to make note of this fact, because it cannot but strike everyone as remarkable.

351. Likewise, that all of our life, as well as thoughts, can be shown to us, [revealing] in detail what we had been like, and all this together with the [subsequent] acknowledgment of them, the grief, the anxiety, the [workings of] conscience, and so on even to our revival. These things were also told to me; and that they are true, no one should doubt, for so much that is confirmatory can be adduced [showing] that if someone had been blinded and carried away by fantasies and passions, it can be conclusively proven to them as if in clear daylight. 1747, the 15th day of December.

352. SPIRITUAL EXPERIENCES

*Souls after death think for certain
that they are living in the body*

352. From much experience, I have learned that the souls of the dead consider it as certain that they are in the body and in the world, so that they will only grudgingly allow themselves to be persuaded that they are in the other life. If they are asked where they are, whether they are standing on the earth or soil, whether they have clothes on, as in the world, and things of this kind, they at once answer that they cannot imagine anything else. But presently, when they reflect upon the matter, they realize they are in the other life; and then some grieve, and some do not, depending on the life they led and the beliefs they held in the body. 1747, the 15th day of December.

*Man has use of a double memory,
and how the double memory passes away*

353. The memory people actually call memory is a memory at the level of nature, because it belongs to the earthly mind and is a memory of personal matters or material mental imagery corresponding with words. This memory passes away when a person dies.

His soul retains the ability to reason and understand due to a certain spiritual memory, or a memory of rational or immaterial ideas, as it is called. It is this latter memory that causes the illusion that one is still in the life of the body. But because this memory was born from the earthly memory, it is filled with fallacies and continues to trouble, to obscure, and if left to itself, to distort truths, so that also this memory gradually disappears to the point where the reasoning power born from it passes away. Nevertheless, this memory is still retained and the person is instructed in the higher knowledge of truth, until the time when it can be erased.

Finally, the human being remains, insofar as it is a human being, which means the remaining part together with the acquired part. This is the soil wherein new or heavenly seed is sown, and out of it arises the new human being, or in the human being the heavenly paradise, with all heavenly happiness, peace and innocence. 1747, 15 December.

Souls and spirits seem to be transported from one place to another, and sometimes as with the speed of lightning

354. It was observed that souls and spirits are transferred upwards and downwards, also from one residence to another, sometimes in an instant or the wink of an eye. But this is an illusion of the senses, just like height and depth.

The reason seems to be that the human organism is designed to interact with the heavens, so that due to given [spiritual] changes answering to movements from place to place, such movements appear in the heavens on account of the interaction. For the most part they are illusions that prevail there, of which there are so many that they cannot be numbered, and at which spirits are amazed. 1747, the 15th day of December.

About the form of spirits

355. Spirits do not sense otherwise that that they are equipped with a human figure, thus with a body, skin, bones, blood (when yet it was shown them that they cannot retain things which are of no use), that they have hair, feet to stand on, and more; from which it would also follow that they have the inner parts, such as a stomach, intestines, bladder, etc., for which, however, they have no need.

When they hear all this, they do realize that they have no need of them, and yet [they see] that they retain their figure, if not an inner one, still an outer one; and in fact, they retain the shame of nakedness from the world, so that they think they are dressed in clothes, considering it a disgrace to appear naked.

Although it is really not known what their actual form is, one can nevertheless deduce this much from the most minute organs of the brain, where the beginnings of the body's form lie: that spirits are forms not unlike those [minute organs], but can still be restored to a form similar to the human one, whenever they focus the thoughts of their mind upon it. 1747, the 15th day of December.

A thousand and tens of thousands together praise God the Messiah with one mouth

356. For much of the night a multitude of spirits was around me, and afterwards a multitude of angels, flowing in accordance with a heavenly pattern that cannot be described to the human understanding; still less can it be described how they move, and speak with one mouth, or with a unanimous voice. This was so perceptible within me, and indeed for so long a time uninterruptedly, that as they speak, nothing could be more clearly witnessed: I saw the pattern, I felt the flow, I heard the unanimity of voice. Each spirit is, and affirms that he is, part of the multitude, thus all together and each one singly, or [all] collectively and [each] individually.

From their flow, one can also sense whether they are as yet initiated to such an extent that they can reach a similar unanimity in respect to spiritual and heavenly truths as well; so that afterwards, there were perhaps tens of thousands of angels around me and indeed, for a long time, whose flow, while perceptible, was nevertheless of such a kind that I could not but assume that they were streaming in an inward heavenly[1] pattern, since I could not perceive any flow in a very inward pattern.

Afterwards they told me that through the entire night, and several wakeful periods, they were doing nothing else but praising God the Messiah, and doing so with an innermost gladness of heart, so they had not wanted to be let out of that state.

From this, one can gather that unanimity is the result of a harmonious configuration; besides other conclusions one could draw from it. [*Cf.* 289–89½.] 1747, 16 December.

Those spirits who have not yet been initiated are urged on by a
certain force as of a river, to join in, or they are
carried along as by a river; hence a river
symbolizes what is spiritual

357. I have also watched still novitiate spirits, who were not yet accustomed [to the afterlife], swept into the spiritual river spoken of today on the previous page [356]. I observed the resistance of those spirits, but still they were forced to join in and were drawn little by little toward the inward regions, and then as they became conditioned, they joined in voluntarily. At length, after being more and more initiated, they were able to flow with them in almost the same manner; but I doubt whether they were able to speak and to praise along with the others, because they are still in a compelled state, and

---

[1] See 262, footnote.

even if they were obliged to speak alike, still they could not do so with the same pleasure as those who are completely unaware that they are flowing, and speaking and praising, in that pattern—the praise coming spontaneously, in an uninterrupted stream, in accord with the pattern. 1747, the 16th day of December.

The memory of particulars, together with pride on account of it, is burdensome at the first entrance into the other life

358. Everyone carries along into the other life the nature which they had acquired in the life of the body; so also do people who possess a great memory, and boast of it, and want to show it off. This memory, so inflated, is [hard], like a callous clinging to the outside. It must soften in the course of time, but meanwhile, it causes a pain in the head as if someone were trying to tear off one's scalp. 1747, the 16th day of December.

In the harmony of many, the pleasure and happiness of all is shared with each

359. It is due to the heavenly pattern that everyone flowing along with that pattern shares their own blessedness with all, and all share theirs with each, so that each one is like a center to all. Therefore, the more there are who make up the Kingdom of God the Messiah, the more the happiness of harmony in the individual groups increases, and it increases according to the levels. From this we can therefore surmise how unutterable the happiness must be, and [how it] must increase! 1747, the 16th day of December.

360. But all must be passive forces, to which active forces, in reaction, respond with a sharing by many with each. This also has the result that the harmony will be the more perfect, the greater a number there is; then the harmony itself also increases.

Daily one should pray for the heavenly kingdom—and thus, What is meant by "daily"

361. By "daily" in the Lord's Prayer is meant every moment, and this can be confirmed by experience, and thus understood.

For those to whom eternal happiness has been shown believe they have been at once transferred to heaven, thus that they, having come out of temptations, must be eternal heirs of the Kingdom—they who have labored in the vineyard and believed they were entitled to eternal salvation, which they then claim as theirs. Yet just the opposite was shown, namely that they were again plunged into crises, temptations, dangers of damnation, and the like.

One may conclude from this that "daily" means at each moment in sequence, one after another, but when in their order one within another, this [sequence of moments] is turned into an uninterrupted glorification of God the Messiah, so that the moments are continuous, without any division. Hence they have an inner sense of [states of] happiness, and it is their portion to receive these constantly from God the Messiah. 1747, the 17th day of December.

A person in the state of integrity can never die

362. I have learned from an experience, that a person who is in the state of integrity or the heavenly state, can never die; but that no one has been in that state, or has been a true human, except God the Messiah Alone. 1747, the 18th day of December.

Who the Water Carriers are
[cf. Deut. 29:11, Josh. 9:21,23,27]

363. Those who think from the Word, but not from a belief grounded in truth, that they deserve heaven because they labor in the vineyard, or preach, and also teach, and therefore think that they merit salvation, are purged in the other life by means of appropriate fantasies, but especially by this, that they seem to themselves to be carrying water from lakes or from a sea surrounding them and pouring this water into a trough, to give a flock to drink. When the trough is filled up, they rest, until they again draw and the trough is filled again to overflowing.

A flock did, in fact, appear to come to drink, but whether the flock appears to them, I cannot yet affirm. 1747, 18 December.

*There are not only fallacies of sense, but also much illusion
and imagination prevailing among souls and spirits,
consequently an apparent actuality*

364. It is remarkable, but souls and spirits have sensation altogether as in the body—touch, as in the body, like when they feel their clothes. The same is true of strong desires and appetites, heat, cold, even sweat, which are just as actual as they are in the body, when yet they cannot be called anything but illusions. But because the sensation is as real as it is in the body, they are as if real.

Conditions of this kind are brought on by a process of mental projection, as I can corroborate by very many instances.

365. The obvious conclusion, entirely beyond doubt, is that we do not live, but suppose that we live—thus that life belongs to God the Messiah Alone, even though people appear to live. This conclusion is so evident and well documented, that it cannot be denied by any souls in whom some power of reason remains. 1747, 18 December.

*Who they are that form the heart and lungs in
the Kingdom of God the Messiah*

366. It was said before [270, 279] that the Heavenly Kingdom is the image of one human being, because every least thing in it interacts with the Only Human, God the Messiah. But as for the heart, it is shaped, so to speak, by those who possess the deepest qualities, or it interacts with them; so also the Lungs. For the flowing, as we have called it [359], of those [angels] is similar, and their thinking is similar [to that of these organs].

A marriage union is displayed by the lungs, through a wonderful reciprocation which was portrayed in me by angels for the whole night, also in wakeful periods. It resembled something that seemed to be flowing, in the heart, then shaping the heart, and afterwards during wakefulness, [doing the same] in regard to the lungs; and it was observed throughout that they had their own breathing, and I my own, and that there was a union between the two breathings by a mutual interaction. 1747, the 19th day of December.

Who they are that form the kidneys

367. Spirits who compose the kidneys are those who like to dispel falsities from truths, and thereby purify spiritual things, which takes place in an incomprehensible way. From this arises the process of separation in the kidneys. 1747, the 20th day of December.

Who they are that form the liver

368. But spirits compose the liver who have something of innocence in them, for which reason also, the liver in infants is the largest organ of the body, and the infant is nourished by it, and it performs the function of several internal organs. 1747, the 20th day of December.

There is an endeavor of the heavens to hold everything together

369. It was proven to me by an actual energy that came to my sensation, that there is such a process of shaping [366–68], and thus of maintaining, the inner organs of the body, consequently, an interaction of the whole heaven with each person. This interaction consists of an imperceptible endeavor of all; from endeavor, action arises, and from action, endeavor. 1747, the 20th day of December.

What bodily Peace is

370. Bodily peace is, of course, the health of the body and of all its members, but besides health, there is also a delicious and perceptible peace of the whole body, which was made known to me by an actual and perceptible operation of spirits into the inner organs of the body, in harmony with the original shaping of the internal organs. From this there is bodily peace. 1747, the 20th day of December.

Those in the life of the body who, from jealous ambition, hope to be the greatest in heaven, and above all others, become devils

371. By an experience of several days, I learned that those in the world who want to stand out above others after the life of the body, and are therefore moved by envy against those who are better than themselves, become devils, and engage in the same kind of scheming. For they want to learn spiritual matters with nothing else in mind than the hope to rise up by means of them, on their own power, above others whom they envy; whereas the heavenly affection is to long to lift others up into heaven, even if one should turn out to be the least.

They who are such as to envy others, and who hope to stand out in heaven above others, are able to be the subjects of many spirits, a fact that has also been observed. 1747, the 20th day of December.

The human power of reasoning and understanding can be diminished, and even taken away from a person or soul, at the good pleasure of God the Messiah [see also 326]

372. From revealing Experience, I have learned that souls can be deprived almost entirely, or partially, of their reasoning and understanding abilities, and likewise have them restored again; for the understanding and reasoning faculty is a gift of God the Messiah Alone. When the reasoning and understanding abilities are taken away, the souls are devils, and they act only from a kind of natural instinct, and just as if in sleep. When these abilities are restored to them, they do not know but that they had been asleep. These facts were demonstrated over a period of many days.

When understanding has been taken away, they behave in that state in accordance with the evil rooted in them—each one according to the nature of their root, and to be sure, against order, against heaven, and its truths. In short, they are devils of diverse qualities.

It was visibly shown that it was taken away from them, as were their natural instincts afterwards. These are not like the instincts of brute animals, but issue from the diabolic impulse to strive continually against things spiritual and heavenly, and to think they have power, and do everything, from themselves. 1747, the 21st day of December.

373. One can also deduce from this the character of a person in whom a native instinct, or a nature derived from hereditary root, goes into spiritual matters, because such people think that they have all and every least thing from themselves, and thus, that they control everything.

About hell, and the cruelty of the hellish gang

374. What the cruelty of the hellish gang is like, can never be described. In their fantasies they carry on in the most hostile manner toward others, committing such cruelties against them that if they should be described, [all] would shudder. For if they were able to carry out the cruelties as in their fantasies, their butcheries would be more cruel than those of even the fiercest wild animals.

In their fantasies they seem to pull out executioner's axes, and other instruments of death; and if God the Messiah did not subdue their savagery, those they intend to torment would actually feel most severely tortured. For the power of fantasies among souls is such that it can bring on a physical-like sensation and, accordingly, one of excruciating pain. These sensations God the Messiah erases, and indeed, He takes the deadly instruments away from them.

In short, there are more horrible things than anyone could ever believe. The human race, which is worse than the fiercest wild animals, would have practiced such cruelties, had not God the Messiah saved them, and redeemed them, and did He not continually free them from the pains of hell. 1747, the 21st day of December.

375. Under my feet, the trembling from their savage and violent commotion lasted long enough for me to fully sense their fierceness. It should be noted especially that spirits' fantasies are of a kind that actually bring on sensation, altogether like physical sensation, when they direct them [at someone]; but God the Messiah erases them. No one will be able to believe this, unless he has experienced it. In fact, spirits could bring on in human bodies dreadful pains, and similar unbelievable effects, if God the Messiah were not constantly holding them off.

Diabolic spirits, by their fantasies, bring not only upon each other, but also upon people on earth, very strongly felt pains and torments

376. For many reasons I can assert that souls and spirits, by mere fantasies, were able to bring painful torments not only upon

FROM THE *BIBLE INDEX* 377.

each other, but even upon people on earth. No one may ever believe this, but still it is so true that I can fully affirm it from experience not only in myself—indeed, quite much and frequent experience—but also from [that of] souls and spirits when they were being tormented, as well as from the strong sensation the souls [experienced] from fantasies like these—which they affirm most emphatically. For every kind of sense is produced in souls as if it were a physical one, such as sight, smell, taste, hearing, yes even desires and appetites—so strong, that they hardly occur in the body so strongly.

So this applies also to sensations of pain. Most violent ones would be brought on by the diabolic gang, if God the Messiah did not save souls from such a hell. 1747, the 21st day of December.

Various fantasies follow souls from their life in the body

377. Fantasies such as they had during their life in the body do not follow souls [into the other life], but they are turned into different ones, unfamiliar to them. Therefore certain fantasies conforming with their life are put on, such as the wood-cutters and water carriers spoken of earlier [151, 271, 273, 330, 363].

1) Those who had been violent on earth, merciless in one way or another, are turned toward incredible cruelty, for they want to slaughter their companions, any of them they come across, hack them to pieces with an axe, torture them by all kinds of methods; and they derive so much enjoyment from these acts, that they are their highest pleasures.

Those who are bloodthirsty, to whom "blood" is attributed [*cf.* Gen. 4:10], enjoy tormenting a person even to drawing blood, at the sight of which they have the greatest pleasure. So an unmerciful life is turned into such fantasies, which are unrecognizable to the souls.

2) From greed, fantasies of offensive and filthy little animals break forth, such as worms, mice, and other kinds, beyond number, that have never been seen on earth, and also, foul lice. They take on a form according to the quality of their greed, and according to the intention that stirs their greed.

3) One fantasy of the diabolical gang is to want to be in latrines. When they look at an outhouse, they think it is their home, finding it exceedingly enjoyable there, and imagining it to be their

heaven. This has become known to me by much experience. 1747, 22 December.

Fantasies belonging to their earthly part, after souls have been created anew, are turned into human images

378. Because all evil is turned into good by God the Messiah, so fantasies of this kind, i.e. of filthy and foul little animals, which are the shapes of the fantasies, are turned at length into human images, varying in beauty. For a person's every least idea or mental image exactly reflects that person in effigy, or [said in another way:] there is a human effigy in a person's every single mental image. 1747, the 22nd day of December.

An outer joy, quasi-heavenly, can come over a person, which is nevertheless filthy, even though the souls thought it must be exceedingly heavenly

379. Today when first awakening, I was surrounded by very many spirits of differing character. Some of them wanted to deceitfully bring upon me their own heavenly joy, which is done by the transfer of one's own joy or delight to another, regardless of what produces that delight—in this case, the diabolic gang under the feet [were causing it] from a cruel fantasy that I clearly felt them breathing into me.

Because of this I felt a delight that took hold of my whole body, even the inner organs, and this in a way that made me think I was in heavenly joy among the blessed; for I was totally relaxed in soothing sensations, like those from soothing warm baths. The causes of these delights were not being felt in me, nor the fact that they arose from any cruelty, nor that they [were brought on] by deception: they were delights in which such things were not felt, because they adapt to those they meet with, and to the recipient's state of mind. For example, in a state when one is peaceful, one looks at all things in peace, even things that are not peaceful; and when one is in an angry state, everything arouses anger—even the playing of little chidren, etc. etc.

2] Besides these bodily, outer delights, also inner ones were poured in, and indeed by different spirits, who wanted to cause me delights because of a kind of veneration. The rest of the spirits I could not recognize, nor investigate the intentions of those from whom the delights came. Still, I lingered for quite a time in the sweetness of delights converging upon me; and I spoke about that sweet feeling as I replied to those who wanted to lead me astray and persuade me that this was heavenly joy.

I do not remember my replies, but because I had not sensed any deception I thought this was indeed heavenly delight, but an outer one, thus flowing forth from outer causes and therefore not able to last, and I wanted to remove myself from it and thus refuse it, because it did not originate from the innermost. It is possible for these [outer] delights as they were felt to serve innermost delights as an embodiment—which is put aside at once, and despised, as soon as the delight from the innermost is felt. But I heard that this body of delights was filthy, which I myself could not feel. 1747, the 22nd day of December.

^{m}I am now being told that this kind of delight was given to Abraham [see 381], but that as it went on, it decreased, as he says, and he doubts whether it can last any longer, now that he has learned that there is an inward or heavenly delight.^{n}

There are other states besides that afflict souls

380.   Aside from the states [of fantasy] mentioned [377], there are also other ones, like thinking they are carrying people on their backs who interrogate them unceasingly until they have gotten the right answer. Carrying such [spirits] is burdensome for them, and they cannot get rid of them before the time for release has come.

Some [are afflicted] differently: they lie on their backs on a downward slope, and there they want to stay. There are some there who comfort them, but they are content with their lot; for their outermost part has been removed.

There are also those who wander about, and wherever they come, ask whether there is any work for them that needs doing. After being answered that there is no work, they go on farther, and they keep this up until they find work. 1747, the 23rd day of December.

381.   SPIRITUAL EXPERIENCES

Some who are enemies of faith nevertheless enjoy a kind of outer pleasure, which they call heavenly

381. As said before [*cf.* 379], there are some enemies of genuine faith who are continually striving against belief and inciting others to disbelief, even alluring them by saying they count themselves among the blessed. But their pleasure is only an outer one such as that of disbelievers in the world, and even if it is more exalted, yet because it is only an outer pleasure and fights against inner or true pleasure, it comes to an end, like the pleasures of disbelievers in the world, and is turned into unpleasantness and grief.

There are reasons why these people are still tolerated and kept in that outer blessedness and apparent joy. Meanwhile, their remaining truths and goodness diminish, so that they finally retain such a small remnant of truth and goodness, that they can hardly be made happy unless they repent while there is still time.

This was told to Abraham and his crowd, about whom I spoke earlier [379]. The same is true of those spirits and furies who are still wandering about in the last heaven [223, 228–29].

Therefore, they who want to enter into truly heavenly joy must undergo temptations, punishments, purgings, which are unavoidable, unless they want to abide in outer [blessedness and apparent joy] and thereby have their remnant [of truth and goodness] eventually go to waste. 1747, the 23rd day of December.

The words of God the Messiah penetrate to the heavens, and to the inward, in fact innermost parts of spirits and angels

382. When the Word of God the Messiah is read, it enters within people according to their own state. So with those who are in the body, it hardly enters more deeply than the bodily senses, whereas in souls of the dead, spirits and angels, it penetrates to each one's innermost parts. And as I can infer from what I was told by heavenly beings, just by the mere reading or reciting [of the Word] by a person on earth, it reaches and has its effect on anyone God the Messiah wishes in the heavens.

This kind of effect and indeed, penetration, does exist; I know for certain from things that have been said, and read, by me, and in fact, several times: namely, that they reached a large number, with varying degrees of effectiveness, and penetrated to their innermost parts.

383. One can see from this quite clearly that the words spoken by God the Messiah filled the universal heaven, and so completely, that everyone would be touched by them. This is the working power of the Word, and this is Its Life. 1747, the 23rd day of December.

*The greedy after death seem to themselves to be shut up
in small underground rooms where there are mice*

384. There are degrees of greed, and also motives of greed. They who are greedy for money alone, which they even bury in the earth in storerooms, seem to themselves to stay in the little rooms where their riches are, and there, in fact, to be plagued by mice the size of mountains, so that they will withdraw from there. Yet they do not go away until they are wearied, when they finally roll away from these rooms, their graves. 1747, the 24th day of December.

*They who love libraries as their riches, and fill themselves
up reading books, likewise stay in rooms befitting
the degree of that passion, and its motives*

385. Those possessed of a passion for mere reading, and for remembering the things read for the sake of praise and reputation, appear to themselves to dwell in underground places, and to have books there, and candles, which now and then go out; and they seem to themselves to be reading. But so that they will tire of these fantasies, it is told, they are sometimes attacked by mice and similar creatures, which draw them away from that passion. 1747, the 24th day of December.

*Those who indulge in promiscuous practices also seem
to themselves to be in underground places*

386. They who had loved a promiscuous life, secretly practicing loose sexuality, likewise seem to themselves to dwell in underground places, like little rooms, furnished with candles, and in fact with women resembling those who were[1] [the objects] of their lewd promiscuity in secret. For fantasies take over when they depart from this life, and are turned into scenes of this kind.

But they too are plagued, in a manner suited to the degree and motive of their promiscuities, as if by mice, and by the type of foul insects that the intentions of their lewdness had inwardly been. And even if they do not know that their intentions had been of this nature, yet these are now revealed to them in the form of foul insects and suchlike, until they abstain from them. For souls are at first led by means of fantasies, from which they are gradually turned away.

Thus instead of sensual pleasure they are allotted dreadful fantasies, which then take hold on them, until they so detest the sensual pleasures that they want nothing more of them, and therefore finally turn away from them, even abhor them. So [the fantasies] are according to one's motives, or hidden loves. 1747, the 24th day of December.

There are filthy and foul little animals that attack and torture them

387. All fantasies that occur because of a forbidden love of the body or mind, have as a companion, or along with them, animals that are offensive, filthy, foul, frightening, stinking, etc., with which spirits are confronted while engaged in their forbidden fantasies aroused by their passions and pleasures, in which they find the most intense enjoyment. As a result, their enjoyments are intermixed with such horror-provoking creatures.

The species of such insects are countlessly many. I have seen some of them displayed, but they are innumerable. Each species is fashioned to image some mixture of fantasies with loves or motives—the fantasies that inevitably follow and accompany earthly-minded persons, who live their life upside-down. From their enjoyments results a most dreadful hell; for as great as the feeling of pleasure in such enjoyments is, so great is the feeling of pain, and of fright, that arises when their worldly and bodily [enjoyments], which they imagine to be heavenly, are turned into hellish ones. 1747, the 24th day of December.

---

[1] The original has *sunt*, which we understand to mean "are [in their earthly life...]."

FROM THE *BIBLE INDEX*

They who want to have worldly possessions for themselves alone,
and to keep them away from everyone else, are
eventually thrown out of heaven

388. The kind of people who long to possess everything on earth and in the world, hating others in comparison with themselves and scorning them as if they should be regarded as the dirt of the streets, have an unfavorable lot awaiting them. At first, they seem to themselves to be living in the highest places of heaven, and in fact, to be enjoying the highest pleasure, like the rest. So they look down upon all as of no account, deep beneath their feet; but the lot awaiting them is just that, namely, that they are cast down and become the lowest, and are degraded to the very level at which they by their hatred had held others. For a love for all is heavenly and Divine. 1747, the 24th day of December.

It is mere fantansy that seems to be real, and in fact,
the kind of illusion that souls in that state
cannot at all distinguish from reality

389. About these states it has been said, and in many places shown, that only fantasies prevail that put on so much seeming reality that [the souls] think they can touch and feel things, like clothing and such, just as in the body. Accordingly, they seem to themselves to be actually in underground vaults, or in a high heaven above the rest, when yet they are scattered over the whole world. If the fantasies are simply bent or turned, those in the lowest places can seem to themselves to be in the highest, and so forth. 1747, the 24th day of December.

About the torment of those who use violence against others, and
feel joy in oppressing them; thus about those to whom is
ascribed blood, violence, oppression [see 377]

391.[1] After life in the body, since life like fantasies continue by which their inward qualities show themselves, therefore they who are violent and oppressors of their fellow man, no matter what the driving passion, are tormented in hell in the following way.

---

[1] 390 is lacking in the original.

With the greatest eagerness, they take those whom they fantasize that they are seizing, and tear them apart, slaughter them, chop them up with an axe, and torment them in a thousand different ways. Those who are bloodthirsty derive the greatest joy from blood, and the greater the torture, the greater is their enjoyment, which is held out to be so great among them that they say it surpasses all enjoyments.

But then these in turn are exposed to the same torment by their companions, who are thereby, in their turn, gladdened in the same way, even until the former have been so tormented, and for such a long time, that they desist; and because a dread of retaliation seizes them, that enjoyment at length passes away, and so they are finally rid of it. 1747, the 24th day of December.

Idol worshippers, like the African and similar peoples, are governed after death by nothing but fantasies, and are thus purged

392. I was shown by a vision what kind of fantasies remain after death with those who are idolaters, or what kind of life follows them. They seem to themselves to be transformed into lowly little animals, dwelling in small houses built of clay, which they go out of and return to. Thus they lead a quite contented life, if only they are not attacked by beings who destroy their little huts of mud. For those they call devils, and while their faces appeared quite human to me, yet they were fierce, or unappeasable, as they say. They destroy their little houses, and maul [their occupants] and, like cats, stalk and bite them; and they are very afraid of them.

So they depart from that place and build little houses elsewhere, but they are attacked in the same way, until at last they become disgusted with that very base life. Meanwhile, they hold to a worship conformable with their idolatry, for there is a marble base on which [figures] resembling living ones are carried around, and these they worship from the heart.

393. After they have become disgusted with this life of repeated lacerations and attacks, then they are transferred into a better condition, and indeed, as it seems to them, into human bodies, but having faces of monkeys or apes, which they can turn forward or backward, and thus look all around them to see that no harm befalls them from their enemies, whom they had fled. Then they live in beautiful houses, like small palaces, and after they have passed through this life, they vanish, because their purging is then completed and they have entirely forgotten their former life in the world, thus their idol worship, and they are instructed, then renewed.

394. There are others besides, who are brought together around a large swan, or a swan with its neck stretched very high, and are following it. Such a fantasy prevails with those of them who seem to themselves to be well informed in the life of the body. 1747, the 25th day of December.

Pleasures can be transmitted from one to many

395. This remarkable phenomenon exists in the other life: not only can the pleasures of one be shared with many others through speech and gestures, and the resulting feelings of each, but also, the pleasures [themselves] can be actually carried over to others, and be felt by them. This fact originates in the heavenly marriage, from which come the delights of earthly marriages, and also the sharing of them between married partners. 1747, the 25th day of December.
^{m}In heaven this is done by the Lord through the language of mental imagery, as well as through their mutual love, in that each one has regard for and longs for the good of the other, which is something imparted by the Lord.^{n}

A comparison of character with trees and fruits
Nothing exists in the world that is not a portrayal of what is
heavenly, and a result as it were of what is spiritual

396. All things whatsoever that are in the vegetable and in the animate kingdom, are portrayals and as it were results of things spiritual and heavenly, and in fact, in a countless variety. For earthly things could never have come forth nor continued, except from spiritual ones, a fact that can be demonstrated in countless ways. Here I will speak only of how character develops in a person growing up. This is seen imaged in trees and their fruits, such as apples and others: the surface or covering is the mother of the fruit in the inward parts or cores; through the surface and the fibers reaching in from it, all the inward parts are developed. The flavor images pleasantness [of character].

After the inward parts have developed from the surface, by means of fibers branching in from all sides, then the hard coverings are separated—as with an almond—and the kernels remain.

So in the comparable process of human development: it commences from higher knowledge, thus from matters of the intellect, whereby character is acquired, which is like the kernel so formed. From the flavor of the kernel it is evident what the juice or sap, that is, the life of the person, had been like. These things were written in the presence of angels and spirits. 1747, the 25th day of December.

Because many human characters, or souls, resemble unripe or rotten fruits, having a stinking odor, therefore they cannot be compared to anything but those fruits which must develop anew in good ground.[1]

A vision by day, about those who are given to feasting, and thus devoted to the flesh

397. At midday, around lunch time, an angel who was with me cautioned me not to overindulge my stomach at table. While he was with me, a kind of vapor clearly appeared to me to be issuing from the pores of my body, having a visibly very watery quality. It seemed to sink down toward the floor, where there was a carpet on which the vapor, coming together, turned into different kinds of tiny worms. These, gathered together under the table, in an instant, and with a crackling sound, just burned up.

I saw the fiery flash, and heard the noise, and judged that all the little worms that can be generated by an immoderate appetite had thus been cast out of my body and burned up, and that I had now been cleansed of them. From this experience, one may infer what sumptuous living and the like, harbor within them. 1745, April. [*See* 93a].[2]

---

[1] This paragraph seems to be deleted in the original.
[2] See also R.L. Tafel, *Documents*, vol. II, pp. 35–36.

About Permissions [of evil]

398. The teachings regarding permissions make up an entire doctrine. Anyone who does not understand permissions, yet draws conclusions about them, falls into doubting and negative thoughts about God the Messiah's power over the Universe. But it ought to be known that without the permission [of evil], no one can be reformed. For opposites have to be brought to bear in order that the shapes of what is true and of what is good will stand out, which acquire their ability to appear, and thus to be seen, etc., from opposites. Hence [comes the need of] temptations, purgings, punishments, persecutions of believers and of the faith, and more.

In short, without the permission of evils—a term which must be understood in the right sense—a person can never be regenerated and guided with any awareness, and consequently with any happiness, into the capability of being bent toward good by God the Messiah. 1747, the 25th day of December.

Evil spirits can, when permitted, bring on almost any seemingly heavenly sensation, when yet it is counterfeit and external

399. This last night I was awakened by very evil spirits, who tried to destroy heavenly qualities, bringing upon me a delicate feeling that resembled the feeling of heavenly delights, and even the feeling of marital delight, so that one could scarcely tell the difference. But being warned, I learned that these [delights] were all fake and counterfeit. For [the spirits] were deriving this feeling from their enjoyment in destroying, by their own methods, what is heavenly, and were transferring it to me in the way you may see described above [379]. So a person can never tell what is diabolical and what is heavenly apart, except from God the Messiah, therefore by belief in God the Messiah. 1747, the 25th day of December.

After the death of the body, departed souls gain many abilites beyond those they had while living in the body

400. The souls of the departed either a shorter or longer time after the death of the body, before being brought into the company of spirits, are quite dull, and know almost nothing. But as soon as they become associated with many, they acquire mental powers. Not only do they regain the keenness of mind they had possessed in the body, but also, when associated with their peers in such a way that they can serve as mediums for thought focussing, then whatever mentality they have is so greatly sharpened that they are much more acute than they were during bodily life.

Add to this the fact that now they do not function with a memory of personal affairs, which distracts them in bodily life, but directly from a kind of instinct. Now they seem to grasp more deeply and more fully the meaning of what is being said, because their mind is withdrawn from the body and its objects—so that the perception of one in the body is not nearly as penetrating.

Moreover, they are able to speak with people on earth in their own language, no matter where they were born. Also, [the spirit] comes into complete possession of the person's memory, to the point where he seems to be the person, thus even [to possess] their power of understanding. But there is the difference, that the spirit retains his own life, that is, the life of his own love or passion, causing him to feel things differently—however, these spirits are deprived of that life while people are being led by them.

Also, they very easily put on various conditions, such as innumerable different states of wakefulness and sleep, among many others. 1747, the 25th day of December.

NB. NB.   *In regard to Permissions: every single thing tends toward the good of the universe, or of all*

401.   There are also permissions whereby spirits who think they are powerful enough to accomplish anything, claim to have the power on their own to arouse evils in mankind, and [engage in] other unallowable and unlawful activities, trying any of numerous methods, even unlawful ones usually employed in working wonders— thus magical arts.

These things God the Messiah never grants, but He is said to permit them [to do] that which, among many things, is to be permitted—as for example, their continually wanting to stir up trouble. So the only things permitted them are those which lead to the improvement of mankind, souls and spirits (other things are not permitted), each and every detail of which God the Messiah so controls and governs that there is not a whit *that they do as if by permission* that does not lead to the good of many, thus of the universe, and of all. *For the good of each can be shared with all in the universe, and shall, in fact, be so shared, when God the Messiah's kingdom is established.* 1747, the 25th day of December.

From peoples afar, many kinds of spirits are being educated by means of their idols

402. A soul brings along with him from the world the adoration of whatever idol he had worshipped in the world. Accordingly, souls are guided right to those whom they had venerated during the life of the body, so as to be instructed there and gradually put off their idolization.

There was one people gathered around their chief—I was told they were from the Indies—worshipping the greatest God. They did this by a ceremony in which, while they were adoring Him, they were magnifying themselves in a certain way, and then straightway prostrating themselves as little worms, due to a notion they had kept with them.

Moreover, it had been more or less instilled into them to visualize the whole human race as being whirled around in heaven, and the great God following along with them from above, watching what they were doing. So [they thought of Him as being] present, zealously watching over the whirling realm.

His spirits had been taught a way of bringing upon their magnate a kind of breathing. His spirits came also to me, and brought the same thing upon me so that I would know this from experience. They were kind, and obedient, and behaving with their simple candor. Their spiralling flow, characteristic of such spirits, proceeded with ease. Later, different ones arrived, who seemed to execute this [action] even more flawlessly. 1747, the 26th day of December.

Mohammedan spirits are very teachable, obedient to their Mohammed, doing him every kindness from the heart, differently from many spirits in the Christian world

403. Once again I spoke with Mohammed [*see* 339, 344], and then spirits were sent to me who had been taught differently, that is, who had been taught how to delight Mohammed in a different and new way, or how to cause him pleasure. He said that he had wanted to pass this delight and pleasure on to me, but it was not permitted. However, he said that he did manage to send over spirits, so that he could show me how teachable and obedient they were.

These spirits were then taught that they should adore God the Messiah Alone, and indeed, both small and great; for everyone is given the privilege to adore God the Messiah, Who governs the universe. By this instruction they were excited, and gave thanks to God most humbly, promising they would take this to heart. 1747, the 26th day of December.

They were taught to cause a kind of washing from the head to the feet, with the accompanying enjoyment.

About the life and punishment of those who during their life want to make profit, and look out only for themselves

404. There were some who during their life had wanted only to make profit for themselves, doing this by the usual technique of eager business people. They get close to those from whom they can gain, eyeing their wealth, which, under a guise of friendship, is what holds their attention.

These people wander around, and wherever they come they ask if they may join those who are there, saying that they are poor. So they are welcomed; but because they stare with longing on their wealth or possessions, they are expelled. So again they wander around and repeat the same behavior, until they have learned how to say one thing while thinking another. This they do with so much skill that spirits can scarcely tell but that they are as they say they are.

In this manner a spirit of that type also came to me, asking whether he might stay here and serve me. I replied to him that I am nothing, but that everyone is welcomed by God the Messiah.

But since they had been like this and would probably say one thing with their mouth while wanting something else at heart, they were given the power of punishing one of their own, miserably. Now there were many spirits disagreeing [with each other], who all wanted to have him as their medium for speaking and acting; and since they were against one another, that medium was being miserably pulled apart, or being torn to pieces by action from both directions. This went on uninteruptedly for about an hour.

In fact, they induced on him the illusion of a kind of body, and were then attempting to tear the whole body and its parts to pieces. How much pain he felt from this, I cannot tell. The pain is milder [or sharper] depending on the degree and nature of the simulation. The one speaking with me said that it had been most fierce. It becomes more and more painful according as the illusion is induced of having a body, with body-like sensations—also according as weariness and resistance come over him, making him long to be freed and let go from them. For it is impossible for him to free himself.

It is a kind of tearing apart into small pieces. The tearing spirits admitted that they had gotten much enjoyment from being able to torment souls in this way, wherefore their fellow spirits were subsequently permitted to torment them one after another, so that they would thus learn to abstain from, and finally abhor, that kind of enjoyment.

2] Thereafter, they were then sent off and, having changed their way of speaking, approached some spirits in order to steal into their company. But once more they were cast out, because the spirits recognized them and said that they were slipping in with the purpose of robbing them of their possessions. For the spirits also create the illusion of having much wealth, which people like these intensely covet.

They told how they had also been punished elsewhere. This is the condition that awaits those who, under a cloak of friendship, lead others on with the sole purpose of obtaining their riches, like very many in the world. They roam far and wide in desert-like places, and when they come upon companions and cheat them, they are punished and cast out. Thus they are more miserable than such a person's ears could believe [if told about it].

These latter words were written from him who had been among robbers, and was pulled apart in this way. 1747, the 26th day of December.

The spirits and souls speaking with me are mediums upon whom many are focussing

405. From experience I have finally learned that the spirits speaking with me are the mediums, or focal points, for many spirits. Because all spirits, including the evil, are grouped into their own kinds and species. 1747, the 26th day of December.

About the coldness of those who are part of the devil's gang

406. Every time a smaller or larger number of the diabolic gang, or those from hell, were allowed to draw near, I was seized with varying degrees of cold, and indeed, in different parts of the body—around the head, at the ears, around the body, on the feet. I could tell by the cold that they were coming, as well as by a usually chilly gust of air; and on almost every occasion I even spoke with them.

As said before [372–3], they are governed by an evil or a wicked nature, as if by instinct, and are entirely irrational, not knowing what they are doing, and yet imagine themselves to be more intelligent than all in heaven and completely in charge. For this reason, since their wickness is ingrafted and they are incapable of understanding, I was obliged out of pity to speak kindly with them.

This surprised some who had not long before departed life in the body and had brought with them the idea that one should not speak with a devil, but rather should constantly chastise them. However, they were then instructed on this point: for when God the Messiah is protecting someone, nothing can harm him, nor does it harm him if the whole of hell should close in on him, both from without and from within, as much supernatural experience has proven to me. 1747, the 26th day of December.

About Mohammedan Spirits

407. Today also, spirits were sent over to me by Mohammed who had been taught by their own methods, while flowing in their spiralling patterns, to depict washings, from the sole of the foot on upwards. They enacted this on me with such realism, that I have no doubt but that they who take pleasure in washings are delighted by it.

Then I also spoke for a while with Mohammed. 1747, the 27th day of December.

FROM THE *BIBLE INDEX* 409.

About some who had been instructed, and not wanting to recognize God the Messiah, were thrust down and cast out of heaven

408. For several days there had been some in the heaven of spirits who were stirring up trouble and persuading others that God the Messiah was not the mediator, besides other hostile sayings inspired by their fantasy. They had led many astray, thus causing a kind of rebellion, in which certain ones joined up with them. While this was going on for several days, God the Messiah, as He had been present before to my spiritual vision, seemed to have disappeared, and so I was abandoned to these spirits' fantasy of recognizing only Jehovah the Father of God the Messiah, without a mediator. All this I was granted to see by spiritual vision, wondering what would come of it.

Presently I heard, and sensed by spiritual vision, that the rebelling spirits had been seized with pain, and that that band had been cast out, and were being miserably tormented. This I am now hearing from them. There is much moaning and weeping. They number near the tens of thousands, as they declare, begging that no one let himself be misled again, if he does not want to suffer indescribable tortures.

This and a like gang is meant where God the Messiah speaks of one who slipped into the feast not clothed in a wedding garment, and was cast out from it [Matt. 22:11-14]. 1747, 28 Dec.

They were cast into a swamp.

About the many and the different ways of flushing out those who find their way into heaven and think they are in heaven because they are welcomed by the heavenly, who love as many as come, and believe all their qualities to be genuine, until they are exposed

409. In an uninterrupted spiritual vision, I experienced, and was also now and then taught aloud, that heaven is purged by various means of those who steal in, putting on what looks like a wedding garment, pretending to be angels. They display themselves in outer form as angels, but inwardly they are wolves who are continually leading believers astray. These are let in by believers because, amongst the multitude being freed from the pit, there are many of the kind who have not yet been purged. These wander among good spirits and angels, slipping into their company in angelic guise, and then, behaving in conformity with their shrewd talents and the sneaky character still with them, they entice the innocent to their side through intrigues that are second nature to them.

They are especially those who are steeped in self-love, and in various worldly loves. They indeed have stored within them the knowledge that there is a heavenly marriage. It is that very wedding feast the whole world is invited to [Matt. 22:9], which they thus slip into, and thereupon seek to destroy, so that they may obtain supreme power and then, from hatred, work against all in heaven.

How these matters stand, and how these spirits were exposed, and how they were cast down from that heaven in bands, would be too much to tell. However, they who have been cast down out of that feast are treated miserably, being thrown into a swamp. When they may again be delivered from there, no one can say, for one's term of imprisonment in the swamp, as well as one's depth in it, differ according to each person's wickness. If the wickedness is only superficial, the punishment is lighter than that of people who, by bringing evil into act, have developed deeper roots.

Very many were surprised that gangs of this kind emerged in that realm, because nothing appears there but turmoil, confusion and condemnation. Therefore, so that they could be shown the nature and magnitude of the heaven of God the Messiah, this was also portrayed by a wonderful flowing movement of countless numbers of stars, and an actual voice then said to them that such, and so great, is the Heaven of God the Messiah. It was added that that gang only appears as a multitude, but that this kind of purging occurs every day and at every moment—otherwise mankind, with all its different states, could never be purified, so as to be able to stay in heaven. 1747, the 28th day of December.

410. Abraham also, together with the gang around him that imagined itself to be at the top of heaven, was also cast out, and is now in the lower parts. This gang, even though they were few, had nevertheless conspired against the Heaven of God the Messiah, and against God the Messiah. As for Abraham, he must be spoken about cautiously; I am told that he also is now being punished. 1747, the 28th day of December.

FROM THE *BIBLE INDEX* 413.

411. I was told that hereafter, they will seek Abraham in vain, because he is not found anywhere, *neither is his place found anymore in heaven* [*cf.* Rev. 12:8].

Words of speech cannot express, much less thoroughly present anything, in the third heaven[1]
Also, about the efficacy of winged speech generally

412. Just from the speaking, and utterance of words, it could be heard and seen what was in them. By a method that is spiritual, and unknown to others, it becomes clear at once that words are inadequate, but what it is that imposes such strict limitations on words, and turns them into a different meaning, has not yet become clear. For even symbolic expressions can be deprived of meaning by the general state of mind of spirits in the lower realm of the third heaven.[2]

Moreover, it is amply certain that human speech is not at all adequate to express inward heavenly[3] matters, for which reason [its words] are given content by God the Messiah, so that they may make their way to spirits and angels, and enter their thoughts in a form adapted to each one's grasp and inner sight, achieving the effect that the speech is intended to produce. Such speech can be called "winged"—but figuratively. 1747, the 28th day of December.

There are three different kinds of people and souls

413. The human race, as also their souls after the death of the body, can be distinguished into three kinds. 1) The first kind, which is the largest and the most common, are like the wild animals of the forest, that is, against order. 2) The second kind is in some order, yet not from a genuine source but from a lower source, still looking downwards like the beasts of the earth. They are able to perform good deeds resembling those that come from true caring, but which regard [only] worldly values. So they are not among those who believe in God the Messiah: and gentiles of good character can be counted among them, who are able to be regenerated more easily than the rest. 3) The third kind is heavenly, due to their belief in God

---

[1] *I.e.,* in descending order.
[2] See previous footnote.
[3] *I.e.,* pertaining to the inward heaven. See 262, footnote.

the Messiah. Their works are acts of true caring, and these acts are the fruits of their belief.

These things I did not hear, or speak about with anyone, but something like this was pictured in my thought in a dream-like vision. However, I can also draw the inference from it that there is yet another kind, perhaps intermediate between the first and the second. 1747, the 28th day of December.

The diabolic gang likes to linger nowhere but in toilets, and similar places

414. It will be astonishing to anyone to hear that the diabolic gang does not like to dwell anywhere but in toilets, which they have several times admitted, even depicting to me how fond they are of staying in latrines, where there is human excrement, nor do they choose any other place, but prefer this above all. Certain other spirits were much offended at this, despite the fact they admitted the same thing to others like themselves. 1747, the 28th day of December.

Spirits know how to shift their own evil to another in an instant; likewise [to turn] good into evil

415. It is amazing how spirits, from what seems to be a natural instinct, are able at once to transform good into evil, and this very expertly, as though they had learned it from long practice. Likewise, how they can transfer some punishment or other, which they have coming to them, to someone else, and even to an innocent person, and thus escape it that time around. This has become evident to me from much experience, which would be too much to cite.

This kind of nature or instinct has no other origin than the habit formed in bodily life of lying, and thereby shifting all blame to another, or causing suspicion to fall upon another, so as to be freed of it oneself. This is what leads to such a distorted character. 1747, the 28th day of December.

416. So instantaneous is both the shifting of good into evil by various methods, and of a penalty threatening oneself to someone else, that there could hardly be anything quicker; therefore, it must spring from an [evil] rooted in by practice, that becomes second nature. *This leads to the conclusion, that hardly anything else holds* *sway in evil spirits, but a root of evil acquired by inheritance and by practice.* 1747, the 28th day of December.

About a change that took place in heaven

417. There were some who had seized the highest place in heaven, because when on earth they had believed they were uppermost, and all but themselves were as nothing. That place was occupied by some whom I am not permitted to mention by name, nor am I allowed to make known the reason. Such [spirits] as these are compared to stars, for they appear to themselves like suns, and souls drifting up from the world worship them. Because they had worshipped them in life, they are just introduced to them, so that they may then be released.

A large one of those stars was yesterday, if I am not mistaken, cast down out of that highest place, and with him, whom they had worshipped as an idol, a crowd numbering about five to six hundred, as I was told. But today they and their chief, lingering in that realm as they had continually before, now began to stir up greater trouble. For this reason their chief, after being instructed once more and warned, and yet not wanting to step away from his upside-down view of faith, was therefore rejected, and for about one or two minutes, suffered hellish torments that made him cry out miserably. Presently, when he was delivered from them, a voice came to him from heaven, [saying] that Jesus Christ is the Son of God. So he then began to think on it and acknowledge it somewhat, but because only the torments had compelled him to it, his confession is not yet acceptable, because it does not yet come from belief.

How permissions are portrayed in nature

418. Pernmissions in Heaven are pictured in nature by the threefold or fourfold atmospheres, the one being a step purer than the other. Each subsequent one is composed from the one before, and acts upon the next composed atmosphere both from within and from without so that in each single part of the last atmosphere, the prior ones are present in their order.

While the last atmosphere is troubled by harsh weather, the one immediately prior to it is working quite calmly both from without and from within in its least parts, thus in the part and in the whole. The atmosphere prior to that does likewise, still more calmly, and the first one most calmly or peacefully, it being the all in all of the following atmospheres both in their parts and in the whole. In this way, by producing a calm, a prior atmosphere, and especially, the first, acts upon the following atmospheres, and through these upon the last one, and restores equilibrium, however turbulent the last atmosphere may be from wind or storm.

So it is in the heavens between the heavenly beings, and the spirits who form as it were a last atmosphere, where there are storms. One standing there would think that the whole heaven was falling because of the appearing storms, downpours, black clouds; yet after their assault, they are peacefully brought back to rest in response to the nod and will of God the Messiah.

These things were thought, but written down in the presence of spirits. 1747, the 29th day of December.

Certain ones, especially the Laplanders and similar peoples, are governed by a fantasy that they are carrying little children, and want to show them to the Lord of Heaven

419. There are some who are completely governed when they come into the other life by the imagination that there are little children in their arms, as many as they can possibly carry in all kinds of positions, just so there is a multitude of them, and at the same time, a line of boys and girls out in front of them. [Approaching] in this manner, they ask where the Lord of the place is, wanting to show Him their infants and children. However, when asked [why], they said that they wanted to nourish their children.

On interrogation, these appeared to be like the people who have long inhabited Lapland, and not unlike them as to dress. But this has now begun, because they have now been instructed, and previously they did not come in this manner, but at the sound of two muffled horn blasts, they would enter with hideous little animals.

Those people, on account of their love of little children, are more acceptable than many others, for the heavens love that love. 1747, 30 December.

FROM THE *BIBLE INDEX* 423.

There are some also who worship Christ as an infant,
and who carry Him

420. There are also those who from innocence, and from harmless simplicity also, worship God the Messiah as an infant. Because of their simplicity and innocence, they, too, are let in (although they do not remain there for long), because they are innocents and simplicities, who have peace in which is innocence. There the heavenly [aura] is constantly present, which I could recognize because of the joy carried over from them.

I am prohibited from writing any more, for the reason that they worship human beings, and exhibit images of them in every temple, in every house, on the highways and at cross-roads, which is entirely forbidden; but with those who do this out of simplicity, and thus out of innocence, this is overlooked. 1747, 30 December.

More are now seeking Peter than before, so as to gain
admittance into heaven

421. It was plainly shown to me that Peter was cast down out of heaven [13a, 67a]. Since that time I heard nothing about Peter until today, when I was told that now more [souls] than ever before are coming and adoring Peter, entreating him to let them into Heaven. The reason may be that something has just been revealed to those called the Jesuits, to the effect that Peter had been let down out of heaven, and that they can no longer approach him, as souls just arriving from the world did previously. Whether there is another reason, I do not yet know.

Quakers especially, when they enter the other life, worship
a cloud, on their knees

423.[1] Someone appeared to me vaguely, like a cloud, kneeling, who was worshipping a cloud. When I inquired what this was, I was told that Quakers are subject to such a fantasy, because they make up a heaven for themselves out of their own fantasy, not knowing what is truly heavenly, or what faith is. For they fashion the heaven they long for, and this is turned into a corresponding fantasy; nor could it

---

[1] 422 does not occur in the original.

be otherwise, because they will not allow themselves to be taught by others, nor by the Word of God the Messiah, but cling to their assumed principles, believing they are ruled by the holy spirit, when yet nothing could be less true.

For there are spirits who do not know what heaven is, and who the lord of heaven is, yet want to be hailed as the holy spirit. That group is being increased by Quaker souls, but they are distinguished from [other] spirits by a white line around the head of two of them, for they usually appear in pairs. "Enthusiastic spirits" is what they call the simple ones who only repeat their adopted principles and teachings, and so arouse enthusiasm. Such enthusiasm they very highly value, so that they can be personalities and can put themselves forth as the holy spirit. 1747, the 30th day of December.

To [new] souls, the Gospel is preached just as it is on earth

424. It may strike everyone as remarkable, though nothing is more true, that the Gospel is preached to souls in the same way as on earth, and in fact with the same sort of preaching, zeal, eloquence of expression. For they all believe themselves to be on earth, as often mentioned before. Strange as this may be, I can affirm that nothing is more true.

But the Gospel is preached only to those who are to be let out of the pit, and to some others as well. I know, too, from much evidence, that different ones also are speaking with souls, and preaching; but the Word has no effectiveness except that which is given by God the Messiah.

There are some who are continually building houses

425. Once again I saw and heard those spirits speaking and giving an account, who build houses and palaces, but which are torn down by others [392–93], and then built again. Whenever they are broken down, they grieve that they cannot live in them because they are torn down. Busy at this work are those who had been seen before with faces on both sides, also some with a single face, for about the same reason as before [393].

FROM THE *BIBLE INDEX*

The souls of the dead, if they do not retain their fantasies and are not led by their fantasies, cannot be guided to inner knowledge, and thus prepared for Heaven

426. At this day, when there is no belief, hardly anyone could be made ready for heaven in the other life, because of the upside-down order of [their] life, unless nothing but fantasies prevail, or hallucinations of the senses. These reside in the [newly arrived] souls in their earthly or lower minds, where the main life of people living at this day centers.

Such souls, filled with so many fantasies, are not broken—that is, their fantasies cannot be dispelled or extinguished all at once, for thus they would be broken, and nothing of their own emotional life would be left, for it is composed of pure fantasy.

This is supported by so much evidence that there can be no doubt about it. There is an insanity in everything, which rules the life and makes up the life of [such] a person. Just now, a certain one was abandoned by the spirits who were functioning together with him, and it then appeared as if he were not alive; when thus deprived of his fantasies, he was thought to be dead. But even this could not prove anything, except that a person cannot enter into the other life like this. In such a condition, he can learn nothing. 1747, the 30th day of December.

Some, due to a special mercy, are prepared by means of deep sleep, and in the sleep by troubling dreams

427. There was also one who kept on saying only, "I am silent," and "I am speaking," and this quite frequently. Upon being asked what this was, he gave no other reply. But I heard from others that he had been let into sleep, and I was taught that some are let into these sleeps and undergo purgings by means of dreams, perhaps also by short awakenings, until they are rid of the fantasies they had carried with them. 1747, the 30th day of December.

There are very many varieties of heavenly pleasures and delights, in which is happiness

428. Those pleasures are called heavenly that come to the sensation of souls as though they were living in the body. There are pleasures which affect them so delightfully, that they can hardly bear any more. But there are delights that come from a still deeper source. In the pleasures there are different kinds of happiness, and in the delights, different kinds of heavenly marital joy. In short, there are very many levels of pleasures and delights, both as to different types and as to intensity; and these pleasures can be shared without lessening them in those who are sharing them. True pleasures and true delights have within them happiness, and happiness has peace, and peace innocence; so that true pleasures and delights come solely from God the Messiah as their only source. 1747, the 30th day of December.

429. Other pleasures are counterfeit, delusory, of the kind that can be imparted, in the world as in the other life, by devils.

There are some who have Jesus with them, and therefore believe

430. At a great distance from the realm (that is, the realm of spirits) in which I was today, there were many gathered into one, who appeared, and said that they had Jesus with them, and saw Him daily; and they are those who have saving belief.

Opposite to them, or below, there were likewise many, who were also saying that they had Christ with them; and they have saving belief based on understanding.

Thus the former are portrayed in the Word by Abraham and Isaac, but the latter, who were at a distance from them, by Abimelech. For Abimelech departed from Abraham and Isaac after the covenant had been ratified [Gen. 21:32, 26:31].[1] 1747, the 30th day of December.

The state of beggars in the other life

431. The fantasy of those who had been begging for a long time and finally had come to take pleasure in it, and thus because of their idle life and aversion for working to procure food and like necessaries, is that they appear naked except for filthy shreds as clothing. They seem to themselves to be in a mass, so bunched together that they cannot be distinguished one from another. Having one with

---

[1] *Cf.* also *AC* 3004–3011.

a cup, they beg for alms, and wherever they encounter people they beg. I heard from them that what is said about beggars is true, that they want nothing but money, despise clothing and food, live wickedly amongst themselves, quarreling, and so forth; that they hate work, sometimes living voluptuously in all luxury, squandering money, harshly demanding to know what each one has gotten; that they had set up a sort of government among themselves, and want this to be a secret. 1747, 30 December. Note that the beggars [spoken of] here are such as had been beggars in their lives. So it is their existence, because they had had no other ambition.

Moors or Africans desire to be white

432. I have heard that the Moors or negroes, like the Africans, in the other life do not want to be black, but white. They consider whiteness to be beauty, after they have been prepared [for heaven], because the angels of God the Messiah are all shining white, and the inward ones love to be clothed in white garments. 1747, 30 December.

Spirits also have the ability, more than people on earth, by various methods to look into and see what kind of a person someone had been, the methods being pictured in different ways

433. Besides the abilities of spirits spoken of before [400], namely, of possessing every human language as their own mother tongue, and of putting on a person's memory as their own, they also have from God the Messiah, the ability to look into people and see the least details pertaining to their life.

Now this was portrayed by some objects being removed from someone, like a bubble, and objects resembling a bubble that also seemed to be taken away; and as if they had been informed in this manner, they at once told what it was. One time this was also done by what looked like a cloud removed from a soul, while in the meantime, the person continues in an altered condition. From me too they removed little bubbles like these (although they are only a symbolic portrayal), and then they saw specific details of my life. So they see such things from one little bubble or part.

Moreover, they also look intently at loves, inclinations, and feelings, as well as matters retained in the memory that are clearly displayed to the eye. I was extremely surprised when [I realized] that they had been able to see with their eyes not only someone's single mental images, but even their tiniest feelings. Spiritual life is such that these things can be brought out for scrutiny, unlike the life of the body. 1747, the 30th day of December.

About the veil of the Jews, also
A kind of punishment by means of the Veil

434. When the Jews want to protect anyone in the other life from being harmed by others, they usually cast a veil over them, under which they are safe, and guarded against harm from others, and so are not done violence.

Certain ones—but Christians—had been put under such a veil by Jews, so that they would be done no more injury by their own. But those under the veil, complaining that they were not able to breathe, were let go after a time.

The reason for this can be deduced: i.e. that those coming from Judaism are safer, being entirely in darkness, like in a thick cloud, than those who are in the light of truth, and yet deny it. This is why the Jews are also kept under the veil continually, during life [in the world].

435. As for punishment by means of the veil, those undergoing it seem to themselves, because of the illusions imposed upon them, to be under a veil stretching out to a great distance, sometimes for miles. The veil is like a thin but unbroken cloud, which thickens according to the power of the illusion. And so they get upset and run about, here and there, far and wide, trying to break out of the veil. They go at varying speeds and with varying force, until finally, exhausted, they either lie down, or are held feet upward and head downward—which can last for a long time, until their indignation has ceased.

A veil of this kind is introduced into the fantasy of those who, though they see the truth, yet—due to all kinds of reasons bursting from their loves—cannot manage to acknowledge it. But since they are constantly becoming displeased for those reasons, so much that they fight against the truth which they nevertheless see, such a veil is suited to their fantasy. And they tell me now that they are being tormented miserably by a longing to extricate themselves—a longing that is flaming up [within them]. 1747, the 31st day of December.

A kind of punishment consisting in running around

436. There are some whom fantasies punish in this way, namely by their seeming to themselves to be running around and around in a circle backwards, either from right to left, or the reverse, depending on to the fantasies. In this way, in quite short gyres, they time and again come back and go out again, carrying something with them that is weighing them down.

This kind of punishment comes to those who let themselves be led along by their desires, and even though they see and acknowledge truths, nevertheless go back on them, drawn by their yearnings. Thus they go forth into the field of understanding and recognize [truth], but being drawn by their desire, fall back into opposing it.

This is especially applicable to women, in whom desires normally take precedence, when they join in like men in matters regarding the doctrines of faith. 1747, the 31st day of December.

A kind of purging by bringing on a childlike uprightness

437. Now to some, a kind of gentle purging process is applied that brings them back into a kind of childlike uprightness, these being the sort who are treated leniently. But in that uprightness there is also, due to their fantasy, a strong desire to surpass others in understanding. Their understanding, however, is taken captive and tied up, for the reason either that they love their own [thoughts], and then can hardly bear it when others utter truer or better ones, or that they do not want the good repute of their own group, consequently of themselves, to be detracted from—thus also because of [a desire] for eminence of self above others.

Being in this state of induced uprightness, they are so tormented by that hidden desire, that they ardently want to be released from it and to return into their original condition. Yet for others, in this [childlike] state one can be happy, because one is then outside of the worrying state. 1747, the 31st day of December.

The last angelic heaven: their happiness is based in settings similar to earthly ones

438. Spirits who had not yet been let into Heaven because disharmony repugnant to heavenly beings still prevailed in them, were speaking with me about heavenly happiness. Because they did not know about it,[1] it was said:

There are separate dwellings, where those are who can live together harmoniously, forming societies. In fact, from a power of illusion or imagination still remaining with them, pleasant and delightful [scenes] seem to be created for them, in which heavenly peace reigns. If they so choose, pleasure gardens also seem to be created for them containing every variety of trees and fruits; as well as cities and palaces, and the like.

But these things should not be described too much for the world, lest it seek what is heavenly in fantasies.

The wickedness of those entering the other life at this day is unbelievable
What left and right are

439. For several days, some who had died and entered into the other life not many years before, were allowed to practice their deceptions and intrigues against true and good qualities, by distorting them, and many more tricks than I could ever describe. They have mediums; they tauntingly urge each other on; they combine their malicious efforts, which are unbelievably wicked. These points show clearly enough that belief has been laid waste at this day. 1748, 2 January.

The entire lower realm, that of spirits coming from earth, is almost such that if a word is let down from heaven, it is distorted, and its meaning can hardly be understood.

The things that lie inwardly concealed in people and have become their own by practice, they bring out at the entrance to the other life, on being let in among spirits. These spirits were portrayed to me as being at the left side in front, toward the middle of the face. Those at the right were the upright. This should be noted, for all at the left, however many, are corrupt, and corruptors, who

---

[1] While the original has *ignorabam*, the context clearly calls for *ignorabant*. By prolepsis, the author wrote *ignorabam, dicebam* and then changed *dicebam* to *dicebatur*.

use such dreadful methods that no person on earth could ever believe it. The things they perpetrate are only the root of evil, for which they have an instinct; but more hideous is the instinct of those spirits who seem to themselves to possess some light of reason. This hellish gang is devoid of the discernment with which nature endowed them.

*About persons who are worshipped as saints,
and as gods and goddesses*

440. Throughout the night, both at waking moments and in sleep, portrayals of people were exhibited to me who are worshipped as saints and gods—even the gods and goddesses of the ancients are still pictured, such as Venus, Diana, Phoebus, Jupiter, and indeed each in their own particular attire—Venus in a beautiful garment, Phoebus with a body having shining yellow skin, and so on. But whether these persons are only fantasies, and continue to exist in fantasies, or whether some spirits put themselves forth as the same, is not quite clear. Some believe they are these deities, and so present themselves—Jupiter, with an unceasing, lightening-like power that is indescribable because it cannot be conceived of, by which all are driven away.

441. It was also portrayed how great jaws like those *of whales* are fashioned, into which spiritual images were being poured and passing into the stomach, one after another, so that when it had swallowed so many that its stomach could be formed, [the figure] turned into a whale, or into a *dragon*.

442. Also a large fish was portrayed, stretched out, that wanted to be stroked, also symbolizing one kind of idolatry.

443. Moreover, of people who were worshipped as saints and thus as gods, only three kinds were depicted to me: namely, those who turned away from that worship, and were among angels and under their protection; then, those who did not want to be among the gods and be worshiped as gods, but nevertheless retain some of the dregs, even though they repudiate it with the mouth. The third kind is profane, accepting that kind of worship and wanting to be acknowledged as gods. They are miserable, silly and stupid. 1748, the 3rd day of January.

How a person is controlled as to his action through the will

444. A live experiment has several times been performed in me in front of spirits, to show how actions are controlled by God the Messiah through the will, which was being bent in such a manner, hither and thither, that they, and I also, thought that I was about to do something, but it was by turns averted. Thus it is only the will that is controlled.

The quality of spirits is also to be judged by the quarters and position [in which they are]

445. As previously mentioned [439], those at the left are for the most part unhappy, and more [unhappy,] the more to the left their quarter lies. Those to the right are blessed. Furthermore, the spirits around a person who are at the back [see 557], are those who want to control his or her body, and believe they are that person, for which reason they cling to the person when they come up. Those who want to be bodies, and also those who torment people after death, cling from behind, nor do they depart until the person has found out what they are after. But those who are in front below the chest and who control the subthoracic breathing, are they who allow themselves to be controlled. Those standing overhead are both those who teach, as those who are easily taught. 1747, the 4th day of January.

It is the nature of angels not to believe anything at all, not even the smallest detail, that does not come from God the Messiah; hence, What peace is

446. I also experienced while I was writing today, that an angel was guiding the things I was writing, and in fact, in such a way as to cause me to realize that there was not even the tiniest occurrence that was not under the auspices and guidance of God the Messiah, because [directed] toward the best purpose.

From this experience I was able to deduce what the angelic quality is, and hence what peace is, because it yields [to God the Messiah] in every single, most minute particular. 1748, the 5th day of January.

About Mohammed: that he drove off a crowd coming towards him, and said they should go to Jesus, the Son of God

447. In a waking afternoon vision, I saw Mohammed becoming angry at a crowd that was coming towards him, and rather forcefully driving them away, and even angrily. He was saying that they should go to Jesus, the Son of God, not to him, because he realized that Jesus was the only Son of God, ruling the whole heaven, to Whom the power has been given by the most high Creator of the World and earth.

This is just what I heard him saying and, I now perceive, hearing these words. And he is guiding [the writing of] them, entreating me to tell this to his worshippers. 1748, the 6th day of January.

The nature of the angels' glorification or speech

448. Today, while I was writing, I became aware that heaven was speaking, but I did not understand anything. Now I am told that they had been glorifying the Redeemer of the human race. I perceived only a surge, as if of a distinct beam, and universal elements somewhat sparkling, so to speak, so that I would recognize them to be universal, having no regard to persons, or to oneself, but only to realities in general. 1748, the 6th day of January.

449. Besides this, I heard a different [kind of] speech during both periods of sleep, last night and the night before—an inward, pictorial speech. It was amazing, beyond the imagination of any person on earth. In sleep or in a sleeping state, not quite, yet almost awake, I was able to grasp what it meant, but since I awakened, I have not been able to express it, no matter how hard I try. 1748, the 6th day of January.

450. Today while awake, I also learned how these matters stand. As for the pictorial speech of the angels, anything whatever that is encountered is taken as an object, whether it be an affection, or an insight, or anything of that order; and by means of these, delicate displays are created. So the objects are realities apart from objects of the senses: such as an affection, an insight, a color. These objects then arrange themselves according to the subjects being thought about. It is due to this, then, that the heavens have communication [with mankind].

451. As for the other [kind of] speech, it is a cosmic thinking in realities withdrawn from objects of the senses, apart from persons, which cannot easily be described.

452. There is yet another, truly angelic speech, which did not come to my perception except as something general from the conversation, and from the feelings it produced.

There are souls released from the body coming into the other life who love to be chastised, punished and tortured

453. There are also souls who are of a character opposite to that of the rest, or of Europeans—I was told they were from Africa—who, upon entering into the other life, love to be chastised, even treated harshly, hoping that good will result from it; and if not punished, they are displeased.

There are likewise some who treat them harshly, whom they call devils, one of whom was shown to me. His body was dirty or yellowish, and gnarled. The bad treatments they undergo are of different kinds. The kind shown to me was one in which an eagle had alighted on their head and taken away their brain, which was done with a pain matching the fantasies—for these produce dreadful ones. Another is by different kinds of sharp punishments, which they love. Yet because of the painful sensations, they finally begin to shun these, and at the same time the spirits who are tormenting them, whom they call devils.

Thus they shed the fantasies, and believe that they are being brought into heaven, which, as they now say, no one can enter but by punishments and afflictions. This is what that people believes and stores deeply in its conscience, for which reason they are treated accordingly, and thereby obtain the reward of coming into joyful states, which they call Paradisal. And they see pleasure gardens, and very many lovely things, after coming to hate the gang tormenting them.

For a long time they spoke with me, and their speaking was accompanied with a kind of clicking sound, like that of a rag [being shaken], by which they can be recognized.

FROM THE *BIBLE INDEX*

These and the things previously told to me [lead to the conclusion] that a greater proportion [of people] from Africa, than from other regions of the earth, are introduced into heaven; for their conscience in these matters is somewhat in the way of truth. 1748, the 7th day of January.

They wish me to write that they are entirely in the way of truth, because they know this from their paradisal [states].

^{m}They say that they do not love their own race only, but all however many there are in heaven, so that they have an ingrained universal love. They detest blackness of the body, for they know that their souls are shining white, but their bodies black, which they loathe. Later, they do not have that clicking speech, but a thinking like angelic thought, and they are overhead, as they now are.^{n}

What those Africans further report, who want to be harshly treated after the death of the body

454. They are drawing near, and want to inform me how things are with them. From the way they are controlling their voices, I can tell that they do not want to say anything wrong, and that they long for deeper things; for they are weighing their words.

They say that when they are being maltreated, then they are black, and afterwards, they put off the blackness, and put on the shining whiteness of the soul, and so enter into heaven. Now they are surprised they had had a painful sensation, which, upon looking back, they attribute to fantasies; for they now say they have no such sensation, but only a pleasant and paradisal one. 1748, the 7th day of January.

How it is to be understood, since God the Messiah leads all by means of spirits and angels so that nothing is theirs, that they nevertheless become guilty of sins

455. It seems questionable that even though nothing that people think and do is theirs, because they are led by spirits, they nevertheless become guilty of sins and will suffer the penalties for the evils committed; but this is grasped through faith. When one has true faith, then one believes, in accordance with the truth, that nothing is our own, because we are being led by God the Messiah in the way of truth, or have true belief; and in this case all evil is bent into good, so that nothing of evil is accounted to him.

But when one does not have true faith, then one believes that everything is one's own, and that we think and do everything of our own power. In this way we are filled with fantasies, which stay with us, and the result of such a belief is that the evil cannot but be accounted to us, because, as we believe, it is from ourselves. For this reason also, evil cannot easily be bent into good, but rather, good is bent into evil, which takes root and increases, even until the person acquires a character, such as remains after death, when he or she is purged of that fantasy by means of punishments. 1748, the 7th day of January.

^{m}Thus when one has not faith, one takes on [false] convictions, which have to be rooted out.^{n}

When good spirits are raised up into a more inward heaven, and then return, it seems just as if the person [they are with] has fallen into a sweet sleep, and sees the more inward regions and their glory, as if in complete wakefulness

456. That spirits also are transferred into very many states of waking and sleeping, you may see told above [319–21]. It appeared to me as if a particular good spirit had fallen into a sweet sleep—something I have been allowed to experience several times when the state of spirits has been communicated to me. This angel, upon awakening (or so it seemed to me) reported that he had beheld the glory of God the Messiah, which I was allowed to see very dimly in his sleep.

Hence I was able to infer that the transfer of spirits into heaven, or of heavenly beings into a more inward heaven, is like a sleep as to their^1 lower mental powers. And I can testify from experience, that during that sleep, things seem just as plainly alive as when one is wide awake. Therefore, the lower mental power comes to rest, as though it did not exist, when the more inward mind is raised up. For what is lower cannot be transferred into what is higher. 1748, the 8th day of January.

---

[1] The original has *ejus*, "his."

An enormous gang of evil spirits desire to steal

457. Because I was being forced by spirits into a sense of their greed, I observed that many times they wanted to incite me to steal, even such things as are of little value, such as are in their market shops. And I saw that this intention and this impulse came from the spirits, who were even trying to move my hand.

From these things as well as from an actual voice, I know that those who had been merchants and were deceitful in their business dealings, trying by any means, right or wrong, to get hold of the goods of others, retain this character. Consequently, such spirits wander about, and wherever they go, seem to themselves to be stealing, thinking about nothing else. But they are penalized, or driven away by punishments. Some use the same cunning they had used in life, so that they do not want people to know this. 1748, the 11th day of January.

In the heaven of spirits a plot was formed to suffocate me, and what it seems to mean

458. When I was going to bed and about to sleep, warning was given that certain spirits were plotting against me with the intent to kill me; but because I was composed, not worrying about it any more than I did about their other threats, I fell asleep. In the night just after midnight, on waking up, I felt that I was not breathing on my own power, but, as I believed, from heaven, which I clearly perceived, so that the breathing was not mine. It was then clearly said to me that the whole heaven of spirits had plotted against me with the purpose of suffocating me, and that just at that moment, when they were trying to carry out their attempts, the heavenly breathing commenced, and so they had to give up on that try. I was told that it was the whole heaven of spirits. (The names of those who were at the forefront were also mentioned, but it is not permitted to name them, except for two, who portrayed charity and the fruits of charity. These were in fact present, but were not agreeing to it.)

Nevertheless, because they thought the whole heaven of spirits was on their side—for everyone who came, they allured over to their side by saying that those whom they claimed the power to let into heaven could not be admitted unless I were first killed—therefore that plot was formed, which ended up thwarted.

Those two who represented charity and the fruit of charity, withdrew, and in fact to the right side, while that incident occurred at the left side. But while the conspirators were being punished, they were driven off, except for their leaders, and treated harshly, while the leaders remained by command of the heavens.

This all seemed to me to signify that the inward elements of the accepted doctrine at the present day, were thus plotting against very inward and innermost things, to which they wanted to attach no belief; but that God the Messiah sustains the life of the very inward and innermost things. That life is symbolized by the breathing that was continued in me by heaven, in no wise by myself but by the heavens, consequently by God the Messiah, Who Alone is the Heavens.

Afterwards, one who seemed to be their standard-bearer, although he was not thought to be present, tried to enter the internal organs of my body and penetrate to the heart, which in his fantasies he still thinks he owns, so as to attack the more inward things, or, as he says, whore with them. 1748, the 8th day of January.

459. When he was admitted into the inward parts of my body, I was let into a kind of heavenly state, so that I did not want to expel those guests, even less avenge the harm done to me. This he also appreciated, saying that it was a peaceable [attitude]; but still, as though deprived of his reason, and still panting for vengeance, he kept on pressing to accomplish his endeavors, and is still keeping on.

About the adroitness of spirits in making up things that appear to be true

460. From one experience today, I was able to realize how spirits can counterfeit the truth, and thus play with human minds. The case in point was their depiction of the inhabitants of Saturn, whom they claim to be little people, for the most part small in stature but still of good character. They say that they meditate more than they speak, that they live in a cold climate, that they cast out from their midst those who are evil (but do not punish them with death, which they say is wicked, but that they are thus banished from society and no longer tolerated by the rest), that they worship God the creator of the universe, and similar concoctions having an appearance of truth. But because they wanted to add on embellishments, I was unable to believe them.

However, I was able to deduce from these things that the inhabitants of that planet, though they did not know Christ Jesus, must nevertheless have been taught by some Divine Word, so as to have a knowledge of Him, albeit a dim one; and that those who had not, like gentiles on our earth such as the Africans, who are destitute of such higher knowledge, can nevertheless be saved. 1748, the 11th day of January.

The abode of some in heaven who are called stars

461. In the book of Revelation [2:3,4], we read concerning the dragon that "he drew down a third part of the stars with his tail." In the zenith, or directly overhead, is the abode of a certain one who calls himself Abraham. He is like a slippery serpent, for at one moment he seems to want to be converted, at another he takes a different attitude. Nevertheless, he unceasingly labors to destroy all those whom he calls gentiles, except for the descendants of Jacob, whom he calls his own children; nor is he interested in other families, such as the scattered Israelites, because he hates Jesus, and continually persecutes Christians and distorts [Christian] teachings. It would be too much to enumerate all his deceptions and devices, which I have only been allowed to learn from experience, for he has been persecuting me now for nearly three years.

He has very great influence, because in his fantasy, he puts himself right in the zenith, and thus looks straight down upon all; so he thinks that he controls the universe, sometimes seeming to himself to be as the sun, surrounded with a like aura. It is only an illusion that he is located at the zenith. For in fantasy, he can be thrust down, and turned about, and driven in different ways, which he cannot help admitting—as happened today in a period of wakefulness. There was one who was said to work by means of fantasies, something most common among spirits, so he placed the so-called Abraham behind me, besides other playful tricks. Consequently he has to admit it was only the illusion of his arrogance that lifted him up and continually holds him there. More about him can be found elsewhere [see 281, 379, 410].

Today he also wanted to deceive me by a fantasy of [his being] the creator of the universe without any intermediary, but he was scared off from doing this and had to acknowledge that there must be an intermediary, and that he himself could never mediate, since he is a wicked person and hates all believers, all devout and innocent people, and allows himself to be worshipped as God. 1748, the 11th day of January (old calendar).

462. At his left in respect to me, or at the right in respect to him, at the same height, there is one who calls himself Jacob, who likewise demands to be worshipped. To him, fewer are said to be coming. He lies on a bed and in this manner receives those who come to him, and promises them heaven, and these, having been sent out by him, return, saying that they find rest nowhere. He answers that they must wait. So the miserable crowd wanders around, without rest. The same day. *Turn the page and see the continuation.*[1]

Continuation about those who are called stars of the dragon

463. Farther to the same side, lower down, is David, who does not receive anyone coming to him, but those who come to him he sends back to Jesus. Thus he lives in heavenly rest, and in happiness. About Isaac, nothing is heard; it is said that because he had hated Jacob, he is not tolerated, or because he had loved Esau.

464. Farther on to the left, or to the right of the one called Abraham, even higher up, so high that no one can ascend unless he is helped by him, is one who calls himself Moses. He boasts that he is the greatest, for which reason, fantasy accordingly raises him up and holds him even higher than the rest. He is said to boast about his miracles. 1748, 11 January (old calendar).

A state of heavenly peace and happiness

465. On first awakening, once again, as frequently before, I felt a state of rest coming from peace, namely a delightful pleasantness—but it was not peace—and at the same time, a happiness that I am unable to describe in appropriate words. 1748, the 11th day of January (old calendar).

---

[1] This annotation appears at the bottom of the manuscript page.

The star in the zenith fell down with the rest

466. Today at about ten o'clock, that star which fantasized itself to be the sun for the rest [461], together with several round about, fell from their place, and in fact, forward to the right, toward a certain sea. To this they were guided down, so that they would look into the sea—which is a swamp.

But this still continues, for he had often been warned to stop, as well by threats and punishments, as by persuasion. He was even thrust down from heaven and severely, though very briefly, punished. Besides, he was sent for several days to wander around (once even, spirited away by God the Messiah, he was hidden) and to search for his companions, and so on; but it was still in vain.

For he had for such a long time been soaking in every kind of cunning, that it became second nature to him. And so he works as if by instinct, and quite slyly, depending on the circumstances: at one time flatteringly, at another imploringly, and often, most threateningly. But because it has become so ingrained, one cannot tell whether there is any hope for change in him. At times of danger and fear, he changes quickly, and says prayers, but he presently returns to his fantasies.

467. That sea which is called a swamp is the punishment of those who set themselves against heavenly truth, and against the One and Only Mediator Himself, Jesus Christ. It is a quite logical result that their fantasy should turn into such a swamp, for thus the very highest turns around to the very lowest, and those who are of this character physically experience the pains of punishment. For their fantasy, which they had thought to be real, does become real, and torments them in a way you may find described in earlier accounts about fantasy [376–77, 461]. 1748, the 11th day of January (old calendar).

About the realm between opposites

468. From manifold experience, I have learned that souls and spirits, once they are convinced of the truth, are for the most part, and almost always, carried away into things contrary, and so, into doubts about truths. The experience I have had in heaven in this regard is so extensive, that it would be a lengthy undertaking to relate it.

The reason for this is that one should not be convinced of the truth by visual persuasion, just as one should not be by miracles—also, that a greater field [of thought] has to be acquired, rendering the person flexible; besides further reasons, which I am not being given at this time. 1748, the 12th day of January.

About the Jews called together by Jacob, and about the greedy in general

469. The Jacob who is now above my head, occupies that vertical position in place of him who let himself down from there and submitted himself. Because he had been deprived of worshippers he is reclining in his usual manner on his bed, grandiose, summoning the rest to his bed [*see* 462]. Many of the Jews came to him as he was thus lying down, which I sensed through much of the night by the stench of mice.

When I could no longer bear it, it was asked in the heaven of spirits whence that stench came. Some declared that they had been troubled by the same smell, but as a result of inquiry, it was found that they were Jews who had been lifted up out of their own rooms, as it seems to them, to Jacob, before whom many were thus gathered together. Thence came the stench of mice.

Jacob told that he was surrounded by so many mice, that he could not stand them any longer, whereupon, being almost ejected from his bed, he betook himself downwards.

Those same people were complaining, because they had not stayed in their rooms, where their money was, which they were afraid thieves might take away.

470. Those who had lived long ago appeared fully bearded, so that their whole face was covered with a black beard, making them very ugly. This was because in old times, they had loved their beard so much.

471. Moreover, they also appeared to be dressed in ragged clothes into which their gold and silver had been sown. When stripped of their clothing, they lament miserably that their money has been taken away.

472. Moreover, they are of two kinds: one whose right eye looks obliquely downward under the left eye, the other whose right eye looks obliquely upward. The reason is that the former regard the earth alone, but the latter regard heaven, praying that riches exist there.

473. Their women appeared all bunched together by themselves, and very much concerned about clothes, which they seem to themselves to be selling. What the clothes were like, was not shown to me.

474. Such a lot, in general, awaits the greedy.

1748, 13 January.

475. I am told that that miserable gang wanders about in bands, looking for a place where they may be fed; and the whole heaven of spirits is said to be full of them. But still no one wants to feed them. Rather they drive them off, knowing them to be thieves. The rest are looking for their patriarch.

The three leaders were thrust down out of heaven

476. Again last night[1], the three leaders, A., J. and M., who were near me, were thrust down. Two of them were also deprived of their power of understanding, so that they were silly—as is normally the case with devils when the faculty of understanding is taken from them and they are left with only instinct. A. was the exception, who still had use of his understanding.

Others were substituted in their place to receive those who came, but these substitutes complained that they could do nothing for them. They describe how they come in bands and ask where A. J. M. are, and how extremely ugly they look, ugly beyond description. They are completely devoid of understanding, unable to discern anything of what is true and good. Therefore they are rather to be wept over. As if insane, they scurry about through the streets of what they think to be the city Jerusalem, and beg. But no one receives them and, as they say, is willing to feed them. Their city is miserable, the streets narrow. 1748, the 15th day of January.

---

[1] See 281, 461-64, 466, 469.

SPIRITUAL EXPERIENCES

About a certain ingenious spirit, or about a second Mohammed

477. In the morning, when I had awakened, there was a certain rather clever spirit who, to the distress of those around me, had adroitly changed all goodness into evil. On awakening, I spoke with the one possessing that talent and found that he was trying to investigate what is true. I therefore proposed at random this and that [problem], which he ingeniously solved, discovering the truth. On account of this he was received into the company of good spirits, among whom he remained for a time; but because he was too energetic, and tried to act on his own, he was sent away and came into the company of other spirits.

From this I am able to infer that some spirits much surpass others in the talent of comprehending, the difference [between their level of comprehension and that of others] being so great, that it would be hard to let oneself be convinced of it.

About Fantasies: how they are shed, and what kind remain

[**477½.**] Moreover, it was also this Mohammed who possessed such an ability to understand what is true and good [477], with whom I likewise spoke about the fantasies that prevail among spirits who first come into that life. For they are only illusions, which must by all means be shed, and are put off only with difficulty and with resistance, because the person favors them and takes pleasure in them. Therefore, these fantasies are removed, little by little, by Jesus Christ, and those spirits are led to inward, and then more inward ones, which interact with, and can be together with truth and goodness. Hence comes heavenly joy and gladness, and in this way they live a life of their own, with delight.

These things [were discussed] with Mohammed of Mecca, and there was another Mohammed also, but who he is, I do not know. It is said that he, too, is adored. Thus both possess the ability to understand truth and goodness, and in fact they confess that the source of all truths and goodness is Jesus Christ, which they want me to testify here from so much experience that no one can ever doubt about it.

478. By the fantasies said to be shed with reluctance are meant the [newly arrived] soul's grosser fantasies, that pertain to the body and the earthly mind. Inward ones, however, that are in agreement and thus harmonious with truly heavenly truth and goodness, remain, causing them to live a life as if their own, with heavenly joy and gladness—and this is the rainbow spoken of in Genesis [9:12–17]. Its harmonious symmetry is created, and shaped, by Jesus Christ Alone. 1748, the 15th day of January.

Spirits are symbolized by "wind"

479. Spirit is likened to wind in John 3:8, and consequently, the spirits present with me at this day, many and most of the times have come with a wind, which stroked my face, indeed even moved the flame of the candle, papers, (the wind was cold,) and this very often when I was raising my right arm. This surprised me, and I do not yet know the reason for it. 1748, the 15th day of January.

The worst of all spirits in the last heaven, are those who had confessed Christianity; then come the Jews

480. From a great deal of experience, I have learned that the worst of all spirits in the last Heaven are those who in the world were called Christians. Most of them have no belief, but attack and hold in hatred everything having to to do with true religion and, unwilling to be taught, persistently trample them under foot. They are so terribly cunning, and contrive such strategems in opposition to the Lord[1], and against faith in Jesus, and against believers, that one cannot be amazed enough. And that [wickedness] stays rooted in their disposition and character, for then they live from their own character, and when abandoned to that, are like furies. Mohammedans are really extremely surprised about this, who themselves are easily taught, and allow themselves to be guided, and easily receive the faith.

After Christians come the Jews, as well as those who had worshipped Abraham as God, the latter also being quite deceitful. The gentlest of all are the Africans, about whom see above [432, 453]. 1748, the 15th day of January.

---

[1] A.W. Acton, p. 142, footnotes: "With the exception of the reference in no. 258 to 'the prayer of our Lord,' this is the first occurrence of the word *Dominus* (Lord), instead of *Deus Messias* (God Messiah). In the next few numbers the term 'God Messiah' occurs, but after this only 'the Lord.'" This is not quite accurate, see 1122.

SPIRITUAL EXPERIENCES

About the language of spirits
Spirits recognize each other, and test by various methods to
find out what the others are like, so that they
may join company with them

481.   That human souls imagine they are people on earth, equipped with bodies, you may see spoken of earlier [207, 296, etc.], even thinking they have clothes on, so that only with difficulty can they be torn away from their fantasy.

They also speak together among themselves, just as they had in this world; for speaking is only the putting together of a series of mental images, which, with people in the body, falls into the words of their native language. It is the mere putting together of mental images of spirits that fall into words with a person on earth, and for this reason, all of them speak in the person's language, even among themselves, of which the person may or may not be aware— or even speak in a strange language, as is well known: for the apostles were able to speak in any language [Acts 2:4], and this came from spirits.

Moreover, there is also a communication of mental images, as there is of words. In fact, by these alone, joined together, they can express more things within a minute than man can express by words in entire hours. I have learned this from a great deal of experience, in the course of which it became evident that souls speak among themselves, and indeed, just like people in this world; and I have even heard that they can also preach in the same way, the one teaching the other.

482.   But how spirits join company, or on the other hand, how they are dissociated, [will now be explained]. Because they are most ingenious, and much cleverer than people in the body, they can tell by various indications that a soul is of the kind that may fit into their circles. They also test that spirit, by leading him into a conversation so that they may follow his mental imagery, and then cause him to speak according to his ideas and their own. Agreement or disagreement is plainly felt, sometimes plainly even by me, and from this they know what things are incompatible with themselves, and what are in agreement.

They lead man also in the same way, for they follow our chain of thoughts, and at the same time, inspire feelings, and thus lead in such a way that we believe we are speaking on our own, whereas it is nothing but a unanimity [of thought]. But when a spirit is intending evil, circumstances of this kind are bent by Jesus Christ to a person's good. 1748, the 17th day of January.

Further about compatibility among spirits, and their simultaneous action

483. When it has been made evident by various methods that spirits are in agreement, they join together and act at one, for they are brought together of their own accord. So it is that spirits find out who and what they are, and actually by a kind of instinct. I do not know all their methods of testing [souls], for there are many. Those spirits who are similar are brought together, the rest dissociated.

484. But even though a spirit may be of a kind to harmonize with other spirits, such as with evil spirits, nevertheless, by the mercy of God the Messiah, these kinds are delivered from their company and inserted into a group of others, so that they may come into the company of the blessed. God the Messiah as it were unites them, so that they may live together.

Thus by the mercy of God the Messiah, they are transferred from one circle to another, and such as the circles are, such is their life. This should be very evident to me, since I have been led from one group to another, continuously, and have come into the life of each one. But in my case—since I have been gifted with a double thought, one more inward, the other inward—when I was in the company of evil spirits, I could still at the same time be in the company of good ones, and thus see what the spirits were like who were trying to lead me, and this almost always happened with awareness on my part. Without this realization that I am in the company of evil spirits, and that it is these spirits who are so thinking and making me feel, I could not but believe that I myself were such a person, and meditated such things. 1748, the 17th day of January.

Besides individual influences, there are also collective ones

485. Today I spoke with evil and good spirits about the collective and the individual influence bearing on every single feeling, evil and good, namely, that there are tens of thousands, in fact many tens of thousands [of spirits] that are responsible for the collective influence, thus the whole heaven of spirits and angels. But there are specific individual influences concerned with each person, which are recipients of the collective influences, and as such they draw upon the collective influence, and are similar to it because they interact.

Thus all spirits and all angels individually are focal points of influences, and such as they are, such are the influences they receive, and share with people on earth, each of whom is likewise an interacting focal point of influences. This matter can be understood on the physical level by means of a great number of phenomena in both the atmospheric and the animate aspects of nature. 1748, the 17th day of January. The angels expressed agreement.

Collective and individual influences could not exist if God the Messiah were not ruling the universe

486. Unless God the Messiah were controlling the whole heaven, both that of angels and that of spirits, there could never be such an arrangement of all things in the heavens and below the heavens into kinds and species, that they could run concordantly in regard to all the lives of men, spirits and angels. For lives are feelings, and unless these derive from the one and only love, Who is Divine, and thus truly heavenly, the remaining kinds and species of feelings could never come forth and relate to one another. Therefore, feelings common [to many] compose a collective form, and one so well ordered that nothing better ordered is conceivable; and without such a horizontal and vertical ordering of feelings, no one could have life, for feeling is life.

Thus do all feelings interact, just as all the parts do among themselves in one body. In this body all feelings exist in a comparable ranked order. Therefore, unless God the Messiah had become [an earthly] Human Being, and thus unless the univeral heaven relates to Him as its body, the universe cannot possibly be kept in that order, and by the universe, thus by God the Messiah, all and each of angels, spirits and men. 1748, the 17th day of January. These things also were written with the agreement of angels.

About the dragon, who took for himself a seat in the vertex or zenith of heaven

487. He who because of his fantasy is seated up high overhead at the zenith [see 461–64, 466–67], had been warned several times not to reproach believers, and persecute them. But still, since many centuries ago he has kept on, and corrupted countless people. When he is frightened, it is his nature to humble himself and to promise repentance and become submissive, but still, it does not last. He is cunning to the core, and because he has practiced his deceits for such a long time, he can by no means desist, however much he is offered grace. He has been shown the punishments and torments of others, and each time he is horrified, and resorts to his own little rituals and utterances, and prays for grace; but still, he returns to his old self, so there is no hope for him.

Of the punishments shown to him, I know three. First, at a given moment he suffered a pain like that of one giving birth, or an internal pain, extremely agonizing, and he wanted to turn this toward his own merit. After that he was let into the swamp, as it is called, to be immersed into it, and was held there for some hours; but he was freed from there. Today he was let into some place of the damned, to behold with his own eyes what he deserved more than those who are there. He was horrified, and for a space of hardly a quarter of a minute, suffered cruel blows. Being freed from there, he is now shuddering and praying again, but one who prays out of fear cannot be heard, only one who prays from the heart. 1748, the 17th day of January. To enumerate his intrigues and tricks, volumes would not suffice.

A great mystery

488. It is a great mystery that the whole angelic heaven has been so formed as to correspond completely to a Human being, as a whole and as to its single parts, and all its members, and that this greatest Human being was completely corrupted by falls, so that lower things were dominating over higher ones. Thence came the necessity that Jesus Christ should come into the world and should conquer the devil, and thereby restore order, and thus be the One and Only Human Being to whom the Universe related.

It is because of this that Jesus Christ is the all in all the parts and that with Him Alone, the angelic heaven interacts; and that the lower and lowest gang has been cast away beneath His feet, like slag or dung. Therefore one who is not in Jesus Christ, or in His Body, is not in heaven. 1748, the 18th day of January.

489. SPIRITUAL EXPERIENCES

About the harmonious hymns of the angels

489. Today I heard angels of the inward heaven[1], very many of them in concert, composing a hymn, which was clearly audible to my hearing. What they were saying I could not understand, because they were angels; nor were the spirits around me able to understand what it was. Only from a certain variation of my inward feeling, I was able to learn that what is heavenly was in it. The angels clearly understood those hymns, which to me were just like a continuous childlike sound, resembling the sound of a flute. They were, to be sure, in a heavenly gyre made up of very many, saying and depicting the same thing at the same time.

Afterwards I was informed what they had said, namely, that by their hymns they had fashioned a golden crown set with diamonds around the Head of our Savior, which was done as well by heavenly displays as by distinct mental images, which are the beginnings of human words, unintelligible to spirit or man; and what is amazing, many say and portray this simultaneously, and one does not command the other in a way that anyone is directing the chorus, but all are mutually leading each other at the same time—in fact the more there are, the more easily it goes. For they are all ruled by God the Messiah.

That harmony is unbelievable to a person on earth, yet spiritual and heavenly harmony is of this nature. Moreover, the angels stream into and are turned about in spiritual and heavenly gyres in countless varying patterns. Some of the more basic ones I myself have been let into and was able to follow; but any who try to act on their own, to command the rest, unwilling to let themselves be led, cannot possibly join in except under coercion. Souls are brought gradually into harmony and unanimity of these kinds, so that they are finally able to live among angels. 1748, the 18th day of January.

490. Those hymns which the two childlike choirs composed, could not be disturbed by fantasies. There was one boastful spirit trying to disturb them, but the fantasies were as nothing. From this I was able to infer what influence fantasies have upon spiritual and heavenly, or angelic elements: they are too gross to be able to bring about any change. It would be as though what is gross tried to enter

---

[1] See footnote at 262.

into what is refined, or the final outcome into the beginnings, or the body into the soul. This, as human philosophy well enough knows, is a contradiction. Similarly, bodily and earthly elements cannot enter into truly spiritual and heavenly ones. 1748, the 18th day of January.

491. Once again I heard hymnists, or those singing the praise of our Savior. In fact, a number of choirs were heard singing at the same time about a variety of subjects, by means of visual displays and mental imagery. And yet they are one chorus, consisting of very many, and acting at the same time as one, without any confusion from each other, so that one was in the other, or inside of the other, even outside of the other.

In this way the whole angelic heaven customarily devotes itself to the praise and glory of the Savior. This is why musical harmony and singing is so delicious to the heavenly ones when the thoughts of a person on earth are concordant with their ideas. I have often experienced in churches, that the heavenly choirs have joined in, with a very deep sense of gladness, unbelievable, and thus unutterable, to anyone. 1748, the 21st day of January.

Continuing about the heavenly Choirs, their provinces in the human body, and their functions

492. While I was awake, again many angelic choirs were celebrating their Savior by their songs, and indeed, many at the same time, with a varying sound I did not understand, even though they were executing each and every note very clearly (for the more subtle or inward the subject, the better articulated it is). They were celebrating God the Messiah in different ways, and even though there were many praising at the same time, it was evident from the tonal modulations that there was wide variety among them. I learned what those varieties are in general, namely three: those who perform solely by visual portrayals; those who do so visually and at the same time vocally, which seemed to me to be very refined, sounding as if subtly winged [*cf.* 412] and as if they were the least of those who can be called lives; there are others who perform by voice only.

493. Moreover, there are also outward angels doing the same thing, whose action reached my perception—pictorial performers as well as vocal ones, and those who performed in both ways at the same time.

But the varieties are such as cannot yet be well described. For these varieties are entirely comparable not only to the lives of individuals, but also to the lives of all our inner parts; because no type [of spirit] exists that does not refer to some member, or to some aspect of an inner part, of the human body, for the reason spoken of earlier [486, 488]. Therefore they are allotted provinces, and functions, in the Body of our Savior.[1]

494. Later I learned to what provinces those singing angels belonged, namely that the purer ones, who are angelic, belonged to the pulmonary functions—something I was also allowed to experience, that is, that they controlled my lungs for a while, which was done so gently and pleasantly, and indeed internally, that I scarcely felt any breathing of air. I felt it from the center to the outside, for the lungs act into all parts of the body, the inner and the outer. Besides these there were some who controlled my outer breathing, which I could feel very well, and they are spiritual, and therefore more noticeable.

495. Moreover, those choirs devoted to the involuntary action of breathing are distinct from those devoted to the voluntary action of breathing. Those devoted to the spontaneous action are governed by feelings alone, while the ones devoted to the voluntary action are governed at the same time by understanding and reason, being those who are in charge of speech, and who do speak. This so happens because speaking belongs to the province of the lungs.

496. It had been told to me that those dedicated to the involuntary action of breathing, also control a person's sleep. For as soon as the voluntary action of breathing is withdrawn, a person falls asleep; then the functions of those take over who are only feelings [for those] who are angelic, or demons for those who are spirits.

497. Every spirit can be controlled through the feelings, and thus be brought to whatever it pleases the Savior. Then they are brought whithersoever it pleases Him; but they should still be carried

---

[1] In the original this sentence is emphasized by the symbol *NB.* written twice in the margin.

along by understanding. This is so for many reasons, the principal one being that character, and thus will, must necessarily develop through understanding in order for the person to participate in it; for without the exerceise of our understanding, we do not realize that our own self is involved. There are very many further reasons, having to do with the human being's regeneration.

About accountability

498. That a person does not have any selfhood when the will is removed, is evident from sleep. In sleep, the voluntary part is absent, so that one does not have control over any part individually, but the whole body lies at the bidding of involuntary impulses. For this reason, one is then accountable for nothing, because of being asleep.

From this also it can be somewhat evident what causes the accountability for evil, and what things, both in men and in spirits, are to be accounted to them. This subject is very extensive, and known only to our Savior. 1748, 21 January.

Continuation about the heavenly body

499. You may see it has been said [486, 488, 493] that the universal heaven relates to the Body of our Savior, Who governs the universe as if it were His body, thus without any difficulty; and that the universe would be dispersed if all and the least things did not relate to His body and were not controlled by Him.

In His body are two kingdoms, so to speak, just as in the human body; one pertains to the heart and the other to the lungs. The one pertaining to the heart is called heavenly, and the one pertaining to the lungs is called spiritual. These two kingdoms are united in a wonderful manner; and the one and the other govern in every single region [of the body], though each in its distinct way.

499½. I have been told that the generative members compose by themselves a distinct kingdom, just as in the human also they are distinct or separated from the rest.

500. Moreover, it was said that those spirits who relate to the kidneys are also partially separate from those kingdoms, but I do not yet know in what respects they are separate [*see* 959 *ff.*].

SPIRITUAL EXPERIENCES

The dragon with his stars was cast out of heaven, toward hell, and what he is up to there [cf. Rev. 12:4, 9]

501. That the dragon was cast out of heaven, with the rest of those who had been his companions, you may see above [32–35, 417, 461–64, 466, 487], namely, from the very top of heaven down even lower than under the tail, or the generative members, where they now live, together with those they had led astray, who think they are walking about in ancient Jerusalem and in its mud, and are attempting continually to rise up, but cannot.

I have seen their attempts, but they still remain in the lower parts, and from there they are continuously scheming against the heavenly regions. This they do by aiming unending blasphemies at the province where the parts are that interact with the heavenly regions, to wit, against the lowest human parts, where the front and rear foundation is. I felt this throughout the night, but it was without any effect, even though, as I was told, the blasphemies were unending. They scheme to do this, because when they were up high, they were attempting by means of their fantasies to enter into the heavenly regions themselves. 1748, the 21st day of January.

About the dragon [see 487]

502. Today again, the dragon was sent for a moment or two to a place of punishment, namely, one where there were dragons and snakes. When he was taken out, he resorted as usual to supplication, asking of course to be released. He was put under the veil in exactly the same way that he himself had done to countless others [434–35]. 1748, the 21st day of January.

503. It was said about him that he had persecuted Jesus when He was in the world, and it was he who had tempted Him the most, and had also stirred up the priests and elders through dreams, both knowingly, as at that time, and unknowingly, for he was the chief of those who are in hell and love themselves. 1748, the 21st day of January.

504. He also said today that he is persecuting the Church, or those who have faith, according to what is said in Revelation, that he persecuted the seed of the woman, Rev. Chap. 12 [verses 13, 17].

505. He is extremely slippery. When he is undergoing punishments and is frightened, he promises all things, and admits the truth—thus from fear, as well as from falsehood or lying—to the point where one cannot imagine but that it comes from the heart, when yet it is only from the mouth. At heart he is entertaining something different. He has so very little left [of what is human], that if purged, he could lose his identity.

The dragon's nature

507.[1] It is the nature of the dragon, spoken of above [501–5], to take notice of all and the least things, so that he does not let anything, either inward or outward, pass him by. Thus he keeps his eyes alert, mixing into every single thing, and then covers up the trails by every means he knows, including denials, so it will not appear that anything came from him—except when he breaks out in overt anger.

Then he blasphemes, brings forth his inner hatred, spares no one who is not a worshipper of him, seeks to fortify himself in every way so as not to be overthrown. When thrust down, he keeps on reaching for higher things, and he is also skilled through continual practice in every kind of subterfuge, exercising many of them, including some that are very filthy and would involve him prostituting himself.

These he also practices in anger, nor could it be otherwise, due to a habit of so many years, and due to the great number of spirits together breathing into him as their own focal point, of whom he is the ultimate medium. There are, in fact, many who are likewise dragons, but they relate to him as their idol. This is why he has this nature, for if he were to be deprived of worshippers, he would be capable of nothing.

This is the chief and the God of the Jews in the life after death, as well as of all those who are evil, even among Christians so-called, all of whom he champions. 1748, the 22nd day of January.

508. He who has just been written about is the head, the rest forming the body. Those who are being led astray by him are even portrayed in the heaven of spirits as streaming into the jaws of a great dragon, and being eaten up, so that they may compose some

---

[1] The manuscript has no paragraph 506.

element of that body which he is striving to obtain. Hence also he is called the Dragon.

About Mohammed

509. Mohammed, in accordance with his own wish, also underwent temptations; that he had this desire, I could also infer from several circumstances, and he was certainly tempted this night by something done by the dragon.

While I was sleeping quite pleasantly and dreaming about almost nothing else than the meaning of the word "Comforter" (*Paraclyti*), spoken of in John [14:16–26, 15:26, 16:7 *ff*.], and matters related to Him, then the dragon pretended in front of Mohammed that I was awake, speaking and answering as though he were I, about which, however, I was entirely unaware.

Consequently, since Mohammed could not see otherwise than that I was so corrupt, and this for the whole night, he was driven to doubts about Jesus Christ, whether His power was so great, since the dragon had been able to lead even me astray in regard to truths.

When I awoke, he said, still undisturbed, what I am like—that I am wavering—and that this surprised him. But when I told him that this had taken place in sleep, and that I knew nothing about the conversation, that I had only been thinking about the comforter, and the like, he was surprised. This was also proven to him by a certain experience, which was, that the dragon tried to force me to sleep. These things show that Mohammed stood steadfast in his belief, even though he was tempted in this way. 1748, in the night between 22 and 23 January.

(See the continuation.)

Continuation about Mohammed

510. When he was finally convinced that those things had taken place while I was asleep, and that I had been completely unaware of it, he was then tempted in a different manner, being put under a veil by the dragon, and thus treated like the others—and in fact, under a thicker veil than the others—and also bound, as I am now told. But still he remained steadfast.

511. Next, he was put to sleep, and the others were thinking he had been deprived of his rationality and then forced to speak as

FROM THE *BIBLE INDEX* 514.

his inclination prompted him, as spirits normally do. However, while asleep he was questioned about Jesus Christ, Whom he then also confessed. From this it can be inferred that he is being kept in the faith, and strengthened by Jesus Christ Alone. These things were written in his presence, and in some cases he has dictated to me the words I have written. 1748, 23 January.

511½. Mohammed now says that he remembers these things now, but that if they had not been written down, he would not have remembered the least detail. 1748, 2 September.

About Mohammed's spirits, how they are instructed and become angels

512. Spirits who approach Mohammed perform similar gyres as the angels, and indeed, along with singing in melodious voices, which I have heard for many days as I awoke from sleep. So they had been performing their own spiritual gyres throughout the night. Twice, and now once more, they were also allowed to enact singing displays, like the angels, one in fact concerning the Savior of the World, which they are said to have performed with a skill comparable to that of the angels, even so well that they were admitted into angelic choirs.

513. Moreover, before performing those gyres around Mohammed, they portrayed the things spoken of before [403, 407], such as baths, and the like, together with the resulting pleasure. They tell also that many things had occurred to them, as if in sleep, concerning the Savior of the World—something which Mohammed had not realized because it had been concealed from him. Thus one by one they had been instructed in the truth, and those instructed had been carried away from him, as he had told me before [345].

514. Moreover, during the morning and even the evening hours I heard angelic gyres being performed, both by those who had truly become angels, and also by Mohammedan spirits who had been competing with angelic ones. And now they are being cheered very much, sending heartfelt emotion through me. Mohammed affirms that he is feeling the same emotion as I. 1748, the 23rd day of January.

SPIRITUAL EXPERIENCES

Two punishments of spirits, namely, that of being pulled apart, and the veil: how they take place in a person [on earth]

515. A person on earth cannot be pulled apart between two contrary [forces] as a spirit can [404], for the reason that neither his body, nor consequently his lower mind—because it adheres to the body—can be torn to pieces without his completely perishing, or dying. Therefore, in place of this punishment, or this type of purging process, a person on earth is held in between evil and good feelings [pressing upon him] from both sides, each of which tries to conquer. Thus he is held in a balance, and drawn hither and thither, and safely his indignation is kindled into anger, then perhaps turned into despair, or to the thought of [eternal] unhappiness for himself through his downfall.

This is how [the punishment of] being pulled apart exists with people on earth; and to these kinds of temptations, they seem to yield.

516. As for the second kind, namely, the veil [*see* 434–5], we on earth cannot be submitted to this either, for we know we are in the body, and cannot be thus concealed from any except a blind eye, nor be thus driven about to seek escape, because we know we are in the body.

But in place of that punishment we have this: when we want to recall truths to mind, or to write them down—even lucid and well thought-out truths—then the ideas are taken away, both in their general and particular form, and we cannot recall anything at all to memory. We are allowed to see something, as when a light is lit and then taken away or put out, and meanwhile we become inflamed with the desire to know it or write it down, and at the same time with indignation, and the determination to proceed, or even a [prompting from] the conscience not to give up.

These things in man correspond to [punishment by] veils with spirits, which are said to be of various kinds and species in spirits. 1748, the 23rd day of January.

About the inhabitants of Jupiter

519.[1]   1) Being desirous of knowing what kind of people are living on other planets, I have also been permitted to become acquainted with the inhabitants of Jupiter. For if there are planets, there must be rational and intelligent beings upon them, who relate everything they see to the glory of the creator—since nothing can exist in the universe that does not finally go back to the glory of God—and thus who are able by these means, to perceive things heavenly and Divine.

Their spirits are of three kinds. They who are of the lowest or reasoning kind, are black, or else dark, and they seek for those by whom they may be led to the One Only Lord, so that they may be changed, that is, become heavenly.

2)   Besides this nation of spirits, there are also others whose faces shine like the Light from candles, and for the rest are dark; and they sit like idols, and let themselves be worshipped by slaves they had kept in the life of the body, for whom they call themselves intermediaries to the one only Lord in heaven, and they do not want them to get there except through their mediation.

3)   Those whose faces are thus fiery are called saints[2], because they had convinced themselves that they had led a holy life in the body; as a result of this, their face shines and they are distinguished from the rest.

4)   The best of these [spirits] are their angels, who are not of a white, but of a most beautiful sky blue color, interwoven with little sparks of gold. These are their angels and constitute their angelic heaven, and these they call the intermediary to the One Only Lord of the Universe.

520.   One of their spirits of the lowest kind was brought to me, so that I might learn from him what they are like. As to his condition, this one was from among those who are dark, who seem to themselves to be flying in heaven, like swimmers in water, with their arms outstretched. This comes from the fact that in the life of the body, they do not walk upright, but creep, yet with their face looking straight forward, but not down, which to them is a disgrace, and

---

[1] Paragraphs 517–18 have been placed, as indicated by the author, after 521.
[2] The Latin is *sancti*, meaning "holy ones."

characteristic of the very lowest kind. Those who look downward, they call the damned, and they are banished, to seek sustenance for themselves elsewhere. Besides this, like the people of our planet, they sit on seats, and are then upright. Therefore the second kind, called saintly, whose face looks fiery, do not swim in heaven like [the first], but sit.

521. As for the planet's inhabitants, the one who spoke with me told, as mentioned, that they creep, and that they sit; and that they are not divided up into cities, and thus communal societies, as we are here, but into nations and families, as we were on our earth in ancient times. Asked whether one nation waged war with another, he answered calmly that they have no need for it, since they have all the necessities of life. (They are naked, ##

Continuation about the inhabitants of Jupiter

517. ## because of the mild climate, and for that matter in a body just like we have on our planet, for a body was shown to me.) Thus they abhor the killing of people, and wars.

517½. They speak very little, but think more, and it is in a language rather of imagery than of words, in which they really excel. They can usually tell from each other's faces what they want, for they are trained to vary their expressions to show this. He tried to speak with me through thoughts alone, as he did not like words. But the power of imagery that brings out his thoughts is like speech without words. This is how he spoke with me, saying that he was a lowly spirit looking for the one and only Lord, so that he could come into heaven, for it was weighing upon his conscience that he had taken something away from a companion, of almost no value and which he believed that person was going to give to him.
    They do not, however, look for their saints, or shining ones; these are only sought by their slaves.

518. Moreover, as he said, spirits also associate with spirits, and spirits with people on earth, which is not surpising considering they are so adept in imagery. But they have three signals to prevent them from saying more to them than they are allowed, namely, that they see a seemingly old man with a white face, which is a sign that they should not say anything but the truth. Therefore they are careful about what they say. The second sign is that a face appears as if through a window, which is a sign that they should depart and speak no more. An old man was seen also by me, afterwards a face as if through a window, and at once the spirit seemed to depart, nor did he venture to speak further with me by that kind of imagery.

Continuation about their worship of the one only Lord ⊙⊙

The Jews worship the dragon altogether as God

522.[1] Today there were Jews around me. I could tell by the stench of mice [*see* 469], and later by a wave-like communication between them and the dragon, who was at a distance. I was able to learn that they worship the dragon as their God because they addressed their prayers to him, as to God. 1748, the 23rd day of January.

⊙⊙ *Continuation about the worship of the one only Lord with the inhabitants of Jupiter*

523. They say that they worship the one only Lord of heaven, whom they do not name by name, but know that the one only Lord rules all people. They therefore look for Him after death, and find Him, Who is Jesus Christ.

1) Asked whether they knew that the One Only Lord is Human, he replied that they all know He is Human, for by many of them, He had been seen as Human, and He Himself teaches them about truth, He cares for them, and they who believe in Him have life eternal.

2) He, the One Only Lord, governs their lives, and they do not worship idols, nor those saints who are intermediaries to the one only Lord for their own servants. So they live in innocence, love one another mutually, abhor wars, have the law written in their conscience or thought, and live according to it; and if they live otherwise, they are warned by their angels.

3) Moreover, because the general principles of how they should worship the one only Lord have been revealed to them in this way, therefore the children learn this from their parents. It is thus a

---

[1] 519–21 have been placed according to the author's indications after 516.

doctrine passed by word of mouth among family members, which does not spread beyond the nation.

4) That He the One Lord had suffered, they do not know, because they live in such a state as to be taught by Himself.

5) After their death, they are led in this same way to His heaven. 1748, the 24th day of January.

524. The first from among the inhabitants of our planet to come to them was one of the worst spirits from the inhabitants of our planet. He could not approach them, for they felt at once that he was evil, even though he was practicing his cunning. Later another came who was good; him they welcomed, and liked to associate with him. Still another came, who was of an in-between character, not yet improved, and they did not want to admit him either. Thus they sense at once what those who come to them are like. So they are kept at a distance from them.

525. Moreover, when their spirits become angels and are raised up to the angels of golden blue, or heavenly in color [519], then Horses, shining as if on fire, appear to them, which I also have seen. By these they are carried up, and so they arrive among the angels, with whom they say they are together, worshipping the one and only Lord.

About the dragon

526. When the dragon had been cast down from heaven to the lower parts—not yet to the lowest, except only to call his attention to the punishment, so that he might repent—finally, after having attempted evil things one after another, and without any result, he then showed himself as a most bitter enemy of God the Creator, Whom he formerly used to say he worshipped. But what kind of worship this had been, I was also allowed to learn, namely, that he placed himself on a par with Him, if not above Him, and even reproached Him because not everything came out as he wished. In fact he became angry, and cursed [God]. For this he was thrust down toward the lowest parts, where he was tormented for yet a little while.

Thereafter, throughout the whole night, as if insane, prodded by no one but himself alone, he cursed me, without giving a reason, he blasphemed, aiming his curses at me because I had opposed him. I could feel this all through the night, so he had been left on his own at that time.

After he was told about this, when I was awake, he admitted to it, as usual. And then, so as to avoid the punishment, he tried to get far away, to the ends of the universe. But whether he is sincere, I do not yet know.

Such a fate awaits those who do not acknowledge Jesus Christ as the mediator, and such is their attitude toward the most high Creator, Whom they confess with the mouth, while in their heart, they consider themselves His equal; and when their evil intents and attempts are successful, then at heart they raise themselves above Him, for they acknowledge no mediator. 1748, the 24th day of January.

Continuation about the inhabitants of Jupiter

527. Neither can those spirits be led astray by evil spirits, because they live in the order of life, and think more than they speak, so that their ability to reason descends from their understanding, and that understanding is instructed, through their heaven, by Jesus Christ, their One Only Lord.

This I was able to see from that spirit who was with me, and still is. For the evil breathing forth from an evil spirit cannot take hold in him, cannot become seated, but is without effect. Nor does this spirit concern himself with anything evil; he is only distressed by the matter he told about [517½], which is so trifling that among Christians, it would be considered nothing. 1748, 24 January.

528. That they can tell the thoughts of others from their face, or speak by means of the face—especially those who speak little from childhood on, and do not learn to put on pretenses—is clear from much evidence. For [when they so speak], all thoughts, in their every least distinction, are marked upon the face. The spirits can display this adroitly by creating faces that pass through all the variations of a single affection in a continuous transformation.

Continuation about the inhabitants of Jupiter

529. One of them also showed me how they speak to each other by changes of facial expression, that is, by tiny little movements of their muscles—especially those around the lips. This is why there are in that region so many interwoven muscular chains. But it is around the eyes, I presume, that their feelings are displayed, that is, their more inward feelings, for the face is a reflection of the inward person, as was explained [528] in regard to the spirits who display faces, with their changing shapes and varying features.

But what they showed me by changes in the tissues around the lips, I could not understand—I could only feel the changes—because my face was not, from early childhood, trained in them and accustomed to them.

The fact that they cannot put on pretenses, but follow the true order of their life, is likewise the reason why they are unable to conceal anything whatsoever from their companions, without their knowing it at once, and knowing what they are like, and what they are dreaming up, and what they have done. So life with them is spiritual, and such persons can at once be singled out, and then taught, and be reformed.

530. They also showed that they do not force their face, but let it go freely, something quite unknown to those who have become accustomed from early youth to put on pretenses, or to speak and act differently than they think and love. Their face is drawn up tight, in readiness to vary itself as shrewdness dictates.

But with the [inhabitants of Jupiter] it moves freely, being especially let out around the lips, which protrude somewhat. In this way, the tissues are afforded the freedom of signalling everything they are thinking, quite differently from here [on earth], where the tissues are contracted, and thus unable to express the things felt by the mind. For if all the tissues in the lips and around the lips were taken apart, the truth would be quite evident: there are muscular and fibrous chains, and bundlings of the same, so complex that they could not possibly have been created only for chewing and speech, but also for expressing the least ideas of the mind, which can therefore be said to be written upon them.

531. It was asked whether they know that their one only Lord is Human. He said that they know this, and indeed from the fact that they see Him often, so that they know that He is Human, and that their one only Lord is Jesus Christ, though not actually calling Him by this name. But that it is the Supreme One Himself, Who is to be

FROM THE *BIBLE INDEX* 534.

called "Jesus Christ," this they all now confess with one accord. He is not only Human but also at the same time God.

As for the name "King," they think it is below His dignity, because the name of King savors of what is worldly. That "Jesus" means "Savior," they also acknowledge, because it is the same as the *Keeper* of all.[1]

1748, the 24th day of January.

Continuation about the inhabitants of Jupiter

532. The one who had been with me was becoming weary, longing for the company of his own people and turning away from those spirits who are from our earth because they were trying to deceive him and lead him astray toward things contrary to belief and truth.

This spirit also said that in the part of his earth where he had been, there was as great a number of people as the land could nourish, adding that the ground is fertile, abounding in all things. Therefore, since all live without greed, seeking only to be nourished, one can infer that there must be a multitude of people. 1748, the 24th or 25th day of January.

533. As for their faces, they are entirely like the faces of the people of our earth, except more beautiful. Two of them were shown to me in their actual shape, and they were beautiful, with bright expressions, beautifully sincere and kind, and showing a becoming modesty. For their angel had appeared behind a bright cloud, with a small face which conveyed to them permission to show their faces. 1748, the 24th day of January.

534. There also appeared to me one of their more holy ones, who in front, from the face downwards, shone with a kind of fiery light. He likewise was splitting wood [*see* 273, 330]) standing, and splitting the wood he had at his feet. When I asked whether he was cold, he replied that he was not warm, even though he appears fiery.

Thus when people ascribe merit to themselves, or credit righteousness to themselves, or holiness to their own abilities, the same lot awaits them all alike in the other life. 1748, the 24th day of January.

---

[1] At the end of this passage, B. Chastanier noted "see no. 3049."

535. Their heaven is separate from ours, both so that they may be with their own people on their earth, and because they believe that the sky blue color dotted with little golden stars is the heavenly color itself; and because they are so convinced of this, they even appear to each other to be sky blue.

Nor do they want to be among the spirits of our earth, whom they know from experience to be cunning and deceitful, and who do not acknowledge the one only Lord; on account of their many wrong notions, they avoid their company. Their heaven is as great as that of this earth, and greater, because the inhabitants [of their earth] are more numerous. 1748, the 24th day of January.

536. It is remarkable that when the inhabitant of the planet Jupiter was shown to me, fiery in front, splitting the wood at his feet, it appeared to me as if it were a person whom he was thus striking, just as it did to the wood-cutters of our earth [271–3, 330], although it was only wood. From this one can infer that the illusion still persists that it is the Lord, even though they substitute wood in place of the Lord. How it looks to them, I do not know; but such an illusion occurs among others also. This shows what is hidden away in claiming merit to oneself. 1748, the 25th day of January.

537. They have little to do with those who are not of their nation. When they come upon them venturing beyond their own borders, they speak with them in a friendly manner, and want to perform for them all the services of charity; but their own circles are within the clan, which can extend quite widely. So they are divided up into nations, families and houses. 1748, the 26th day of January.

About the Dragon

538. It is amazing that although the dragon, or the "old serpent," does not cease to persecute believers—so very cunningly that I cannot describe his wiles and poisons—he has nevertheless admitted several times that he knows better than all others that Jesus Christ is the God of the universe, and governs the universe.

Moreover, spirits can also speak with him, and I have spoken with him just as with another person, often exposing his tricks in front of him. But I have done this only [through] spirits. Those who are in the heavens do not speak except through spirits.

Continuation about the inhabitants of Jupiter

539. As told before [518], the inhabitants speak with their own spirits, just as the sons and daughters of the most ancient Church did with both good and evil spirits, as may be evident from the creation story. For in the most ancient Church, there was not so much of speech and memory, but more of imagery and thought, so that they were able to share their thinking and mental images. Those living in a comparable state, on a different planet, are likewise able to communicate the mental images of their thoughts.

But in the course of time, to the extent that mankind was carried off into outward things, he began to speak, and to use the memory, and this causes him to forget the powers of thought.

540. With the inhabitants of Jupiter, almost all their speech is an inward mental image, or what we call a mentally materialized or imaged idea. It is not so much sensory or outer mental images, formed into words, that constitute their speech. This they have also, but in such a way that it supports the inward speech, and in certain cases, objects are expressed by it that are of use to their life.

541. As regards their speaking with their spirits, there are two kinds of evil spirits who molest them.[1] One kind is their worst. When he comes, a trembling and a kind of fear seizes them collectively, such as also seized me visibly when he came to me, so that I trembled, deeply frightened.

Looking at him as he was placed before me, I saw that he was a dark being, like a dark cloud, with several stars in front of him. He came up to my left side, retreating toward my back. He spoke with me, trying to talk with me in the same way as he did with them, but he was prevented by their angels, about whom something will be told presently [542]. He said that he could find out all that they had thought and done, which he does actually draw out of their memory. This is easy for spirits to do, when the Lord permits it.

Thus he wanted to reprove me for things I had thought and done, which he wanted to bring out, but it had been forbidden him. Still, he said that this is how he reproves others, surprised that he could not do so with me. He said that he is also allowed to chas-

---

[1] The second kind is spoken of in 545.

tise them by punishments, such as pains in the joints, even to such an intensity that they can bear it no longer—such as a twisting of the joints in the fingers, and feet, and also by some pains like gentle pricks in the face—subject to permission.

542. But their angels are present instantly, and occupy the region of their head, which they fill up by a special method, not used by the spirits of this earth.

The spirits of this earth as it were take possession of the brain and the head, and sometimes with such force that it feels as if they are squeezing together the scalp, or pulling off the skull, very often with some sense of pain; so that if any other than an experienced person were to undergo this, they would believe it was pulling off their skull, or even squashing their brain.

But the spirits of the planet Jupiter approach with a gentle blowing action, occupying the brain in a kind of gentle and coordinated glide, for they fear that the person might be hurt and feel pain from them. They came to be within me by this gliding movement. They are the ones who restrain evil spirits from doing something worse to them than they have been permitted by the Lord to do; so that an evil spirit is held within limits, and controlled. These are their angels, who preserve them. I have spoken with them also. 1748, the 26th day of January.

543. A person on earth should not speak with any spirit, but a spirit may with the person on earth, and they were surprised that I spoke so much with them. From this fact they were enabled to learn that I was of a different kind. The person is only permitted, when he is being punished, to speak these words, that he will do so no more. Nor is it permitted him to tell anyone of his own people that he had spoken with a spirit. This is severly punished.

Continuation about the inhabitants of Jupiter

544. Spirits are permitted to speak with earth dwellers, but these are not permitted to speak with a spirit, except those words, when being chastised, that they will do the thing no longer. If they do it again, when they had promised not to, they are punished even more severely; for the spirit comes back, and easily proves them guilty. For he can tell from their memory everything they have done, as angels can from their conscience. So spirits know from their memory what people have done, and angels know from their conscience whether there was evil intent, and they therefore temper [the punishment] according to the factors that present themselves. What it amounts to is that the angels judge between the spirit and the person.

545. The second kind [*see* 541] of these spirits who reprove, and at the same time teach them, also appear dark, as if they were dressed in sackcloth. These also come up to their left side, more to the front; and such a one came up to my side and spoke with me, saying that while he does frighten them with threats, he nevertheless brings no evil upon them. But when the people are afraid, he teaches them how they should think, and live. So these are their instructors.

545½. Moreover, I was also shown a dead head, or a skull. The highest part of the head was bald, bony. It was said that those see such a head who will die within a year, so that they may prepare themselves for death. They do not, of course, fear death, except because of leaving behind their friends, parents and children; but knowing that they are going away to heaven, they are not saddened by it.

546. The lifespan of people there is for the most part thirty years. Those beyond that age are said to be unteachable, so that the spirits do not venture to reprimand and chastise them, for they say they know these things as well as the spirits. Therefore, because they are not flexible and docile like their young people, spirits are less desirous of speaking with them.

Moreover, it is of the Lord's Providence that they do not live beyond those years, lest the population grow too large. For their offspring are multiplying, because famine and thus scarcity of food does not withhold them from the sense of obligation to have children, as on this earth. Therefore they are brought together [in marriage] in their earliest youth, nor do they want anything more than to have children, caring little for the other delights, as they are here called. They are eager only for offspring.

547. Moreover, their faces are bright, and they guard them from the sun's heat. As for their bodies, they wash and groom them to be sure, but they do not care about them, for they say it is only body. The face, however, they do not call body, because they speak and think by means of it. Because, as they believe, thought is of the face, they therefore do not want it to be body; so they care for the face, keeping it bright and clean. They have a wide head covering made of light blue tree bark, with a wide brim circling the head, but no such thing for the body.

By their thoughts they showed me how they conceive of the face, namely, as speaking only, almost without any bodily element. Although it is of muscular composition, still they consider it to be devoid of muscles and tissues.

1748, the 26th day of January.

Continuation on the inhabitants of Jupiter

548. Their dwellings or tents were also shown to me. They are small, only roofs, open round about, made of light blue tree bark, which looked to me as if dotted with stars.

In addition, they also have another tent, constructed of the same material, of the same color, and likewise dotted. It was rounded, but stretched out lengthwise. Into it they betake themselves lest their faces be harmed by the heat of the sun. Their face they guard very closely, since they do not consider it as the body.

549. Moreover, I spoke with them about their saints. Their holiest ones who become wood-cutters, as said before [534, 539], do not call our Savior "the one only Lord," but "the highest Lord." In this they are distinguished [from the others], for they want to be hailed as lords also, and want their slaves not to worship the highest Lord, but themselves, who will convey their prayers to the most high. This is why they are tormented by this punishment of being quite cold, and splitting wood.

The spirits do not approach and chastise these, either [*see* 546], as they do the others, for they do not allow themselves to be taught, being unbending as well as cold. For while the spirits are coming toward them, they recognize because of the cold that they are such a kind, and therefore cannot approach. Such spirits seem to themselves to be, not like our wood-cutters, beneath the feet[1], but rather high up, towards the front, in heaven. This is a sign that they are arrogant.

550. When I spoke with them, saying that no one can do anything good of himself, but from the only Lord, Who is Good Itself, and the fountain of all goodness, their angels replied modestly that they thought they could do good, and could not tell differently than that it is they who are doing the good. But after that, on being shown that all good that is thought and done, comes solely from the Lord of the Universe—and shown in such a way that they could comprehend it—then they replied that they are speaking in accordance with human custom, and we in a heavenly manner.

So they did acknowledge, but said it was simpler to think as they did. This too was explained to them, namely, that the Lord leaves those who live in that simplicity free to think in this way, just so they know. They were also present, but from afar, when I was writing these words; yet in such a way that they were nevertheless present, through mediating spirits.

551. They intensely contemplate the starry heaven, which they call the dwelling of the angels, not knowing anything about the many solar systems. Moreover, they are much wiser than our spirits, of whom they say that they speak much and think little, and are thus unable to grasp many matters more deeply, namely, whether [theirs] is truly heavenly goodness—therefore that they are outward people. But this they only say about spirits in whose company they do not want to be.

552. Furthermore, their angels are separate and, except for their very inward and innermost angels, cannot so well be together with our heavens; for the inward angels' own qualities, when they mingle with heavenly and spiritual angels, do not harmonize. Their fantasies, and similar phenomena to which they are subject, are different, for which reason they cannot so much be together, except by a general influence. However, the very inward and innermost angels make up one heaven throughout the universe.

1748, the 26th day of January.

---

[1] See *Arcana Coelestia* 4943.

553. SPIRITUAL EXPERIENCES

Continuation about the inhabitants of Jupiter

553. After the evil spirit had come up to me [541] and their angels were keeping hold of my head in the way described [542], restraining the spirit from bringing on anything evil, angelic choirs came from our angelic heaven. One after another, they performed their harmonious pictorial gyres, and delighted [their angels] so much that they decided they had been swept up into a higher heaven—I could faintly feel their delights—and they wanted to tell this to their other angels.

Moreover, one choir after another kept coming, and thus, as it appeared to them, the entire heaven. This delighted them most deeply, so that they confessed that their One Only Lord governs all in the starry universe. Those melodious angelic choirs continued for around an hour, and [the spirits of Jupiter] were present, and they were amazed, and were deeply moved.

554. They were further surprised when I said that I would tell the inhabitants of this earth this and that which I had heard about them. This they did not want at all to happen, for it is forbidden for them, and punishable, to publish anything spirits tell them. They were likewise surprised that such things could be published throughout the planet, because they are unfamiliar with any region beyond their own, where their relatives are.

555. Their Moons shine on them, so that they live in light. Those who want to be worshipped [*see* 519]—being those who call themselves the holiest ones, and who call and name [the Lord] "the highest lord" and not, like the others, "the one only Lord"—do not like to call the sun "sun," for they believe it is the dwelling place of their Lord most high.

They are therefore nature worshippers. It is also for this reason that they want to be fiery, as they even appear to be, and why they have continually suggested to me "the most high Lord" [549], because they strongly desire also to be called lords. These are the ones who do not want to call the sun by name. The others said that they are lying, because they know that the sun shines larger than their moons, or great stars, and with intense heat, which they seek to avoid by withdrawing into their tents.

556. In short, even though they live so simply, they are much wiser than spirits and souls who want to be learned. For they see on their own what is good, not even wanting to name "evil." Twice I wanted to say "evil," but they were averse to it. This I can declare, that they are much wiser. The details in which our people place wisdom, they reject and call worthless. They say that there is nothing of wisdom in them, on the contrary, that they obstruct the way to wisdom, which is indeed most clearly the case—something that can be seen much better by spirits, and even by people on our earth who have not acquired a taste for philosophical jargon and petty opinions. These cannot but laugh within themselves that any should think themselves wise because of such things, whereas they are like thick clouds that overshadow and obscure all the light of true understanding. For they not only hide and take away the light from them, but also blind them, being the source of all doubts that cannot be dispelled, because they lie so far away from truth.
1748, the 26th day of January.

About communication of spirits with mankind

557. As has been stated and demonstrated [319, 445], when spirits, who are the souls of those dead as to the body, are present with people on earth and stand at their back, they believe that they are in every way those people. And if they were allowed, they could be entirely engaged in the life of the world through a person who speaks with them, although it could not be done through others. In fact, this could be done so openly, that through that person they would be able to communicate their own thoughts by words, even by letters. For several times, in fact quite often, they controlled my hand while writing, entirely as if it were their own, so that they believed it was they themselves who were writing. This is so true, that I can swear to it. Indeed, if they were permitted, they could write in their own style, which I know also from a bit of experience; but they are not permitted to do this. 1748, the 26th day of January.

About the inhabitants of Jupiter, continued

558. Their greatest concern is how to tidy up their tents, which they do not decorate. They only want to keep them clean, and also [to have enough] to eat. They do not have clothes. They do not strive to become richer than is needed in order to be nourished and to live. Besides these, their greatest concern is the upbringing of their children, whom they love most tenderly.

559. When they walk, they keep their face directed frontwards, wearing a spacious covering above it, and because they are almost jumping along, repeatedly lifting themselves up in their course, they do step upon their feet. When they take steps forward, they help themselves a little with their hands, thus raising themselves up. All these things were shown to me, and were seen and confirmed by their spirits, who do not dare to say anything but what their angels allow them to say. 1748, the 26th day of January.

560. Those who were with me saw horses, then said that many such are to be found with them, but they are in the forests, and they fear them greatly. Even though they do no harm, there is nevertheless a certain ingrained fear of them. The cause of this lies in the fact that horses portray knowledge, and that it was personal knowledge, or knowledge [obtained by] the senses, consequently pertaining to the body, self, and the world, that had led the most ancient Church astray and caused the fall—the same thing as is meant by the tree of knowledge, which led them astray [Gen. 3:6]. Herein lies the cause of the fear of horses, and from this it follows that they should not learn sciences, for thus their understanding is darkened and blinded, and thus the loves of self and of the world begin to dominate, which originate from and reign in darkness.

561. The question whether there were too many horses was answered in the negative—from which it can also be gathered that the fish of the sea are not multiplying out of bounds, nor certain harmful animals, such as crows, and others, even though they are not being exterminated, etc. etc. All of this shows clearly the Providence of the Lord, in general and in particular. This they understood, saying that the Lord governs in such a way that each may have its own existence. 1748, the 26th day of January.

562. The advantage of spirits in comparison with people on earth is evident also from the fact that [spirits from the] inhabitants of that earth could even understand letters, both those I was writing and those I was reading, as if they had been taught. Thus they come into possession of the things that are in a person [they are with].

Continuation about the inhabitants of Jupiter

563. Those who are the worst of them worship the Sun, calling it the face of the Lord. But while those who call themselves saints persuade their own people that this is so, yet they say that they themselves do not worship the sun, but the Lord on high, whose abode is in the sun. These, however, are their worst ones, and the others shun them. From them, even spirits stay away, as said before [549], on account of the cold. So they are shut out from communication with heaven.

564. Moreover, I was able to grasp many things from them because they only think, and are not interested in particulars.
1) For example, when I was considering what the Light of understanding is, namely that it is the light of truth flowing in from our Lord, and in fact, a higher knowledge of universal truths, such as that our Lord governs all things, then [I understood] that personal knowledge obscures this light, and that such details, or truths about details, are in that general light like the variations that cause colors in the world—for which reason regeneration is also compared to the rainbow.
2) I further understood that it is the thinking that makes a human being's quality. When the thinking only clings to worldly and bodily things, then the understanding attaches itself to them to such an extent that the person cannot possibly speak with the Heaven of spirits; for the thought rushes outwards, and into oneself, the world, and nature, causing persisting fantasies in the other life that must be shaken off and die, which takes place by a painful separation process. It is different in the case of those who are absorbed only in thoughts about the Lord, thus about things of heaven.
3) There is therefore a twofold arc of the rainbow: one, which [newly arrived] souls love, arising from fantasies joined to what is spiritual; the other, arising from a spectrum of spiritual and heavenly elements, without anything of nature, and such is the very inward heaven. 1748, the 26th day of January.

565. For people who give themselves over to the will of the flesh, only personal elements emerging from words, and double meanings, and the values they place in worldly and bodily things, count for anything. These qualities draw to themselves all higher thoughts, which are then engulfed in them, and thus perish—because to them, those things are everything.

But they who are absorbed in thoughts about heavenly life have no interest at all in anything of this kind, but regard it as something to be laughed about, seeing it as a little cloud in front of the sun, which they at once chase away. For they love the light without little clouds; while those living in an upside-down order love the cloud without the light. They find their light in clouds, and in this their ingenuity consists, that is so admired throughout this planet.

Such [obstructions] also are philosophical terms—consequently, the totality of manmade philosophy. 1748, the 26th day of January.

Continuation about the inhabitants of Jupiter

566. The inhabitants dwelling below the equator, like the inhabitants of this earth in Africa and in the warm zones, go about naked, as said [521, 558], as we read also about the children of the most ancient Church under the name "Adam," namely, that they were naked [Gen. 2:25]. In a state of innocence, nakedness is not shameful. The shame of nakedness arises from sin, and in fact, from the wiping out of heavenly love. Then follow loves which cause nakedness to be shameful, for which reason Adam also knew at once that he was naked, and also Eve, and they hid themselves.

So it is with those who live on this planet in the equatorial regions. Nakedness is no great thing to them, for they desire nothing else than to have children, for the sake of heaven.

567. They do not walk on four feet like animals of the earth, or four-legged animals, but more or less jump, at the same time helping themselves along with their hands, so as to go faster. From time to time they stand on both legs, but bent at the knees, and they sit gracefully, almost like the Mohammedans, wherever they may be; and they rest in the same posture.

The fact that they move forward by jumping, arises from their inward nature, because they are of the earth, and at the same time look toward heaven. But the people of our earth, and spirits, mock them for this, being evil themselves, and born into wickedness, and boasting that they walk upright, whereas this is more a result of being arrogant. Clearly, the erect position of the body is not natural, but artificial, learned by training and habit over a period of time. Nature prefers that they walk in this manner, and if [the people of our earth] had so walked, it would have become good manners from custom, just as nakedness did in the warm regions of our earth.

568. Those from that earth are now saying, while I seem to be speaking with them through spirits—which is an easy matter for our Lord in His omnipotence—they are saying that their friends do not mind in the least that they are naked, that they are never surprised about it, nor do they ever consider it improper.

569. When an evil spirit of the earth Jupiter was at my side, wanting to reprove me for things I had thought and done, the angels of that earth were also present, as mentioned earlier [541–42]. They were then holding up my face, especially the area around the lips— my mouth open, and my expression ever cheerful and laughing. Later I was told that this is the way they keep the inhabitants of that region, so that they have a cheerful countenance, not a sad one, for the reason, as it seems, that angels are present.

The evil spirit did not know otherwise than that it was an inhabitant of his earth at whose side he was standing. 1748, the 26th day of January.

570. Besides the spirits of that earth spoken of above [519–20], there are other spirits who urge toward things contrary, for everywhere there are also opposite spirits, and these are their spirits who have been banished from their society and have become evil. When they come up to anyone, something like a flying fire falls near the front parts of the person, passing thence to his back parts lower down, and from there he speaks toward the higher parts, and in fact in a rough and forked voice, such as cannot be adequately described, almost as if he spoke with a forked tongue. He tells them contrary things, namely, that they should not live according to the teaching of the angels, but free from restraints, and things of this kind that are contrary to what the teaching spirit had told them previously. For the most part they come not long after the teaching spirit has left, and then tell the person the opposite, urging him toward a licentious life.

But because the people there know that these spirits are of that character, they do not heed them. They also learn in this way what evil is, for without a recognition of evil—inasmuch as there are such people—their life and understanding cannot develop; but they must be taught what is good by means of evil, and thus they learn to avoid evil, and to strive after good, as well as to be moved by what is good. 1748, the 27th day of January.

571. Those spirits who present themselves as saints, are cold. In order that I might feel their cold, a certain spirit approached, and appeared as though he were in me, with the result that I could feel his cold condition. He said that he felt warmth from me. 1748, the 27th day of January.

Continuation on the inhabitants of Jupiter

572. Their good spirits were anxious that I should not publish anything I have heard from them, for among them it is forbidden, and punishable, to divulge what spirits speak to any outside of their family—thus except to closest friends and married partners, and children to their own parents.

1) But I replied to them that on this earth, the situation is different in that spirits and angels do not speak with people, nor do people hear what a spirit is saying, because their thoughts are immersed in worldly and bodily concerns. And it is their nature not to believe anything the senses do not grasp, so that many do not even believe there are spirits and angels, thus that there is a heaven, or a life after death, still less that the one only Lord rules all things and all people—these facts they comprehend all the less because they judge from the ideas of the outer senses, which are so limited, corporeal and material, that they grasp nothing of that kind, but cloak it all in darkness, and consequently in doubts, causing people to deny inwardly.

2) In fact today, even these things that have been seen and heard by me concerning people on another earth, many do not believe, but roll up in various wrappings, calling them fantasies; and if they dared, they would even call fantasies anything they read in their holy Word—so unbelieving they are! So what they will have thought about these matters among themselves, I do not yet know.

573. They were extremely surprised that our spirits do nothing but mock them for helping themselves along in their steps with the use of their hands, and for being naked, remembering nothing at all of the things said [in the Word] about their own heavenly life. This is an indication that they think only the lowest, or bodily and earthly thoughts, and that higher things are of no concern to them.

574. It can be inferred from their facial speech that they understand quite fully and quickly whatever a companion, and what their spirits speak, and of course, those who are more perfect, what their angels speak. For it is a speech free of elaborations that distract the thoughts and break them up into main points. Thus they can see the thoughts as a whole, for there are many things in them simultaneously, as when a person thinks or sees what is pictured almost at a single glance, as they say, together with all the feelings that are in it; so they are able to recognize what feeling lies within the speech.

Therefore with them, the face speaking is the index of their true feelings—and around the eyes, even of their mind. And they are not at all able to dissemble, and therefore their inward and more inward life itself is in their speech.

So they are able to speak with their heavenly beings, because their ideas are not thus immersed in earthly and bodily matters. Such an immersion causes the inward parts to be cut off, and, on this earth, makes people outwardly like angels, but inwardly like wild animals. They are surprised that any beauty can exist on the faces of this earth, and that they are not deformed. But this results from a different cause. 1748, 27 January.

Just now I spoke to those spirits from Jupiter who were present, saying that the evil people of this earth in the other life gradually become so ugly and deformed in their face, that they cannot look at them on account of their ugliness. I was told that their beautiful faces come from their infancy, which is innocent. 1748, 4 Sept.

About those in the afterlife who seek to warm themselves by cutting grass with a saw

575. About the wood-cutters, you may see what has been said previously [271–3, 330, 534–6, 549]. There are also some who saw, not wood, but grass, and by this means seek to warm themselves.

When I inquired who these were, [I was told] that they are those who live morally well in life, doing no one injustice, thus who are reputed as good in civil life, and also give to the needy and poor, so they believe that on this account they deserve some [reward]. But although they know that Jesus Christ our Savior is the way, and the only one to be worshipped, because He is the one only Intercessor, Human, and God, thus the one only Lord, nevertheless they still pass Him by and believe in their heart that it is sufficient for us to acknowledge the one only God, creator of the universe—by whom they mean the Father. Consequently they doubt, or rather deny our Lord, thus scorning His the Only Intercession.

These after death are the kind who are cold, and who seek to acquire warmth for themselves by sawing grass into tiny pieces.

576. Furthermore, they go about, asking among all whom they meet whether they would like to give them something to make them warm. When they receive something, and indeed, something of warmth from others, even this does nothing for them. For they are trying to obtain an inner warmth, not the outer warmth they get from others; and they finally become so afraid and sick of the others' warmth, that they go back to their sawing, to acquire warmth for themselves.

Their coldness also, I have felt, which is very intense, and they could not bear it if I either warmed myself at the fire, or warmed my feet with shoes, or anything of that kind.

576½. Moreover, they are always hoping they are to be carried up into heaven because they have done good deeds in their life, even deliberating how they could force their own way, or lift themselves up, into heaven. But it is in vain, for they still become cold.

577. Still, these are quite perceptive spirits, as I was able to infer from one who had been elevated into the realm of higher spirits. The spirits there could not harmonize with him, because they were too dense, for they could not penetrate the things that he was thinking—until he came among some who had been like himself. But even in their company he could not remain for long, because that same quality was still clinging to him. 1748, 27 January.

About the Characteristics of good spirits

578. Good spirits are distinguishable by many characteristics, as by their warmth when they came up to me, by the gentleness of their action upon me, and by the softness of their speaking; likewise, by their gentle pliability when they move in the company of many, and especially by the fact that when they are working in the company of many, it is openly seen that there are many functioning at the same time—thus not completely as one, like the angels.

They are distinguished chiefly by the fact that they do not want to say anything evil about anyone—like one in their company who was speaking, and called evil spirits by a bad name because they are wicked. Him who had said this and had thus set himself apart from them, they estranged from their choir, saying that he should first be taught not to hurt anyone by some smart remark.

Thus it is recognized at once in their circles, whether they are alike, or harmonize; and so they are also tested. 1748, 27 January.

About angelic choirs

579. Many angelic choirs have been heard round about me for several days, which I cannot well identify, except for the Mohammedans [*see* 512–4, 3040]; for the whirling movements of the ones I was able to watch differ. There are those who complete a gyre without a sign of any partition. There are those who go through and terminate a gyre in two parts—so that the beats, as it were, heard in a whirling movement may be threefold, fourfold, fivefold. There are those who reach six quite perceptible beats in each whirling movement, which is so fast, that one whirling movement scarcely lasts one second. 1748, the 27th day of January.

About the inhabitants of Jupiter

580. I have heard from their good spirits about the death of those who live on that planet, namely, that they die in their youth, for the reason advanced earlier [546], that is, so that the population does not increase too much. But they rarely die of sicknesses, as on this earth, except those who have lived an evil and superficial life;

instead they die calmly, and as if in sleep, thus entering through sleep into the other life.

581. There were some spirits from that earth who listened as I was reading Chapter 17 of John. They were surprised that the One Only Lord had become a human being, and had been on earth like another human being, but still they said afterwards that all things [they heard] are Divine. Spirits of our earth, who were disbelievers, were constantly interjecting that He was human, that He was crucified, that He was born human, and was like any other human being.

They listened to these remarks without saying anything. Later, however, they declared that these spirits were altogether devils, because they take the things they are saying from what is worldly, bodily, and the like, which they on their earth reject as waste and consider as nothing. On such refuse these spirits like to base their speaking, which blinds minds and casts darkness over the light of truth.

And now they are warning the spirits of our earth that so long as they stay in such rubble, and develop their arguments therefrom, or judge therefrom, they are no different from their own devils, whom they completely reject from society, casting and spewing them out beneath their feet, or into the mud.

The spirits of Jupiter could also judge their evil character from the fact that of all that the spirits of our earth had heard about them, they entertained in fantasy nothing else but the fact of their nakedness. Other matters, which are heavenly, they do not even think about, which leads to the conclusion that there is almost nothing heavenly in them. 1748, 26 January.

582. As for their gait, I have watched them helping themselves along with their hands, and jumping [567], because it was also granted me to see how they walk. Every third step, they turn around, performing a full circle with face and body, and then sit. They do this so that they will not be seen except for the face, for they very much like their faces to be seen, but they hide the other parts by so sitting, in their own fashion, whereby also their foreparts are concealed, which they do not like to be seen either.

583. Furthermore, some of their spirits were present with me, to whom I was showing the inhabitants of this planet, whose faces at the time all seemed to me smaller than usual. This happened because they were seeing the faces of the people of our earth as smaller than the faces of their earth's inhabitants, and they said that the faces were not beautiful, both because they were smaller, and because they were quite ugly on account of (koppor, koppärrig[1]). They said that among them such faces are not to be found, nor people who were blemished in the face by red pimples and the like, because they do not get sick. Some faces they smiled at, namely, those in which the region around the lips somewhat protruded, and those which widened so as to be laughing faces. Sad ones they did not enjoy, because worldly concerns imprint such expressions on them. Thus from the faces, they are able to recognize of what character people are. 1748, 26 January.

The annual movement of Jupiter is twelve years, and the diurnal movement six hours.

Continuation on the inhabitants of Jupiter

584. About the inflow of the angels of the earth Jupiter, it is allowed only to note that it is soft, and comes in alternating waves, so to speak; therefore it is gentle, like the character of these angels, who also think in this manner.

584½. From time to time, I have engaged in conversation with them, through their spirits, for of course, what the angels are thinking, this the spirits speak, as if on their own. In general, the thought is drawn away and taken up by spirits who, without reflecting on these circumstances, believe that they are speaking entirely of themselves.

I have discussed the same matters with some who had been from another earth, and they understood them better than I. If I only intimated or attended to what I was thinking, they grasped a fuller meaning of the matter, so that they said they understood me better than by outright speech conveyed to them by speaking spirits.

585. Furthermore, their understanding far excels the understanding of the educated and wise on our earth, especially of those

---

[1] In the original, two Swedish words, *koppor, koppärrig*, meaning "pustules, pockmarked," appear here in parentheses, and in the margin the Latin word *maculati*, meaning "blemished."

who are from Europe. These regard themselves as learned because they dissertate on philosophical matters, and are enraptured by nothing but terms and trivia, which take away all the meaning of a thing, as when the mind is intent upon the words of a speaker and not upon their sense—so that if the terms were gone, the mind would perceive the meaning clearly.

This the spirits of Jupiter well understood, and they said that such terms are only little black clouds, which get in the way, and which they do not want to let in when they are portraying their starry heaven by a vision. That is where it becomes evident what a difference there is. When they wanted to portray the one only Lord changing wrong feelings so that they might become good ones—which amounts to changing evil into good—then they pictured the mind devoted to understanding as a beautiful figure, and its activity as a feeling harmonizing with that figure. Then they tried to show me how the one only Lord bends bad feelings into good ones, which they did for some time in their own characteristic manner, and so adroitly that they were warmly praised by the angels.

The learned of our earth, however, could not grasp this at all, when yet they were scholars, and thought themselves wiser than those spirits. But they think themselves learned if they merely can dispute about what form is, what measurement is, what substance is, what matter and non-matter is—which the spirits of the other earth laugh about and call insanity. They love real things, while the former love nothing but filthy scum. They are now telling me these words.

586. Again regarding their gait [*see* 582], it is not creeping, like that of animals, but half-upright, with their chest and face leaning forward and upwards and their feet resting on the ground below, so that they can easily help themselves along with their hands or palms, and quickly turn, and quickly sit down.

587. Moreover, when I was in bed, they did not want me to turn over facing the wall, but wanted me always to look forward, that is, away from the wall. And when I said that it was not possible in this case, because I had to lie on both sides for the sake of rest, they said that this was done by their people by completely turning over end for end, and rapidly, for they want to look outward, because they believe the Lord to be there. This has also often happened to me

before, but I did not yet know the cause of it, namely, that spirits of this kind were acting with the others in a group.
1748, the 28th day of January.

588. Also shown to me was the head covering of those who boast that they are saints. It is a dark, towering cap. The head beneath it was snowy white, but whether because of gray hair, I did not inquire. In this manner their saints cover their head, namely, with towers, so to speak.

About one kind of punishment of the evil spirits from the planet Jupiter

589. A kind of punishment that their worst undergo was shown to me. They are held as if in a tub, so bound up that they cannot move themselves at all. Meanwhile, they are troubled by dreadful fantasies about their own imprisonment, and a longing is aroused to come forth from their bonds. This being futile, the longing is joined by anxiety and torment, and they are told that they must bear these things until they have paid everything, even to "the last farthing" [Matt. 5:26]. Even so, they are set free. The appearance of their face was brought before me, and it was ugly, and as if it had been torn apart.

This punishment corresponds to both of the fantasies of the hellish crowd, that of being in a kind of tub [285–86], and also that of punishment by a veil, spoken about earlier [534–35]. It is said that they are then tormented miserably; but they were told that if they had paid the very last farthing, it would have taken forever. It was for this reason that the One Only Lord bore the cruelest tortures on our earth, in order that they may thus be freed, when yet they have borne this for only a dot of time.

590. Learned spirits of Europe, who are constantly trying to lead them away from truth and belief in the Lord, held forth that His act of salvation took place in a given time, and almost four thousand years had elapsed before He came into the world, and yet that also previously, spirits had been saved. The spirits of Jupiter could not help laughing at their inventing such charges in regard to Divine matters, since, as they were told, past and present are one with God;

for to Him all things are present from eternity to eternity, so that promised and done is the same thing with the Lord.

There are other objections besides that they very often raise, wanting to corrupt all spirits, whomsoever they meet. Such are the Europeans, who are called Christians, and in fact inwardly, many are of this character; for in the world, they dissemble, saying one thing with the mouth while bearing something different in the heart. Hereafter, spirits or souls cannot but speak from their acquired character and therefore from the heart, consequently from a life of self-love, which had consisted of nothing but passions, with the result that their understanding, so-called, had consisted of nothing but falsities.

For there is no other power of reasoning that stays with people [after death] but what springs from their love, so that such as the love is in the body, such is the life, and such is the behavior. That love is recognized in the other life so easily that nothing is easier. When they utter but one word, or when they divulge, or only think, one mental image, their whole spirit is exposed at once, as well as what they had been like in bodily life. So they are put in the company of similar spirits, who all act in conjunction.

591. There was also conversation with spirits of the other earth on the manner of philosophizing here, namely, that when those here are describing spirits, souls, and similar invisible entities, they remove all elements on which human ideas can have a grip, such as locality, components, shapes, and the like, and leave no idea and consequently no term, by which to express those things which have to do with spirits and the like, calling them immaterial, etc., thus wrapping them in terms, finally [assigning them] occult properties. Thus they end up doubting whether there is anything within, or beyond, those things which the senses grasp, and many deny that there is (at least at heart). So they deny the existence of spirits, they deny spiritual things, they deny heavenly things, supposing that they will die, as all other animals do, from which they do not even know to distinguish themselves—and nevertheless they want to be thought learned. Moreover, they connect together their terms and thereby develop many themes that are nothing but scholarly terminology which, if unwrapped, exhibits a simple, easily expressible meaning.

The spirits of the planet Jupiter laugh about these and similar matters, and again they are calling such people insane—and manure, if their thinking is immersed and bound up, or entrapped, in such things.

1748, the 28th day of January.

About a punishment of women, especially, who lead an indulgent and idle life

592. [I have seen] the punishment of women who lead an indulgent and idle life, characteristic of those in some regions when they have become wealthy, and for one reason or another rise to prominence above others—who thus reside in pleasures, letting themselves be waited on like queens by servants and attendants, not having to worry about anything, just indulging their inclinations in elegance and indolence, reclining on couches, dressing up, and sitting at tables and desks; and in this fashion they pass their lives.

But having seen the fierce punishment that such women undergo in the other life, I was told two times that they were not the type of women who had been born into such conditions, such as queens, or who were brought up in them from early childhood and thus accustomed to them, for these have known nothing else. The type of women that are meant here are those who, because of some distinction, or because of riches, and the resulting arrogance, in the course of time have thus given themselves up to voluptuous living.

593. Those who are like this, upon coming into the other life, seem to themselves at first to be among their like, and thus to carry on in the same way as they had done during their life in the world. But this scene is changed into a cruel one, for those same women clash vehemently among themselves, bruise and tear each other, pull each other's hair and tear each other's scalps, so pitiably that one cannot stand looking on. Also, they even hang them up naked like pigs, cutting off their feet, tearing them apart in a thousand ways, one after another. In fact blood flows so abundantly that I shuddered, and it is a horror to describe such scenes, but nevertheless, such is their punishment. The spirits around me, frightened, wanted to flee away.

What kind of women they are, you may see above [592]. These appeared to me in front, toward the left, in a certain higher place symbolizing the fantasy linked to arrogance. 1748, the 28th day of January.

About the disbelief of European spirits

594. When I was reading something about the suffering of our Savior, certain European spirits who had been called Christians, brought in this and that, wanting to lead astray spirits of the earth Jupiter, with the intent of drawing them away from the true faith so that they could communicate to them their own scandalous thoughts, which are many and relate to the passion and crucifixion of our Savior.

However, I said to the inhabitants of Jupiter that among those telling these offensive things, there might be some who in the life of the body were able to be public preachers, and when they were preaching about the Lord's passion had been deeply stirred, and had moved the common people to tears; and yet now they are such scorners, because now they are speaking and reasoning from their character and their heart.

Then the inhabitants of the other earth were amazed at this, and dumbfounded that there could have been such a disharmony of their inward parts that they had been able to speak in this manner, and yet have something else at heart—which for them, as they say, is impossible, for their face cannot speak something different than their heart. 1748, the 28th day of January.

About someone among the most learned

595. One spirit who had been extremely famous and most acclaimed on account of his doctrines, came upwards toward me from below, thus from the lower earth. He was cold, as I plainly felt from the cold blast. He said that he had heard what I had discussed with others, but that of the heavenly and spiritual things, he had understood nothing, even though he had been one of the main writers on those subjects; nor did he understand what even a spirit of the lower sort knows, or even want to learn it. He was therefore rebuked and told that this was one thing necessary in this life. He did not know that he was in the other life. 1748, the 27th day of January.

More about the inhabitants of Jupiter

596. In regard to the taste of foods, they do not prepare foods for the taste, but for the use they have to their body. A food that is more useful to their body, is accordingly more savory to them, and seems sweeter. Consequently, they are not carried away by the sense of taste into luxuries that undermine the health of the body, causing the mind to suffer, which is sound in a sound body if the body is taken care of for the sake of the inward person. This is different from on our earth, where taste is in command, and so, the body becomes sick and the mind unsound.

About the burning desire of spirits

597. There are spirits who are easily enkindled with desire, so that they become exceedingly impatient, and seemingly burn with a desire, and in fact, for something of no use to them. One even admitted this, since it happened now and then that I burned with the desire of possessing and buying this or that, and realized that it was not I who was thus burning with longing, but that it was spirits. They spoke with me, confirming their desire, and saying that they could hardly exist if they did not obtain those things. Their desire persists a long time, sometimes even until I have acquired them. In fact, this happens even with those who know that the items they want are of no use to them, but only to me, as I also showed them. One said that he knew this, but still could not desist. The yearning for those things is inflamed by many other spirits of the same kind who are in society together, for whom they act as intermediaries with the person on earth. So that I might understand this better, that desire was changed within me in an instant, which was caused by the fact that different spirits had then taken over.

Thus it is spirits who arouse desires, longings, and such, as has happened with me so often that I cannot number the times. And so there are demons through whom the Lord governs people and allows them to be aroused, for various reasons, both for the purpose of punishment and for the purpose of their uplifting. 1748, 29 January. There are evil spirits who even arouse that pleasure of sitting for a long time in toilets, and staying there beyond the required time; for devils delight exceedingly in toilets, as you may see mentioned previously [377, 414].

About spirits properly so called, who are not demons, but are speaking ones

598. Spirits properly so called are only those who love to speak and are mediums of the speech of many. These are also divided up into kinds and species, as well as into classes. They want to be called intelligence, or knowledge, and think they are the only ones who know, indeed who control all things, each in a different way. At each level there are such spirits, to whom pertain the spiritual matters; yet they think little, although they believe they think more than others. But I cannot as yet enumerate the different kinds among them.

599. It is remarkable how, when something comes up, such as if anything occurs in the other life, they then immediately think they know what it is, and speak as though they know, saying it is this or it is that and describing it as if they knew all about it. This they do one after the other, each differently, so that they form different opinions about the things that occur and touch any one of their senses, at once convincing themselves that it is as they say. Many spoke with conviction, one after the other, about one and the same object. They also love to lead me, when I am writing. 1748, 30 January.

About a collective glorification in the heavens

600. For quite a long time I was kept in a broad vision, which almost withdrew me from personal ideas, or those on the bodily plane. There appeared a kind of lively sparkling of light nearby, like the light of diamonds, and this continued for quite a long time. I cannot describe that light in any other way, for it was very general, and it drew me away from ideas on the bodily plane, in fact, from the body. When I was in it, then I was looking at bodily things as if below me, and I did feel them, but as if remote from me and not belonging to me, and thus not being part of me.

Several times, the spirits and demons said that I was absent from them, and that they did not know where I was, nor what I was thinking. They complained that because of this, I was being removed from them, and thus the gladness which they had felt from speaking with me, and from being one with me through direct communication, had passed away.

601. Moreover, it seemed to me at that time that I was in that glory as to the head, but not as to the body—but in such a way that I was without a head, which had diffused itself into their common head, while the body was below that realm. From this it was granted me to learn how they who are in heaven are able to hear and see those things that come forth in the realm of spirits, namely, as being remote from them, and below them, nor are they allowed to see and know anything but what it pleases the Lord [to show them].

602. The influence of evil demons I have also felt, but without any effect upon myself at the time, because they could not have very close communication. One of them who is a dragon, encircled at that time by very many evil spirits and demons, enabling him to work more forcefully, was then laboring and using every device to find his way in and attack. But he eventually admitted that it had been to no avail, and he wanted to persuade his crowd to depart.

603. Due to some bodily elements that were attached to spiritual ones, something seemed to me to have entered him, but this did not cause any anxiety, for it passed away at once, and was as if dissipated.

604. Moreover, when I was in bed, before I fell asleep, I heard a general singing of heaven around me, by many angels of the inward heaven[1], and at the same time I was then in a visual glorification. That glorifying which came to my hearing, while it was audible, at the same time it was general, because what they were portraying and singing, I could not understand at all. I was told that the universal heavens continually ascribe glory to the Lord, and glorify Him in this way.

604 1/2. That such glorification goes on and on, I was also able to infer from the fact that whenever I took a breath while humming a song, I would be following those who were likewise singing by means of gyres, so that I could tell that the glorification was perpetual.

604 1/3. But this was just the glorification common to all; the angels have distinct spiritual and heavenly mental imagery, which no

---

[1] See 262, footnote.

one can see except one who is in the heavens. I am told that it is most clear to those who are in heaven, that is, heavenly glorification, as well as spiritual; and that whatever of it comes forth in the realm of spirits, appears in such a way that they are able to know and learn nothing but what the Lord allows them to.

605. There is also a collective breathing, about which I was able to observe the following, namely, that I was then somehow taking part in a collective breathing that was easy and spontaneous; and indeed, that the collective breathing of heaven related to my own breathing as three to one, as did my heartbeat also. Nevertheless, because of the collective respiration, all can breathe in accordance with this rule, that the contiguous collective breathing turns into something continuous, so that from that continuum, all have their own breathings, of every variety.
1748, 30 January.

Continuation about glorification

606. The angels look upon everything pertaining to the realm of spirits as beneath them, nor do they have any communication, except when it is granted by the Lord that they may look upon them and observe the nature of the spirits and things there. I have been shown by actual experience how this takes place. Still, they can control nothing, as I have also been shown, for they cannot influence them on their own, but the influence is controlled in an imperceptible manner by the Lord.

607. When I fell away from that realm of collective glorification, spoken of above [600 *ff.*], into any imagery derived from some grosser feeling, such as pertains to the world, it was then said that it looked to them just like a fall—that I was therefore falling down from them; and whenever I fell into imagery having to do with the body, it was said that this looked to them like clouds.
1748, the 30th day of January.

608. During that state of glorifying that I was in for almost a day, or half of a day, I had no thoughts of a personal nature—no thinking in mental imagery that was familiar to me, because this was a celebrating of the Lord at which I was present, Who was being glorified in different ways by choirs of angels. Yet it happened in such a way that I seemed to be among them as to my head, so that I was able to know about the things in the realm of spirits as if they were in the body. Therefore, it is no wonder that the inhabitants of Jupiter say that the face is not body, and that they look down upon their body [547]. 1748, 30 January.

About philosophy—that it is worthless

609. Today, as I was on my way home and got back, I was moved with sadness, and I knew that the sadness originated with a certain spirit, who was upset. He came up to me, saying that in his lifetime he had been a philosopher, probably among the most famous, and had applied his mind to studies of that kind; and now, when he thought them over, he said that he was upset and moved by a great sadness, because he now saw and realized how worthless such pursuits in the world are, and that they are illusions, which take away all light from spiritual and Divine matters. He calls them manure, which is to be thrown away, and had prevented him until now from knowing spiritual, and even more, heavenly things. He is now with me, and sees me writing, and directs me. 1748, the 30th day of January.

In the other life they meet their acquaintances

610. Those in the other life, when they first arrive there, still have things of the earth clinging to them. They do not know but that they are in the world, still living there. This has been made clear to me in many ways, for [some] did not know after many years that they were in the other life, nor could they realize it except when it was proven to them, so that finally they admitted it. Thereupon they also recall to mind the companions they had had in the life of the body, and then they are also permitted by the Lord to come upon them, and to speak with them as they did on earth—but still, [to say] nothing other than what is permitted and granted. Thus all can find their own friends, parents, and children; however, they do not remain together there any longer than they are allowed by the Lord.

611. As they find their friends, so also they run into their enemies, especially any whom they had persecuted in hatred. From this one may infer how dangerous it is to persecute anyone in hatred. There no one can pretend, that is, contemplate one thing in the mind, and say in words and show on the face something different; but the feelings of the mind show as in broad daylight, so that pretense gives way to open hatred. How these persons, therefore, can be admitted into heaven, anyone can judge.

Heaven does not see words and names, but things

612. From what has already been told about spirits, it is clear that the bodily elements themselves must be laid aside—which is accompanied by pains of various kinds—and thus given to death; and later, so must the earthly elements clinging to spiritual ones. For that nature cannot enter heaven. Finally, there remains in the spirit or mind what is spiritual and heavenly.

Since, therefore, they must shed bodily and earthly elements, which in themselves are dead, before the soul is able to enter into heaven, it is most clearly evident that Heaven can never hear or understand the things in words that pertain to the body and to nature, but the things that are spiritual, heavenly and Divine, and consequently far, farther, and farthest removed from the literal meaning.

Just as when we would think more lofty thoughts than others, we are not concerned with the words, but the meaning emerging from the words, and the even loftier meaning emerging from the direct meanings—so it is absurd to think that Heaven hears, and understands, the Word according to its letter, or that it understands the names of men, women, cities, and the like; for heaven perceives the realities concealed within them, while the meaning of the letter does not reach beyond the air, or sound in the ear, consequently not beyond the body. So why would you believe that the Lord God, our Savior, attends to things that are merely bodily and merely earthly, when He Himself is heaven, and causes heaven to hear? 1748, the 31st day of January.

About the spirits of Jupiter

613. A company of Jovian spirits came to me, whose silent approach and presence, as well as their active influence, was so gentle that it could be described as sweetness. For they are all upright, and live uprightly together, wanting nothing else than to perform kind deeds for one another; so that there was a feeling of generally shared uprightness. Because of the gentleness, or sweetness, of this company, one can readily tell them apart from a company of good spirits from this earth.

614. If the least disagreement should arise among them, it is signalled by a thin white ray, like a lightening flash—which, I was told, is a sign of disagreement—as well as by the appearance of a cluster of bright little stars. Thus disagreement does exist, but it is quickly resolved.

615. Furthermore, when little stars appear, it is a good omen, as they have appeared to me more than six hundred times—small ones, still smaller ones, even single ones, also several one after the other. Moreover, it is also common knowledge to spirits of that earth, that when some kind of starry heaven appears, it is good.

616. From this it is evident that spirits of different earths cannot be together, because they are distinct as to their individual characters, as well as the characters of their societies as a whole. Thus when the Jovian spirits approached and were with me, the spirits here could not bear them, as if they had a strange odor, so they fled away. However, I admitted that I had not smelled it myself, but that it had been a suggestion inspired into me by the spirits of this earth. 1748, 1 February.

About temptations

617. How deceitful the devil's gang is, can never be expressed in words. During temptations they simulate not only angels, but indeed, even the Lord, feigning them in every way in keeping with the person's fantasies. [The devil] knows these fantasies in an instant, for he impersonates people and then searches out what is in them without their knowing it, and amazingly, remembers it when an opportunity arises.

Moreover, when so disguised, he breathes in suitable feelings that seem either good, or evil, and manipulates them in a remarkable way, skilfully bending them toward evil. He sees clearly how the feeling is developing, constantly striving to bend it toward evil.

Furthermore, he even breathes words into our thought and mouth that harmonize with that feeling, and instantly causes us to think they are our own words. They who are not aware of this, cannot believe otherwise than that they are their own words, when yet they are the devil's—to which I can testify from manifold experience. And so he proceeds from one artifice to another, which he does in an instant by a natural instinct acquired in the life of the body, which may be surprising to anyone. Such [spirits] have the nature of a wild animal, something they actually acquired, making them the more cunning in the other life, because from their nature they now act like wild animals, although with a life as if they were human.

To enumerate their tricks would fill up countless sheets; wherefore, if the Lord Jesus does not keep the devil in bonds, and restrain and reverse his attempts, a person could not but succumb at every moment. ^{m}1748, 1 February.^{n}

About the stench of intemperance

618. One evening when I had taken a lot of milk and bread, more than the spirits thought I needed, they kept their feelings fixed upon [the idea of] intemperance, of which they accused me. This caused an odor of human dung, coming from the solids, and a foul urinous smell from the liquids, to invade my nostrils. It persisted, and I was told that this happens to me because they hold their feelings fixed upon this kind of intemperance. They say that they smell no such stench themselves. 1748, 30 January and 1 February.

The difference between life in the body, and after bodily life

619. In the body there is a different life than afterwards. In the body, anyone can do well to enemies and to those whom they hate, for any worldly reason whatever, because they are governed by a variety of motives and loves pertaining to the world. Thus they are able to dissemble and call themselves friends, when yet they are enemies.

But this is not true of the other life, since everyone then behaves according to the character they had acquired. One who harbors hatred keeps on hating, until the hatred is wiped away by means of a purging process. Otherwise, if they try to pretend, as they did during bodily life, this is at once recognized, and in fact, out in the open.

620. Moreover, they who are governed by the Lord are passive, and have no powers from themselves, being incapable of doing and feeling anything from themselves, and they know this. [m]With them there is only a passive force.[n] These are called "poor," and also "miserable," and are looked upon as such by others who think themselves strong. But those weak ones, who can do nothing from themselves, are governed by the Lord, He Himself taking care of them.

Those, however, who think that they live from themselves and govern themselves, are called "strong," and they possess active powers, while those just spoken of possess only passive powers. Those having active powers from themselves, are the ones who stir up evil thoughts and feelings in the others, so that the evils which they think and toward which they are urged are from the active powers of such spirits as inspire them. This was shown to me by a spiritual method today, and once before, so plainly that there can be no doubt of it. About these matters, I also spoke today with the spirits around me, who cannot but acknowledge it. 1748, the 1st day of February.

I have been together with my acquaintances and friends in the other life for a long time

621. To this I can testify, that I have associated and spoken with many friends and acquaintances in the other life, who had been with me almost constantly, barring some interruptions; and that a certain friend had been at my side continually for the space of more than a month, as he attests. How many there have been, I cannot count, and who they were I am not permitted to say, even though they desired to tell this to their friends; but such a wish is not granted.

This I can aver and testify, that I have associated and spoken quite long with many in the other life who had been known to me in this, or bodily life, and that many conversational exchanges have taken place concerning the state of the unhappy, and the state of the happy. These very states were even shown to them, and they were amazed that no one in bodily life knows that they live immediately after death in another life, and that they are among spirits, whose life is a continuation of bodily life, such that they do not know but that they are still in the life of the body—so much so, that no difference exists except such as that spoken of elsewhere now and then; for their state changes in accordance with their life in the body, as you may see stated elsewhere [*cf.* 619]. 1748, 1 February.

Continuation about the spirits of the inhabitants of Jupiter

622. The punishing spirit who was speaking forcibly, as was said [541], as if by forward thrusts of the voice, and standing at the left, below the mid portion of the body, came up to me and wanted, according to the custom on their earth, to punish me because of things I had thought and said. And those angels, as they call them, stood at the region of my head in order to guide him, to permit him to punish according to the circumstances, and thus to moderate.

But he was not permitted to do anything to me, except to show me their various kinds of punishments, one being to cause a painful contraction around the midriff, like that of a sharp belt being tightened, which, they said, was attended with great pain to their people. Another kind was a privation of breathing, such that they finally came into a shortness of breath caused by the intervals of stoppage. Yet another was to announce their death, and the consequent loss of joy from their married partner, children, companions, or from those who are dear to them; for these spirits are able to find out in an instant what they love.

623. Moreover, they are divinely guarded from falling into distorted opinions concerning the one only Lord, both by means of penalties, and by threats and warnings; and if perchance any did fall into them, they are banished from society. On an earth such as this, things of that kind cannot fail to be rooted out, and if any families should backslide, they would be utterly removed. For to these, death is announced, which takes place for the most part by the uplifting of their spirit by spirits, and rarely by illnesses, as on our earth. So they are raised up, as they say, into heaven, nor do they call this dying, but being heaven-made.

624. Neither can their better spirits easily be together with the spirits of our earth, but must live separately. For they derive a different character from a different life, implanted by parents through the ages. As a result, they have an altogether different life, consequently a different nature that is closely associated with the heavenly ones, as observed before [564] when a rainbow was portrayed among the angels of their inward heaven[1]. And now, because their nature is closely joined to the heavenly ones, figuratively as the colors of the rainbow [are joined], and the natures of [their spirits and ours], being from a different root, are divergent, neither can the inward angels [of the two earths] be associated together.

These are their angels who love golden sky blue. They do not want to allow the word Spiritual—as I now observe, because they are guiding my thoughts, thus my hand—for they say they do not want to know what is spiritual, but only what is heavenly. Many of them are guardian spirits, which is due to the fact that they speak little [cf. 598], but they do think, and their thoughts consequently derive from feelings.

625. They have a sweet, silent approach [613], a prudent way of living and conversing, so they are careful what they think and say, weighing and measuring the smallest details. But if they come across in anyone the slightest thing contrary to their order, they are of a mind to punish them, so as to compel them to goodness. This they do to spirits who come fresh from their earth, bringing them back to obedience with some force. This I have also been able to observe, as I have told them, because when any such thing came up, I at once sensed their chastising thoughts. 1748, the 2nd day of February.

626. I was able to observe their presence [with me] when they themselves did not, by a widening of my mouth, or the region of the lips and cheeks, for they have this effect [569]. And as they then think I am like they are, that region of my face was disposed into that shape as a result of their imaginative power.

And so it is evident that the angels of the inward heaven[2] are separate because of their earthly-minded characters, as said previously, while the angels of the very inward and innermost heaven are together throughout the universe [552]; for no discordance can

---

[1] See 262, footnote.
[2] *Ibid.*

exist among those who are truly spiritual and heavenly, but only among the earthly-minded. 1748, 2 February.

627. Their inward angels also were instructed that the Lord never punishes anyone, much less does evil to anyone. And because at first they did not want to admit this, firmly believing that the Lord does chastise and punish, it was declared to them aloud that even their angels do not chastise or punish, nor do they speak harshly to people of their earth, but only permit the punishing and reproving spirit to carry out and speak the punishments and threats, while they temper them, and decide of what kind and what intensity they shall be.

From this they were able to deduce that since their angels do not punish and say harsh things to any person, so much less does the Lord, Who is the Best, the Fountain of all Goodness, He Who governs the angels. Hence because of their own modes of behavior, they could not help acknowledging, but even affirmed in a public declaration, that the Lord punishes no one, speaks harsh words to no one, still less does evil to anyone. 1748, the 2nd day of February.

Continuation on the spirits of the inhabitants of Jupiter

[628.][1] From their method of chastising their people, it is evident that their angels exercise a kind of judgment upon a person, or that they judge their people, and their spirits also. For as said, they stand by, control the punishers, moderating or allowing, so that a kind of judgment can be ascribed to them. Nevertheless, they had been clearly told that while they may think they are judging, yet the Lord Alone is judge, and that He so moderates their lives that they know no otherwise but that it is they who are judging.

629. Moreover, their cold spirits [534, 549, 575] also came up to me in great number, but from where—whether from those who had been with me, or whether from others—I do not know for sure. It occurred to me that those who had been with me were entirely cold, creeping up like a chill. 1748, 2 February.

---

[1] In the manuscript this number appears to be deleted.

*The angels must ever be perfected, and can
never be perfect or holy*

630. However it may be that souls are admitted into the very inward and the innermost heaven, yet they are not perfect, but some earthly element always clings to them which must be corrected. This is done when they are let back among spirits. Then it appears at once what residue from a rooted in nature they still retain, which is then corrected; and this betterment goes on by their being let back many times.

Therefore it is a rule that an angel can never be perfected to a point where he can be called perfect and holy, thus never to eternity. The only perfect and holy person is the Lord, Who is Perfection and Holiness Itself. 1748, the 2nd day of February.

About the inhabitants of the earth Jupiter

631. Among the punishments belonging to their penance, there is also this one put upon them, that they should eat no other food than bread, while at the same time an appetite is aroused for eating other things. Whether they make use of any other food besides greens, herbs, fruits, and then the seeds which they grind into flour, it has not been granted me to learn.

632. As for their horses, which are forest animals [560], they are very tall, and larger than our largest, nearly as tall as camels. For this reason these horses frighten them very much, as they told me when a horse of great height appeared to them—which they portrayed to me as small, and asserted to be so when speaking about the horses.

633. Moreover, they take pleasure in dining for a long time, not on account of the luxury of foods, but because companionship is more enjoyable while they are also sitting and eating. They do not sit on chairs or benches, nor on elevated grassy mounds, nor on grass, which they avoid like something unclean beneath them; but they put leaves under them, and when I wanted to know what leaves they were, they affirmed it when I named them fig leaves, such as Adam and Eve girded themselves with [Gen. 3:7] before they were provided with sheepskin tunics. 1748, the 2nd day of February.

About the deceptions of the dragon

634. The dragon can be called two-headed in several respects. First because he makes an oral show of penitance, speaking as though he repented, while at heart he is fostering deceptions—and this at one and the same moment, very much like those false people who can pretend [friendship] in facial expressions and gestures while they harbor enmity at heart. This ability, which rarely exists with spirits, is nevertheless found in the dragon; for he can speak pleasingly, while at the same time plotting evil—as he did today, when he called together evil spirits with the purpose of secretly attacking good ones and destroying their belief.

Then besides this, he also meddles into every single thing that the spirits closest by are doing or thinking, so that he has more attentive ears than any other evil spirit, watching for [the chance to do] evil things. He has very little ability left to do what is good. 1748, 2 February.

About the fact that we are governed by spirits and angels; also about faith, and the active and passive principle in us

635. Because it is the truth, it should therefore be believed that the Lord governs heaven and earth, and that no one lives except the Lord. From this belief, when one is gifted with it by the Lord, follows another point, namely, that a person cannot commit sin, knowing that spirits who think they live from themselves and govern themselves, arouse evils in us, and that though they are in us, yet they are not aroused by us, because we are then living passively and letting ourselves be governed. Being in such a state, one can also be gifted with peace by the Lord, for then one trusts solely in the Lord, and is not at all worried about other things.

Thus a person who would live in peace must be in a passive state, not ever in an active one [*see* 620] except by reaction and responsive action, which likewise come from the Lord, so that the state is still a passive one, resistant or compliant. Such is the state of the angels, who live in peace, while the rest, believing they govern themselves, are continually being disquieted. For they lead themselves into various desires, thus into anxiety; and even though they are [really] being aroused by others, and in fact by very many, nevertheless each and all believe that the [evil aroused in them] is their own, or from themselves. This is why it remains with them, and takes root as something pertaining to or proper to themselves, something their own, and so also it is accounted to them. Because it is the truth that the Lord governs heaven and earth, He gifts believers and angels with this faith; but it cannot be given to those who have not a saving faith, even if they imagine they want to think this way because they know about it. This is impossible unless they have saving faith, and are therefore governed by the Lord. That this is the case, I can testify because of long and daily experience. I have spoken about the matter frequently with spirits, so that nothing has become more familiar to me. 1748, 3 February, ##

638.[1] ## Souls or spirits who want to govern themselves think that [to be so governed by the Lord] would be to lose all pleasure, and the whole will in which pleasure resides, and thus all freedom, consequently all life and its pleasantness—as they are now dictating to me.

But because they do not know what life truly is, and what pleasure truly is, and what freedom truly is, therefore it should be known that we for the first time have true life and the things which make life's happiness, when we are governed by the Lord alone, and when we are only acted upon. It is then granted us to live as if on our own, and to partake of heavenly joy.

But the reason it seems otherwise to those souls or spirits, is because they are judging from their own active state, in which there can be nothing but unrest, and finally unhappiness—the result of exercising their imaginary freedom. This freedom is license, or the rule of passions, and of evil spirits who arouse them. When they are under the control of evil spirits, or of their own desires, then they believe they are being governed by themselves, whereas the contrary is the case. 1748, 3 February.

Nor indeed, can the one type of person be distinguished from the other by the outer aspect, the inner aspect being what makes us such as we are and that in which happiness resides. Indeed, there are those who judge me insane when I speak in this way, when yet countless experience has confirmed this to me, and confirms it in me every day.

---

[1] 636–7 will be found after 638, in accordance with the author's instructions.

636.

Who spirits are, and what they are like, can also be recognized from the quarter [they are in]

636. When spirits and angels have acted, whether from afar or nearby, I was able to know where they were, or in what quarter in relation to my face, howsoever my face was turned; for the directions are determined by the face. Those who are at the right side, obliquely toward the front, are good; those obliquely toward the left are evil. Far from there toward the left, lower down, is Gehenna; toward the front a little more to the right, is a swamp; beneath the feet is the earth of the lower ones, towards the left is hell. Above the head are those who boast, and who raise themselves up in fantasy, the higher the haughtier, where they are likewise arranged according to the quarters.

637. The case is the same with those who come up to a person on earth: behind are those who want to command. There, clinging to the back, at the left side, lower down, are those who want to chastise, as said above [445, 541, 545]; then above the head, those who moderate the one who chastises. Those at the right side are angels who inwardly in a person on earth—especially when they fill up the whole person—likewise protect him from the injuries threatening in other ways. In addition, there are those from the [region of the] head in the cerebrum, in the cerebellum, as I have seen many times; but what these circumstances mean, I have not yet been able to observe. 1748, 3 February.

About the spirits highest up in heaven

639.[1] I also became aware of spirits who, because they were in the highest part, above where the dragon was, made me wonder who they were. Speculating that they were such or such—knowing that the higher the place to which they lift themselves up by fantasy, the more wicked they are, because the more haughty—I was told that they were demons, who exert an influence, not by spoken words, but maliciously and very cunningly by an inflow of evil desires, which I have also experienced. They streamed in with concealed malice so great that I could hardly be held back.

---

[1] 638 has been placed after 635, in accordance with the author's instructions.

FROM THE *BIBLE INDEX* 641.

I was told that they are not let loose or do not act freely, because they have the serpent's poison stored up very deeply within them, but are kept bound up there—although not there, but in hell. For, as was also told and shown to them, only their fantasy is there, while they are in Gehenna. Moreover, when they wanted to be let loose, different spirits were attached to them, who tempered them to keep them from pouring forth their poisons. About this they complained—and also about being compelled to speak, which they are reluctant to do because they want to operate in hiding, or secretly. 1748, 3 February.

640. It was surmised that these were the worst of them, who in bodily life had striven to own the heaven of our Savior, by their own power, and had thus misled the innocent. They were said to have an influence, but one that was tempered in various ways. Even on the way, before their cunning or poison reached me, it was taken up by spirits in between, and thus also tempered.

These seem to be the ones who inspire the trickery in those whose ambition is to own heaven, or to possess all power in heaven and on earth. They are among the stars of the dragon and should rather be called "the beast of Babylon," spoken of in Revelation [17:3 and elsewhere].

About hiding spirits

641. There are also spirits who hide, and do not show themselves, and do not act in the open so that their fantasies, cunning arts, and deceptions become apparent, as do those of other spirits. These are in the zenith, that is, overhead, higher up than the dragon, who does not operate so secretly. Such spirits imagine that no one can discover their destructive tricks. Therefore they also think they are safe, and cannot be harmed or punished by anyone, because, as they suppose, they have withdrawn into the more subtle [parts of] nature. On this account, as they say, they do not fear anything.

Nevertheless, their deceptions appear openly whenever this is granted by the Lord, and are exposed as destructive tricks (truldoms konster[1]), by which they imitate the character of good spirits by streaming in softly and gently, so that their poisons are not

---

[1] The original has the Swedish for "witchcraft," *truldoms konster*.

noticed. In this way they could lead even the good astray, if the Lord were not protecting them. They slip secretly into the obvious deceptions of other spirits.

642. Moreover, they thought that they were exempt from the same punishment others received, because, as they believe, they could withdraw within the more subtle [parts of] nature, and so be hidden away in secret. But they were disappointed. They were not only sent under the veil [*see* 435], but also glued together, like the beggars [*see* 431], and thus deprived of all freedom. And the more they wanted to free themselves, or cut themselves loose from each other, the more tightly they were bound. The punishment for them is a very intense torment, because it responds to their secret poisons.

643. These are they who persecute the Lord on earth, under angelic guise, and do so for self-promotion and profit; and who have been successful in these intents. This is the source of their violent and in fact, extremely wicked practices, which could not be disclosed to me because they are so abominable.

They admit that they cannot do otherwise

644. The same ones who were continually plotting deceptions, and were so intent upon them that they hardly paused, were warned by the others to stop. But they admitted that they could not, even if it meant they should die. Others, too, on several occasions have admitted the same thing, that is, that they could not possibly stop. And each time they were told that this is no excuse—for if it were, all devils would exculpate themselves—but that they should go away, or else be driven away, until by fitting types of punishment they begin to feel disgust at doing such things.

So by different methods of punishment, they must be divested of evils, as usually takes place. Hence one may infer that it is their natural instinct, acquired in bodily life, not only to feel the greatest pleasure in such evils, but also to be possessed of such a desire for them, that they cannot desist from them, just as wild animals cannot refrain from tearing apart [their prey]. 1748, 5 February.

Spirits also alter the taste

645. Sometimes, in fact quite often, it has happened that something which tasted good seemed to be offensive, or to have a different taste. Twice, if I am not mistaken, I even experienced sugar as almost salty, feeling a kind of salty taste from the sugar on my tongue. I could actually taste that the moisture on my palate had a saltiness in it, which had been pressed out of my bodily fluids by spirits.

This happened when the Jovian spirits thought that sugar was salt. Indeed, they thought that anything divided up into grains, as sugar, was therefore granulated salt; and because they thought it to be salt, [it tasted salty to me]. So in regard to other things, a person's taste is thus changed in accordance with the fantasies of spirits. This they sometimes do to deceive; for they can bring on this kind of thing through deceptive fantasies.

646. Moreover, there exists nothing whatever affecting the senses, whether it be outward or inward, which they do not strive to reproduce. They imitate whatever they see and feel, and counterfeit it as if it were real, when yet it is only the outer [appearance], and artificial. Therefore it requires the highest degree of good judgment to tell apart what is true and what is counterfeit; nor can these ever be distinguished except through belief in the Lord, and thus by the Lord, Who gives the ability to discern. The same is true in the life of the body when such demons are present and try to lead people on earth astray. 1748, 5 February.

Speaking and coaxing are of no avail when the heart is longing, moved by a love

647. Through much experience with spirits, I have learned that persuasion contrary to the feelings is of no avail whatsoever. For very often my heart has been moved by some feeling, and meanwhile, spirits as well as angels would coax, saying that this should be done, and not that; but as long as I was still gripped by that feeling, their coaxing could have no effect whatsoever, as I even told them in response on several occasions.

Also this, that if the feeling shifted only a little, then at once my mind was changed, and I would yield to the persuasion.

From this and from many actual experiences, I was enabled to learn that all persuasion contrary to one's loves can achieve absolutely nothing.

This is the reason why those spirits who are demons, who operate through the passions, are the most dangerous. On the other hand, the angels' way of working is to bend minds toward good through the feelings, the Lord so directing. 1748, 5 February.

648. From this can also be deduced what a belief based on the understanding [alone] is worth, or what preaching is worth, when a person is being carried along by desires, and whether a faith based solely on understanding can save! For in love there is life; in the understanding of such things there is nothing but memory.

This was told to souls after death, or spirits, and corroborated in such a way that they admitted they had been completely mistaken during their lifetime, and acknowledged their errors with sadness.

Man, who is an instrument, fallaciously thinks himself or herself to be the acting force in every single action

649. That human philosophy has [indeed] discovered many truths, is evident from the fact that people know that the acting force and the instrumental force work together as the cause [of something]. But this is where a fallacy arises, causing the human (who is only instrumental, or an instrument) to suppose that he or she is the acting force, because the accomplishing cause issues from the two forces combined. Because of this sense-deception, we ascribe to ourselves, the instrument, what belongs to the Lord, Who is the only acting force.

This was said to some in heaven, and they recognized it to be so and likewise the fact that a person may know many truths, yet know nothing whatever in the practice of them, the instrument still thinking itself to be the force. This results in a distorted order of life, causing the fantasies that so torture their souls. 1748, 5 February.

650. Thus philosophy can assist when it is subservient, as can also sensory experience, provided it serves in enlightening those who believe nothing but what is philosophically true and which they want to grasp with the senses.

About the sight of spirits

651. There are four kinds of sight that have been made known to me. The *first* is a sight of sleep, just as real as daytime sight; so I said while actually asleep that if this was sleep, then wakefulness must also be sleep.

The *second* kind is vision with the eyes closed, which is just as real as with the eyes opened, and by which similar objects are presented to view, even more beautiful and pleasant. The same kind can exist with the eyes open, and has occurred two or three times.

The *third* kind is in a state with the eyes open, when those things are portrayed which are in heaven, both spirits and other things. This kind causes symbolic vision, which has become very familiar to me; but it is rather obscure, differing entirely from the commonplace human imagination.

The *fourth* kind occurs when a person is separated from the body, and in the spirit, and then one cannot tell in the least but that one is in a waking state and is then in possession of all one's senses, such as touch, hearing and sight, and I do not doubt, of all the rest. It is more than the sight of a waking state, because it is an exquisite one, nor does one perceive that state as any different from wakefulness—unless one lapses into a waking state of the body.

652. Spirits have all these states, some the former, some the latter. When they are in the latter, life is felt more keenly than bodily life. One spirit told me he was in that state, and he could not tell in the least but that he was in conversation with others in his own room. In the same way, gardens and countless scenes depicting the pleasures of life are displayed. In this kind of life are angelic spirits.

653. As for the fourth kind of sight, this has been granted me four or five times—an experience attended with much pleasantness—and during a waking state as well, when I was two or three times similarly led by the spirit.[1]

---

[1] See *AC* 1884, *SE* 56; also 1 Kings 18:12, 19:8, Ezek. 12:3, Acts 7:55–6, 8:39.

About the punishment of those who want to counterfeit what is holy

654. Those who like to counterfeit what is holy, thus deceive people by sacred illusions and the like, receive this punishment: what is holy separates itself from them, resulting in sores upon their body, scabies, leprosy, lice, and similar afflictions, depending upon [the nature of] their profanation. I was given to understand this from spirits who had been up to such practices. 1748, 6 February.

What a miracle is

655. A miracle is what is done by the Lord, when there is something that concerns Himself, belief in Him, His Heaven, or the Church as a whole, which then passes through His Heaven, and is then carried out by spirits without any of their own cooperative power [entering into it]. This is a miracle, and is called "the finger of God" [Ex. 8:19, 31:18, Deut. 9:10, Luke 11:20].

656. False miracles, on the other hand, are those which are contrived by evil spirits or devils through artificial means, and indeed, for no other purpose than [to satisfy] some extremely corrupt passion. This type of miracle is also permitted, and it looks the same in its outer aspect, but has no inner one; and it is not distinguishable [from a true miracle] except by those having faith in the Lord.

657. Evil spirits, when freed of restraints, work at nothing else than to to corrupt goodness into what is evil, and to imitate the qualities of heaven with the purpose of misleading minds by means of imitations and shams. These are their main endeavors, because each of them wants to be lord. 1748, 6 February.

About the passion for stealing

658. Those who in their bodily life had coveted the possessions of others and [sought to obtain them] by various tricks, either business dealings or other means which they justified before men as allowable, in the other life go about and continually seek to take away the goods of others. When they approach spirits like themselves, or different, those spirits recognize their character at once, and with a fine or a lashing, throw them out. So they wander about, seeking, and wherever they go they are punished by whippings or other methods. Spirits like these have come to me several times, complaining, and I learned that they had been businessmen—even, to my surprise, well-known ones.

659. Moreover, no sooner did I look at something in the stores, or at money and such, than the craving of these and similar spirits became evident within me. For, thinking that they were myself, it was as if they instantly wanted me to reach out my hand, quite contrary to my usual behavior, and in addition, slipped their own passion into my mind.

About that passion I have subsequently at times spoken with the spirits, saying that I had realized such spirits were present. This they could not deny, but were obliged to affirm it, explaining their character, and what comes over them. 1748, 6 February.

About the life of those who are wise from themselves

660. A certain spirit whom I believe I had known during his life, having died only a few years earlier, three or four, came to me and spoke with me. But about his life in the body I knew no more than that he was devoted to studies, and at the same time, devoted to philosophy. From this I was able to infer that he also wanted to be a philosopher in the mysteries of faith and thus to comprehend them, and that he would only believe something when he understood it philosophically.

He had been present with me for nearly a quarter of an hour, so that his life's belief was streaming in, as I could plainly sense from the fact that I began to doubt, feeling cold in regard to the Lord's government over least things, while admitting it over the whole. As a result, whatever particular detail then flowed in, I seemed to want to reject—as if the Lord ruled heaven and earth only by a universal, not a singular providence.

The cold was that of a belief based on intellect, or truths, not so much on affection—as I am now telling that spirit. And he is standing by, and even guiding the selection of words. 1748, 6 February.

661.   SPIRITUAL EXPERIENCES

Evil spirits are eager to kill and torment every single person, but in the person they are with, they are restrained in a twofold manner

661. Evil spirits, or rather, the devil's gang, desire nothing more than to destroy people, both body and soul, as well as to torment them in a thousand ways. This is evident from numerous experiences involving not only those who have been within me in bands, attempting to [destroy me] in many wicked ways, but also souls in the hells, who take the greatest pleasure in barbarically tormenting each other, one after another. And if the sensation were not intercepted by the Lord, the one being tortured would undergo unspeakable suffering.

Evil spirits who flit about freely are also of this nature, and yet they are joined to people in order to arouse their life, as told before [635]. However, because they do not know otherwise than that they are the very one with whom they are present, therefore they do not want to bring any harm upon that person, for this would be as if they were doing it to themselves.

This is the first reason why they do not direct such attacks against the person with whom they are present, but nonetheless, if they were not restrained by the bonds of law, they would try to treat companions who do not worship them as gods and give them all of their resources, in the same way they treat each other in hell. This is quite evident from their souls after death, when their nature is not restrained by any such bonds of law. It is also plain from kings, from soldiers, and others.

The second reason they do not torment and destroy the person is that at the same time good angels are also present, and the Lord controls them in accordance with the permissions and allowances spoken of elsewhere [398, 401]. 1748, the 6th day of February.

After death we retain all the faculties and sensations we had in the body, except for several earthly functions

662. After death people lose nothing of the faculties they had in bodily life, but retain them all, and more are given to them, which have been spoken of here and there [333, 400]; but they are gifted with different ones.

For example, when a spirit confesses that he cannot help doing evil, then by chastening methods he is tempered in such a way that he is able to desist from them, and finally turn away from them. After that he is also given the ability to accomplish something good. So it is an ability he is simply given as a gift, while he still retains his former faculties.

Faculties for doing good that are added or given, are a gift of the Lord, and as soon as this gift is taken away, a spirit returns to his original nature. This happens sometimes to angels, who, when restored to their original state, are evil spirits as before—indeed, who had been in heaven for ages, and several thousand years.

From this it follows that anything souls do from their own power, is evil, and that they can do nothing good except from the Lord Alone, the fountain of all goodness. Therefore, as soon as this gift ceases, the soul returns to its inborn and enrooted wickedness.

It also follows from this that the ability to do good is only from the Lord, and it is given, and not that anything of good has been enrooted or becomes enrooted in him. 1748, 6 February.

663. Indeed, it is true both of man, and of the newly arrived soul, that there is nothing whatever except evil coming from themselves. In any thinking or acting from oneself, it is impossible to conceive of anything so small and insignificant that it is not evil. In fact, it is evil when one thinks about wanting to do good from oneself, or wants to turn oneself [to God]. And sometimes I have been so distressed that I did not know what I should think or do that was from myself, that would not be evil. So also were the spirits distressed, as they clearly showed, and acknowledged.

It is different when one does this from innocence, for then the Lord is guiding, and whatever is from the Lord in a person is good. 1748, 6 February.

About the dreams of spirits

664. I awoke in a dream, and there appeared to me one spirit who kept on with the dream. From this I was able to learn the state of spirits in dreams, which is not really different from man's, for the still remaining outward and bodily elements in a spirit quiet down like the bodily elements in us do in sleep. I saw this plainly, for he could not fix his attention upon anything except what was going on at the time in his mind. He was speaking, as though not knowing that he spoke. His outer elements were sleeping, his inner ones thus [active] in the dream. 1748, 7 February.

Continuation on the provinces in the body that are allotted to the angels

665. There are two as it were kingdoms in the universe. As has been explained [499], one is heavenly, the other spiritual. The heavenly kingdom encompasses those provinces of the body that are under the command of the heart; the spiritual kingdom, those under the command of the lungs or respiration.

666. There are individual internal bodily parts, members, organs and sensory functions that constitute provinces, and in order for souls to be in heaven, or in the body of the Lord, they must by all means be in one of the provinces, and assigned to one member.

667. As a result of this, there exists an immeasurably great variety, just as in the body, where no particle can be completely the same as another, and if it were, it would not harmonize.

668. Nevertheless, the state of mind of souls and angels changes as they are perfected, so they are transferred to better positions in the same member or province, in fact even to different provinces that are nobler. For there is a continual purification, and as I may call it, new creation, nor can ever any angel arrive at perfection itself, to eternity. The Lord Alone is Perfect, or Perfection Itself.

669. There are also those who interrelate with the mouth, who likewise are afterwards transferred elsewhere. They are those who continually want to talk, from which they get their enjoyment. Insofar as that enjoyment is purified, so that they do not want to speak anything other than what is useful to their companions, to the community, to heaven, to the Lord, or insofar as the desire to regard themselves in talking, or the effort to be thought wise, passes away, so far they are raised to a more distinguished place.

This was shown to me today by a gold coin, which a hand representing the hand of the Lord, took and gave to one who was indignant after having been given to know that he was in the province of the mouth.[1] It meant that he can be transferred, and even to the region of the heart, if he is found worthy. 1748, 7 February.

The province of the eye

670. The eye pertains to the very inward angels, because it is in the face and projects from the brain. The mouth indeed is in the face, but it leads into the body, that is, into the stomach and into the lungs, as well as away from the same; so that they who are in the province of the mouth are less esteemed than those in other regions of the face.

The eye is the noblest region of the face and also excels the rest of the senses, and it pertains to the spiritual class, over which it presides, because its sight interacts with spiritual sight.

About spiritual love

671. Moreover, there is also spiritual love, but how it is distinguished from heavenly love is not yet apparent to me. 1748, 7 February.

About the heavens

672. I was told that before the coming of the Lord into the world, there had been no other heaven than the inward one[2]. For as yet no one on this earth could understand the very inward, much less the innermost matters; and because higher knowledge must precede, therefore no other heaven could come into being at that time.

The inward heaven[3] is such that something earthly is joined to their spiritual part. Consequently, when angels formerly spoke with people on earth, and through the prophets, the Word had to come down directly into earthly forms. This resulted in the prophetical style that the Lord also chose to use in part. For otherwise they would not have been able to understand inward, much less very

---

[1] In the original, a deleted footnote is here referred to: "He said that he had not been able to hide the coin wh..."
[2] See 262 and footnote.
[3] See 262, footnote.

inward, spiritual matters. For this reason also the Lord spoke in parables.

About this subject I spoke with those in heaven, who seemed to me to affirm them, that is, that there had been this kind of a heaven for the sake of the inhabitants of this earth, but that a very inward and innermost heaven had nevertheless existed from others in the universe.

673. Of the same origin are symbolic portrayals, into which [spiritual] realities come down, besides very many other phenomena.

About the millennium

674. I have also spoken with those in heaven about the "thousand years" in Revelation [20:2–7]. They said that the thousand years do not mean a certain or fixed number of years, or a thousand, but a great amount of time, and that by the "first resurrection" those are meant, spoken of just above [672], who are in the inward heaven[1]. These are certain that they will remain there and that many will be admitted into the more inward heavens. Thus the first resurrection is for those who have something of nature joined to their spiritual part, so that they may live, and have lived, in heavenly pleasure.

675. But those who are to be admitted into the very inward heaven must put off what is of nature. So they come into the more inward joy, for without shedding outward elements, no one is able to be admitted into what is very inward. Therefore man must die on earth, which is a dying of the body, then die again in the other life when the attached nature element must be abolished. Failing this man cannot be let into the very inward heaven. Then again the nature element must be abolished in order that the person may be admitted into the innermost heaven[2], thus into heavenly glory.

---

[1] See 262 and footnote.
[2] The manuscript appears to have the words *interius coelum* and *intimius* respectively, where the context calls for *intimius coelum* and *intimum*. After making this revision, we noticed that A.W. Acton had done likewise, but without a footnote.

[A conversation] with a certain famous philosopher about certain matters in Philosophy

676. A philosopher who had died several years earlier spoke with me, for whom I clarified how certain philosophical terms should be understood.

In regard to "forms," I told what they are like, one within the other, and that a more inward one cannot be entered upon except by a dissolution, or death, so to speak, of the outward one, so there is an ascending from one level to another. Nature everywhere has such levels; so there are likewise degrees of the body's life, and of its vital organs, etc.

Then I said that there is nothing which does not consist of varieties of its form, and that the more inward forms can vary immeasurably more than outward forms; and that there are many varieties among the different changes of condition.

In the purer regions, I said, forms of force and forms of substance signal mental imagery; as well as other similar points.

Because he was in the other life, where they are more receptive to understanding matters of this kind, he affirmed them point by point, vowing that the world would do better to acknowledge such things than to get stuck in terms and argumentation about words, which entirely distract the mind from an understanding of the actual realities—as when a speaker dwells on words rather than the sense of the words. In this way people are plunged into trivia, out of which they cannot be raised up; besides other points as well. 1748, 7 February.

About very inward things

677. What "very inward things" are, no one among men or spirits, scarcely anyone among the angels of the inward heaven[1], as yet knows. For, something very inward, those who are inward cannot understand, thinking that [what is more inward] would dissolve them, and they would become as nothing, because of regarding inward things as everything—just as a person living [on earth] does in bodily things.

---

[1] See 262 and footnote.

But there is as great a difference between them as between what is vile and what is precious, or between a cottage and a very large city. But that which they cannot see, they think to be nothing, when yet it is the ineffable, which "no eye has seen, nor any ear has heard" [Is. 66:4, 1 Cor. 2:9]. And it is that from which everything comes that is harmonious and inwardly or more inwardly delightful within the symbolic displays of the inward heaven[1], while the inward heaven itself sees only the outside, or the shapes.

678. [The difference] was further shown today to a certain extent by a spiritual angelic choir, speaking, and saying that there is now no one [who knows, 677]. For this choir divides up and separates its lovely contemplations into mental images, which come down into words, while the more inward choir is like something continuous, which expresses more in one instant—and very clearly—than the inward choir does in an hour.

679. Moreover, there is also a mental imagery in the very inward and the innermost [heaven], but because it is not a mental imagery like the sense impressions of sight, but rather like those of the understanding, therefore, for the sake of distinction the expression *mental imagery* can be applied to inward [angels], *contemplation* to very inward ones, but *[true] thinking* to the innermost. 1748, 7 February.

About very inward things

680. The relation of very inward things to inward ones also became apparent when it was visually demonstrated how mental images, followed up by words, streamed into a spirit's speech, namely by a white cloud divided up into particles. At another time it was also shown to spirits and angels, I believe, how feelings streamed in in the same way.

These demonstrations show that those things were flowing in through the very inward heaven, or from very near to that heaven. One may therefore conclude that there are thousands of things in one seemingly uncompounded idea covered by only one word of speech, thus that there are thousands of things within a con-

---

[1] See 262 and footnote.

templation of the very inward heaven, or of the very inward angels, which appear simply as one thing to the angels of the inward heaven[1].

681. This can be still more clearly evident to us from the objects of our sight, to which mental imagery or a material idea almost answers on its own plane. In any object of the eyesight taken as a single entity, when it is looked at through the microscope there appear thousands of things of which it is composed. Thus a hundred tiny insects take up but one ray of vision, appearing as one point, and a faint one at that; while to the artificial or optically aided sight, not only a hundred little living animals are revealed, but even the internal parts of each.

682. So it is also with a Rainbow, in which nothing but the most general form appears, namely, bands of successive colors, when yet each color is made up of countless rays flowing into it separately and producing this most general effect. The eye perceives the myriads of rays only as a unit, and even then indistinctly. That indistinct unit appears simply as some one color which is [actually] an indistinctness thus made up of many shades.

Since the sight perceives myriads of myriads as only a single entity, and an indistinct one at that, why should it be any different in the case of the earthly mind, whose sight is no deeper than the sight of the eye? That mind, consequently, does not understand where mental images come from, which are likewise [composed of] myriads of more inward ones.

If these latter were not flowing forth in distinct forms from an innermost life, and this from the Lord, nothing distinct could ever be conceived of in a mental picture. But since a mental image is not in itself a matter of understanding, but does come forth as it is by the agency of the understanding, it can therefore be understood by means of mental images.

Therefore it is evident how general, in fact most general or most vague, that is which one thinks to be clear, sharp, wise, ingenious—which, however, is anything but intelligent and wise.

---

[1] See 262 and footnote.

SPIRITUAL EXPERIENCES

683.   It happened, when I was picturing [these things] to spirits around me by a spiritual display—specifically, by depicting ideas as forms of forces, which in turn consisted or were built up of myriads of things unseen, and each of these, of myriads of myriads of more inward ones—that then, because souls and spirits are sensitive to such depictions, immediately it was as if they had gone out of their minds, as one of them who was with me admitted. He did not know how they could help perishing from insanity. For if this is the case, [they thought] nothing of life would be left [to them], and even if there were, they would still have no spiritual life coming into them.

So a life like that, devoid of a living spiritual influence, is comparable to the life of vegetation, in which there is life, to be sure, but a kind called vegetative. Therefore all things even in the vegetable kingdom reflect the Kingdom of the Lord, each in its own way; in fact, they reflect the human being, having lungs and the rest, as is known. Hence the Divine is in the vegetable kingdom, but without animate life. 1748, 8 February.

About the excellence of the faculties of a soul or spirit, compared with the faculties they had while living in the world

684.   Besides the superior faculties a soul acquires after being released from the body, spoken of previously here and there [400, 433, 662], there is also the fact that they grasp a much richer meaning in mental images, or in a given subject. This is due to their pictorial mental imagery, but what it is like cannot be adequately described. These images are ideas, shaped in definite, diverse ways so that they at once see the meaning, which appears as if shaped to the sight. Thus they receive a fuller meaning of things, in a way that is not possible in the life of the body.

685.   For in bodily life there are different objects that move the senses and arouse a person, even to distraction; and besides these there are desires, which are inner objects, that cling like glue or something sticky. When we are infected with these desires, then no matter what someone else says, we stick to our desires, that being what is generally dominant in us.

Therefore, a grasp of matters like that spoken of [684] cannot exist in a person while living in the body, but it exists in a soul upon arrival in the other life and joining in the company of others. I also told these things to the spirits around me, and they affirmed them. 1748, 8 February.

About the inhabitants of Jupiter

686. Spirits of the planet Jupiter suppose, as was said before [547], that their face is not body, and therefore they have the firm impression that after death their face will be larger or wider, of a round shape. This face has been shown to me. It is sky blue, or more or less light blue in color, with little stars. This impression persists [with them] for that reason.

687. Moreover, they even believe that they will also see a fire that will warm their face. I was shown a fire, indeed a warming one, as has happened before, a hundred times. For it has been and is a common occurrence for me to catch sight of fires, and indeed of various kinds, as well as flames. These [I have been seeing] over a long period—but now for the first time, a fire that warmed my face, such as they want for themselves. But I was told that their flame, which they highly prize, is of a spotted light blue color. A flame like this, most cheerful, was once shown to me. 1748, 9 February.

About horses that were seen

688. Many times I have seen horses, as well as horse-drawn carriages, and in fact, of various colors and various sizes, as mentioned previously [302, 560, 632]. I have learned today that these stand for human erudition—in the good sense, intelligence, but in the bad sense, that erudition which distorts true intelligence.

And once earlier, I learned that one can also tell from the horse's position what it stands for. When the rear end of the horse is turned toward the face, then it symbolizes a distorted order and a distorted belief, brought on by learning—that is, when as a result of learning, people have become insane, or entirely stupid in spiritual matters, believing in nothing but what is earthly and worldly, and that they will die like animals, having no life remaining after their death. In this case their knowledge suffocates all understanding and belief regarding spiritual life. To such as these, the rear end of the horse is turned, indeed, they are cast into the horse. Although unwillingly, they are thrust inside, to their great distress and shame. 1748, 9 February.

Continuation about horses

689. From the position of the horse, one can tell what it stands for. When its rear part is turned toward the face, it means there is a distorted order of spiritual life brought on by knowledge, wiping out belief. It is different, however, when its side is turned toward one's face, or when its head is facing one: then it symbolizes that by means of the sciences, all things contained in the Word of God the Messiah have been supported. 1748, 9 February.

About two persons shortly after death with whom I spoke

690. There were two I had known during their bodily life, [whom I met,] one about six months, the other about two months after they had died. They were as if in dreams, because in their fantasy, they were entirely unaware that they were in the other life, thinking they still lived in the body. Speaking with them a little, I pointed out that they were in the other life, and they still could not believe it until it was vividly proven to them. They behaved exactly as they had in bodily life, clinging to the same fantasies.

690½. One of them had been quite learned and esteemed in earthly matters. His belief was communicated to me, and it was such, as I was able to learn in a spiritual way, that there was none at all—it had been completely suffocated by earthly knowledge. He did not believe in a life after death, in the existence of spirits, much less in a heaven, to such a degree had his faith been buried in the sciences.

691. I discussed with them the need of knowledge for life, saying that the only thing necessary is to know those matters which belong to a true belief, and that other things are of small value, although they can be of support; but one should not consider them as everything.

692. In addition, I was allowed to tell them what kind of a life awaits them, namely, that they are first taken into the company of good spirits, who warmly welcome recently arrived souls; but that when they are unable to harmonize with these spirits because of their distorted beliefs, they are then separated from them as if spontaneously.

Now they are received into the company of other spirits; and when they do not harmonize, they are also rejected by them. Next they are associated with spirits who are not good, and when rejected by these, they are also penalized and punished. Finally they are left all alone, and so wander from door to door, seeking where they might find welcome and, at the last, begging to be given food, and warmth.

When they are taken in, and then desire, as they did in life, to stand out above others, and to be more esteemed, and if besides that they are eager to steal what belongs to the others, which they cannot help doing—while such people are punished in bodily life, here they are severly punished and driven away. After this they wander alone in tattered clothes, begging. This goes on until their arrogance and sense of superiority over others is wiped out, or the desire to take what belongs to others ceases.

So they are finally chastened and can be let into the company of such spirits as harmonize, and this sometimes takes very many years, a few hundred they say—even a few thousand; for the purging of some takes a long time. 1748, 9 February.

All and the least occurrences in the other life are aimed toward a joining together through love

693. Whatever happens in the other life, such as punishments, purgings, and many more things, all and the very least tend toward the goal of developing societies [whose members] harmonize as if they were one person, and this takes place only through a love for the Lord and thus for one's companions.

This love is never achieved when one person wants to be greater than the other, which results in disunion and rejection, nor when one wants to stand out above the others in some respect. On the contrary, it is achieved when one wants to be the least, and to serve the rest. Thus when all mutually want to serve one another, they are united, and each receives happiness from everyone individually, and thus from the whole. These words were spoken in the presence of spirits and souls. 1748, the 9th day of February.

About belief

694. Again today I spoke with souls and spirits about belief, saying that the belief of Christians at this day is a memorized faith, only recited by mouth, and therefore outside of the person; while a belief that is inside of the person is today almost non-existent. For their works reveal what their belief is, namely, the opposite of belief. Such is their character in the other life. There, when [souls and spirits] want to search out where someone's belief resides, it is [found] outside of the person, as far away as the moon is from the earth.

695. But whether [that kind of faith] contributes to the ability to receive a saving belief, and is therefore like bark through which the sap or life passes into the tree, or into the branches, and thus into the fruits—this is another question. 1748, 9 February.

About the life of souls and spirits, and its diversities

696. Each spirit has his life's own instinct, which is noticeable at a time when he is either left to himself, or is in the company of his like; but it vanishes when he is in the company of better spirits. I have seen that change [in a spirit], as well as his being brought back suddenly to his natural instinct of wanting to take something that was not his, although nothing of this was apparent to the company he was in.

Moreover, the life of a spirit not only changes depending upon the kind of companions he has, but is also degraded, which was likewise shown, namely, that by diminishing the number of companions to a few, his life was likewise diminished from a clever one to a rather stupid one. So the lives of souls after death are joined to different societies, and in this way also it is discerned what their character is, and with whom they harmonize.

In whatever society they are, souls think that they are alone and live from themselves. They are likewise explored during several states of a society of similar spirits, so that the spirits find out, as do the souls themselves, what they are like. For one is not the same in one state as in another. But societies of angels must be the same throughout changing states, because they must all let themselves be led by the Lord. 1748, 9 February.

FROM THE *BIBLE INDEX*

ᵐThese words [were written] in the presence of some who constituted one society.ⁿ

About admission into the inward heaven[1]

697. It is said in the Word [Matt. 25:10–12, Luke 13:25], that the door was closed and they could no longer be let in; also, that they had come too late, and knocked, so they were not admitted. How these matters stand was shown to me vividly.

698. In a dream, I observed in a spiritual manner how good spirits, or good qualities, had been stolen away by evil spirits, and that there was dispute over their possession between the evil and the good; and finally, that the good qualities were given back. These things were depicted in a spiritual way.

699. When I awoke, certain societies of spirits, one after the other, began to declare in a singing, loud voice, that the Wolf had wanted to steal them away, but the Lord had snatched them from the wolf, and that they had then been restored to the Lord. On this account they rejoiced from the depths of their heart. For they had been in despair, extremely afraid that the Lord had rejected them, and that the wolves would therefore seize them and the Lord no longer wanted to keep them. They feared that there was an overabundance of spirits or angels in heaven, so that no room was left to receive more. This was the generally shared thought, which I perceived clearly.

700. When one society after the other had declared with a loud voice, as if in song, that the Wolf had stolen them away but that the Lord had snatched them back and restored them to Himself, this saying was passed along farther away from me, from one society to the other, or to one choir after another. Also, at some distance, it was uttered by those of one choir rather doubtingly, with falling voices. This choir, however, being brought back to the proper state, was taken in by the twelfth society; they said that this was the character of the twelfth. (There had actually been eleven, but still a twelfth was also admitted.) Afterwards about eight more societies came,

---

[1] See 262 and footnote.

declaring the same thing, whom I thought to be of the other sex, or of a different kind.

701. After these events, they were introduced into the inward heaven[1], as I was told by a clear voice saying that they were admitted in this way when they had been in the heaven of spirits for a certain length of time. Therefore no one more could be let in, however much they cried out and insisted. This is what is meant by those who had come too late, because they had lacked oil in their lamps. They received the reply that they could no longer be admitted, whereupon they were turned away.

702. However, it was said that this process goes on continually throughout the universal heaven, as if in a chain, from one place to the next. So in this case also, after its own cycle, so to speak, an admission of this kind repeats. And it was said that heaven can never be filled, but that this fantasy that all the places were already filled had taken over because of the prevailing despair of ever being let in, because there was no room left—brought on, no doubt, by the wolf, or evil spirits. 1748, 10 February.

On admission into the inward heaven[2],
a continuation from the other page [702]

703. I also heard, or saw, the reason why no more than twelve societies were admitted at the same time, and after that about eight societies of the other sex. It was because they were thus being distributed into heavenly societies that had been formed there and for many reasons could not be brought in all at once, but only in succession. For as soon as they are let in, they are received by angelic societies according to a secret mode of distribution ordained by the Lord, into their own *inheritance*, so to speak. This can be called their lot, because it is done by the Lord in secret, or the Lord providing.

Admitted in this way, everyone to their own societies, they are welcomed wholeheartedly and with joy, and all love and friendship is shown to them. But when they do not freely want to remain in those societies, they are received by different societies, and so on, until they come to a society in which there is harmony and

---

[1] See 262 and footnote.
[2] *Ibid.*

unanimity. There they remain even until they come out still more perfect, and so one after another is lifted or raised up into greater glory.

704. But it should be noted that a transfer from one society to another does not take place through a rejection by the society where one is, but through an act of will, and the desire to be elsewhere—to where according to that desire one is indeed transferred. Thus everything is done from freedom, and consequently, of their own freest will.

705. It was said, moreover, that heaven is never completely closed, even to eternity, but that in this case it is closed for the reason given [701], also and especially for the reason that the remaining spirits have not yet been prepared, and not anyone can be let in before being prepared. If it happens that anyone is admitted due to a [Divine] permission for special reasons, as a kind of ferment, that spirit is then rejected thence in the greatest disgrace.

706. One group of spirits who were agitating to be let in, recieved the reply that it was not yet time, but at another time, if they came prepared. Watching this incident were also some souls whom I had known. 1748, 10 February.

About the spirits of the earth Jupiter

707. Those from among the spirits of the earth Jupiter who had been with me for some time were then at the same time also admitted into the inward heaven[1], for they were longing for it; and others followed them, who were also let in. Now still others have succeeded those, who, I think, are staying for the time being with me, also waiting to be admitted.

708. Moreover, I could not but marvel considerably at how gentle and calm the spirits of the inhabitants of Jupiter are. This I was allowed to learn due to the fact that for several days now, if not for a week, they have been with me, and obtained a place in my head [542, 553]. They are very gentle, and do nothing but think, and their

---

[1] See 262 and footnote.

thoughts are so yielding, that they allow themselves to be bent, simply at the good pleasure of the inward heaven or of their angels, and thus at the will of the one only Lord. They are patient, so that hardly the least bit of indignation is observed. When they notice that this or that is not granted them, they acquiesce at once, nor do the doubts of other [spirits] cling to them, but seem to leave them untouched. They are so [calm] that unless I had known of their presence from other indications, I could scarcely have known it from some change in their state of mind. *Content in those things which are enjoined on them*: these are their words. 1748, 10 February.

About the heavenly joy of those who are being received, spoken of on the adjoining pages [697–706]

709. I heard more from those who were admitted, besides the fact that they were received in friendship and brotherhood and brought into their societies: namely, that everyone, as suits his own pleasure and pleasing imaginations, obtains whatever he could possibly set his heart on, and a thousand times more.

710. For example, some [longed] to be clothed in most beautiful white and clean robes, such as young men and boys very much enjoy wearing. Their joy reached me, so that I could feel their gladness; for when dressed in this way, besides being in most beautiful white garments, they also know that they are angels.

710½. Some are delighted most deeply by an abundance of lovely things, such as those of pleasure gardens immeasurably surpassing every human conception. For there is nothing that is not springing up, blossoming, bearing fruit, so that all things are laughing, thereby revealing a very inward heavenly gladness in each and every leaf, issuing from their innermost parts. For I believe that such things spring from the very inward heaven, and that therefore the symbolic portrayals of them are as if alive. From this there is gladness in every detail.

711. A decoration was shown to me which then came up— just a decoration on a gate by itself. It was, by its constant variation, of a kind to surpass beyond measure all human imagination. For one decoration follows upon another, in entire processions, as far as the eye can see. This is now being displayed to them, as well as its continual changes one after another, and its seemingly live mobility. In short, it cannot be described, nor conceived of, and this is only the least and first [kind]. The yet deeper kinds are even more ineffable, not to mention the very inward and innermost kinds.

712. Moreover, the Light those who are in heaven have is such as to surpass beyond measure even the solar light on earth. I was shown this light. Some angels, shining white, who had been let into it, were sitting there, and that shining light appeared. I was told that brighter and more vivid light cannot possibly exist, because the Lord is their Light.

713. Those who are let in afterwards, or at intervals, come veiled over with a bright cloud, and are received in this way. The bright cloud was also shown to me.

714. Besides the lovely gardens of delight, there are also what are called heavenly abodes, that is, magnificent palaces, within which there are these most wonderful ornamentations, one after another, seemingly alive, countlessly diverse, and indeed, [seen] much more vividly than things looked at with the eyes of the body. 1748, 10 February.

About the rejection of evil spirits who try to slip into heaven by craft and deceit

715. Sometimes evil spirits are permitted to do this, as well as those called wolves, who, earlier, carried off some who fear them for the reason then given [699]—but only during the first period, before they have been initiated into societies.

They clothe themselves, as if in shining white garments, but they are recognized immediately by the angels, because it only is an outer layer, as if painted on, not anything living. Therefore, it is impossible for them to be received in any society, for to be received into heaven is to be received into heavenly societies.

This, then, is what is meant by there being a gulf between hell and heaven [Luke 16:26], because it is an impossible thing; and if it should be permitted, then they would at once be rejected as something entirely contrary, like scum.

716. Moreover, they who even attempt to gain entry into heaven under a shining white, angelic appearance, are turned at once into animal shapes befitting the disposition of each one. These were likewise shown to me. For the lower mind, or attitudes, or the passions, are pictured in the heaven of spirits by animals, even though they are nothing but passions and their varieties, thus shaped. So some vaguely appeared to me as birds, some as animals—but I was surprised that they were white. This happened to show that they wanted to couterfeit a shining white angel. 1748, 10 February.

717. Furthermore, there is a way to heaven, as said above [697–706]. Below is hell, then the lower earth (these are known by another name as well), then the heaven of spirits, next the inward heaven[1], then the very inward, finally the innermost. Everywhere the same process is occurring, but with much difference in this respect, that in the lower earth, and in the heaven of spirits, they obtain what is delightful to them, thus being transferred from one society to another; while evil spirits [undergo this process] in the opposite manner, namely, by punishments, and thus unwillingly. 1748, 10 February.

About those who desire to be the highest in heaven

718. In regard to those who desire to be the highest in heaven, I observed that during their bodily life, other, similar inclinations had become attached to them, to want to surpass others, either in worldly glory or in other respects. And therefore they ambition more or less the same thing in the other life, even though this is opposed to the love of the neighbor.

Such people in the other life are deprived of all rationality, and become as though they were not humans; for not knowing what they are doing, they go about everything from instinct, and as if in sleep, as said before [372, 696]. And because they had thought there was something good in such ambition, they are allowed to follow their instinct most zealously in whatever they do. So, trying to copy all [good qualities], they appear as good.

When these are permitted, they seem to themselves to fashion wings, and so to fly aloft. And then out of sheer fantasy, they

---

[1] See 262 and footnote.

fly so high that they believe it hardly possible to be any higher, as has also been shown to me. So far does their ambition uplift them. 1748, 10 February.

A difference of spirits

719. When a spirit is deprived of rationality, so that he acts from mere instinct, then he is pardoned for whatever he does since he is acting as if in sleep; also because no one can help pitying their condition, seeing that they act in this manner.

However, when the same spirits are rational while so acting, the rationality does nothing other than strive to hide their instinct. Thus a habitual pretense is usually present, from fear and from other causes, because the rationality in bodily life had hardly been anything other than a means of hiding their natural instincts and distorted loves. This I was able to gather today from actual experience. 1748, 10 February.

These points spirits were able to understand as well as if the subject were exposed to the senses, but I am doubtful whether people living in the body can understand them.

In the absence of reflection, spirits do not see by means of the human body they are joined to

720. I have often walked through the streets of a city among a large crowd, not reflecting on the spirits around me, [supposing] that they, too, would be noticing everything along with me. This reflection happens by my simply looking inward and then tacitly calling things to their attention. Almost on every such occasion and so, quite often, they told me that during that time, they had seen and heard nothing, but had all the while been attending to thought in my mind.

So also, any spirit whatever whom I reflected on was summoned up, so to speak, and this happened very often. From this I was able to infer that the spirits, when present with someone whose inward parts are not opened toward the Lord through faith, absolutely cannot speak with that person, nor see through his or her eyes. They only make use of the person's memory and so of their reasoning power, just as these spirits with me use mine, who have very often confessed that they had not been able to tell otherwise than that they were living my life. This also occurs in a group of many spirits, each one of whom thinks he lives his own life, unaware that the rest also think the same.

721. Those reflections I could best compare with people's reflection on themselves. They are unaware that their hand or face is cold, or that their foot is pressed when they walk, or that they are speaking words when they speak, or that any other condition anywhere in their body exists, unless they reflect on it, or direct their thought toward it. There are besides many similar confirmatory examples, such as the fact that if we do not reflect upon the sounds of bells, or on the objects of sight around us, we are entirely unaware of having heard or seen them. 1748, 10 February.

Man can live in both lives

722. The human race was so created by the Lord as to be able to be both in the world and in heaven, the outer person in the world and the inner one in heaven, consequently to be able to speak with spirits and angels as well as with fellow human beings. This was so that heaven would be united with the world, and the world with heaven.

This has also, by the mercy of the Lord, taken place with me, and indeed in such a way that when I was mixing with people on earth, I did not differ in the least from myself as I had been before, nor could anyone tell me from an [ordinary] weak human being. But when I was with spirits, I was then as if separate from my body, yet at the same time joined to it, because my spiritual part was then with spirits—in fact, so much so, that when I wanted to write something like "the other life," I could hardly realize that it was the other life, or the life after death; for the spirits wanted "in this life," because I was with them.

About a kind of spirits who do nothing but engage in robberies and commit butcheries
And about the kind who, because of them, seem to themselves to flee to cities, and then dwell in a large city

723. A kind of roving spirit was shown to me that engages in nothing but plundering and robberies. There first appeared to me a spirit wearing dark blue, and on his head a twisted cap of the same color, like the [headdress] of certain Turks. He came toward me, waving his right hand. Another spirit then told me that he was fleeing, and was terribly afraid of some who do nothing but search for and find people to torture, put to the sword, torment, burn up with fire, boil, and who cruelly maltreat all whom they come across. But about this spirit who waved his hand, he said that such a one usually appears to them, warning them to beware of those robbers, because they are then near at hand.

724. It should be mentioned that before the latter appeared to me, I had been removed from the company of the spirits who were with me before. As a result, they spoke with me from far off and cried out that I was being taken away, or moved far from them, while I thought I was being transferred to the inhabitants of a different earth.

725. Those robbers are, as the spirit speaking said, entirely black from head to heel. Soon afterwards, one such did appear to me, very black, who was one of the robbers.

726. The same appeared close to me, his right hand stretched out straight at full length, threatening, in case anyone were there whom he might thus torture.

727. Presently others appeared, three in a row, among whom there was even one woman. They were cunningly awaiting the opportunity to steal something. One, at the left, secretly looking for my purse, wanted to slip his hand into it. Another, facing me, was cunningly saying he did not want to take away anything, yet his craftiness was apparent from his speech. His looks were not unattractive, nor were the woman's. Whether she had been sent out as a decoy, I do not know for sure.

Someone also appeared who was taking away boxes as though he were carrying off plunder, 1748, 11 February.

Continuation on the robbers and about the Large City,
spoken of on the adjoining pages [723–7]

728. A spirit, when I asked him where he came from, explained to me, saying that he was fleeing and was afraid of the robbers, who kill, slaughter, burn, boil people. He was looking for someone with whom he would be safe. I asked where he was from, whether from such and such a region, and he said that he did not know which land, but which city. He did not want to hear "land," or the word naming it. For he said afterwards that the land is the Lord's, but the city belonged to them; that they were in the city so as to be safe from the robbers.

729. Afterwards I talked with a robber who spoke with a deep voice, like a giant, and I asked him who he was. He said he was looking for plunder to carry off. I asked where he stored his loot, and whether he realized that it would be taken away from him, since it was nothing but an illusion.

When I asked him where he was, he said that he was in a desert, or in deserted places, seeking opportunities to plunder, and that those whom he comes upon, he torments in the manner described. Thus the robbers were together [with the others]. He finally acknowledged that he was a spirit; yet still, because he is with me, he does not reallize it, thinking he is still living on earth.

730. Now I realize that they are like, if not the same as, the Jews who roam the desert in this way, and upon meeting anyone, are of a mind not only to seize whatever they possess, but even, if no one knows about it, to kill, slaughter, burn, or boil [them]. That they have a mind to do this, although they do not dare, may be amply inferred from their passions, attitudes and inclinations against even their own people and companions, as well as from their wicked life when they had been given power over their enemies, whom they could not treat cruelly enough to satiate their lust for cruelty.

731. Therefore that generation seem to themselves to be living in a very large city, as they call it, where they are safe, nor do they dare to go out of it. For this reason, when they do go out of their city, unless they are like [those robbers], they are warned by a spirit wearing dark blue like the one mentioned [723], not unlike their rabbis, to beware, because the robbers are not far off. 1748, 11 February.

732. Something that surprised me very much is that when I was saying the Lord's prayer, such a robber was present with me and said it together with me, as very often happens, and I noticed that he did so with such devotion that I was unable to make out whether or not he had true belief; for I could not discern that his mind was unfamiliar with the meaning, as I could in others. Thus he was at the time worshipping the Lord as if from his heart, [praying] that He might protect him.

From this I was able to infer what that generation is like, namely, that when they are in danger, and afraid, their covetousness is entirely unnoticeable, as though it out of sight, or as if it passes away, and they perform devotion, all on account of the danger of death. This is borne out by many incidents in their history. Nevertheless they bear such intentions in their hearts [729], and, as I was able to sense, they derive this hereditarily from both dragons. For as soon as they come out of danger, they are the same as ever, except now using the heart to lie. 1748, 11 February.

About reflection

733. I was just conversing with spirits and angels about reflection, to which I do not know whether people have given enough attention; and it was said that if they give it some thought, they will discover more secrets in the doctrine of reflection than in any other.

What reflection achieves can be quite clear to everyone from the fact that we perceive no sensation of the body or its parts, and are unaware of having a sensation, unless we reflect upon that part of our body. Then we perceive heat, cold, pressure—we even feel what that part is suffering. If we reflect on our breathing, then we feel and know that we are breathing, and in this way a voluntary factor joins in; besides innumerable other instances.

734. Likewise, when we do not reflect on the things in our own mind, or our motivation—how we are thinking, what we are thinking, what we are doing, what is motivating our actions—without reflection we know nothing, except that we are, and nothing else, not what we are.

On the other hand, if we reflect upon ourself from [the viewpoint of] others, or allow others to reflect upon us, and to say what we are like, then for the first time we are able to know ourself. Otherwise we can never learn, but remain in our own illusions, and from them, reflect upon others. So one thinks truths are falsities, because one is judging from one's illusions. For such as the starting-point is, such also is everything that follows.

735. Spirits especially, stay after death in a state devoid of reflection. This is also the reason that they cannot tell but that they are earthly people, living in the world as before. So they remain in their illusions and live on as the character they had been at death. But as soon as the power of reflection is given them by the Lord, they know that they are in the other life—a belief to which they can hardly be brought until they are given something, or rather many things, to reflect on. But illusions rooted into their character still remain.

736. Consequently, spirits cannot at all help thinking that they are better than the rest, especially those who had been arrogant in life, who also dislike being reflected upon. However, when they are brought into a state of reflection, they are brought into a state of better life, for then for the first time they are able to know themselves, and know more truly what they are.

737. Moreover, even the doctrine of faith accomplishes nothing at all with people, unless the Lord enables them to reflect. That is the very reason why people learn what is true and good from the Word of the Lord, namely, so that from what they learn, they may reflect upon themselves, as to whether they are as they ought to be. This reflection is given them at certain times, especially times of distress. It is of the utmost importance, therefore, to learn truths. Without spiritual knowledge, there can be no reflection, thus no reformation.

738. However, they who fall into passions and illusions, are unable to reflect from a viewpoint of truths, until those chills and those shadows have been dispelled. 1748, 11 February.

About reflection

739. The doctrine of reflection is an entire doctrine, and without it no one is able to know what inward life is, not even what the life of the body is. In fact, without reflection from a knowledge of truths, no one is reformed. For this reason, the Lord is delivering to the people on this earth, because they are living in a corrupt state, written down truths. From these, as from a wellspring, they may draw a knowledge of truth that will enable them to reflect on themselves—or more truly, from which higher knowledge, inscribed upon the memory, the Lord may cause people to reflect upon their falsities, and the like. Therefore, without spiritual knowledge, reformation is not possible.

740. It is different on the earth Jupiter, where spirits warn them, and raise up and display before them whatever they had wrongly thought and done. So reflection there takes place through revelations, as mentioned before [523, 539–45].

Revelations cannot take place on this earth, because the door toward heaven has been closed, and people's thoughts are only drawn up to heaven by the Lord at certain times. The rest of the time, they are concerned with nothing else but bodily, worldly and earthly matters, and upon these they reflect.

If in these circumstances the door toward heaven were opened to them, as it was to Cain, with whom spirits could even speak, then falsities would so mix themselves together with truths that they could never be separated. Thus they would be damned to eternity. This is therefore guarded against. 1748, 11 February.

About spirits' appetite for learning

741. In place of the appetite people in bodily life have for eating and drinking to nourish the body, spirits have an appetite for, or enjoyment of learning. The angelic appetite is for learning only what is true and good, but that of spirits is for anything whatever that is new. This desire is almost constant, taking the place of the appetite for nourishing the body with earthly food. So in every heaven, there is a most intense feeling for understanding truth and goodness, or matters of belief. This brings on reflections, by means of which they are perfected more and more. 1748, 11 February.

Every word of this was written in the presence of many spirits and angels who were reflecting on what had been written, and affirming it

About the inhabitants of Jupiter

742. The presence of the inhabitants of Jupiter was recognizable to me not only from the influence of their feelings, but also because they made my face appear smiling and cheerful, something they did constantly. For so they dispose the faces of the inhabitants of their planet, so that from heartfelt pleasure, they are almost laughing, or radiating joy. That it was joy of heart, I was able to learn also from the fact that they shared their calmness with me. It was so pleasant that I felt it fill my chest and my heart. Moreover, they do not let themselves be swayed by the passions of others, but remain in their own pleasant calm. Thus they are free of concerns such as the spirits of our earth have, who are stirred up by all kinds of emotions, and are continually in a state of restlessness. From this it can be inferred quite surely that the life of the inhabitants of the planet Jupiter is very far more pleasant than the life of the inhabitants of our earth; for it is passions which render a person restless.

743. Besides, they do not fear death, except on account of the loss of their married partner and little children; nor do they fear for them, since they live in tranquillity, and know for sure that their life is continued through the death of the body, and that they thus become happier, and heavenly angels.

744. [They know,] however, that there is a still deeper state of happiness, unknown to those who are with me. So they would be receptive of a more inward happiness that is not possible in those who take pleasure in a corrupt way of life, in passions and fantasies. For these people, inward things are annoying, and disquieting— which is not the case with the spirits of the planet of Jupiter.

About the robbers in the desert, and about the city

749.[1] About the robbers in the desert, see above [723–32], as well as about their cruelty, which I am not even permitted to describe; nor were they permitted to show it to me. In addition, it can be said that they are not in the habitable land, but are in the desert, because they go alone and do not put up with a companion, because it is their nature to want to torment, slaughter, burn up, and boil anyone they meet, this being their great enjoyment.

750. There is a boundary point beyond which they are not allowed to pass. From it, a line extends away in both directions

---

[1] 745–48 appear after 754, as indicated in the autograph.

FROM THE *BIBLE INDEX* 753.

toward two cities, so that a triangle is formed when lines are drawn from the boundary point to both cities, and from one city to the other. One city, a city of the evil, is not far from Gehenna but more to the left, where the dragon appeared several times when he wanted to call together his own evil spirits to form a wicked society or conspiracy against the good, that is, against the Lord. Thereabouts is the city of the evil. Those who seem to themselves to live there, in fantasy rush around the streets, ankle-deep in mud, moaning and complaining miserably.

751. The second city lies between Gehenna and the swamp, almost equidistant from them. There, the better ones of them seem to themselves to dwell. This city sometimes appears magnificent to them, with palaces and quite beautiful houses. But sometimes the same city is suddenly turned into countryside, or small towns, sometimes even into stinking swamp, practically nothing but mire, in which they are being buried. So the illusion varies for each individual who is there, and is not the same with everyone—for they are dominated by illusions. Therefore, depending on their various passions, and punishments, as well as refreshing enjoyments at intervals, they experience these fantasies as if they were entirely actual, quite unable to tell but that they are real. In this city, it is a common expression that the city is theirs, but the land the Lord's [*cf.* 728].

751½. I inquired who was the governor of the city. This they did not know, and told me that no one was, but that they were nevertheless together, for fear of the robbers wandering in the deserts. Thus they are held together because of fear. It is clear that the Lord controls their illusions in this way, through fear, so that one does not attack the other, as in the deserts, which would happen if they were not under the Lord's auspices.

752. Now the line drawn hence is the boundary, which, running to each city, and from one city to the other, forms a triangle within the space of which the robbers are.

753. On that boundary, a spirit almost snowy white appeared to me, and an angel also, almost shining. And as another spirit was coming up, the spirit standing there welcomed with outstretched arms the one approaching, who, bowing himself to the earth, passed under his feet. Then, having quickly turned around, being on his back or with his body downward and face upward, he was driven under his feet and then thrown forward on high, and so he fled away. This they call admission towards the city. So they are not harmed, because they say that [the spirit] is obliged to admit them.

754. But there was another one who crawled under those feet, back and forth, or under the feet and back several times in the way described. These are the ones who will worship [the robbers, *see* 748]. 1748, 12 February. # #

Continuation about the robbers in the desert, and the city

745.[1] But there was also one who in his crawling got wrapped up in a fine net, so that he was unable to pull himself out of it, but was anxiously crawling greater and greater distances and being tormented. These are the ones whom they want to temper by torture, before admitting them, but likewise afterwards by a spear which the spirit kept holding in his hand, and which formed a leg of that angle [750, 752], and around which a veil was wrapped, under which the spirit [being tormented] had been put. Finally he broke out near the point of the spear, but together with the veil, and not within the boundary toward the city, but toward me, on high. So this is a sign that such a spirit would not enter into that place, or that city.

746. But there was another man wrapped up in the net, thus two of them—for what reason, I do not know. Perhaps so that he could show me these matters. For the dragon does not want them to be disclosed, and has therefore often tried by his illusions to invalidate my visions, as well as even to steal them away so that I would not know of them, as he is also doing now. It is a severe punishment to be let under the veil, because they are thereby tormented pitifully. The one who fled away [*cf.* 753] drew the net with him, like a tail, because of an illusion joined to the fear in fleeing.

---

[1] 745–48 are placed here in accordance with instructions in the manuscript.

747. They who live evilly even in the city to the right or halfway between Gehenna and the swamp, are penalized with severe punishments.

748. From these particulars it is apparent what the fantasy of the Jews, who during their earthly life thought that they were still to possess Jerusalem and the holy land, brings with it in the other life. Few, if any, believe in heaven or a life after death—one devoted to mere greed never can believe that there is a life after death, or a resurrection, just as they did not believe it in the Lord's time. Specifically it brings with it the consequence that this fantasy remains, and so, they come into a city—the worst ones, as soon as they die, into a city to the left, the better ones into a city to the right. And their holy land to which they think they are coming is profane, and filled with robbery, that is, plundering and wickedness. They call it the land of the Lord, for as such they are obliged to worship the robbers, in order to be supplied with what they regard as the necessaries of life. 1748, 12 February. These are the consequences of their belief and life.

About the difference between the delights of pleasure, and true happiness

755.[1] When I was feeling deep delight, or pleasantness, I did not know their source; for it is very difficult for a soul or spirit to distinguish between false or counterfeited delights and true or heavenly ones. Their sensation is still so gross that they cannot tell. For this reason, I discussed these delights with spirits around me, as to where they came from, and it was said that false delights or pleasures sometimes so counterfeit true and heavenly ones, that they cannot at all be distinguished. In fact, unless the Lord inspires a recognition of the difference, a spirit cannot ever find out.

By false delight of this kind, evil spirits, in fact the worst ones, very much mislead and enchant those in the other life, who then think it to be the epitome of heaven, whereas it is completely hellish, because it turns into what is hellish, and into torments. Thus they not only inject the most deeply felt pleasantness, but also counterfeit the beautiful shapes of various objects, even like the gardens

---

[1] Following the author's instructions, 749–54 have been put after 744.

of paradise. For evil spirits, especially those high overhead, constantly seek to copy such things, and thus lead souls astray or entice them to their side, so that they will join them.

756. The difference is like that between artificial fruits, artificial flowers, leaves, artificial human figures of wax, reproductions that are clay on the inside (it is only the outside that counterfeits and leads astray, in fact so cleverly sometimes that the untrained and simple are easily fooled), and genuine fruits, flowers, and human faces. In the latter there is life, and the deeper and deeper one goes, the more spiritual and heavenly the life is. These endure, and develop, and the more deeply this takes place, the more beautiful and the happier they become; whereas with the former, as one goes inward, the outer beauty and pleasantness falls away, or collapses, betraying nothing but what is filthy and hellish. 1748, 12 February.

Such is the life of pleasures in the body.

About the circle to the understanding, and thence, through the will into actions

757. There is an obvious circle starting with the senses—especially the hearing and sight, which present objects that arouse inner sensation—to the understanding, and from the understanding into the will, then from the will into action, either of the mouth, i.e. speech, or of the face, or of the bodily members. This is the natural circle.

But because [human] nature has been corrupted, so that objects can only pass from the senses to the understanding, but not into the will, because this is being controlled from a different source, therefore there must be a process of regeneration whereby the true order, or circle, is restored. Then, finally, the will holds full sway, and from it, the understanding, both striving together for the fruits of charity. Then all evil that is slipped in by evil spirits is turned into good in the understanding. For the Lord, through the will, that is, through love, and mercy, which is His alone, is guiding the person whom He has regenerated and gifted with these abilities. 1748, 12 February.

FROM THE *BIBLE INDEX* 760.

Those who in the life of the body have greatly excelled in cleverness, but only in outer matters, are stupid in the other life

758. Someone slightly known to me during his bodily life, who was brought to me just for the purpose of conversing, but had nothing to say, was so dull and seemingly stupid that he knew of nothing that we might talk about. His dullness was communicated to me, so that I could learn about it. It cast such shadows over my thought that I could hardly understand what I was writing.

During his bodily life, this man had been cleverer than others, although only outwardly, so that due to his sharpness of mind in regard to trivial matters, he was highly acclaimed.

Thus ingenuity in outer, worldly and bodily matters turns into stupidity. But I do not yet know whether this was the result of his being left to a company of similar spirits. In this circumstance any spirit is stupid, and still more one who, like this one, had only died a few months earlier [*see* 400]. 1748, 12 February.

759. Moreover, there was also another person who had likewise surpassed others in cleverness during his bodily life, and who was nevertheless among good spirits, and capable of perceiving the deeper things of heaven.

On hatred during life in the body: what it causes in the other life

760. A certain person, owing to various misfortunes and for various reasons, during his bodily life had nursed a hatred against some he thought had persecuted him, and on account of the length of time [he had persisted in doing this], it had taken root. I was able to tell this from the acts of his life, as well as from conversation with him. When he saw someone whom he had hated in bodily life, it was as if he had suddenly been torn away from the conversation he was having with another and had been hurled from above like a bolt of lightning, casting himself at the one whom he hated, intent on destroying him—but he was not permitted to do so. Only to me, it appeared that he took something from [the other's] head, but this then fell out of his hands.

So he was brought to me, and he remained for some time, almost as in sleep, absent from himself, constantly thinking about the one whom he had hated. Afterwards he spoke with me, and I showed him that he could have no reason for hating that person, because I had never heard that person speaking of him, either well or ill, nor had that person ever hated him, but what he had done had been done by necessity and by agreement.

Finally I noticed that the hatred in him was allayed, showing that he was still capable of moderating his hatred. This I can infer for the reason that when he suffered misfortunes during his bodily life, the Lord had been merciful to him. 1748, 13 February. This was written in his presence.

Continuation about the robbers

761. Again one of the robbers approached me like an entirely black cloud. He came up to my right side, striking fear into those who were with me, though not into me. For the mere presence of these robbers is such that it strikes those whom they approach with fear, terror, and even trembling. With all his energy he was bent on attacking me with his crafty tricks, but it was in vain. He even stretched out his right hand [*see* 726], trying to exercise an imaginary power, but he could accomplish nothing whatsoever. By the way, when that black robber appeared, he had stars around him, as well as a starry sky.

761½. Just this one observation occurs to me as worth mentioning, that he portrayed women with beautiful faces [*see* 727], and then wanted to sneak them in with the purpose of gaining the opportunity to steal, which he also attempted to do by use of his illusive arts.

762. Moreover, this type of robber also appears to have fierce dogs with him, which he sets upon those he encounters to terrify and devour them. The dogs I have also seen.

763. His face was also shown, as it looks to those whom he frightens, namely, no face [was seen] except a very black something, only his mouth, opened threateningly and fiercely, so that it was rather a gaping maw showing rows of teeth. In short, he was like a mad dog with gaping jaws. It was jaws, not a face. 1748, 13 February.

About truth and good

764. I spoke with spirits about showing respect to anyone, and I was informed that respect, as well as fear, is attributed to truth, for it is truth that is feared, and thus respected; whereas love is attributed to good, for what is good ought to be loved, because goodness has that quality in it. By a regenerated person, however, as by the angels or by the heavens, both good and truth are loved, because good is the source of truths.

About the year 1657

765. In a vision, I was shown 57, or 1657, the numbers being written before my eyes; but what they mean, I do not know exactly. 1748, 13 February.[1]

The powerful and the rich in the world are saved equally as the lowly and poor

766. I spoke with some after their bodily life who had been powerful, with Kings, and queens, with whom all was well, and who can be counted among the more happy. On the other hand, I have also encountered very many of the lower class and the poor who are in a wretched condition, especially beggars and the like.

So worldly power, and worldly riches, do not hold a person back from attaining Life eternal, nor does a pitiable condition or poverty promote it. The determining factor is rather the inward person and the productiveness of one's faith and charity, consequently one's motives and the use to which one's goods, power and riches are put.

Therefore, there is no distinction between the two types of people except on the plane of religion. 1748, 14 February.

How the different sciences take hold of the human mind, and limit it

767. I was talking with spirits about the different sciences, such as philosophy, and others—how they develop human minds.

---

[1] J.F.I. Tafel, first Latin editor of this text, wrote: "Why not 1757?" (the year of the Last Judgment).

As for philosophy, every aspect of it up until now has done nothing but cast shadows over minds, and thus has closed off the way to a contemplation of deeper matters, as well as of universal principles, for it consists solely of terms, and of disputes about them—even more so does rationalistic philosophy, which constricts ideas in such a way that the mind dwells upon nothing but petty details and consequently on trivia. Besides, it not only obstructs the channels to what is deeper, but also causes blindness, and completely banishes belief. Therefore, in the other life, a philosopher who had clung fast to such details and given himself up to them, is now stupid, and by far less knowledgeable than others.

768. As for Mechanics, when people gives themselves up too much to the practice of mechanical science, then they develop the mental attitude that nothing exists but what is mechanical, not only the whole of nature, but spiritual and heavenly things as well. Then if they cannot trace these to mechanical principles and their powers, they believe nothing, and so become bodily and earthly people.

769. As for Geometry and the like, this also strongly focusses the mind, as it were, and prevents it from going into universal principles—except in presuming that nothing exists but what is Geometrical, or mechanical. Yet the scope of Geometry does not extend beyond earthly and physical forms.

770. As for historical studies, they do no harm, provided they are not merely matters of memory.

771. They who indulge the memory alone, or studies that are a matter of memorizing, or other studies but only for the sake of the memory, in the other life understand very little about what spiritual truth is, still less what heavenly truth is. They remain fixed in their own personal ideas, which form a kind of callus surrounding their brain like bone, or skull; and this callosity has first to be cast off, before truth can penetrate, and before spiritual and heavenly knowledge can have any abode.

This callus is dispersed only with difficulty, and in fact, only with pain, or if perchance without these, then it has to soften, as it were, over a long period of time. Many experiences have shown this to me, and each time, the depiction of a callus amazed me.

772. Experimenting with nature, such as horticulture and similar studies, does not hinder the knowledge of what is spiritual, [or prevent those who are educated in this science] from being spiritually perfected equally with those who are not—something I have also observed in the case of a certain person.

773. Not any knowledge is hurtful or detrimental, provided it is not considered to be everything in itself, but a further goal is looked to. It is spiritual wealth, on which the understanding of realities can be based. It is just the same as with riches or wealth, and with power: if one values them only for the sake of riches and power, then one is very badly off in the other life, whereas if they are valued only for further ends, so that they are only means, and are thus regarded as nothing apart from the end, then they do no one any harm. 1748, 14 February.

About an entirely infernal gang

774. At the left side there is a hell where there are demons, as they ought to be called, who live from mere instinct, their rationality having been taken away. They are not so evil, but think when doing evil that they are doing good. So that place is for those who consider evils to be good and who, having been deprived of the ability to reason, abide there and think that they are ruling the universe. But they are then in a dream, as they themselves also said when they returned to themselves and their rationality was restored to them.

775. Not far from there, more toward the right of the same left quarter, is a dark place I had not yet seen, where there are devils. These store up the more secret types of poison. Today I observed one of them going out from there and speaking quite intelligibly, using his own wit and reason. But soon after this, a hellish poison exhaled from that place, that is, a poisonous persuasion regarding life, heaven, and the state of departed souls. This was conveyed to me first, and soon after that, the same devil, coming up to me, wanted to speak with me without anyone hearing. But because his poisons had already been recognized, he was not permitted to utter them but only to think them, so that he was, I realized, being compelled to speak differently [than he thought]. He is now present.

776. Here is true hell, and the thought is being inspired into me that these are the kind who are sent out especially to people in the world who corrupt others, and are inwardly extremely wicked. 1748, 14 February.

About certain rich and luxurious people in the world

777. There was a spirit who had lived in luxury in his bodily life, having become rich from gifts, so that he was reckoned among the more wealthy and served a sumptuous table, though he was not born such, but became such. After the life of the body, such people wander around asking for food like beggars, and they go in tattered clothing, not knowing but that they are in the life of the body. Thus their condition is changed to the opposite, which must be painful for them. 1748, 15 February.

About the sleep even of spirits

778. It has already been told, I believe, that there are various changes of state with spirits, many more than with people on earth [319, 651–52, 696], so that there are perpetually changing states which they undergo. Therefore they also have a state of sleeping and waking and all the states in between.

779. Once while a spirit was sleeping, I was awake and paying little attention to his sleep. Then there was another spirit who was sleeping and displayed what that spirit was feeling. At the same time there were also angels, who were inspiring this dream, who are always awake. Therefore, dreams like this one come from heaven, and there are angels who cause them, from the Lord, and there are other spirits who then believe they are enacting [the dream]. I even heard how this spirit was working, and what was being said. 1748, 15 February.

To strive after any honor on earth or among people on earth, is not heavenly

780. I spoke with some who had died not so many years earlier, but were still among good spirits not yet let into heaven, who inwardly still desired honor in the world, or some kind of acclaim for

FROM THE *BIBLE INDEX* 786.

their name among mortals on earth. I was also enabled to feel this their ambition. Then I spoke with them, and I said that this is something worldly still remaining, and that a heavenly attitude is to desire nothing of the kind, but rather to scorn it.

781. Speaking further, I said that in heaven, all since the very creation [of man] are gathered together, thus an enormous society, with whom they may become acquainted and even associate, with the resulting enjoyment and pleasantness, without any one of them desiring for whatever reason to be greater than another, but feeling themselves less. There is no comparison, therefore, between a name in heaven and a name on earth, especially among the kind of people who know nothing of what is good and heavenly, just as there is no comparison between glory in the world, and glory in heaven. Being hereby convinced, they affirmed this, because they perceived from the Lord that it was true. 1748, 15 February.

About the state of life after death

782. From a soul after death, the first thing that must be shed is the earthly element, as well as the bodily, this being love of self and love of the world, consequently the delusions that stream forth from those loves and go together with them.

783. After this souls undergo preparation, so that their earthly part harmonizes with their spiritual part, then they are let into the inward heaven[1].

784. There they are divested of the earthly part, and thus prepared for the very inward heaven, where the spiritual element is still dominant.

785. Finally, that dominating spiritual element is put off, and then they are let into the innermost heaven, where that which is heavenly dominates.

786. These stages of divestment are symbolically portrayed by clothing being taken off, and are almost the same process.

---

[1] See 262 and footnote.

787. However, they can be clothed again with these garments, one by one, and be brought back from the innermost to the very inward, and then to the inward regions, and into the heaven of spirits.

788. For they retain everything they had drawn with them from the world. These are resources with which they have been gifted only by the Lord; so that by putting on clothes, this process is portrayed, whereby from being angels, they can thus be reduced to spirits.

789. But they are brought back, or they thus put on those elements one after another, for the sake of being perfected. For the elements still clinging to them, of nature, of the world, of the body, joined together, while they are gradually being resolved are like a ferment, so that their life ferments, so to speak. In order for these elements also to be as if separated, or to become harmless, the souls are brought back to their original state, thus being made still more perfect.

790. No one reaches the very inward regions without being prepared, so an [unprepared] soul cannot ascend, but descend. 1748, 15 February.

The odor of offences

791. I perceived a general feeling of spirits that was so made up of offences[1], that they would not acknowledge the Lord as the Lord of the universe and Savior of all. This was the general feeling that I sensed, so I was comparing it with a certain odor. For everything of this kind is so comparable to an odor, that it is even presented by means of an odor; and whenever it so pleases [the Lord], it is indeed smelled as an odor, both by those on earth and by spirits.

Then I became aware of the kind of odor like that of stinking water, or water polluted with garbage; and I was told that this is the odor [of offences]. 1748, 15 February.

---

[1] *I.e.*, offences against the faith, or stumbling blocks.

Spirits who had not believed in the life after death are dumbfounded when it is proved to them

792. A certain spirit, about whom I know he had not believed in a life after death during his bodily life—even though in his last hours, I think he had been persuaded by a priest [to believe]—when it was proved to him in various ways that he was in the other life, was so dumbfounded, so amazed at being in another life, that he could hardly be convinced. He said that he had been living without reflecting, when yet all this long while he had been in the company of [spirits] like he now was. But he was among infernal ones. 1748, 15 February.

About one who is lukewarm

793. One of those who are devils, and who from hatred persecute truth and goodness the most, coming up to me, did not want to do anything [wrong] at all, behaving as though he had repented. Nor did I sense any deceit, even though I did think that he harbored deceits within, only awaiting the opportunity, but meanwhile putting himself forth as a good spirit, and converted.

Someone fleeing far away from him, told me that he could not bear his presence, because he smelled like vomit, which made him want to vomit. This was because he was like the one of whom it is said, that he must be spewed out [Rev. 3:16]. 1748, 15 February.

794. These [devils] are more dangerous than all the rest, because given the place and the opportunity, they are crueler than others.

795. One of them later spoke, and did, unspeakably horrible things, which therefore must not be made known, for he viciously attacked everything [true and good]. And amazingly, because such spirits have this nature, they can never let up, but once they are permitted, then no matter how they are persuaded and how well instructed that such acts should not be done, they nevertheless commit them. Their nature and instinct drive them to it and they carry them out with pleasure, because a passion for such [wickedness] clings to them. 1748, 15 February.

About the raising up of whatever resides in a person's memory, by spirits

796. It has often struck me as amazing how spirits can raise up the appropriate items from a person's memory, and indeed, instantaneously, in any situation. This is due to the fact that [something in it] interacts with their desire, which then works in secret upon the memory.

797. Moreover, in a person's memory they can also read, so to speak, what is stored there, and find out anything the person had thought and done. And this they did, sometimes, when I knew nothing about the things they had seen. So they read it as if it were a written book; and more besides. 1748, 15 February.

The universal rule regarding the life after death, that it is allotted to each according to his motives in bodily life

798. It is known that the created universe is but a complex of means toward the goal of goals, Which is the Lord, because He is Heaven. Intermediate goals range in their own series and levels, one after another, from the lowest to the higher, then on to the highest. The arrangement of these means, and series of means, is order.

799. Therefore, whatever kind of means, or intermediate goal, people are in their own goals, such is the character they acquire, and such their life at first becomes after bodily life; and such also is the abode they are allotted in the greatest body or Heaven, thus in the Human Himself, that is, in the Lord.

As for still deeper regions, and the very inward and innermost, these we do not discern, nor consequently, where our heritage will be. This the Lord Alone discerns, because these matters are too inward to be able to open up before our very dim human sight.

800. According to the goals that we set for ourself during bodily life, in every respect—regarding ourself, society in common, heaven, the Lord—we are assigned a place after bodily life as a member [in that greatest body].

801. That people's goals or motives determine their placement is clear from the fact that our life consists of our motives, which are mostly the same as our loves; and our motives, taken together, are like our soul—and such indeed does our soul become. For one's soul looks only toward purposes, and is a bundle of purposes [26]. So it is that during bodily life, we develop a soul for ourself, which is our character and instinct.

802. That our purposes determine our place is also clear from the fact that whenever people are looking to a personal goal, such as themselves, or something connected with themselves, even if they are benefitting the community, so that the common good is thus served, they are still not at all rewarded for that, because their motive was not the common good, but a personal goal. It is same as when devils are striving for the harm and destruction of a person, of society, and of the human race, and the Lord turns it into something good and salutary: yet that devil who had had an evil, a most evil, intention, remains nevertheless a devil, and becomes worse.

803. The worst purpose of all is that of one whose goal is self. Then common and universal interests are focussed upon oneself. Next worse is the purpose of those who have the world as their goal.

Purposes in bodily life induce the character and instinct
we bring with us in the other life

804. Some examples were shown today of how peoples' purposes in bodily life had determined their character and formed their instinct.

805. A certain person had thought and talked of nothing else but giving phrases and words a clever twist; whatever came up he would bend in such a way that in one phrase or another, something witty would emerge. I wondered who this was, because one could not distinguish him from the other spirits except by the way his speaking and thinking were directed to things of this kind.

But I was informed that these are the kind whose only goal in the life of the body had been studies dealing with their own favorite ideas, which they loved, such as critical analyses, variant readings of classical authors and of the Sacred Scripture; or who had just loved to compile dictionaries, or who in their everyday life had loved nothing more than eloquence with words, double meanings, or plays on words.

I was shown what his, or their, life was like. It was as though I could sense nothing living in them, but only words, and scarcely anything else but words. While they were certainly alert mentally, able to speak at length, still their thought dwelt on the details just mentioned. Of these their speech also consisted, as if it were something lifeless, like something in which none but the very least life was present.

Yet, he was not evil; he could simply not stretch his thought further, but confined it to some special feature of words, as well as to the least characteristics of speech. Consequently he did not look like a living being, but like an artfully carved, talking statue.

806. But these are they who had loved only such things, and considered them as essential, while they are but the lowest means. These people always imagine such things to be most important, as is commonly done, because they are means for coming to inward, and so to very inward principles.

On account of his love of these pursuits and the delusions it causes, in his thoughts this person did not rise beyond them, much less come to universal principles. Consequently, he did not have the purpose of putting them to a further use.

807. One who loves only memorized facts and considers them to be wisdom, going by the rule that a person is the wiser, the more he has stored in his memory, has a kind of callus enveloping his thought, as said before [771]. When this callus is removed, he laments, thinking he has lost his whole life, and that there is nothing left; but as it seemed to me, he then for the first time is in a state where he can be perfected. And the reason it seemed that way to me was, I think, that he also had, inwardly, some goodness, so that some goodness sweated through. 1748, 16 February.

Continuation on the life after death according to one's purposes in the life of the body

808. There were also some of the kind who had done no thinking at all, but were only followers, so to speak, so that whatever was said, they followed. In these likewise there did not seem to me to be much life, because they did nothing on their own, only following others, as if they themselves were nothing—for if they do nothing of themselves, then their presence goes almost unnoticed. I was informed that this is what those become who during their bodily life do nothing except on impulse and who in considering, understanding, responding to anything, are like little bursts of flame. What they are to say or answer back occurs to them on the spur of the moment, so that they commit themselves spontaneously, without thought, or deliberation. During their bodily life such people are easy and flexible, and at the same time also demons; for they readily flare up, although the fire is soon put out. The flame is a visual image of their speech; besides many other details.

809. These people in the other life are apparently compatible with many [groups], for they do almost nothing else but promote what I may call harmonious movements of spirits. They can almost be called lubricants, because they facilitate [these movements], especially where some passion has not become deeply rooted.

Among these there are both demons and spirits, as well as intermediate types. Thus they are as it were mixers, which struck me as being connectors; but they are mixers, for promoting the flowing movements of spirits.

810. There are also some in the other life who are sticky, so to speak, holding onto anything that antagonizes them; nor do they let go before either having taken revenge or seeing an end to it in some other way. They are the kind who in bodily life had harbored revenge over long periods. They are almost sticky, as has often been noted previously.

811. There are others, also, who perform a quite important use. They seize upon whatever is thought, and do not reason about it, but believe and are convinced. But the ones who are good are not convinced by anything other than what they understand to be true and good. In bodily life, they had been people who had believed others obstinately, and had seized upon things that they had simply heard, without any effort to think for themselves. They are of important use, and near to the angelic heaven. When they are led astray, they are angered and grieve. Among them are also those having spiritual innocence, which arises from ignorance of more inward truths. 1748, 16 February.

812. The former ones [810], who are obstinate, or sticky, have been allotted a place before the face, a little to the left, near to the upper region, but not high up.

813. The latter, however, have been allotted a place toward the right side, and they appear to me as though they form a lesser segment of a circle.

About those who are allotted a place within the body

814. I was surprised that certain ones were allotted a place within the body, while others are outside. But I was instructed that they are allotted a place within the body who during their life had loved what is good, and had not hated anyone, but had put a good interpretation [on others' actions], desiring to do kindness to every individual and likewise, living in accordance with established order, thus showing heartfelt respect toward those who were in charge. 1748, 16 February.

About the first entrance of souls into the other life

815. As soon as souls come into the other life, they are for the most part received among societies of good spirits, unless they had been such as had led a contrary life or had been completely evil. Those in whom there is goodness and uprightness, or any such qualities, are received by societies of good spirits, and by them are shown every kindness, in fact, even to introducing them into heaven, or into companies of angels—although only for the purpose of showing them heaven and its happiness and glory. For afterwards they are let back into their original state, and then examined by spirits, both secretly and openly, as to their quality; so they are either separated from the society or brought into it, depending upon their character thus tested.

816. For this reason, when souls are let into heaven, or into other regions pleasing to him, one cannot judge from this that they are to be angels and more acceptable than others, as it is commonly supposed. But because all things take place by permission and consent, they are therefore sent back, as it were, to the spirits, so that the spirits may find out as if on their own, secretly or openly, what [these souls] are like, and more or less judge about them in their own way. Nevertheless, all these circumstances are governed by the Lord. 1748, 16 February.

An appetite for eating can also be brought upon spirits

817. That spirits have desire, and induce their desire on people, I have observed clearly and frequently [*cf.* 597, 741], so that they desire things which are entirely unnecessary to them, such as articles of human clothing. Indeed, they burn with an uncontrollable passion for them, even while they know that such things are not for them, but for the person [they are with], as for myself for example. I spoke about this matter with a spirit, and he knew and confirmed the fact, but did not rest until I had bought a certain sort of clothing.

818. Moreover, even an appetite for eating is aroused in spirits—even though they know, and say and affirm that they know, that they cannot eat—and in fact an appetite for specific foods is aroused, as happened today. Then when I promised to eat the foods in question today, the spirit quieted down.

Therefore, purely physical appetites do exist in spirits, which can be aroused by objects near a person, and then be aroused in the person by the spirit. 1748, 18 February.

By various experiences it has become clear that spirits believe they are people on earth

819. By much experience over a long period, it has been made clear to me that spirits do not know differently than that they are the same as myself, so that they have admitted it many times, with full assurance, declaring it to be so both when separated, and when joined to me in different ways. I was instructed by reflections, and by experiences, that spirits strictly believe that they are the person [they are with], both in respect to the person's reasoning power, or thinking, and to the body and bodily actions, even those that are characteristic; thus they imagine to be their own what the person thinks and does, indeed, that the whole person is themselves.

820. But of what quality they are can be recognized from their location with a person. The experience has been so abundant, and made so plain, and so sure, that if I were to bring forth all the instances of experience, it would be a larger undertaking than I would want to guess.

Spirits are educated my means of people on earth

821. That spirits are educated by the Lord by means of man, and in this way obtain enlightened knowledge, is most clear to me, having been borne out now by the almost continuous experience of two and three quarter years.[1]

822. That they likewise learn through other people who are not aware of this, is plain to me from many things that had happened to me before I spoke with spirits; and if I had reflected upon each incident at that time, I would have been quite certain about these facts, and able to assure everyone by experience alone.

Although this [instruction] is also accomplished by means of spirits, and a thousand other ways unknown to us, yet it should not be doubted that it is by the omnipotence of the Lord.

823. The reason [they are educated by the Lord] by means of man, as a spirit, is that they put on the whole person, and they put on everything of his or her memory, and are thus enabled to learn instantly—differently from people on earth, who must be instructed starting in infancy.

About permissions

824. The doctrine of permissions [*see* 398] also involves this, that evil spirits claim dominion over those who are evil, consequently over the evils in a person. They claim this as theirs by right, one even declaring that [evils] are theirs, because injected by them, so that they belong to them. For this reason, they claim dominion over every person who speaks falsely. And over one who is driven by passions, and thus evils, they also strive for dominion; but because

---

[1] See A. Acton, *An Introduction to the Word Explained*, pp. 113 *ff.*

every human is evil to the core, they are not given permission to rule except over those evils in a person that are added by actual life. But the permission does not extend beyond the purpose that the person may, through punishments and purges, be cured of these evils. This is one of the rules governing permissions. 1748, 18 February.

There are spirits who depict the kidneys and the bladder in the human being

825. Spirits who depict the kidneys, ureters and bladder in man are at the left side of the face, but toward the front, at the opening between the side of the temples and the forehead, closer to the forehead. They are of the kind who are not concerned with inward matters, much less very inward ones, nor do they understand them. Therefore when I spoke of and questioned them about such subjects, they said they did not understand them, although other spirits had understood them well.

These same ones also easily become indignant, as if from a kind of envy. They were indignant, for example, that good spirits were standing by and present with me, and they wanted to irritate them in various ways, so as to drive them away. Thus they do many things out of indignation, they are restless in spirit, and are not content with their lot—so that some property of the urine can be traced to them.

They are present, and I am speaking with them—they grow angry, go away, come back—there are many of them, and in lines. They are not deceitful, because they do this from a kind of irritable jealousy but not from deceit, and are like those in the life of the body who are called simply bad-tempered.

826. Moreover, at the left side appeared large swine joined together, by which are portrayed the earthy matters present in the urine, and being separated from the liquid. Thus depictions of earthy matters in urine are made by means of pigs so joined together, large ones, at the left side, not far off, on almost the same horizontal plane, if not somewhat higher. # #

829.[1] ## These same spirits sometimes ruminate over things said previously, which they retain in their memory and then become angry, wanting to find out the reasons why they were said in that way. Thus there is a kind of stickiness in them, also [*cf.* 810, 812].

827. The same ones who are like Kidneys, ureters and bladders, do not understand man's thoughts well, either. They do not penetrate to any but those that are superficial. Sometimes they ask whether something was said about them, when it concerned others, or whether something is true, when it is quite otherwise. 1748, 18 February.

There are also those who relate to the skin

828. There are spirits who relate to the outward human coverings also, but with these I have not spoken, only perceiving from them that they brought on warmth caused by exhalations through invisible pores. Now they are indeed speaking, saying it is they who cover all; but what they are like in other respects has not yet been revealed to me. 1748, 18 February.

There are spirits relating to the large ventricles of the brain

830.[2] The large ventricles of the brain are the chambers into which liquids flow from the spaces between the tissues, and from elsewhere, as is known. Thus they are, so to speak, the urinary bladders of the brain, where fluid, or lymph, is mingled with [animate] spirit and whence in turn, [animate] spirit and better elements are secreted, one after the other.

831. Those spirits are above the head, quite high up—not directly overhead, but a little toward the front, very little. They are good spirits, and they, too, spoke with me, quite pleasantly; for they operate, even speak, with a very pleasant flowing motion. They said that they constantly aspire to come to heaven, for they are not aware that they had been in heaven, and then been removed so as to be

---

[1] This paragraph is inserted in accordance with indications by the author.
[2] 829 is placed after 826, following the author's instructions.

better perfected, thus returning once again into heaven when the heterogeneous parts have been cast out from them. The case is just as it is with that fluid in the ventricles, part of which is absorbed by the choroid plexus: part is expelled from them, part seeps elsewhere; part passes over into the third ventricle under the pineal gland and thus through the infundibulum toward the pituitary gland, where it is separated into three quantities, which are borne through various paths, canals and cavities, towards the jugular vein, going to meet the chyle coming up through the thoracic duct. Mingled together there, they are carried toward the heart, thence into the lungs, then back into the left ventricle [of the heart] and thus onward, part toward the head through the carotid arteries, part downward toward all the internal organs of the body.

All these events conspire to the purpose of forming the purer blood, or animate spirit, and thus the red blood, so that by a uniting of material and spiritual elements, they may bring about a harmonious life. 1748, the 18th day of February.

About a state of innocence

832. Certain souls who had been with me were let into a state of innocence, and from it spoke with me through spirits; and they declared that it is a state of such joy and gladness, that the human ear, eye, mind, and understanding is incapable of perceiving it, for it is their innermost parts that are moved.

833. Where they were was above the forehead, upwards, a little toward the front.

834. They were with those of their parents, grandparents, great grandparents, and thus the whole family for two centuries back, who were together, and had been let into that heaven at the same time. The joy is such as to be entirely unutterable, as they are now telling me through spirits.

835. But they were only in the inmost region of the inward heaven[1]. For at each level there are three heavens, a spiritual one, one of peace, and one of innocence. Into the very inward heaven that is at the [next] higher level, no one can be admitted, who had not

---

[1] See 262 and footnote.

[first] been in the inward one, without being dissolved. 1748, 18 February.

About those who worship nothing except holiness in the world, and do not know any specifics about what true belief is

836. There are some who love to teach people only to worship a kind of holiness in general, without any knowledge of true belief. They are the kind who simply hear masses, which they pay no attention to both because they do not understand them, and because they do not care to understand. They only come into the temples to worship holiness; thus there are many places of this kind everywhere.

837. But holiness is of two kinds, namely, of those who put on an outer holiness in order to deceive people, and of those who so doing think themselves holy, believing this because they are so persuaded and completely ignorant of other matters. There are intermediate kinds besides, countless in number, the abovementioned being the two extremes.

838. A certain one appeared to me who believed himself to be holy and had persuaded those who were overhead to call themselves holy. But he was cast down from them, and presently they began to chant "holy, holy," in a melodious voice, and nothing else but "holy," for a full half hour, until he wearied of hearing it.

839. Such are those who love only a general holiness, who in the other life, chant "holy" until all feeling of holiness is gone and afterwards nothing living is left—only a bare term, in which they nevertheless place piety. Thus they worship something dead, in the same way as those who place piety in prayers and praying, even when their mind is far away. With this type they are somewhat comparable.

840. Near them there was a spirit being spun around, so that his nakedness appeared in an indecent manner, who portrayed a saint whom they adore in that holy state. The spirit was turned around and around, until his private parts showed. Such is the adoration of those who only worship holiness.

841. Moreover, someone naked also appeared, flame-colored, or like a flame, on bent knees and with his palms toward the Lord. Who he was, I was not told; I suppose that those are of his kind who believe they deserve salvation merely for their prayers, the flaming color meaning that they want to justify themselves, like [the Pharisee] in the temple [Luke 18:9–14], by their own merits. 1748, 18 February.

Mankind is completely unaware of being led by spirits, and by means of spirits

842. It is ever so clear, and known to everyone, that people are not conscious of being led by spirits, and by means of spirits. But that they are neverthelss so led, and quite obviously, is evident from manifold experience—for I have seen, perceived, heard, how one spirit was led by others, and then by still others as a group, and yet the spirit knows absolutely no otherwise than that he is leading himself, entirely like a person on earth.

It can be recognized what kind, or particular sort of spirit is leading another spirit, though not by that spirit being led. Spirits also can be led in the same way by a person on earth when in the spirit, as I have sometimes been given the ability to do. I then know it, and the spirits in company with me know, perceive, and more or less see [it happening], while the spirit who is being led is quite unaware of it, thinking that he is speaking on his own. This has sometimes been done by myself, and I was amazed that the spirit did not notice it, for it was obvious to me. 1748, 18 February.

About a city on this side of Gehenna

843. To many there also appears a large city, with tall buildings, situated in front of Gehenna [751], where many seem to themselves to dwell. Some who were there told others that they are in a calm city, where they do nothing but kindnesses to one another, and all things are done fairly, so that one does not harm another, but wants what is right. Such are allowed to stay in that city, but not others.

844. The city also appeared to me. The buildings are tall, sometimes with dark streets because of the tall buildings, nevertheless such that the whole length of the streets appears, and the sky shines through, showing the city's skyline, as in other large cities. Presently, when one could just make out its streets, then the closed in city appeared, and an unbroken line of very high buildings was displayed to me, the roofs of which I did not see, perhaps because they ended in the clouds. They had many windows, covering a square area on two sides. The color of the buildings on the outside was almost brick-like, or dark brownish.

845. This city and these buildings were almost joined together, and not divided up into houses, so that the city was all together, or like one building stretching out to all sides, and I was told that their rooms were also joined together, so that they could pass on the inside from room to room, thus throughout the whole city, as through a building covering a large area.

846. The rooms also were shown to me. The interiors were [built] of greyish colored boards joined together—single boards, but made into a one, only the joints in between being slightly visible. There was also something black portraying a fireplace. Their rooms are like this throughout the whole city, except for some varieties not shown to me; for the different types come forth according to the souls' fantasies, to which they correspond, presenting the same elements, and presenting them entirely true to life in the world. I spoke with some who were finding out for the first time that they were fantasies. They soon acknowledged that it was so: thus those who see, agree. 1748, 18 February. # #

Turn the page, and this is continued[1]

Continuation about the city in front of Gehenna

847. The rooms, as said above [845–46], are connected, and inside of a greyish color. As soon as they see little black clouds on the wall of a room, or black stripes like a cloudy black belt, then they at once leave that room for another, and so it goes on. Thus, to their delight, do the scenes keep changing.

848. Now and again, the vision of the city even fades away. Before this happens there commonly appears something like a large back stretched out in the room, or a voluminous form like the human

---

[1] This appears in the original at the bottom of the page.

back, which raises itself, stretched out, even to the roof. The roof then appears, with beams joined together in the form of a triangle, as roofs usually are in cities of the world, and up to it that back or voluminous form raises and stretches itself; and then it appears as if there is an opening at one side, of a sky blue color, yet in such a way that the beams of the roof are still visible. Then the illusion of a city passes away.

849. They who live there, or seem to live there, had said they live justly and fairly, and that they do not harm one another, but rather perform for each other civil kindesses. Some are even distinguished by a little flame on their caps, indicating that they want to justify themselves, or are self-righteous.

850. Moreover, there are also displayed to them many scenes with city buildings, such as arcades at ground level, long entryways, courts laid out along the arcades, and indeed, very magnificently, because the courts are joined together, communicating with and opening upon one another. Thus there are countless scenes, depending on the fantasies of each individual.

851. And although they sometimes seem to be living together, the city does not appear the same to one as it does to another, but according to each one's fantasized righteousness, or merit from self-righteousness, this being because the one is unable to see the other's fantasy or portrayal of the city, or to tell how it differs.

But the things which have been told about the city are common features; the various scenes cannot so well be described, but they relate to the same common features, as particulars. The outer and inner profiles are common [to all], as well as the height of the buildings, etc.

852. It seems that this city is the judgment of Gehenna [Matt. 23:33], for they want to live self-righteously. Thus [the city] seems to be able to condemn all to Gehenna who, according to their fantasy, do not behave and live righteously. From this attitude we find out what they are like, that is, those who think themselves most righteous from their own fantasy, not from true belief; hence this city is called the judgment of Gehenna.

1748, 18 February.

853. SPIRITUAL EXPERIENCES

See the continuation ♀ ♀

[♀ ♀] *Continuation on the city in front of Gehenna, and on the view of Gehenna from there*

853. That city is on almost the same plane as Gehenna, but somewhat, only a little, higher; so there also appeared to me a bridge leading from the city toward Gehenna. The bridge was of the same color as their rooms, namely, grey, but was raised on either side, so that it was quite safe to cross. The bridge was rather pretty, but at the city end of it, I saw a black spirit.

He was said to stand there so that they would not cross over; for they hate what is black, and shy away from it, while grey, which is a combined color, namely, white mixed with black—the color they also usually paint the ceilings of their rooms—symbolizes self-righteousness. For white is [the color] of righteousness. But black, although it is in their white, they shun, thinking it right and even devout to do so, thus damning others from their fantasy. And so they evaluate and examine the lives and the belief of all. Indeed, all the heretics who damn to Gehenna everyone who does not believe, think and act as they do, are like this.

854. Such are the ones who tarry there. The black [configurations] that prompt them to go off into different rooms [847], are fantasies, which they get rid of one by one; for that is the purging process some undergo, and indeed, it can take a long time. If they fail to get rid of them, something violent slips in and strikes terror, so that whenever they go back to the same fantasies, they are secretly frightened, and thereby also purged. But those who think it is calm there [843], and who love such dwellings, are purged the most slowly.

855. On the other side of the bridge mentioned above, there appeared the kind of glow that shines out in the sky from a huge fire, at no great distance from the other end of the bridge; and there, it was said, was Gehenna.

About a certain plane in man as to his feelings

856. There is in man something like a plane, which is portrayed as a soft substance lying beneath the outward, callus-like part of a person produced by bodily and worldly elements. This underlying plane or substance becomes visible when the superinduced exterior is removed. Yet I cannot rightly say how it is removed—only that the matter is portrayed in this way, that when it has been cast aside, something like a round, soft body or brain is portrayed, and that the person subsequently, when living from this body, now acts in accordance with his or her inward character, by which they govern their outward elements.

But because the outward elements are heaps of the individual's personal [qualities of life], they cannot be governed by the gentle inward body in such a way that it shines forth, except by a constant reflection upon one's actions and life, these being the criteria from which the wise will usually judge a human character.

That beneath this there is again a similar substance, still softer, I cannot doubt, because inside are the remains [of goodness] that are preserved by the Lord, and which the Lord Alone knows of. 1748, 18 February.

About a Spirit who confessed one God the Creator of the universe

857. A certain spirit came forth boldly and confidently, and during a conversation with others in which we were speaking about the Lord, asked self-confidently, so that I could at first suspect nothing else but that he believed, "Who is the Lord about whom you are speaking?" I said that He was Jesus Christ. He said that he did not know who this was, and that he had not heard of him, but that he only believed in the One God the Creator of the universe.

When I wanted him to inform me where he came from—whether he was from among the inhabitants of this earth, from India, Japan, Africa, or elsewhere—but was unable to find out, I could therefore not yet reply to these words, because spirits must be instructed according to the circumstances of their belief during earthly life. Therefore he moved on, saying that he wanted others to tell him who else was Lord, other than the one Creator of the universe.

2] But I was still able to speak with him, and said that no one can be saved without true belief; whereupon he asked what belief is, and how a person can be saved by belief—this also self-confidently. Finally I told him that anyone who does not believe in the Son, cannot believe in the one God, Creator of the universe, because all power has been given to the Son in the heavens and on the earth [Matt. 28:18].

858.   SPIRITUAL EXPERIENCES

In the end he was also unwilling to learn what the Son of God is, and that He is, because he cannot understand it; and he said he would never be able to understand that anyone was God's Son. Then I answered, that matters of belief are mysteries to the believers, which we should believe, even if we do not understand; and if we do not believe in the Son, it cannot be avoided that such are damned to hell [Mark 16:16]. But he insisted that he did not understand, therefore did not believe.

But I found out that there was a league of evil spirits for which he had served as a medium, and that he had been sent out to play this part, when yet he had known very well. Meanwhile these spirits, or this league, were as usual inspiring this same faith in general, and it was as if the whole realm were half-filled with that same opinion, or falsity.

858.   When, therefore, he had self-confidently expressed surprise that anyone believed something he did not understand, it occurred to me to bring forward something on the worldly and bodily plane that he believed, even though he did not understand it, namely, first, whether # #

Continuation on the spirit confessing God the Creator of the universe

859.   he understood how people on the antipodal side of the earth can walk, when, from our point of view, their heads point down. (For when this is portrayed in a spiritual manner, and a person is placed in the opposite region of the globe, spirits almost detest it, and suddenly vanish, because they do not understand it, as has sometimes happened.)

Then he denied any such thing, but when I convinced him that nothing is truer, as all experience testifies and proves, then this is what he had to admit: that he did not understand it, even though it is true, and he therefore ought by all means to believe it.

860.   Later I said to him, "Do you believe you are a human being, dressed in clothes, and thus a person on earth?" And he touched what seemed to be his clothing he thought he had on, he touched his hands, which he believed he had, and I asked where he stood, whether he had feet; he said that he did. But when he was asked what ground it was that he was standing on, whether it was not in a realm above the earth, he acknowledged that it was, so I brought him to realize whether these things are only fallacies of the senses, and illusion, because he was a spirit.

Being thus convinced, he wanted to flee away, and said that he had been persuaded by the others to behave in this way. So he was able to recognize that they were mere sensory fallacies, of which there are thousands, all false; so that if we only believed what we understand, we would believe only things that are false, to speak only of worldly and bodily matters. How then could anyone say that he wants to believe nothing in regard to spiritual and heavenly matters, which he does not understand, when they are very far, in fact the farthest removed from the senses—[knowing] also that unless a person believes those things which are true, and is thus in the way of truth, he can by no means be admitted into heaven? 1748, 18 February.

861. Consequently, since the human understanding is so full of fallacies arising from the bodily senses that it is formed by nothing else but fallacies, and into nothing but fallacies, so that there is only darkness in it, therefore it is amazing if anyone of sound mind, wanting to think aright, would decide or maintain that he would by no means believe matters of faith, or of light, or of heaven, or even more, which are Divine, unless he understood them.

About the callus, or the bodily and worldly elements which form the callus

862. It is remarkable that that heap which is built up of bodily and worldly elements [*see* 856] is pictured as a hard callus, or as an outer crust. In some, this callus appears thicker and harder; in some it does not appear, but it is nevertheless there. That callus is a heap of fallacies of the senses, consequently of falsities glued together by the loves of self and of the world, which must indeed be softened, but not broken, for it has its roots from the inward parts, and this callosity from the more inward.

When the removal of this callus is being pictured, such as it appears by a spiritual display in the realm of spirits, then an underlying medullary substance is seen, almost such as exists in a person on earth, in whom the callous substance is depicted by bony skull, and the inward parts by medullary brain tissue.

863. Scattered within this callus are also good and true elements which sprout forth from the medullary body as a root, and are thus implanted. It was portrayed to me how those good and true elements scattered in the callus were removed [along with it], but withdrew themselves toward the inward parts. Thereupon those from whom they had been removed, crying out, said that now they did not believe anything—that there is a heaven, a God, or anything spiritual and heavenly, and that it appeared to them as if they were nothing, or nobody. A number underwent this who nevertheless are believers, or had been before these elements were taken away.

864. Hence it can be evident that the Lord permits these same interspersed elements to be taken away from people in the world, that is, to withdraw themselves toward the inward parts, for many reasons spoken of in His Word. But as soon as they were restored, they returned to their original state of belief. 1748, 18 February.

865. Calluses in which elements savoring of deceit are mingled, as in those who had tried to cheat their neighbor, cannot readily be softened and dissolved, for which reason this is done by means of the punishment of being pulled apart by opposites, spoken about previously [404, 515]. The person is placed between two contrary actions, or spirits working at cross-purposes, unable to get away from them and so, is being pulled apart with the greatest of pain. The like happens to those, especially business people, who, without conscience and at every opportunity—when not prevented for various reasons, such as the laws, profit motives, etc.—try cunningly to take away their neighbors' goods, thinking that this does no harm to the conscience. There are also others having the same intention, who may not have carried it out, but had wanted to, and only place and circumstance had prevented them from proceeding to the act. 1748, 18 February.

Philosophical studies so limit the human mind that in the end, they can see nothing [see 609, 767]

866. Philosophical studies have, since their first centuries, and for about a thousand years now, consisted only in terminology and syllogism. And because what [philosophers] avidly dwell upon are only terms, such as what "form" is, what "accidents" are, what "modes," and so forth, it cannot but turn out that their mind is bounded only by ideas without any life, because without light. For they do not connect them to rational elements, and those they do so connect are nevertheless mere terms. In arguing for these terms, they are like one who is learning the words of a language, not for the sake of expressing the meaning of a thing, but only for the sake of talking. Thus they so confine and restrict universal elements of the mind into that which has no life, or which is only material, and so doing, form such a dark callus, that no light can pass through.

It is similar also with syllogistic philosophy. It so encloses the ideas of the mind, that there is hardly a crack for the light [to enter]. Wise people of this kind are consequently much more blind, even more stupid, in spiritual and heavenly matters, than the least person in the crowd, or than farmers. 1748, 18 February.

On the torture of spirits who want to be high

867. There are some spirits, or troops of spirits, who wander around, periodically arriving back at the same places. [I was told] that souls and spirits are extremely afraid of them, for they torment them with a certain kind of torture.

I was afterwards instructed that these are they who portray the inner basal lining or upper part of the bladder in general, that is, the parts which there insert into the bladder, such as the umbilical ligaments, the muscles, the nerves, which spread out from there and come together towards its sphincter.

These same ones who were with me today, therefore, are those who relate to the sphincter of the neck [of the bladder], or the entrance to the urethra; for their torture is like strangury, and indeed, from the beginning even to the outlet of the urethra.

868. Those troops of spirits return periodically, because they portray how that sphincter must operate periodically, or at its own proper times, and in the meantime must be at rest until those substances have been collected which are to be cast out and evacuated. A similar process occurs in the realm of spirits or souls with regard to falsities.

869. When these troops of spirits come, they apply themselves to the back side, down low, almost at the tailbone. Their presence is noticed from their operation; otherwise they do not appear.

870. Their method of working and torturous twisting is rapid, consisting of quick back and forth motions, which no one can hold back. It is even accompanied by sound; and they direct their quick binding and tightening motion upwards, above the forehead. Their operation appears like a cone coming to a point upwards, and anyone who comes within this cone, especially toward its apex, is pitiably squeezed together, and twisted in every least joint of the body; so that in the spirit being thus tortured, there is nothing but a twisting of all parts, back and forth.

The torture was visible to me, especially that of the joints of the arm, and that of the rest of the joints of the body below the head. This twisting back and forth appears cruel, and spirits told me that it is crueler than anyone could ever conceive. When one of them has thus been twisted, others follow, as many of those present as have accumulated such urinous elements. They have to be cast out, for they are fantasies engendered by falsities, to which urine in the material world corresponds.

But they do not twist the region of the head, because there are situated the calluses engendered by desires. By the joints of the arms and of the chest or thorax are portrayed fantasies resulting from reasoning, so they have to do with spiritual matters, and belong to the spiritual class, as do all those who assist [in this torture]. For there had been some who assisted from above, which displeased me, so they were indeed sent in, and they were those who composed the province of the kidneys, and thence of the ureters, because these insert into the bladder, and assist. Also they stood at the side like the ureters, which come in at the side, but, as said, from above, while those who had worked the sphincter and portray it, did so from below. They say that the torment is severe, and annoying.

871. Those are inserted [within that cone] who are puffed up by their fantasies and, on account of delusions engendered by their [false] reasoning, consider themselves to be above others. This is clear from the location where the torture takes place. 1748, 19 February.

Some others, also wanting to undergo the same tearing apart, were just below the left foot, and they said that they had never felt anything so painful, or believed it to be possible. 1748, 11 September.

FROM THE *BIBLE INDEX* 875.

About a spirit who desired most intensely to come into heaven

872. A certain spirit from among those of Jupiter came to me and earnestly requested that I intercede on his behalf, so that he could come into heaven. He described his own state: that he was unaware of having committed evil, that he merely threatens the inhabitants of the region, and afterwards instructs them. He was one of those at the left side, below, who speak as if they had a forked tongue. These have been discussed earlier [570].

873. He also had the ability to arouse pity, so that I could not answer him in any other way than by telling him I cannot bring about anything, and that if deserving, he, like other worthy people, may have hope of coming into heaven. But when he was sent back among the good spirits of that earth, they said later on that he cannot remain in their company, because he is not like them.

874. Again he came to me, and from an innermost longing, he begged them earnestly, saying that he desired heaven most intensely; and he would not stop. When this was heard, he was received into the company of good spirits from our earth, but these declared that he could by no means remain in their company. He was called by spirits of his own earth a *skorstensfejare*[1], meaning that in his bodily life he had cleaned chimneys, causing him to be of a black color, though he himself says that he is brown.

875. All this leads me to conclude that it is spirits like these who constitute the province of the seminal vessels, where the good seed gathers, together with the liquid it combines with so that it will be fit to be emitted, and later broken down in the neck of the womb; for the seminal vessels store up this substance.

His desire to go to heaven indicates his desire for regeneration, or to enter the womb so that he can be reborn a new man. In spite of his having this kind of outer form, it is by virtue of the inner form that he longs for, or desires outwardly, nothing but heaven; and it is for this reason that he was able to arouse pity. Such a desire is indeed characteristic of the particles contained in the seminal vessel.

---

[1] Swedish for "chimney sweep."

876. His function, that of threatening somewhat, indicates the same thing, because it is the duty of such spirits to do so, though not as severely as others. But thereupon he instructs them as to how their life should be improved, thus outwardly, how a person should be made ready so as to have truths, since the knowledge of truths serves that purpose. So if he were allowed to teach about heaven, he would also want to do so, but he is not permitted to because he is still among spirits of that kind and has that outer form.

877. After this form is put aside, like the calluses spoken of previously [862–65], then the new or inward person arises, who is prepared by the Lord Alone. This is portrayed in the world by little worms being transformed into nymphs, and presently, with the wings given them, flying in their own heaven, or joy, or in the air—having their own heavenly [lives], suited to their nature, and playing amongst themselves, laying eggs, and gathering delightful foods from the flowers appointed for them; besides other circumstances that pertain to them, unknown to us. 1748, 19 February.

About some rooms belonging to good spirits of the female sex

878. Rooms belonging to certain spirits of the female sex were shown to me, which are fashioned for them, and which they see as clearly as people on earth see theirs. There are entryways that open into their longer sides. They sit in the room to the side of the entrance, so as not to be gazed at. The walls are designed in many patterns, with floral combinations and similar lovely displays spread out across the wall; but I cannot describe the various scenes because they are countless, following in turn one upon another, with now brighter now lesser degrees of light, in different colors, sprouting forth delight.

879. The room is lit up, sometimes more than things illuminated by our own daylight, but sometimes the scenes following one upon another are rather dim; and when these imaginative pictures vanish, then something that seems to depict a window appears on the wall and grows wider and wider. Yet it is still dark, and no light enters, [the rooms] being for the most part dark in color. After a while some sky appears, with a cloud in it, and far off, little stars. In this way their rooms are changed into more pleasant ones.

880. Those virgin spirits, who had been here for some time, began to burn with the desire to return to their own chambers, saying that they have their greatest enjoyment when they are there, because the scenes are so delightful; and they cannot possibly tell otherwise than that they are real. They are telling me now with assurance that they are—something I too can affirm, only in the sense that the imagery with which they are portrayed is so vivid. For I have seen things like these so many times, with closed eyes, in their own light—altogether as in daylight—that nothing has now become more familiar to me. In fact, all things whatsoever in the inward realm can be shown in such a vivid way, that nothing seems out of the ordinary: even written material can be placed right under my eyes, so that I can read the writing as if from an open book—and this when I am in a wakeful state, at the same time engaged in lively discussion with spirits.

About a bare arm shown to me [see 1754]

881. Again an arm was shown to me, but a bare one, bent forward. Then I was given to know that arms depict strength; for such arms convey the fear for power—as on a previous occasion, when I was frightened [*cf.* 541]. The force of that arm is so great that if it were allowed, it would break the bones of a living person. This is true, even though no one can believe it except from experience, frequently spoken of elsewhere sporadically.

882. Another property of this arm was, that a kind of warmth exhaled from it, which I felt, and was told about. 1748, 19 February.

Angels can improve to infinity, that is, to eternity, yet
never become perfect

883. I spoke with the spirits around me about the fact that no one is perfect but the Lord Alone. The angels are not perfect, for Heaven is not holy before the Lord [*cf.* Job 15.15]; nevertheless, the angels can improve more and more, and even to eternity, yet never become holy in themselves, or as to what is their own.

Because this struck spirits as odd when it had been pictured in a spiritual manner, it was therefore illustrated by similar occurrences in nature, specifically, that there are things approaching infinity, as they call it, *yet which never reach it, like the asymtotes of a hyperbola*[1]; *but we may pass over these examples, since many do not understand them. Universal principles fall more readily under [the view of] the understanding.*

It was shown, moreover, that angelic minds are only instruments for receiving the beliefs of religion, and must therefore be developed; hence, that they grasp only the most general principles; but the details, which are infinite, even in every least object, can be filled in, although never completely, but only as to the most general ones, since the angels are finite instruments. So those details, when they are as it were inscribed by the Lord on their general principles, are what more and more perfect the angel; and because they can be filled in even to infinity, and the angel thus developed and perfected to infinity, he can never arrive at perfection, and therefore not at [a state of] holiness, so that heaven can never be holy in the Lord's sight. 1748, 19 February.

About the spirit longing for heaven

884. The same spirit spoken of earlier [872], who so ardently longed for heaven, came to me once more, and was dressed in I think even shabbier clothing. He said that he was really burning with desire to come to heaven; but he was still seemingly reproachful, being among those spirits of Jupiter who are eager to punish. This time he showed me a new action he had not known of before, namely, a kind of gently pulsating one around the part of the back above the hipbones, where a motion occurs like that of shaking at the knees; and he explained that he was now in this condition. I told him that this was a sign of shortly coming into heaven, for the reason that I knew him to be one of the sort who correspond to the genital vessels, where the generative particles are clothed with something like crusts, membranes or mantles, so that they can safely tarry there and eventually be safely transferred into the womb, there to be broken down gradually until the enclosed spiritual elements find their way to the ova.

His new kind of clothing told that he was now prepared for the exit; his action, that the moment was now at hand, for this is how the generative particles in the seminal vessels behave, when the

---

[1] The manuscript has *parabola*, but see *Divine Providence* 335.

time is at hand. His garment was now more crude, and in fact, having been told to cast off his clothing and thus come into heaven, he from his strong desire cast off his clothing so quickly that nothing could have been done more quickly. But this happened only for the sake of testing him, and of teaching me what the desires are like of those who relate to the seminal vessels in the other life. But he could not be received, as said [873–74], so he returned into his original state. Now he spoke with a forked tongue even worse [than before, 570], and was below the region where he had been before, being now in a shabbier condition on the outside. Those who later reach the point of passing from these bodily conditions to inward ones, and then on into what is heavenly, are brought by a way at the back, then between the knees, and are so raised up. 1748, 20 February.

About the determination of souls toward definite goals,
as well as their development in the other life,
and about the inward memory

885. Such as people have developed in their bodily life, and such as they therefore are at the point of death, so they remain. They first of all encounter the circumstances that had existed at the point of death, and during the terminal illness, or final period of life. Next they are introduced into different groups made up of good spirits, whose place it is to discover what their natural inclinations are like. This duty they perform as if it were their own [judgment], scarcely knowing otherwise [628]. So, depending on how they are found to be, they are either received into better circles, or they are received into worse circles, as befits their natural character. So this is done by a method of consent, or of love and aversion, all and the least details of which are arranged by the Lord.

These things I have learned through manifold experience, and I have seen, heard and sensed them. They have told what [the souls being examined] are like in this state, what they are like in that. For of course, they are at first carried along largely by opinions and convictions they had adopted [in the world]; but experience teaches [the examiners] whether they are of this nature, or that. Meanwhile they are in their element, and almost their very life, when they can test the spirits coming up to them by their own and diverse methods. The reasons for this are many, in addition to the dominating one among spirits, namely, that they are curious, and eager to know what others are like, and what is what. Enlightened knowledge in general is spiritual food, wherefore these longings and desires [to know] correspond to the bodily appetites for eating and drinking. For this reason, higher knowledge is also called spiritual food, and hence come the deeper meanings of bread, grain, wheat, milk, water, and so on.

886. Moreover, I have observed that when souls are kept in a universal, indefinite state, they are thinking almost nothing, but dwelling upon something general without any clear idea, almost as people on earth do when they seem to themselves to be thinking nothing. Nevertheless, this what might be called general contemplation has its own focusses and consequently, changes, unfamiliar to man, but recognized in heaven.

However, in this state I was able to realize, as was also corroborated by spirits, that as a result, a soul cannot be reformed as to outer life, before he is brought back into a state where his mind is directed toward mental images familiar to him, or dominant in him during his life. Then for the first time, [thoughts] conducive [to his reformation] can be inspired and take hold.

887. The memory of spirits or souls is, as has been said, an inward one, but not a memory of personal affairs, like that of a person on earth. For a memory of personal matters is useful to one on earth, meeting the needs that living in the body and the world dictate.

But the memory of spirits is an inward one, unfamiliar to [recently arrived] souls, so that whenever I have spoken about it with souls, they thought it did not exist—which happened quite often, for during their life they had been unaware of it. Yet their reveries, and like phenomena, which they love, pertain to that memory, and their passions are the result of an imaginary harmony in fantasies, comparably as some enjoy instruments that are not harmonious, but harsh sounding and out of tune; while others enjoy only those which harmonize rightly and well.

888. As for that inward memory, and how spiritual knowledge is instilled into spirits, this cannot be understood except from things that take place in the life of the body, as that a person from early childhood learns to speak, learns to think, and this little by little, and does not know at all how these abilities, still less the faculties of understanding, thinking, judging, forming conclusions, are instilled into us. Likewise, an adult person in learning languages; or, as I have noticed in my own case, that I have been instructed in this same way in the duties of my office, so that they became fixed in my mind by experience alone, without any memory of particular [methods]. *(The latter instance is mentioned only so that it can be understood what the nature of that memory is, not so as to insert something about myself.)* 1748, 20 February.

Continuation on the inward memory

889. The deeper memory develops like the disposition, or the native character, and like the understanding, as well as many other human faculties (see above [888]). For whatever gives the memory of personal matters its ability, is directly due to the inward memory, but [ultimately,] that power, regarded in itself, is a property of life.

a] That there is a deeper memory, and what it is like, can be understood from the fact that in dreams, where the memory of personal matters is not so active as when one is awake, people normally appear with all their features, and every characteristic of their body, their speech, having the same walk, etc., more than the person [dreaming] had ever known from the memory of personal matters, nor could describe in such an abundance [of detail]. Similarly, we recognize people's moods or changing states of mind from their facial expressions, also from their eyes and the surrounding region, as well as from their tone of voice, and many more details beyond description. And people do not know where they learned to do this, except only from practice, without [previous] knowledge.

890. So that these facts might be portrayed to me in a living manner, a spirit of the kind who can be persuaded of anything whatever came to me; for there are very many such spirits. They themselves know absolutely no otherwise than that they are the very ones [whom they impersonate]. Therefore, different persons can be produced through them, almost as in real life. Consequently, lest anyone with whom spirits speak be misled, let it be known that this phenomenon is most common and familiar in the realm of spirits.

The spirit in question was examined by many, so that they might find out who of my acquaintances he had been during his bodily life. Finally, there was a certain person—whether he had died I do not know, about a half a year ago he was alive—whom they took him to be, because his personality could be put on so precisely. So he came into the company of spirits who could find out from me what that acquaintance was like, since, as just said, they are gifted with a cognition of inward properties. So that very person was portrayed as vividly as if it were he himself, in most respects. They are still convinced that it is he, and this, to them, amounts to the same thing as if this [persuasion] were being induced on me, as I said before. Nevertheless, I kept saying it could be that he is that person, but that I did not feel convinced, since such phenomena do occur. 1748, 20 February.

891. Moreover, even good spirits were not able to tell but that it was that same person, because all and the least details can be counterfeited so as to corroborate it. Inward angels, however, know [the truth], as I was told and shown.

He who is led by the Lord, sees in every least thing he does whether it is [merely] permitted, whether consent is given and the thing is pleasing [to Him], in short, whether it should be done

891[a].[1] There is with those who are being led by the Lord a certain inward sight or consciousness in regard to things that are to be done, especially in the act of doing them. This sight is so clear to those who are led by the Lord, that they do not do any least thing unless it is either by the Lord's good pleasure, or by His consent, or by His permission. These are distinct from each other, and the person is also given to see them distinctly, but this fact cannot be understood by anyone except by such a one.

Others, no matter how well the matter is explained, along with all the circumstances, still do not believe it, because they do not understand. For example, even spirits who are quite intelligent still cannot be convinced that it is so. They who know it, and do not want to think from themselves, and are therefore in the way of truth, acquire such a sight. The main reason why others cannot believe this is that they think they would then be deprived entirely of their own free will in doing and thinking what they love, supposing

---

[1] In the original, the number 891 is repeated here and 892 does not occur. It is left unchanged here because it is referred to in the index.

they would thus be as if dead. I said to them, however, that then they are alive, because living from oneself is rather death, because there is nothing of good from what is one's own. Therefore no one should be surprised if someone says he sees what should be done; because this is truth, and it is part of faith. 1748, 20 February.

About those who relate to the pancreatic duct, the hepatic duct, and the gall bladder

893.[1]   There are spirits relating to these three members, who, while distinct among themselves, are nevertheless brought together in relation to the state of those spirits whom they work upon. Especially, they stand by at chastisements and punishments, which they want to direct, so to speak; and the worst of them are so stubborn that they never let up, unless compelled by punishments, or things that frighten them, whereupon they promise they will no longer do all those things. But immediately thereafter, they return to the same nature.

They are those who had clung to their own opinions and illusions very tenaciously, yet who do not act out of hatred, but out of a natural perverseness. (Such appear as little old women of the kind who grow old in their passions, stubbornly holding on to them.) In their normal state, they think about and dwell on nothing else—and I do not know whether they take pleasure in anything else—than being allowed to engage in such activities, and to chastise, whip, bite, and the like cruel behavior, just as do those biles, especially the gall. All they want is to be engaged in their foul [practices]. 1748, 20 February.

About the speech of angels of the inward heaven[2]

894.   Today angels spoke among themselves, for quite a while, but their speaking was not at all understandable to me. I perceived it only as a gentle, wave-like motion overhead, up and down. The spirits around me can also perceive the same thing, but can understand nothing.

---

[1] See the footnote to 891[a].
[2] See 262 and footnote.

Moreover, they also speak clearly amongst themselves, saying many things simultaneously in one connected utterance, which I could make out from the fact that many things were said on a certain quite lengthy subject, and it was done in a matter of moments, as has also happened several times before.

895. Some may be surprised at this, but when a written text is being read, and the reader is not paying attention to or understanding the words written, then the meaning and understanding of the subjects rises up to the angels more clearly than when the earthly human mind participates. When the meaning of something has to be grasped more clearly, then it is as if the bodily senses must be withdrawn from the inward mind. The result is that the mental image always becomes clearer, because freed of hindering objects. It is like when the mind does not dwell upon words or expressions, which are the body of speech.

This may seem amazing, and thus paradoxical, namely that the angels understand the meaning of something written, even if the person [reading it] does not understand it; nevertheless, it is most true, for it was proven today by experience. From this one may infer that when little children are reading the holy Bible, angels understand and see the meaning of the Word more clearly than when grownups are reading it, as has also been told to me before. 1748, 20 February.

Souls have a memory of personal circumstances when these are displayed to them spiritually

896. Whenever any soul who had been known to me during his bodily life came up to me, not knowing that he was in the other life, but thinking he was still in the body, or the world, and I then displayed to him by spiritual mental images, as if they were actual, persons, places, cities, houses, rooms, where he had been or which he had seen in bodily life, then he recognized all things, just as they were.

Thus souls can have such personal matters recalled to their mind by others, although they cannot do this of themselves. But it can be done by a person with whom the soul is, and in this way also he may learn that he is in the other life, as well as by various questions, such as Where does he suppose himself to be, in what place? 1748, 20 February.

About inward sight and conviction

897. Souls and spirits can never understand that a person can see and be convinced from the Lord, what should be thought, spoken and done; for they do not believe any other insights are possible than those which spring from themselves or from what is their own. Thus they never wanted to acknowledge that such inner sight exists—even those who were quite sharp, or clever, in the life of the body, and in the afterlife, and seem to themselves able to penetrate and to understand every single subject.

Whenever this sight and conviction came under discussion, they could not conceive otherwise than that if their own or proper self were absent, then they would no longer exist, but that it would be someone else who was thinking, speaking, doing, so that one would be like a kind of implement, in which there was nothing living, like a wooden machine or something of that kind. For they cannot conceive of any life other than the life that is their own, thinking that if this were taken away, they would either not be alive at all, or, as one is now saying, be too stupid ever to be a soul or spirit.

898. Those souls or spirits, however discerning they may be in other matters, and receptive of understanding, nevertheless cling so hard to these ideas that they do not doubt them, but deny [any other life]. The reason for this is, as said, that when their own or proper self is taken away, then they think there is nothing left but something they reject. And I told them that the difference of life between those who do not have this inner sight and conviction [and those who do], is like that between something very faint—so faint as to be nothing—and heaven, or such as the difference between darkness and light, or indeed between what comes forth from man's lowest parts or rectum, and what descends from the universal heaven. In fact, a kind of vat was portrayed to me, almost like the infernal one [285], thus it is just like the difference between this tub—where hellish spirits imagine that they possess the whole heaven (for they think that the vat or tub is the universe, under their sway)—and the universal heaven with its flames and light.

899. For there are two routes to the human understanding, namely the way through the senses, that is, the lower way, by which the human understanding is born, and there is the way through heaven from the Lord, which is the higher way. Whatever is born by the lower way is bodily and material, while what is born by the higher way is spiritual and heavenly. Unless the higher door is opened by the Lord, it can never be believed that such communication exists that one may see and be convinced. Yet from this source, there is conscience in many people. However, this conscience for the most part regards actions, and consists of a recognition of those things considered as matters of worship and duty; so it is not a true conscience, except faintly in some good people and spirits. But in angels it is clear, so that they know, perceive, understand that a thing is so, and that there is no life without that manifest conscience and conviction of realities, made manifest in various ways.

900. They were extremely surprised whenever I have said that I can do nothing from myself, when yet they had often seen how many duties had been done, from me. And when I repeated that these had not been done by me, but through me, so that I seem to myself to have performed them, when yet I had not performed even the least particle from myself, but it was the Lord, then they were still more surprised. It struck them as a paradox, whereas it is a truth that can never be contradicted, and is not contradicted by any of the angels, but corroborated. And after they had heard the corroborations from heaven, they seemed to themselves to believe it is so. But they do not believe it, because they neither see, nor understand.

901. Besides the corroborations from heaven, other confirmations were also added from experience, of which there are very many. When they then directed their minds to them, they were able to understand that it is true, because, by a spiritual method, revealing experience was set right before their eyes. But as soon as the experience had passed, together with its reality, or light of understanding, they slipped back into their former ignorance, and could not grasp that this can exist, and that this is life. This is because they consider a mere earthly glow, in itself darkness, to be light, and to them, light cannot appear as anything but darkness. But where, and of what kind the darkness is, can only be seen in the light, or by those who are in light, the Lord Alone enlightening and revealing it. 1748, 21 February.

902. Such inward seeing and conviction can never be obtained without belief in the Lord; for it is His, and therefore His gift, and not one whit thereof belongs to man, soul, spirit, or angel.

About spiritual harmony, and happiness

903. There are heavenly, and there are spiritual elements, which are distinct both in people on earth and in the heavens. Those who are spiritual are allotted their own provinces in the human body, and those who are heavenly theirs. Everything related to the lungs pertains to spiritual elements, and everything related to the heart to heavenly ones, and so with the rest.

904. The spiritual have their own proper types of happiness that differ from those of the heavenly, as the gladness of the spiritual does from the joy of the heavenly.

In order that spiritual types of gladness or happiness may be understood, an idea of them can be gotten from the harmonies of sounds, as well as from visual harmonies. Harmonies of sound, including speech, especially the meanings of speech, pertain to spiritual harmony, and the gladness resulting therefrom is spiritual gladness, due to which the music of the Church of old, and due to which singing in the heavens, is so delightful. Likewise, visual harmony, and the various forms of beauty therefrom, which touch the mind— and beauty in general, such as that of pleasure gardens and all things of that kind, or of buildings—these also pertain to spiritual gladness. More deeply, so does [the beauty] of understanding, hence the love of truth itself, or of truths, and consequently of enlightened knowledge. Spiritual gladnesses are the forms of heavenly qualities, which are—or if they are not, yet should be—their very essence.

905. The remaining senses, however, such as touch, taste, and smell, belong to the provinces of the heavenly, for they are not spiritual enjoyments. From this, the difference between spiritual and heavenly happiness can be learned, as well as what a person would be like if deprived of this or that sense.

906. An angel was telling others by an angelic method how many kinds of happiness there are in the inward heaven[1]. He did this

---

[1] See 262 and footnote.

by an enumeration and an angelic portrayal of them to the clear sight of the angels. But that display was not visible to me except in the form of wave-like motions, and from them I was able to learn in a general way that only the kinds of happiness of the inward heaven were being gone through. Those enumerated and vividly portrayed during the first 4 to 6 minutes amounted to 478, thus almost 500; so I would put it at 500.

Since there are that many kinds of happiness in the inward heaven, one can infer from this how many species there are, since countless species exist in each kind, and in turn how many individual types of happiness there are, since a countless number of these exist in each species. And there are many further subdivisions, such as particulars of the individual types, when each of these in turn is taken as a species or as a whole kind, lower or higher, as it is within a society where that specific or individual type of happiness abides.

907. It can also be inferred from this how numberless, and how ineffable, are the things that can be told and displayed by an angel within one minute, which would take such a long time to describe in spoken words, and even then cannot be described. 1748, 21 February.

About the greedy, and their life after death [see 384]

908. There are many kinds of greed, and many species. Those who are stingy, and thus by frugality have gathered and heaped up money and wealth, are penalized in a different manner after the life of the body than those who exercise greed by cheating others and acquiring wealth by any means, right or wrong. Here we refer only to the kind of greed in those who amass riches, setting the heart upon them, and placing the happiness of life therein, even though they do not do so by unlawful means.

909. So that their life might be described, a dark room appeared to me, which I do not remember [seeing before], and leaving it was a person who, during his life, had been the kind who could get hold of the goods of others by cunning or trickery. For wherever something profitable was to be expected, there his mind was; so that he placed himself in many such situations where he might, on some plausible pretext, carry off something. This kind dwell almost where the worst deceitful hellish spirits are, at one side of hell, at man's back somewhat toward one side, verging toward the left flank. For deceits are of many varieties, these having gain as their object. They are about at the level of the shoulder blade.

910. I heard a heavy rumbling, like that of a huge mill. It was nearly at my left side, above me, but I did not know what it was. Presently, someone was lying near me at the left side, around the same region, who, as if in sleep, said nothing but "I am nothing, I am no one, I am no one, jag är ingenting[1]." I supposed that this was the kind of purging, or desperation, that occurs before they are raised up from the lower earth; it must also be another way of expressing that he ought to be pitied.

When he sensed that I was near him, I began to speak with him, and I was able to find out that he was from that crowd that pile up riches, keeping their mind on them and deriving their deepest thrills from them, especially if there is silver and gold in their strongboxes—without having done anything deceptive or unlawful in acquiring them. I further realized that such spirits speak this way from a kind of anxiety, namely, because there are in the vicinity those who covet what belongs to others and want to acquire it deceitfully, or by trickery, and are able to justify this on various pretexts by which they cover themselves, not at all fearful for eternal life.

These [covetous spirits] being in the vicinity, trouble them, and for this reason they thus lie on their strongboxes or riches, wondering whether such are present, for they are very often molested by them. Therefore they cry out amongst themselves loudly enough that the robber will hear them, that they are nothing, that they are pitiable, and will refrain from plundering them. Such are the miserable lives of those who get their deepest joy from silver, gold and riches.

That mill, or sound like the grinding of a mill, consisted of the murmurings, each in his own way, of many such spirits, fearing that their riches might be seized.

---

[1] Swedish for "I am nothing."

911. Moreover, because these had not acquired their money and wealth by deception or by any indiscriminate means, fair or foul, inwardly within that lamentation that they are nothing and that they are to be pitied lies something good into which later, after some time, those sayings on account of the robbers that they are nothing and are to be pitied, are gradually changed. Afterwards, when they forget the robbers and the money, they only fear spiritual robbers, and acknowledge themselves to be nothing because they can do nothing in their own defense. Then also they cry out, that the Lord may have pity on them. Thus insanity is turned into this kind of quality. 1748, 21 February.

The evil spirits also have stars around them

912. An evil spirit from the earth Jupiter, and also evil and even treacherous spirits from this earth, often have stars about them, and a view of heaven as well. This symbolizes the spiritual element that flows into their reasonings, and also the fact that they are able to understand something of faith. 1748, 21 February.

About those who depict the funnel[1] in the brain

913. First a face appeared to me at the top of a sky blue window, which soon withdrew inside; then a little star appeared in the vicinity of my left eye; presently, farther away from me and higher up, some tiny little stars, twinkling. These were spiritual stars, because they sparkled with white (som brillianter[2]). Then I saw walls, but not a roof, the walls being only at the left side, then a starry sky, with many stars. Because this was at a somewhat lower location, on a level with my arm, and near the quarter where treacherous spirits are, I was thinking that something horrible would meet my sight. But soon the wall and the sky vanished, and a well appeared to me, out of which issued what seemed like a bright mist, or vapor, like a hardly visible smoke. It also seemed as if some substance was being pumped out of the well.

---

[1] The Latin word, *infundibulum*, is also the English term.
[2] Swedish for "like diamonds."

914. When I asked what these things mean, or depict, I was told that this is how the infundibulum in the brain is portrayed, the nature of which is patent from the term that describes it, namely, that it receives solute spirits from the blood that have been moistened along the way by a suitable liquid so as not to escape through the pores, and so they are carried down along many paths into the large ventricles, and from there through their foramen under the pineal gland into the cleft, or third ventricle, and from there into the funnel, and so into the pituitary gland. There a separation takes place, and by certain routes they are brought down to the ends of the sinuses and into the jugular veins.

Thus do the [animate] spirits resolved from the blood globules and joined there in the cortical beginnings with new spiritual essences travel, brought down through their own tissues into the ventricles, and then through the funnel into the blood, so as to vivify the dry and lifeless blood at the ends of the sinuses, and to be brought then to meet the chyle just arriving from the body, and to be combined with it in the heart, thus vivifying the blood stream in the heart.

All these details, and the whole process, so lengthy to describe, were told by angels to other angels, and took but a moment, or about one second.

915. So that it might be plain to me what those spirits are like who constitute the province of that funnel in the heavenly body, there was a company of them, acting as one person. He heard me speaking, and [although] I did not manage to speak with him, nevertheless he either applied to himself whatever was said, thinking it was being said about him, or he became indignant, constantly scurrying toward me and away from me—in imitation of that fluid in the ventricle, which is constantly being driven back and forth from the vertex to that horn of the funnel. They are quite impatient and cannot be held down, are quick, attentive to details. Whether they are bound by definite principles, cannot be determined. Thus they are also among the inward excremental materials—cowardly, inconsistent, suspicious.

916. Now such spirits, and others also, since they are organs, relate to the same organs in the human body, but the fluids of the internal organs reflect the elements in us such as our reasonings, fantasies, and the like, which behave in the same way, activating us and making our life. However, there is a life deeper than those fluids, for they have vital substances stored up within them, which are liberated whenever they are to serve some use. 1748, 21 February.

917. Such spirits are in the region of the forehead, forward at the same level. They run forwards, sometimes to quite a distance, and then back again, reporting everything that happens, and what they hear.

918. There are many kinds of these spirits, and consequently, still more species, for similar fluids exist in almost any internal organ, though they differ as to function. Every internal organ has its own excretions, which are not cast out, but put to a use; and their nobility should be evaluated on the basis of their uses. 1748, 21 February.

919. Their lot after life is restless. They can have no peace, and they are also annoying to others; wherefore they must by all means be brought back, through suitable anxieties, into better states.

919½. Those discussed here are of the sort that is intermediate between the good lymph and the waste lymph of the brain. Relating to the waste lymph, are those who draw spiritual truths down into earthly things and thereby defile them, so that they end up in filth, as has just been shown to me. These are in front at a distance, rather high up, at the right side of the nose. They have the habit of taking spiritual and heavenly truths, and drawing them down toward earthly filth.

Those who relate to bones, on which vital motions come to rest as on their fulcrums

920. There are some in bodily life, or after bodily life in the other life as well, who, for special reasons, think only in a general manner, or do not keep their thought directed toward anything definite. Thus they are withdrawn, as if they were not in the body.

Spirits of this kind brought to me a similar general mental image, without objects to which the thought might be directed. Such are those who relate to bones in man. They are also slow and dull-witted, nor can anything become fixed in their memory, nor, consequently, drawn forth from it, except in a focussed state.

There is in them not only a sluggishness in performing their functions, but also an inertia in coming to judgment and action—yet no disquietude. For worries do not really penetrate [to them], but disperse so to speak into a generality, and pass away. And they are not malicious.

About the examination of souls, as to their various states

921. It has been explained previously [867–71] that when [newly arrived] souls come among spirits, or among those souls who wander freely in the lowest heaven, as if in a second world, the latter examine them to the best of their ability.

There are some who examine only the cruder states of mind in a soul, and can be quite mistaken. They get him to say only what they have planned and have put to him, and if he responds agreeably to the discourse of those who are leading the soul to speak as he does, then they at once make up their minds that the soul is of a certain character, when yet he is not. For they induce upon him a state like their own, and in that state, he speaks affably with them, as one of them, so they think he is like that.

Sometimes, inducing evil things, they condemn him out of prejudices or opinions they have adopted—as they did in the case of certain persons known to me in life, about whom I was not always able to think in fairness, because I did not know them so well; and so they judge them on that basis.

922. This is the judgment of those who search out only the cruder aspects of a soul, or are permitted to search for the grosser qualities of a person. And even though they are influenced by bad opinions and are thus abusive toward the soul, it is nevertheless conducive to his welfare and betterment, for nothing else is permitted by the Lord.

923. Indeed, when spirits like these examine, they do not see things except crudely, and thus do not see the inward quality of the other's speech. [For] as I was able to observe, it was not very sympathetic and harmonious—something that is seen quite plainly by good spirits, and especially by angels.

924. Those examiners belong to the kind that constitute the province of the human secretory organs, such as the kidneys, the ureters, the bladder, for these parts likewise do nothing else but examine every single element that comes their way, which in fact they seize and carry off, as is known.

925. In general, all those who examine souls and spirits, and are eager to do so, and take pleasure in it, belong to the provinces of the secretory organs; so that there are as many kinds of them as there are human internal organs. For there is no organ that does not in one way or another perform a secretory function; and thus there are countless kinds and species, existing in great abundance, because all the glands, of which there are two kinds, are of this nature. 1748, 22 February.

About the examination of souls

926. In addition to this, there is a still more subtle examination, for there are yet more subtle spirits, who see more deeply into human souls, or into their more universal feelings, that is, those that are more dominant and that people conceal in different ways. In this examination, the spirits cannot be so mistaken as were the former spirits in theirs.

927. I was also enabled to see how their dispositions then become apparent. There is a certain kind of aura emanating [from each soul], and in this case that aura, not being harmonious with my thought, immediately turned mine into the thought which the soul had, without the soul knowing it. For instance, when I thought the soul was in that place behind me, then at once, without his thinking and planning beforehand, that is, without premeditation, he made his way forward, so that I was scarcely aware but that he was in front below, whereas he was in back below.

This was because he had been such in his life, that he did not want anyone to know on which side he stood, because then he would not be able to be in their company and know what they were planning, and would thus be deprived of opportunities (to profit [from them]), as the saying goes, or (to gain) honors and riches.[1] He behaved the same way in every case, unconsciously and unpremeditatedly distorting my more universal thoughts—so skilfully, that I hardly knew otherwise than that I was of this character—causing indignation in me, at being held in such a base feeling. And so it was in numerous instances that I have forgotten.

In this way, their prevailing, or more universal, passions could be discovered; but the angels identify them easily.

928. Such is the examination of the dominating passions in a person, for one is subjected to it by spirits relating to some human secretory function, some gland or other. But who these were at that moment, I do not know—whether they related to the head, to the lungs, or to the body. I only know that twice, bright streaks appeared in front of my eyes, like curved streaks of lightning, but very thin.

929. At times, something like very sharp little spikes appeared to me, threatening the head of this soul, so that I feared he might be hurt, for such things usually bring on pain, generally fright, as if sharp points or the tips of swords should fall on someone's head. This means that such souls are thinking something different than they would like to say, as I was also told, for everything that is sharp symbolizes deceit, or cunning. 1748, 21 February.

930. Thus they can also be examined to find out what kind of an idea they had had about the Lord, about heaven, about the life after bodily life, and such matters, and others having to do with society in general and in particular. There is a kind of field emanating [from them], and quite actively working so as to distort or change the thoughts of another, persuading [the soul] upon whom they are acting that [their thoughts] are his or hers.

Their action is stronger or weaker, depending upon what has taken root in someone by actual deeds aimed to achieve more or less their desired goals. Thus the goals one had set for oneself can also be determined, because of the means employed. Spirits who are weaker, and those susceptible to the operations of another, can easily be brought to believe that they are like the other, whose condition is

---

[1] The parentheses are in the original, for what reason we do not know.

induced upon them. But such conditioning does not work on angels. 1748, 22 February.

931. This cannot be illustrated in any other way than by comparison with an aura of effluvia emanating from the body, being such that when anything strikes against it, it either repels it, or changes it to agree with its own character or nature. So they themselves do not know that they are like this, and have this effect.

All spirits are surrounded with this kind of aura, such as those who frighten, or strike with fear, and the like. Nothing is allowed to enter within that aura that is repugnant, or opposes, unless it is an aura having a stronger action, in which case it causes pain, because the person and the aura make one. However, enlightened knowledge that does not approach with passion is able to enter it, and to be received. 1748, 22 February.

Continuation on the examination of spirits

932. The more difficult for spirits to examine are souls who can actually be brought into a state of benevolent feeling, as is usual even with the wicked in the world. When they are engulfed by misfortunes, sadness, temptation, sickness, at such times they seem as though they have changed completely, but if their former character is still there, they readily fall back into it. Therefore, with souls also, such states of mind can be created, and when they come into them, they appear to be different, as I was taught today by actual experience in the case of one who had been cunning in bodily life.

But if they take on a stance of goodness out of cunning, the pretense immediately becomes apparent before the angels, as if seen in broad daylight, but not so before cruder spirits, whom they can fool by brilliant simulations. Pretense does occur among souls, for they bring this with them from their bodily life, thinking nothing else than that they can fool spirits in the same way; but their pretenses show plainly. And if those pretenses are natural to them, they are punished as though their inward and outward elements were being split apart [from each other], by [various] kinds and species of [the process of] being torn apart described before [404].

933. Souls who have a strong action through their aura [931], and who change and distort the aura of thought belonging others,

FROM THE *BIBLE INDEX*

doing this because of tendencies ingrained in their character, not only as it were twist goodness around into something agreeable with their nature or aura. They also, sometimes and if circumstances invite it, twist evil into what is good, but with the purpose of deception, and also because [in life] they had liked to twist everything in order to hide what they were after. 1748, 22 February. These are cases based on experience.

Swords and sharp points appear whenever souls are speaking differently than they are thinking

934. When souls speak differently than they think, as, for instance, if one says something good for the reason that it seems the right thing to say, then a sword appears, [or] as told before [929], sword points [appear] overhead, which look as if they would fall on the head of the one speaking. And even when we are not deceitful, but it just somehow seems to us that we should say so because we realize it is true—while yet our feeling does not agree with it, but dissents—then a sword appears behind the back, indicating danger. Thus do swords or their points threaten in various ways, depending on what kind of discrepancies there are between thought and speech. 1748, 22 February.

About those who constitute the province of the mammillary processes in the brain

939.[1] The mammillary processes are those appendages which absorb the phlegm of the inward or medullary substance of the brain through their own interstices, and secrete it as phlegm into the nostrils, casting it out as the entirely useless waste that the mucus of the nostrils is. For it is not discharged into the throat, where it would besmear the foods, and spoil the appetite.

940. They who constitute that province are those who persist in hatred, and are obstinately revengeful once they have conceived hatred against someone. But the malignity of hatred differs according to its reasons. Hatred and revenge has its reasons, or motives, which can infect [the whole] person, and so take root.

---

[1] 935–38 were written, and properly belong, after 948, where we have placed them.

941. Such spirits are in front, a little toward the left, at the level of the face but at a distance. And when they come in sight, a large and wide brown-colored vat appears, in which they are confined because they are infernal; for they imagine that from there, they rule the universe [*cf.* 285, 898].

942. When these spirits speak, they do so with wavy tones sounding like ocean breakers; for so they want to be perceived, and are therefore heard in this way. There is a large gathering of them there.

943. Those, however, who [had harbored hatred] for some better, and what seemed to them good reason, do not dwell so far distant, but near the face, in a similar [tub-like place]. But they are within a wall that is curved at the front and, in fact, is white, as if coated with plaster, and has beautiful carvings in plaster—because their reason for contracting hatred and vengefulness had appeared beautiful to them.

A wall like this appeared to me, near my face. It was snowy white, with beautiful carvings, and it grew wider, the carvings being erased, and at the same time higher, so that eventually I could not see the top. It became less white in color, but on the inside verging toward a kind of sky blue. So it is for those who cling to such a feeling, not for an evil reason, but for some other, looking to the common good, and finally to heavenly good.

This flat wall went up and raised itself upwards, offering me the opportunity to look at it on the inside also, and I was told that in it, at the bottom, are snakes and dragons—which, however, I did not see—symbolizing hatred and revenge, which are then dispelled.

Grievous punishments of revenge

944. Those who have adopted a spirit of revenge for reasons that appear good, such as that it would be princely, and dignified, also having taken it to be just, are grievously punished so that they may realize what meanness and filth it is.

945. As for the first punishment, it is so filthy that it cannot be described, and so also is the second; for body and face are so disfigured thereby that nothing human is left, but the face appears like a raw, round, wide cake, and all that is human perishes, together with everything that is worthy of man.

946. Thus disfigured, the person, with seemingly outstretched arms, is whirled around, the arms extended and motionless—which are not arms, only rags, slightly white, stretched out in this way. And as his body keeps being spun around, he is carried toward heaven, and it is proclaimed in front of all that he is of this [revengeful] character, so that the deepest shame may seize him. Thus he must become a supplicant, pleading [for forgiveness], and it is dictated to him what he must say in his plea.

947. After this he is brought toward Gehenna into the miry swamp and there rolled in the mud, and sunk into the mud as though he were to be suffocated, so that he becomes like mud. Such punishments exist for those who persist in their revenge; and unless they refrain from it, these punishments continue, time and again, though it be to eternity. 1748, 23 February.

948. These things concern myself, such as I had been, and someone else whose name is here withheld, because he had been of this character from early childhood, and in fact, against me, whom he had seen in a dream and had burned with murderous hatred, but did not know that it was I.[1]

About the punishment of revenge and hatred, continued

935.[2] The punishment of revenge is such as you see it described on the whole page visible here [939–48], because there is within revenge the most filthy meanness, that is so portrayed—namely by bodily parts thus turned hideous.

Such hideousness and meanness, therefore, are latent in revenge and hatred, and it is unavoidable that punishments of this kind result from them. And for such spirits there is a muddy swamp to the left of Gehenna, in a place lower than the feet [*see* 938, 947].

936. Later there appeared the head of a dragon, with large jaws and rows of teeth, altogether fiery inside, so that he was all fiery

---
[1] See 6110½, and footnote.
[2] See the note at 939 above.

flame in his gullet. This punishment is afterwards inflicted, thus it is a "consuming fire." Into such jaws they are then cast.

About those who punish hatred and revenge

937. It is a most wicked spirit who punishes revenge. He can impersonate anyone. Now he takes the guise of this person, now of another, so that one can scarcely tell who he is. He counterfeited many when he punished. He is one of the most wicked spirits, pitch-black, from the region of the colon.

938. The spirits who punish in the miry swamp, are wicked women, being from the province of the bladder.

Goodness is not credited to a person who is evil; and evils are blotted out when a person is good

950.[1] This was clearly shown to me today in a mental image, that is, that goodness is the Lord's, and cannot be credited to evil people, because they are immersed in evils and, ascribing goodness to themselves, think that it is their own, which can never be. To a good person, however, goodness is accounted, and evils are then blotted out. These matters can be more clearly seen in a mental image than described [in words]. 1748, 23 February.

Angels are able to examine a person's mind as if it were separate from the person

951. Now once again [*see* 542], it was as if a part of the skull had been raised up toward heaven, and looked into, and as if it had been read what the person had been like, both what he had been like in regard to his desires, and then also what he had been like in his early childhood, what he had had in mind or intended; likewise, what thoughts he had had, and what dreams.

In fact, two faces were shown to me bearing the same expressions they had when they had appeared to him in his boyhood. They resembled those against whom he had burned with rage. One of the faces was said to be like mine, although I could not recognize it;

---

[1] 949 is lacking in the original, and 939–48 have been placed after 934; see footnote there.

the second face was certainly a man's, but attractive like that of a rather adult virgin.

In short, nothing in a mind being examined that the Lord allows to be disclosed, is left uncovered—neither thoughts, nor character acquired by deeds, nor anything else.

952. However, there yet remains with that same man a softer kind of substance, like medullary brain, but harder, from which the person keeps on speaking and thinking, but differently. By this means they can search out what his slightly deeper person is like, compared with the outward one. 1748, 23 February.

Angels see people's pretenses, even those which seem to them most hidden

953. When a soul or person on earth tries to pretend, to think one thing and say another, it can become as obvious before the angels as a large black cloud before the eyes. There are indeed some who can pretend with their thought, as if they had a double thinking, as I do, and they imagine they can simulate so well as to deceive even angels, as one of them said. But I was enabled to learn that such [deception] is also seen—by myself and by spirits as a thin vapor, but by angels as a cloud, or as smelly smoke.

Thus things which are very hidden to man, are this visible to angels of only the inward heaven[1]. By angels of the very inward heaven, they cannot even be noticed, due to their grossness—only if there is something more deeply hidden that does not agree with them, or like circumstances. 1748, 23 February.

About those who constitute the province of the mammillary processes

954. This only is to be added [*see* 939-43], that those who constitute the province of the mammillary processes, when they come up—which is to the face, not to the body—emanate heat. Because revenge is fiery, or is portrayed by fire, therefore heat came from them.

Thus from the heat, and the quality of it, as well as from its place and distance, and every circumstance connected with its

---

[1] See 262 and footnote.

location and with the objects around them, it can also be learned of what character a soul is. 1748, 23 February.

Angels accurately know natural truths, so that scarcely a detail is missing

955. Only as a matter to be borne in mind, not as a proposition, it should be mentioned that when I read several items from my writings on a certain internal organ of the body, together with the hypotheses inferred from them, angels were able to tell very well whether a thing was the truth or not, which I in turn was enabled to learn from them. Thus they know in anatomical, in physical, in philosophical material, what is true, and correctly developed, and this without previous knowledge through the sciences. 1748, 23 February.

A quite profound acuteness of thought can sometimes exist in those who are corrupt

956. No one can judge about anyone's life by the sharpness of their thinking and penetration in various matters, for the evil may be sharper than the rest, rather than the good. For example, swindlers, even the worst ones, and thieves, can better penetrate the thoughts and intentions, and the feelings, of others, than any; if not, they are not diligent thieves. But they direct all [their sharpness] to falsehood, evil, deception, or to whatever is consistent with their desires. Thus devils in the other life are so sharp, and so occupied in contriving treachery, that no one could ever be brought to believe it.

Those who are praised for their acuteness, therefore, are not on that account to be praised for their life, for no one can hope for any reward in the other life because of a capacity for sharp thinking. 1748, 23 February.

957. In the other life, they abuse their acuteness and corrupt goodness into evil so skilfully, and so instantaneously, that one could never believe it. For during their bodily life, such persons are like snakes, whose eyes are almost every moment watchful to see how they can do harm.

About the hardness or softness of calluses

958. The calluses that are taken out, and by which they examine the souls' outer or bodily qualities brought with them after bodily life [862 *ff.*, 951], are harder or softer, depending upon the state of the actual life they have led.

Those that are hard must be softened, which is done by various punishments. Before they soften, the better outer qualities cannot be joined with inner ones, nor can evil qualities, together with their associations, be as it were blotted out. These must be torn out, so to speak, by a spiritual method.

Those having harder calluses suffer great, in fact tremendous, pains, and deeper torments, because the roots are affected; while those having softer ones, do not suffer such pains, as I was taught by experience when this same requirement, or [action of] being pulled apart, was performed on me, as on anyone else [404, 932]. 1748, 23 February.

Those who constitute the province of the Kidneys, ureters and bladder like to examine

959. Whenever any soul comes along and is met by those who constitute the province of the kidneys, ureters and bladder, these are at hand to examine, or explore, hoping to have grounds [for punishing] and anxiously seeking to find them wherever they can; for they like to explore for the sake of chastising and punishing—a passion in which they take great pleasure.

But they only examine those things which the soul has taken along with him from the body; for the kidneys, ureters and bladder only discharge the worn out and defiled elements from the blood, thus from the bodily parts 1748, 23 February.

Those who are in the province of the kidneys and the adrenal glands, divert grosser elements into themselves, and thus purify those which must be very pure

960. It may be known that both the urinary Kidneys and the suprarenal glands divert unclean elements into themselves, the Kidneys specifically, unclean elements of the serum, and the suprarenal glands the more unclean elements of the spirit of the blood. It is for this reason that the spermatic vessels descend from the organs devoted to waste.

961. When the purer thoughts are raised up from a person, then bodily and thus more unclean elements also follow along in double file, or like pace. Those elements are compatible with [the spirits] who constitute the province of the Kidneys, and who bring them into it. Those in that province therefore concentrate their mind on them, and thus draw them away from the purer elements, so that the purer elements are raised up toward heaven without an unclean companion.

962. Therefore, the suprarenal glands remove the impurities in the blood spirits, and the Kidneys the impurities in the blood serum, accomplishing this in more or less the same way. They work by a process of attraction, this being the way the organ functions.

In like manner do the spirits in that province work, because that is their nature. No sooner does a corresponding [spiritual] condition arise in the purer realm, whereby bodily elements a person or a soul brings along cannot be separated, those spirits, by a cooperative force that works in proportion to the outreach of their field of energy, join in. They arouse and attract [those bodily elements], and thereby free the better and purer elements from the more impure—in fact filthy and rotten ones.

It is evil spirits, therefore, who wipe them away. But they do not become the worse for it, but are obliged to perform such functions before they become better, or are reformed.

963. When spirits keep their imaginations fixed upon elements of this kind [961], and if this is portrayed before spirits' eyes, it appears as though something were being lifted up, like the bodily callus you may see spoken of earlier [862, 958]. But it is simply a concentration of their minds on these elements, so that they quiet down and cannot act together with inward elements. When they are no longer visible, then a substance like the interior medulla appears. But because they are keeping their eyes upon outward elements as their goal, therefore that something appears to be lifted up before their eyes, thus brought under their sight.

964. That there is this kind of attraction is quite evident from the attraction that has become familiar to me from various and manifold experience, when they drew up my skull [see 542], causing quite a marked sensation, sometimes pain. The noticeably painful feeling was nothing but the clinging of their inner sight to outermost elements, so that inward ones might be visible to the better spirits, and so on.

965. Also, when consent is given to angels to look into anyone's spiritual and heavenly elements, then something quite similar appears, which is raised up into heaven, but it is nothing but the concentration of angelic minds upon those things which are harmonious with them. 1748, 24 February.

966. The suprarenal glands, then, draw toward themselves the fluid of the [animate] spirits, or of the purer blood. They do this by fixing their inner sight on the elements that are not so grossly unclean, but inwardly unclean—they attract them because they fix their inner sight on them, and thereby the purer elements, freed of them, are raised up unimpaired, and so on.

This method is one of the cherubim, [guarding] lest the more unclean things should reach the Lord; so that He in His Divinity may thus be in the heavenly and spiritual regions, and from these as from centers, rule the universe. 1748, 24 February.

The Tongue belongs to the spiritual and heavenly parts

967. By a vivid experience, it has become known to me that the Tongue belongs as well to the spiritual as the heavenly regions, and that through it a passage stands open in both directions, namely, from the spiritual to the heavenly, and the reverse, on which account also it is at the forefront of both the lungs and the cardiac system. This appears more clearly from the double function of the tongue, in that it belongs to spiritual parts through speech, and to heavenly parts through taste; so that those who constitute the province of the Tongue are the kind through whose midst one passes from spiritual to heavenly regions. 1748, 24 February.

968. SPIRITUAL EXPERIENCES

*On those who constitute the province of the renal capsules,
a continuation*

968. The function of the suprarenal glands prevails throughout the fetus, because at that stage they perform the duty of many of the internal organs that meanwhile go without a function. But later, they have the function of attracting the purer blood when it is about to circulate, so that it will not be absorbed by the spermatic vessels, and of urging it, through a short circle, into the vena cava, and so into the heart, thus enlivening the blood from its direction, as the brain does from above. But this occurs only so long as the spermatic vessels, or genital parts, are not strongly active; but when they are strongly active, seizing the better elements of the blood, then the renal capsules are deprived of this vital blood, and so the purer serum is taken away from them.

969. This, too, I have learned from actual experience, for there are also some who constitute the province of these capsules and perform the duty belonging to them. This is to draw the purer reasonings to themselves and pass them on, so to speak, although it seems to them that they keep them. But they are still communications with heaven.

Consequently, when my thoughts were of the kind to be directly taken up by heaven, some female spirits from this province said that they were moved with great anxiety, and they did not know its source. Yet is was caused by the fact that in this case, they were not drawing to themselves the spiritual and heavenly elements and communicating them, as before, and for this reason, were feeling an unusual anxiety.

970. They who constitute this province are chaste virgins, very prone to anxiety, afraid they might be shaken from their condition. They lie quiet at the left part of the side, almost inside but at the side, about where the suprarenal glands are located. They anxiously fear that there might be a [direct] admittance into heaven; for they think that if deprived of their function they would perish, being without any use. So they are among the best, heavenly spirits, who work in silence; and if there is the least thought about their being deprived of their function, they immediately sigh, and are worried.

I have felt this several times, and wondered where it came from. Their anxiety, having now been communicated to me also, shows itself clearly as a kind of holy shiver, which I even openly witnessed, when communication was taken away [from them] and diverted directly to heaven. Beyond this they do not speak at all.

They sometimes said that they felt as if they were being deprived of their function when I came to writing down matters contained in the Word, because they thought that then a direct communication was taking place, thus not through them, so that they were deprived of their spiritual food. 1748, 24 February.

[m]They are those undergoing a purging process, as I realized today, who despair of ever being able to come into heaven. For this reason, these female spirits are extremely troubled at the least thought about heaven, and do not know why. I have spoken with them about this. They easily become tearful. 1748, 12 September.[n]

971. When my thoughts were drawn to little children, how their tender little bodies were governed, which takes place through the agency of the Liver and these glands, then those female spirits felt a special comfort and inward joy, as one of them openly declared.

972. When something is being thought in which there is nothing heavenly, then also these same virgins are distressed. This, too, was clearly apparent, and was pointed out, as when I was thinking about earthly matters.

It is also reflected in those capsules, for example, if the productive or good element is taken away from the blood by way of the spermatic vessels. After an excessive seizure of this by the spermatics, sadness usually ensues, which may also be caused by this, as well as by the fact that at such a time the better blood to be brought to the heart becomes deficient in the blood stream. 1748, 24 February.

How in the earliest Church they spoke in different languages
[see Acts 2:4, 10:46]

972½. Because the world is such at this day that it does not want to believe anything but what it understands, and because such things do not occur today as they did in the case of those who spoke

972½.

in strange languages, I have had occasion to converse with them and question them, and thus to be informed.[1]

---

[1] See A.W. Acton's footnote, *Spiritual Diary*, vol. 1, p. 269.